The Aristocracy of Talent

The Aristocracy of Talent

*How Meritocracy Made
the Modern World*

ADRIAN WOOLDRIDGE

Skyhorse Publishing

Skyhorse Publishing books may be purchased in bulk at special dis-
counts for sales promotion, corporate gifts, fund-raising, or educational
purposes. Special editions can also be created to specifications. For
details, contact the Special Sales Department, Skyhorse Publishing,
307 West 36th Street, 11th Floor, New York, NY 10018
or info@skyhorsepublishing.com.

Skyhorse® and Skyhorse Publishing® are registered trademarks of
Skyhorse Publishing, Inc.®, a Delaware corporation.

Visit our website at www.skyhorsepublishing.com.

10 9 8 7 6 5 4 3 2 1

Library of Congress Cataloging-in-Publication Data is available on file.

Cover design by David Ter-Avanesyan
Cover illustration: Shutterstock

Paperback ISBN: 978-1-5107-7555-8
Ebook ISBN: 978-1-5107-6862-8

Printed in the United States of America

For
Simon Green
il miglior fabbro

Contents

CONTENTS

PART FIVE

The Crisis of the Meritocracy

Introduction

A Revolutionary Idea

It is now a commonplace that the ideas which have shaped and sustained Western societies for the past 250 years or more are faltering. Democracy is in retreat. Liberalism is struggling. Capitalism has lost its lustre. But there is one idea that still commands widespread enthusiasm: that an individual's position in society should depend on his or her combination of ability and effort. Meritocracy, a word invented as recently as 1958 by the British sociologist Michael Young, is the closest thing we have today to a universal ideology.

The definition of the word gives us a sense of why meritocracy is so popular. A meritocratic society combines four qualities which are each in themselves admirable. First, it prides itself on the extent to which people can get ahead in life on the basis of their natural talents. Second, it tries to secure equality of opportunity by providing education for all. Third, it forbids discrimination on the basis of race and sex and other irrelevant characteristics. Fourth, it awards jobs through open competition rather than patronage and nepotism. Social mobility and meritocracy are the strawberries and cream of modern political thinking, and politicians can always earn applause by denouncing unearned privilege. Meritocracy's success in crossing boundaries – ideological and cultural, geographical and political – is striking.

The one thing that the most successful politicians in recent decades have in common is their faith in Michael Young's neologism. Margaret Thatcher regarded herself as a revolutionary meritocrat, engaged in an epochal struggle with languid establishmentarians in her own party and thuggish collectivists on the left. Ronald Reagan pronounced that 'all Americans have the right to be judged on the sole basis of individual merit, and to go just as far as their dreams and hard work will take them'. Bill Clinton declared that 'all Americans have not just a right but a solemn responsibility to rise as far as their God-given talents and determination can take them', a formula reiterated by Barack Obama.[1] Tony Blair repeatedly identified New Labour with meritocracy.[2] David Cameron declared that Britain is an Aspiration Nation and that his government was on the side of 'all those who work hard and want to get on.'[3] Boris Johnson praised meritocracy for 'allowing the right cornflakes to get to the top of the packet'.[4] Such praise for meritocracy is hardly surprising: opinion polls repeatedly show that large majorities of people are deeply opposed to interfering with the meritocratic principle. A Pew poll in 2019, for example, found that 73 per cent of Americans, including 62 per cent of African-Americans, say that colleges should refrain from taking race or ethnicity into account when making decisions about student admissions.[5]

Meritocracy straddles the East–West divide. In his address to the National Congress of the Communist Party of China in 2017 President Xi urged the Party to select officials 'on the basis of merit regardless of social background'.[6] His acolytes never miss an opportunity to point out that China's relative success in fighting the Coronavirus pandemic compared with the West is proof of its superior ability to choose its leaders. Singapore pays top civil servants more than $1 million a year in salary and performance bonuses. South Koreans worship the American Ivy League even more fervently than Americans do themselves.

And the divide between the public and private sectors too: successful civil services the world over have introduced elite streams and merit-based promotion; successful firms, such as McKinsey and Goldman Sachs, sell themselves on the basis of their brain power; the tech industry regards itself as meritocracy incarnate. The 'citizens of nowhere' that Theresa May once tried to demonize are, in fact, citizens of the global meritocracy.

Our culture reverberates with the sounds of meritocracy in action. The term 'smart' (American for 'clever') has crept from people ('the smartest guys in the room') to technology ('smartphones') to policy ('smart government', 'smart regulations', 'smart foreign policy').

During his presidency Obama used the adjective in the context of policies more than 900 times.[7] Companies boast names such as the Economist Intelligence Unit, IQ Capital Partners and Intelligence-Squared. Bill Gates advises schoolchildren to be nice to nerds on the grounds that one day they will be working for them. Sports stars and managers routinely boast that their sports are 'meritocracies' in which all that matters is skill.

Politicians are alternately boastful and defensive about their IQs. As well as declaring himself a 'very stable genius', Donald Trump has repeatedly boasted that he has 'a very good brain' and a 'high IQ'. During his first run for the presidency back in 1987, Joe Biden ticked off a voter who asked him about his educational qualifications by retorting, 'I think I probably have a much higher IQ than you do ... I'd be delighted to sit down and compare my IQ to yours.'[8] Boris Johnson has been known to rag David Cameron because he was a King's Scholar at Eton, a sure sign of mental ability, while Cameron was an Oppidan, or regular fee payer.

This is not just froth. The meritocratic idea is shaping society from top to bottom. A growing proportion of great fortunes are in the hands of people with outstanding brain power: computer geeks such as Bill Gates (Microsoft) and Mark Zuckerberg (Facebook) or financial wizards such as George Soros (who pioneered hedge funds) and Jim Simons (who helped to found computer-driven 'quant investing').[9] The world's richest man, Jeff Bezos, graduated *summa cum laude* and Phi Beta Kappa from Princeton and makes a point of surrounding himself with academic super-achievers. High-IQ types are even thriving in the more rough-and-ready corners of capitalism: six of the seven biggest Russian oligarchs of the 1990s earned degrees in maths, physics or finance before becoming natural-resource tycoons.

Bill Clinton's belief that there is a tight connection between earning and learning is proving truer by the day. In the United States, for example, a young college graduate earns 63 per cent more than a young high-school graduate if both work full time – and college graduates are much more likely to have full-time jobs.[10] This college premium is twice what it was in 1980 and is continuing to grow. Raw intelligence is one of the best predictors of success in life. Peter Saunders, a social-mobility researcher, estimates that performance in an IQ

3

test at the age of ten predicts a child's social class three times better than their parents' social class does.[11] A study of a cohort of British children born in 1970 found that those in the top quartile of IQ scores at the age of ten were much more likely to reach elite social positions (28 per cent) than those in the bottom quartile (5.3 per cent).[12]

Education and IQ also determine where we live. In post-war America people with degrees were evenly distributed regardless of region or the urban–rural divide. Today only 10 per cent of inhabitants of Detroit have degrees compared with more than 50 per cent of inhabitants of San Francisco, Boston, New York and Washington, DC. Once-proud regional elites are being subsumed into a national elite defined by education and headquartered on the coasts. In Great Britain, talent is now concentrated in Greater London and an archipelago of high-IQ towns such as Oxford and Cambridge. A study of the whereabouts of almost half a million Britons who volunteered to have their DNA recorded in the UK Biobank suggests that people who leave deprived areas are brighter and healthier than those who stay behind.[13]

Parents the world over labour on the same treadmill of meritocracy-driven hope and anxiety: British parents provide their teenage children with an average of ten hours' extra tuition a week, Chinese parents with twelve, South Korean parents with fifteen and Bulgarian parents with sixteen.[14] In South Korea, some parents pray every day for a hundred days before their children take exams then sit outside school on the day of the exam, praying. In Singapore, the global capital of meritocracy, students erect shrines to the 'bell curve God', referring to the normal distribution curve, the 'omnipotent, inscrutable force that rules over their lives'.[15] These tests don't stop when we leave school or university: global estimates suggest that companies use aptitude and personality tests for 72 per cent of middle-management jobs and 80 per cent of senior ones.[16]

DOWN WITH MERITOCRACY!

Even at the best of times, ruling ideologies provoke sharp criticisms. In volatile and dyspeptic times, they can quickly become an object of hatred. The meritocratic idea is coming under fire from a formidable range of critics who roundly denounce our ruling ideology as 'an illusion', a 'trap', a 'tyranny' and an instrument of white oppression. This criticism has yet to shift popular opinion, which remains stubbornly loyal to the meritocratic idea. But it is already gaining traction not just in the ivory tower but also in influential public-policy circles. The criticism comes from a wide range of different sources – from elite academics as well as angry populists. It feeds on some of our most profound anxieties about everything from racial injustice to the psychological strains of hyper-competition.

The Black Lives Matter movement is one of the most powerful protest movements of recent years. Its prime target is brutality, particularly police brutality towards African-Americans – it was ignited by the killing of Trayvon Martin in 2012 by a member of the neighbourhood watch and then re-ignited, on an even larger scale, by the killing of George Floyd by a police officer, in 2020. But it has also popularized critical race theory, an ideology that was incubated on American campuses from the late 1960s onwards, and which provides the intellectual underpinnings of a succession of successful books, such as Reni Eddo-Lodge, *Why I'm No Longer Talking to White People about Race* (2017), Robin DiAngelo, *White Fragility* (2018) and Ibram X. Kendi, *How to be an Antiracist* (2019).

Critical race theorists start from the premise that Western society – particularly American society – is structurally racist. Racism is not confined to intentional acts of discrimination committed by immoral individuals. It is part of the DNA of society – structural rather than just intentional, and unconscious as well as conscious. Critical race theorists are fiercely hostile to the meritocratic idea, which they regard, at best, as a way of justifying social inequality as natural inequality and, at worst, as an offshoot of eugenic theory. They reject the intellectual building blocks of meritocracy: that people should be judged as individuals rather than as members of ethnic groups; that it's possible to produce colour-blind assessments of individual educational abilities; and, indeed, that it's possible, through progressive policies, to escape from the burden of history.[17] For them, the legacy of slavery and colonialism is present in everything we do, racial identity is all-pervasive, and colour-blindness is not just impossible but, by

5

denying reality, a form of racism in itself.[18] Supposedly objective tests are saturated with cultural and therefore racial prejudice. 'The use of standardised tests to measure aptitude and intelligence is one of the most effective racist policies ever devised to degrade Black minds and legally exclude Black bodies,' argues Ibram X. Kendi.[19] Educational institutions, including the most self-consciously progressive universities, are vectors of race-based inequality. The only way to forge a better future is through collective struggle for collective ends. Critical race theorists frequently drive their point home by pointing out that many of the earliest exponents of mental measurement, such as Francis Galton, were out-and-out racists.[20]

Conservative populists may be on the opposite side of the ideological divide from critical race theorists, but they share their fierce hostility to meritocracy. Populists delight in criticizing meritocrats for being 'smug', 'self-righteous' and 'out of touch'. They also have more substantial objections. They complain that the so-called cognitive elite has done a dismal job of running the world: the financial crisis was driven by highly qualified 'quants' who built a mathematical house of cards, while the Iraq debacle was masterminded by neo-conservative intellectuals who promised that the entire adventure would be a 'cake walk'. Tucker Carlson, one of Fox News's most prominent pundits, also argues that meritocracy acts as a 'leech' on society as a whole, crowding successful people together in self-obsessed enclaves and dulling their empathy with their fellow citizens:

> The SAT [Scholastic Aptitude Test] 50 years ago pulled a lot of smart people out of every little town in America and funneled them into a small number of elite institutions, where they married each other, had kids, and moved to an even smaller number of elite neighborhoods. We created the most effective meritocracy ever ... But the problem with the meritocracy [is that it] leaches all the empathy out of your society ... The second you think that all your good fortune is a product of your virtue, you become highly judgmental, lacking empathy, totally without self-awareness, arrogant, stupid – I mean all the stuff that our ruling class is.[21]

Some of the sharpest critics of meritocracy come from the very heart of the meritocratic system itself. Daniel Markovits is the Guido

Calabresi Professor of Law at Yale Law School, an institution that admits only 1 per cent of applicants and then offers them a golden ticket into the new American elite. In *The Meritocracy Trap* (2019) this self-acknowledged uber-meritocrat argues that 'merit is nothing more than a sham'.[22] Meritocracy is now the opposite of what it was intended to be, he argues: a way of transmitting inherited privilege from one generation to another through the mechanism of elite education. Members of the elite spend millions of dollars purchasing educational advantage for their children, sometimes by moving to the right school districts, sometimes by sending their children to the right private schools, but always by providing them with a rich diet of extracurricular activities. At the same time, poorer children are trapped at the bottom of the ladder, weighed down from the get-go by poor infant care, poor schools and general lack of opportunity. This palace of illusions is also a factory of misery. The successes of the system are crushed by overwork: documents to read late into the night; emails to answer at all hours; an ever-buzzing smartphone.

Michael Sandel is the Anne T. and Robert M. Bass Professor of the Theory of Government at Harvard University, Yale's perennial rival for the top slot in America's meritocracy machine. In *The Tyranny of Merit* (2020) he presents an equally uncompromising message. For him, meritocracy is nothing short of 'toxic'. This toxicity is inherent in the meritocratic idea for reasons that Michael Young laid out sixty years ago: because it says to those at the bottom of the pile that they *deserve* their fate, thereby diminishing them as human beings. But it is rendered even more lethal by contemporary social developments: the stalling of social mobility, the destruction of manual jobs by a combination of technology and globalization, and the rise of a technocratic elite who have little in common with ordinary people. Sandel looks forward to a more balanced future in which we stop fetishizing merit and put more emphasis on democracy and community.

The Markovits–Sandel fusillade is the latest example of the 'revolt of the elites' against the very ideology that is the foundation of their elite position. *The New York Times* and the *Washington Post*, the elites' favourite papers, regularly contain op-eds arguing that 'our elites stink' (David Brooks)[23] and that 'it's time to abandon the cruelty of meritocracy' (Steven Pearlstein).[24] Publishers have invented a new form of misery memoir that stars disillusioned meritocrats grappling with the intellectual and moral emptiness of life in elite educational institutions: read Ross Douthat's *Privilege* (2005), David Samuels's *The Runner* (2008) and Walter Kirn's *Lost in the Meritocracy* (2009) and shed a sympathetic tear.

There is truth in all these complaints. The critics are right that the theory of meritocracy can often be a disguise for class privilege. Privileged children who begin life with supportive parents and then waft along on a cloud of good schools and extra tuition have a much better chance of realizing their full potential than poor children. Oxford and Cambridge recruit more students from eight elite schools than they do from 3,000 state schools put together.[25] Ivy League universities have more students who come from households in the top 1 per cent of the income distribution than from the entire bottom half.[26]

Critical race theorists are right that black people are often the worst affected by the uncritical assumption that everybody deserves what they get. Black people start off with significant material disadvantages, with the typical American black family possessing only an eighth of the wealth of the average white family.[27] They encounter more disadvantages as they grow older: more pollution, worse schools, a higher chance of arrest, ingrained attitudes. It is no wonder that meritocracy can seem like a crown of thorns rather than a liberation.

The critics are right that the distinction between winning and losing can be much too sharp. It sometimes seems as if we are now living in the world of the 1992 film *Glengarry Glen Ross*: 'We're adding a little something to this year's sales contest. As you all know, first prize is a Cadillac Eldorado. Anybody wanna see second prize? Second prize is a set of steak knives. Third prize is, you're fired.'[28]

They are also right that meritocracy is an unbending taskmaster. Most professionals spend their lives on a meritocratic treadmill, rather like prisoners in one of Jeremy Bentham's panopticon penitentiaries. They spend the first twenty-five to thirty years of their lives acing exams, getting into elite universities, finding slots in brand-name companies, and the next twenty-five to thirty years trying to win promotions, please their bosses, make their names in the world. Then, as they grow older, they visit their meritocratic obsessions on their children. Today's parents worship Oxbridge and Harvard with the same devotion that earlier generations reserved for God and His prophets.

We should nevertheless be cautious about rejecting an idea that is so central to modernity. Critiques of liberalism or democracy, even if they are partially justified, have led us to some dark places. We need to beware that the same thing might happen with critiques of meritocracy, particularly in the wake of a Trump presidency that has trashed meritocratic principles in government through the wanton use of nepotism, political favouritism and the systematic denigration of expertise.

At the very least, a few questions are in order. What exactly is the problem with the meritocratic idea? Is it that it supports the status quo (the left-wing criticism)? Or is it that it keeps everybody in a state of constant anxiety (the communitarian criticism)? Are meritocracy's problems inherent in the idea itself? Or are they the product of a failure to implement meritocracy vigorously enough? Is there a sensible compromise between having 'you're fired' as third prize and giving everybody prizes? Professors Markovits and Sandel worry that meritocracy is producing intolerable pressure to succeed. But aren't there other compelling explanations for this pressure, such as slow economic growth, which is increasing competition for desirable jobs, or the relentless increase in the amount of knowledge that needs to be mastered, which is forcing would-be professionals to work ever harder?

And is there a better system for organizing the world? The relevant question is surely not whether meritocracy has faults. It is whether it has fewer faults than alternative systems. Meritocracy's advocates don't argue that it's perfect. They argue that it does a better job than the alternatives of reconciling various goods that are inevitably in tension with each other – for example, social justice and economic efficiency and individual aspiration and limited opportunities. Critical race theorists suggest that race should be taken into account in all decision-making. But isn't there a danger that this will reinforce racial divisions and turn all ethnic groups into political interest groups? Progressives have taken to arguing for getting rid of SATs and other tests and replacing them with more holistic modes of assessment. But this opens the way to favouritism or politically inspired rigging. Michael Sandel wants to distribute university places on the basis of 'a lottery of the qualified'.[29] But this risks making American universities even more impersonal than they already are: rather than choosing to study a particular course with a particular set of professors, students will simply have to hit the right numbers to reach the threshold and then will see their names put into a giant sorting hat. It also undermines one of the central tenets of higher learning: that academics are capable of making fine distinctions about the quality of people's minds. That is, after all, what tenure committees and academic referees spend much of their time doing. Or perhaps we should also distribute named chairs and tenured professorships on the basis of a lottery of the qualified?

One reason why the current debate about meritocracy is so frustrating is the lack of a historical perspective. Meritocracy is not an abstract idea that came to the world, like Minerva, fully formed from the head of Jupiter. It is a way of thinking about the world – and indeed organizing the world – that has evolved over time in the light of economic pressures and political agitation. How can we judge whether meritocracy is a tyranny or a liberation unless we can see it in its historical context? And how can we tell whether it is a sensible way of organizing the world or a trap unless we can see how it came about?

The fact that there is no convenient history of meritocracy is remarkable, given that it is one of the great building blocks of the modern world – and an increasingly controversial one. There are dozens of histories of the other building blocks – democracy, freedom, capitalism – many of them excellent. There are still remarkably few studies of meritocracy, and the best of the lot, Michael Young's *The Rise of the Meritocracy*, is as exotic as it is brilliant, a strange combination of history and science fiction. Anybody who wants to understand the subject has to venture down some obscure byways labelled 'the history of education', or 'the history of the civil service', or, most obscure of all, 'the history of IQ testing'.[30] The aim of this book is to fill this void: to explain where the meritocratic idea came from, how it replaced feudal ideas about 'priority, degree and place', how it evolved over the centuries and why it eventually became the world's leading ideology. In the process I also hope to offer some perspective on roiling debates about whether it is a mistake that needs to be rejected or a still-progressive idea that can be a force for good in the world.

HISTORY LESSONS

The history of meritocracy reveals three things that are vital to understanding our current condition.

The first is that meritocracy is a *revolutionary* idea, the intellectual dynamite which has blown up old worlds – and created the material for the construction of new ones. For millennia, most societies have been organized according to the very opposite principles to meritocracy. People inherited their positions in fixed social orders. The world was ruled by royal dynasties. Plum jobs were bought and sold like furniture. Nepotism was a way of life. Upward mobility was discouraged and sometimes outlawed.

The meritocratic idea was at the heart of the four great revolutions that created the modern world. The French Revolution was dedicated to the principle of 'a career open to talents'. The American Revolution advanced the idea that people should be allowed to pursue life, liberty and happiness without being held back by feudal restrictions. The Industrial Revolution unleashed animal spirits. The liberal revolution, which was headquartered in Britain but influential across middle-class Europe, introduced open competition into the heart of government administrations and educational systems.

The meritocratic idea transformed Western society from the inside out. It changed the tenor of the elite by reforming the way that society allocates the top jobs and the nature of education by emphasizing the importance of raw intellectual ability. It did all this by redefining the elemental force that determines social structure. 'When there is no more hereditary wealth, privilege class, or prerogatives of birth . . .' Alexis de Tocqueville wrote, in one of the earliest attempts to understand what was going on, 'it becomes clear that the chief source of disparity between the fortunes of men lies in the mind.'[31]

The establishment of this 'chief source of disparity' at the heart of society entailed a momentous intellectual revolution: the rejection of the aristocratic ethic and its replacement by a meritocratic one. Examine the basic building blocks of the meritocratic world view – assumptions about individualism, intelligence, hard work, the family, social mobility – and you discover that they are at variance with the attitudes that dominated most previous societies. The rise of the meritocracy entailed a comprehensive revolution in the way people think about the world.

In meritocratic society, people are individuals before they are anything else: masters of their fates and captains of their souls.[32] This is particularly true of the elites: Scott Turow calls the new elite 'the flying class' or the 'orphans of capital', who regard it as a 'badge of status to be away from home four nights a week'. (For several years, Nicolas Berggruen, a successful investor, took this to extremes as a 'homeless billionaire' who spent his life flying from hotel to hotel in his private plane.) In traditional aristocratic societies, what matters is people's relationships with family and land. The first question aristocrats asked about somebody was 'who are his people?' British aristocrats come with place names attached; the higher the rank, the bigger the place. The German *von* expresses the link between the *Herr* and his *Herrschaft*.

In meritocratic society, people are judged on the basis of their personal qualities: if examiners take background into account, they do so in order to come to a truer assessment of a candidate's inborn abilities. In aristocratic society, they were judged on the basis of their connections and relations. When the future 10th Earl of Wemyss attended his interview for admission to Christ Church, Oxford, in 1837, he was asked just one question: 'How's your father?'[33] In meritocratic society, people are supposed to refrain from overt influence-peddling. In aristocratic society, influence-peddling was the stuff of social life. A popular story about the Habsburg empire features a charming young man who, 'at dinner with his father and some well-placed family friends, ate soup as a cadet, the main course as a lieutenant, and dessert as a captain'.[34]

In meritocratic society, coming from nowhere is a badge of honour, while being what Warren Buffett calls a 'member of the lucky sperm club' (by which he means being a child of a member of the elite) is a defect to be explained away. For most of history, established elites have looked down on parvenus as offences against the natural order. Forgetting his own petit-bourgeois origins, Dr Johnson insisted that 'mankind are happier in a state of inequality and subordination'.[35] Hannah More satirized the tradition-loving squire of Hanoverian England:

> He dreaded nought like alteration,
> Improvement still was innovation.[36]

One of Victorian England's favourite hymns summed up the doctrine perfectly:

> The rich man in his castle,
> The poor man at his gate,
> God made them, high and lowly,
> And ordered their estate.

In meritocratic society, raw intelligence is the defining human quality. The marriage announcements in the *New York Times* list university affiliations and post-graduate degrees where they used to list family pedigrees. Joe Biden's wife, Jill, makes a point of calling herself 'doctor' to prove that she's more than just an appendage of her husband. Several German politicians have lost their jobs because they fabricated their doctorates. Aristocratic societies were at best ambivalent about 'smarts'. Walter Bagehot observed in 1867 that 'a great part of the "best" English people keep their mind in a state of decorous dullness ... They think cleverness an antic, and have a constant though needless horror of being thought to have any of it.'[37] As late as 1961, Lord 'Bobbety' Salisbury (the fifth Marquess) is thought to have scuppered Ian Macleod's chances of becoming prime minister by describing him as 'too clever by half'.

Ideas have become the currency of the global elite. Bilderberg and Davos invite 'thought leaders' to address corporate titans. TED conferences are so enthusiastic about ideas that they can seem like religious festivals. 'We don't have castles and noble titles,' says Andrew Zolli, the organizer of an ideas forum called Pop Tech, 'so how else do you indicate you're part of the elite?' Aristocratic societies regarded ideas as either dangerous in themselves or, if they have to be indulged, things that should be taken only in measured quantities, like wine with a good meal. 'I'm not sure I like boys who think too much,' Endicott Peabody, Groton's most famous headmaster, once proclaimed. 'A lot of people think of things we could do without.'[38]

This revolution of values applies particularly starkly to the question of hard work. Aristocratic societies regarded hard work as proof of low birth and conspicuous leisure as proof of superiority. Today's rich, by contrast, have replaced conspicuous leisure with conspicuous work – and the 'effortless superiority' that was supposed to distinguish the Balliol man with 'effortful superiority'. Daniel Markovits calculates that more than half the richest 1 per cent of households include someone who works more than fifty hours a week – a far higher incidence of overwork than you find in the rest of the population.[39] Prominent businesspeople have taken to giving absurd interviews to the press about how they get up at 4 a.m. (Indra Nooyi, boss of PepsiCo), immediately leap on an exercise bike, work out furiously in the gym (Tim Cook of Apple), and then spend their days in a whirlwind of activity.[40]

Before it took over the world, meritocracy was the rallying cry of the oppressed and marginalized everywhere. Feminists demanded that they should be allowed to compete for jobs and educational distinctions and judged by the same standards as men. Mary Wollstonecraft's *A Vindication of the Rights of Woman* (1792) argued that girls and boys should go to school together and learn the same things. John Stuart Mill's *The Subjection of Women* (1869) argued that 'the principle of the modern movement in morals and politics' is that 'merit, and not birth, is the only rightful claim to power and authority', meaning that women had to be freed from Victorian restrictions.[41] One of the seminal moments in the early history of feminism came in 1890 when the Cambridge examiners had to rank a woman, Philippa Fawcett, 'above the senior wrangler' (i.e. top scholar) because she got the top mark, despite being formally banned, as a woman, from taking a degree.

The working classes seized on the meritocratic principle to prove that they were just as good as their supposed social betters. Working-class autodidacts performed astonishing feats of learning in hostile circumstances. Working-class scholars forced their way into elite universities by dint of superior brains and effort. Working-class politicians went out of their way to prove that they were just as well educated as members of the establishment. Ramsay MacDonald, the illegitimate son of a Scottish ploughman, who was prime minister in 1924 and 1929–35, was fond of pointing to all the working-class autodidacts he knew as a child who were far more learned than university academics. A tubercular watchmaker introduced him to Shakespeare, Burns and Charles Dickens. A local ragman kept a book propped open against his barrow and presented it to the young MacDonald when he showed an interest. It was a translation of Thucydides.[42] The result of all this intellectual effort was a revolution: the powers that be were forced to concede that it was not only inefficient but also immoral to deny opportunity to talent wherever it appeared.

The same was true of other marginalized groups who used meritocratic standards to confound ancient prejudices. Great Jewish intellectuals such as Albert Einstein made a mockery of Nazi ideas of the master race. Great black intellectuals such as Frederick Douglass and W. E. B. Du Bois proved that blacks could hold their own in the corridors of intellect. Martin Luther King was such a morally compelling figure because he held out the hope of a future in which everyone would be judged by the content of their character rather than the colour of their skin. Marginalized groups can be at their most influential when they appeal to universal standards and collective hope – and shaming the ruling class can be a much more effective way of persuading it to hand over power than attacking it.

Socialists seized on the meritocratic idea to give substance to their vague hope of a better society. Sidney and Beatrice Webb, the intellectual father and mother of the British Labour Party, argued that socialism was about making sure that everybody had a job suited to their natural abilities – which, given the natural abilities of Britain's traditional rulers, meant a social revolution. John Spargo, one of the leading lights of the Socialist Party of America, devoted much of his 1906 classic, *Socialism*, to demonstrating that 'not human equality, but equality of opportunity to prevent the creation of artificial inequalities by privilege is the essence of Socialism'.[43] Émile Durkheim, one of the French left's greatest thinkers, argued that social solidarity depended on the proper use of individual talents.

By contrast, conservatives treated meritocracy as a threat to the social order. In 1872, George Birdwood, a high Tory, predicted, angrily, that civil service reforms would produce a world in which men were 'tested for the public service by means of positive Chinese puzzles' and that schoolchildren across the country would be trained in solving these puzzles.[44] In 1898, W. H. Mallock, a popular novelist and conservative polemicist, criticized equality of educational opportunity on the grounds that it would institutionalize social disharmony by encouraging the masses to entertain ideas above their stations.[45] In 1953, Karl Mannheim, a German-born sociologist at the London School of Economics (LSE), argued that conservatives should champion the group, such as the nation or association, rather than the individual, on the grounds that groups have distinctive collective identities that make them the modern equivalents of feudal estates.[46]

The second lesson from history is that meritocracy is a *protean* idea. We can all agree on what 'meritocracy' means in a general way: allowing people to rise as high as their talents and efforts will take them. But what does this mean in practice? The notion of 'talent' has changed over time. Until the early twentieth century, 'talent' carried a moral as well as an intellectual connotation. Plato believed that the character of his philosopher kings was just as important as their intellect. Enlightenment thinkers talked of 'virtues and abilities', not abilities alone. The twentieth century saw the progressive demoralization of 'talent', thanks to the invention of IQ testing (which identified ability with measurable intelligence) and the rise of technocracy (which fetishized technical skills above moral outcomes).

Terms such as 'allowing' and 'as high' are equally problematic. In the nineteenth century, policy-makers interpreted 'allowing' to mean removing barriers to competition. But was it enough just to remove barriers if some children were given superb educations and others left school at ten? This reasoning led progressively to mass secondary-school education, to mass higher education and to affirmative action. Some meritocrats have interpreted 'as high' simply to mean rising as high as your talents will allow. Others have interpreted it as an argument for giving political power to the most intelligent.

There are, in fact, lots of different types of meritocracy. There is *political* meritocracy, which argues that the merit principle should be applied to the heart of the political regime. Plato dreamed of a brave new world in which the most talented ruled the state. The Founding Fathers gave Supreme Court justices jobs for life so that they wouldn't be compromised by democratic pressures. Liberals such as J. S. Mill and Friedrich Hayek have argued in favour of giving people with qualifications more votes or creating a second chamber of highly educated people. There is *technocratic* meritocracy, which emphasizes technical expertise to the exclusion of things such as character or virtue – or indeed to the old-fashioned quality of judgement.[47] There is the *businessperson's* meritocracy, which emphasizes the importance of the battle of the marketplace, and the *academic's* meritocracy, which focuses on academic results. Different versions of the meritocratic idea have come to the fore at different times.

The third lesson is that, precisely because it is both revolutionary and protean, the meritocratic idea is capable of *self-correction*. There have been notable occasions in the past when it has looked as if meritocracy was degenerating into a defence of the status quo. In mid-nineteenth-century America, it looked as if the 'men of merit' who fathered the American Revolution were handing on their leadership positions to their children. Then vital new forces such as the Jacksonian Democrats and new immigrant groups such as the Irish and Italians displaced them in the name of open competition. In the late nineteenth century, it looked as if a new elite of robber barons was transforming America into an aristocratic society. Again the meritocratic spirit renewed itself: Teddy Roosevelt declared war on the 'malefactors of great wealth', civil service reformers embraced the merit principle and 'captains of learning' revitalized the universities.

Many of today's sternest critics of meritocracy think that it is beyond reform. A growing number of left-wingers who march under the Social Justice banner argue that society should resort to explicitly non-meritocratic principles such as race consciousness or equality of outcome. In fact, the historical evidence suggests that it is eminently reformable. Marginalized groups can use the principle of merit to shame entrenched elites into levelling the playing field. Institutional reformers can emphasize the extent to which supposedly elite institutions fail to live up to the meritocratic principle.

Today's critics of the meritocratic idea nevertheless get one big thing right: that the meritocratic elite is in danger of hardening into an aristocracy which passes on its privileges to its children by investing heavily in education, and which, because of its sustained success, looks down on the rest of society. The past four decades have seen one of the most depressing developments in the history of the meritocratic idea: the marriage between merit and money. The new rich, having done well out of global markets and booming asset prices, have entrenched their positions by buying educational privileges for their children. The old rich have embraced meritocratic values in order to add education, or at least certification, to the long-established fortifications that surround their estates. With levels of social mobility declining, an idea that was designed to promote social mobility is morphing into its opposite, promoting social closure and the return of caste.

I called this book 'The Aristocracy of Talent' for two reasons. The first is that so many meritocrats have used such terms themselves. Plato talked about 'philosopher kings'. The French and American revolutionaries talked about 'natural aristocrats'. A character in Thomas Mann's *Buddenbrooks*, distilling the revolutionary mood of the late nineteenth century, proclaimed that 'we, the bourgeoisie – the Third Estate, as we have been called – we recognise only that nobility which consists of merit'.[48] More recently, people have taken to talking about 'the best and the brightest', 'the great and the good' and 'the leadership class'. The second reason is to sound a note of warning. An aristocracy of talent ought to be an oxymoron. The aristocracy of talent can survive only if it is constantly recruiting new talent from the rest of society and downgrading members of the elite who don't quite make it. The 'aristocracy of talent' can and should be celebrated when it upsets the status quo, but if it distorts the meritocratic principle, using it as a way of entrenching its position at the top of society, then it needs to be challenged.

THE PLAN OF THE BOOK

Part One introduces the pre-meritocratic world, a world in which people's stations in life were fixed by tradition and jobs were allocated on the basis of patronage, nepotism, inheritance and purchase. Poets condemned self-seeking individuals as enemies of the heavenly order. Patrons gave away senior positions on a whim. Governments sold off jobs in the civil service and the military. Dullards acquired Oxford and Cambridge fellowships for the simple reason that they were related to the people who founded the colleges. Even as the old world went on its merrie way, there was another world in the making: a world of intellectual aristocrats, mandarin scholars, 'pauper born' bureaucrats and roving intellectuals and entrepreneurs. Part Two examines the history of meritocracy before modernity. Plato's *Republic* provided a blueprint for a world run by carefully selected and rigorously trained guardians. China introduced a system of examinations designed to select top scholars from across the empire. The Jewish people have always put a marked emphasis on intellectual success for both theological reasons (they see themselves as a chosen people guided by a rabbinical elite of scholar-priests) and practical ones (they have often had to make a living as entrepreneurs, middlemen and fixers). The great organs of medieval society, the Church and the king's household, invented mechanisms of (limited) 'sponsored mobility'. If meritocracy has a relatively short history, it has also had a long prehistory.

Part Three focuses on the three great liberal revolutions that created the modern world – two of them bloody (the French and, to a lesser degree, the American) and one of them peaceful (the British liberal revolution, which transferred power from a landed elite to the liberal intellectual aristocracy without a shot being fired). These revolutions were all driven by the same underlying force so succinctly identified by de Tocqueville: 'The mind became an element in success; knowledge became a tool of government and intellect a social force; educated men played a part in affairs of state.'[49]

The American revolutionaries wanted to replace the 'artificial' aristocracy of the land with a 'natural' aristocracy of virtue and talent. David Ramsay, a South Carolina historian, celebrated the second anniversary of American Independence by arguing that America was a unique nation in human history because 'all offices lie open to men of merit, of whatever rank or condition'.[50] Thomas Jefferson, the most committed, if also the most contradictory, of the new breed of philosopher-meritocrats, wanted to discover 'youths of genius from among the classes of the poor' and provide them with a free education. Later, Americans rejected this top-down view of society in favour of opening opportunities for upward mobility. But the essence of the American experiment remained the same: create equality of opportunity but expect that equality of opportunity to lead to a highly unequal outcome as people sorted themselves out according to their abilities and energies.

The French Revolution was a messier affair as well as a bloodier one. The revolution was inspired by a similar revolt against the 'artificial aristocracy': the revolutionaries declared that all men should be treated as equal before the law and that all careers should be opened to talent. Feudal privileges were abolished; the purchase of jobs was prohibited; elite schools were strengthened. Yet the result of this explosion of energy was confused: Napoleon mixed dynastic and meritocratic principles indiscriminately; and the Restoration brought back some of the most dubious features of the old regime. The France that emerged from the revolution was a strange mixture, half furiously meritocratic, half nostalgically aristocratic.

The most idiosyncratic revolution took place in Great Britain. The revolution was led by the intellectual aristocracy – a group of intermarried families with names such as Huxley, Darwin and Keynes – who owed their success to their sharp brains rather than to their broad acres. These reformers first subjected established institutions such as the civil service and the universities to open competition and then gradually built a ladder of opportunity for scholarship children.

Chapter Eleven looks at the rise of IQ testing. IQ testing provided a convenient way of testing mental ability and expressing that ability in a single number – so convenient, in fact, that, only a few years after IQ tests were invented, the US army used them to classify millions of recruits in the Great War. IQ testing also addressed three questions that anybody who takes the meritocratic idea seriously must confront. Is intelligence inherited or acquired, and, if both, in what proportions? How can we distinguish between innate ability and mere learning? And how much social mobility can we expect in a properly meritocratic society?

Chapter Twelve looks at the triumphant march of meritocracy after the Second World War. This was the glorious era in the history of the meritocratic idea: an era in which the left and the right could agree on the importance of giving everybody a chance to develop their natural abilities; an era in which opportunities were expanding in the form of university places and white-collar jobs; an era in which society as a whole celebrated the power of intelligence, as represented by scientists, engineers and even public intellectuals.

Chapter Thirteen re-examines the story through the lens of sex. The story of the rise of women is often written in terms of collective struggle for group rights. This chapter argues that it is just as important to recognize the role of liberal intellectuals such as J. S. Mill (and his wife, Harriet Taylor), who argued that the meritocratic revolution could not be complete until women were given a fair chance. The shift in the overall balance of the economy from brawn to brains made it inevitable that women would perform just as well as men. The feminist revolution thus represented the logical continuation of the introduction of open competition in the nineteenth century.

Part Five tells a darker story. Chapter Fourteen details the revolt against the meritocracy on the left. This revolt started in academia, with various specialists questioning both the power of IQ tests to measure intelligence and the deeper theory that IQ testing rested upon. This revolt was particularly fierce in Britain because of the role of the 11-plus in dividing children into sheep and goats. Academic doubts about IQ tests fed upon deeper intellectual currents. Egalitarians argued that the principle of meritocracy smuggled the principle of elitism into the heart of the socialist project. The proper aim of the left was equality of outcome rather than equality of result. Communitarians argued that the principle of meritocracy was dividing communities into the educational equivalent of the saved and the damned. Radical intellectuals such as Michel Foucault deconstructed every imaginable boundary – between the sane and the mad, the good and the bad, the law-abiding and the homicidal and, of course, between the bright and the average – as the product of bourgeois power. Increasingly, the debate was between egalitarians, who believed that all should have prizes, and super-egalitarians, who believed that prizes were just part of the 'bourgeois problematic'.

Chapter Fifteen examines the recent marriage between meritocracy and plutocracy. The egalitarian revolution in the state sector was a failure not only because it deprived working-class children of an avenue of social mobility but also because it coincided with a meritocratic revolution at the top of society. The privileged discovered the importance of intellectual success: British public (i.e. private) schools and American Ivy League universities put increased emphasis on school results. The children of the meritocrats who had thrived in the 1950s and 1960s devoted their considerable resources to passing their privileges to their children. Even during the Great Depression, when, in Charles and Mary Beard's phrase in *The Rise of American Civilisation* (1930), poverty was 'stark and galling enough to blast human nature', Americans still believed that there was 'a baton in every toolkit'.[51] Today, thanks to the widening meritocracy gap, they, along with the citizens of other advanced countries, particularly Britain, believe that the baton has been taken away. That is a dangerous situation as well as a sad one.

Chapter Sixteen looks at the more recent populist revolt against the meritocracy – a revolt that takes up many of the themes of the 1960s (that the elite owes its privileges to a rigged system rather than hard work and ability) but mixes it with powerful cultural resentment. The populist rebellion is driven by a revolt of the exam-flunking classes against the exam-passing classes. In Britain, one of the strongest predictors of how you would vote in the Brexit referendum was educational level.[52] In America, the proportion of people who voted Republican in presidential elections in the hundred best-educated counties, judged by the proportion of degree holders, shrank from 76 per cent in 1980 to 16 per cent in 2020.[53] Donald Trump, who was particularly successful at appealing to blue-collar workers, even declared, 'I love the poorly educated.'[54]

Chapter Seventeen returns to one of the themes of the earlier part of the book: the Far East. Singapore is the closest thing the world has seen to Plato's Republic or Confucius's mandarin state. This is significant in itself: Singapore's success in making the leap from a swampy backwater into one of the world's richest societies demonstrates the power of the meritocratic idea in producing prosperity. But what matters even more is that China – a giant economy that is rapidly catching up with the United States – has decided to model itself on Singapore. China has not only embraced educational meritocracy: Chinese schoolchildren increasingly tread the same path as their mandarin predecessors, only this time they study engineering rather than the Confucian classics. It has also embraced political meritocracy: China prides itself on eliding the difference between political and administrative positions and promoting politician-bureaucrats on the basis of a succession of increasingly demanding tests. Even middle-aged aspirants for high office have to sit written examinations.

The more the West abandons liberal meritocracy in favour of plutocracy modified by quotas, the more it will cede the future to China. But how do we revitalize a meritocracy that is degenerating into plutocracy? And how do we live with this most demanding of taskmasters? That is the subject of the conclusion.

PART ONE

Priority, Degree and Place

I

Homo hierarchicus

In *Troilus and Cressida* (1609) Shakespeare's Ulysses presents a view of society that is as repugnant to the meritocratic world view as possible. Society is divided into estates and degrees. People are born into a fixed place in the world. The social order is a reflection of the divine order. Fail to 'observe degree, priority and place' and everything will collapse in ruins – the natural order as well as the social order:

> What plagues and what portents! what mutiny!
> What raging of the sea! shaking of earth!
> Commotion in the winds! frights, changes, horrors,
> Divert and crack, rend and deracinate
> The unity and married calm of states
> Quite from their fixture! O, when degree is shaked,
> Which is the ladder to all high designs,
> Then enterprise is sick! How could communities,
> Degrees in schools and brotherhoods in cities,
> Peaceful commerce from dividable shores,
> The primogenitive and due of birth,
> Prerogative of age, crowns, sceptres, laurels,
> But by degree, stand in authentic place?
> Take but degree away, untune that string,
> And, hark, what discord follows!

This hierarchical view of the world was the dominant view in Europe until relatively recently. It also found striking echoes in other pre-modern societies such as India with its caste system of Brahmins and untouchables and Japan with its rigid hierarchy. I will focus on

Europe because it was Europe that first saw the 'prerogative of age, crowns, sceptres, laurels' comprehensively challenged.

THE THEORY OF INEQUALITY

The pre-modern world conceived of itself as a hierarchy of social groups – estates, orders or corps – that were ordained by God and defined by their relationship to two great verities: their social function (those who prayed, those who fought and those who worked) and their position in a hierarchy of status that stretched downward from the heavens (the word *état* is derived from the Latin for 'status').

Charlemagne instructed his subjects in the early 800s to 'serve God faithfully in that order in which he is placed'. The 843 Treaty of Verdun, which divided Charlemagne's empire between his three sons, proclaimed the principle that 'every man should have a lord' with the same certainty that the United Nations proclaimed, in 1948, that human rights are universal. In 1079 Pope Gregory VII declared that 'the dispensation of divine providence ordered there should be distinct grades and orders'. In 1302 Pope Boniface VIII reiterated that the members of each social order should not aspire to the prerogatives and honours of people in higher social positions.[1]

This theory of fixed estates was a distorted image of reality, of course. There were plenty of occupations that didn't fit into this simple tripartite hierarchy – merchants, millers and strolling players, for example – and the number of misfits increased as society became richer. People nevertheless continued to be wedded to a status hierarchy that defined everything in terms of its relationship with manual labour. Those who lived a little like priests – for example, men of letters or lawyers, or, at a pinch, teachers – had a high position in the hierarchy. Those who soiled their hands with manual work had a lower position, even if they grew quite rich. Money could never wash the stain of manual labour from your hands.[2]

The hierarchy of status was reinforced by a hierarchy of legal rights and obligations. T. H. Marshall, one of the founders of sociology in Britain, noted that in a society of estates 'people have a position (status) to which is attached a bundle of rights, privileges, obligations and legal capacities enforced by public authority'.[3] Nobles were entitled to trials in special courts, where they were judged by their peers, and even to particular punishments suited to their rank: in France nobles were entitled to be decapitated if they were found guilty of a capital crime, if decapitation can be counted as a privilege, rather than being tortured to death. They were also exempted from various taxes on the grounds that they were already serving the state through their military prowess. Nobles were also bound by obligations to fight for their king (or other feudal lord) and to provide for their dependants, starting with their family members. Removing group-specific legal rights and replacing them with individual rights was at the heart of the Enlightenment project in the eighteenth century.

The hierarchy of status doubled as a hierarchy of honour. Honour determined how people treated you: the more honour you possessed, the more deference you were owed. Honour also determined how you treated other people: because you possessed honour you were obliged to treat other people with a (measured) degree of civility. Honour was a demanding taskmaster. If someone insulted your honour, they could not be allowed to get away with it: hence the plague of jousts and duels that took so many young noble lives. '[A] hundred and fifty years ago, we would have had to fight if challenged,' says Ivor Claire, the aristocratic hero 'with feet of clay' in Evelyn Waugh's *Officers and Gentlemen* (1955). 'Now we'd laugh. There must have been a time . . . when it was rather an awkward question.'

The world of special rights and privileges extended to corporate bodies. Some of these bodies, such as aristocratic assemblies and universities, were reserved for the elite. Others, such as town councils, provincial estates and professional guilds, might involve 'middling sorts' or even below. A striking proportion of the population of pre-modern societies enjoyed special privileges, either in the form of rights or exemptions, by virtue of their membership of certain estates or corporations or guilds or by virtue of their birthplace. This meant that pre-modern regimes were both enormously complicated and enormously hard to define: you might discover that a person from, say, Ludlow, had a claim on an Oxford college for a subsidized education for no reason other than that he came from Ludlow and a wool merchant had forged some special link eons ago. What mattered were the ties of nature and custom that bound you to your superiors rather than the universal rules that ideally govern opportunities in a meritocracy.

This organic view of society rested on both ancient and biblical authorities. Aristotle talked about 'natural' rulers and 'natural' slaves: some people were designed to rule, some to obey, and that was just the way things were. The Bible is full of passages emphasizing the importance of obedience. 'Obey them that have the rule over you,' thunders Hebrews 13:17. 'The powers that are be ordained of God,' St Paul says in Romans 13:1. 'Render ... unto Caesar the things which are Caesar's,' Jesus says in Matthew 22:21. Across Europe a black-coated intelligentsia took every opportunity, from their regular Sunday sermons to celebrations of births, marriages and deaths, harvests and holidays, to repeat these passages and add fulminations of their own. The message is well summed up in a nineteenth-century British ditty:

> God bless the squire and his relations
> And keep us in our proper stations.

This belief in natural hierarchy found its most elaborate expression in the notion of a great chain of being, a chain that stretched from the foot of God's throne to the 'meanest inanimate object'.[4] This governed social thought in the Middle Ages and became even more elaborate in the sixteenth and seventeenth centuries with the doctrine of 'correspondences'. Shakespeare's contemporaries saw a correspondence everywhere they looked: between hierarchy in the divine world and hierarchy in human society, or even between the human body and the body politic, with the monarch acting as the head and the labourers as the hands. Walter Raleigh's *History of the World* (1614) contains a fine passage on how the social hierarchy is an extension of natural hierarchy (though not fine enough to save him from being beheaded in 1618):

> Shall we therefore value honour and riches at nothing and neglect them as unnecessary and vain? Certainly no. For that infinite wisdom of God, which hath distinguished his angels by degrees, which hath given greater and less light and beauty to heavenly bodies, which hath made differences between beasts and birds, created the eagle and the fly, the cedar and the shrub, and among stones given the fairest tincture to the ruby and the

quickest light to the diamond, hath also ordained kings, dukes or leaders of the people, magistrates, judges, and other degrees among men.[5]

According to this view, an untuned string meant more than a single discordant note. It meant disharmony on a universal scale – cosmic anarchy in which the universe ceased to obey laws and disorder was unleashed on every corner of God's creation. Thus Othello worried that 'chaos is come again', Ulysses talked of 'this chaos, when degree is suffocate', King Lear's madness reflected the anarchy that comes from the rebellion of children against their father.

If all this sounds more like a literary trope than a guide to everyday living, it is nevertheless true that the theory of priority, degree and place was woven into society. To demonstrate this point, let's look at the way the theory of inequality worked in a particular society at a particular point of time: in the England of the Tudors and Stuarts. This England – Shakespeare's England – is of particular interest because many of the old assumptions of hierarchical society were being tested by a new commercial society and a new philosophy of Renaissance humanism. The defenders of the old order had to explain themselves because they were being challenged for the first time. In 1642–51, a quarter of a century after Shakespeare died, Britain exploded into a Civil War that sounded many of the themes of a new meritocratic social order.

HOW HIERARCHY WORKED

In a society in which the most important economic resource was not the brain inside your head but the land under your feet, the most powerful people were the ones who owned that land. In the Middle Ages landed aristocrats had held their lands – 'fiefs' or 'fees' – in return for providing military service for the king. Members of the landed elite invested psychologically as well as financially in turning themselves into warriors. They spent most of their youth learning how to fight, most of their leisure time sharpening their skills in hunting and jousting, and most of their surplus money on equipping themselves with horses and armour.[6] They organized themselves into morale-boosting fraternities such as the Templars, the Knights of

St John and the Teutonic Knights; told romantic tales about knights on horseback who went off in search of honour, adventure and, through the Crusades, religious salvation;[7] and otherwise bound each other together by three adamantine bonds: shared danger, shared breeding and shared myths.

The cost of warfare was nevertheless exorbitant in both blood and treasure. By the thirteenth and fourteenth centuries knights were tanks in human form: mounted on horses for mobility, covered with heavy armour for protection, equipped with lances and swords for offensive power, serviced by a retinue of lesser soldiers such as servants and shield bearers, and expensive to operate. According to one study, almost half of the male members of British ducal families born between 1330 and 1479 met a violent end.[8] So it is not entirely surprising that, as the Tudors established a centralized state, aristocrats spent less time fighting and more time cultivating their estates and politicking in Court.

The principle of hierarchy governed every social relation. Masters ruled over serfs. Husbands ruled over wives and children ('I know not which live more unnatural lives,' John Taylor, a seventeenth-century poet quipped, 'obedient husbands or commanding wives.')[9] Men ruled over animals. Society celebrated hierarchy in everything from the most elaborate rituals, such as state dinners, to the smallest gestures. The two great symbols of this society were the hat and the whip. People were forever doffing their hats in deference to their betters – and those who refused to doff their hats were frequently given a whipping or put in stocks.[10]

The social order was founded on entitlement: certain people were entitled to a certain treatment because of who they were rather than what they had achieved. Aristocrats regarded themselves as superior to the common herd by virtue of generations of careful breeding. 'If there are races among animals there are races among men,' Margraf Karl Friedrich von Baden wrote. 'For that reason the most superior must put themselves ahead of others, marry among themselves and produce a pure race: that is the nobility.'[11] Still, members of the ruling class inherited duties along with privileges: they had to keep the machinery of government going (for example, by serving as lord lieutenants of their counties) and they had to provide an example of good conduct. 'In the greatest fortune,' observed Richard Brathwaite in his *English Gentleman* (1630), 'there is the least liberty.'

> He sinnes doubly, that sinnes exemplarily: whence is meant, that such, whose very persons should bee examples or patternes of vigilancy, providence and industry, must not sleepe out their time under the fruitlesse shadowe of Security. Men in great place (saith one) are thrice servants; servants of the Soveraigne, or state; servants of Fame; and servants of Businesse. So as they have no freedome, neither in their persons, nor in their actions, nor in their times.[12]

The basic unit of society was not the individual but the family. The aristocratic family was defined by its relationship to two great existential facts: place and time. 'We belong to our possessions, rather than our possessions belong to us,' Lord Montagu of Beaulieu put it as late as 1974, speaking for his caste down the generations. 'To us, they are not wealth, but heirlooms, over which we have a sacred trust.'[13] The only thing as important as land was lineage – the individual landowner was 'the ancestral baton-carrier in the relay race of family destiny', as one historian puts it.[14] Rights, status, laws, property, all were justified by inheritance rather than utility, by tradition rather than reason.

John Galsworthy summarized this outlook in his novel *The Country House*, written in 1906, set in 1891, but relevant through the ages. 'I believe in my father, and his father, and his father's father, the makers and keepers of my estate,' the local squire proclaims, 'and I believe in myself and my son and my son's son. And I believe that we have made the country, and shall keep the country what it is . . . And I believe in my social equals and the country house, and in things as they are, for ever and ever. Amen.'[15] The Curzon family motto made the same point more concisely: 'Let Curzon holde what Curzon helde.'[16]

The best way to justify change was to present it as a return to tradition. Pre-modern societies actively willed themselves to be 'stable', in the same way as modern societies will themselves to be 'mobile', citing traditions wherever possible but, if they couldn't find them, simply inventing them. As soon as new men had made enough money to become respectable they either married into an established family or purchased a coat of arms that 'proved' they belonged to the ancient aristocracy.[17] Daniel Defoe captured this in *The Complete English Tradesman* (1726):

> We see the tradesmen of England, as they grow wealthy, coming every day to the Herald's Office, to search for the coats of arms of their ancestors, in order to paint them upon their coaches, and engrave them upon their plate, embroider them upon their furniture, or carve them upon the pediments of their new houses . . .[18]

The flip-side of deference to tradition and lineage was dislike of change and rootlessness. Sir Edward Coke, an Elizabethan and Jacobean lawyer and one of the fathers of common law, advised everyone to 'Hold all innovations and new ways suspicious.'[19] Lord Salisbury, three times prime minister in the late-Victorian era, pronounced gloomily that 'whatever happens will be for the worse and therefore it is in our interest that as little should happen as possible'. In Anthony Trollope's *The Prime Minister* (1876) Abel Wharton, QC, vigorously opposes his daughter's marriage to Ferdinand Lopez – rightly, as it turns out – because he doesn't know where Lopez comes from and who his people are. He might be clever and plausible – but he has no roots and no history, and 'no one knows anything about him'.[20] He is a man fallen out of the moon.

Medieval and Early Modern societies worked as hard to put limits on people's freedom to improve themselves as today's societies do, at least formally, to boost social mobility. Governments laid down rules about how much land different sorts of people could buy, what sorts of clothes they could wear and what sorts of sports they could play: archery was for the plebs, bowls and tennis for the toffs.[21] It also devoted a great deal of effort to tying people into elaborate apprenticeship systems. 'If any young man unmaried be without service,' a sixteenth-century legal scholar thundered, 'he shalbe compelled to get him a master whom he must serve for that yere, or else he shalbe punished with stockes and whipping as an idle vagabond.'[22]

Educational mobility was a particular bugbear. In the early sixteenth century James I forbade people who were 'not gentlemen by descent' from entering the Inns of Court.[23] In the seventeenth century Oxbridge colleges introduced the status of Fellow Commoner (Cambridge) or Gentleman Commoner (Oxford) so that well-bred undergraduates could sit with the Fellows rather than with run-of-the-mill undergraduates (for double fees, naturally). In the sixteenth century, continental universities drove poorer students from student lodgings and obliged them to do domestic work, frequently looking after richer students. Paris, Bologna and Perugia deprived poor students of the right to vote and become members of academic councils, while Louvain obliged paupers to wear a white shoulder piece, instead of the traditional black, for graduation ceremonies.[24] In the 1720s, Bernard Mandeville, supposedly a great champion of the liberal order, attacked charity schools on the grounds that they would make the poor discontented with their lot in life: 'it is requisite that great numbers of [the poor] should be Ignorant as well as Poor'.[25]

Up until remarkably recently the best sort of people had little time for the three great articles of faith of today's meritocrats: hard work, ambition and education.

Living nobly meant avoiding all forms of manual work, including trade. Christianity taught that work was a punishment for the Fall – before the Fall, Adam and Eve had not had to labour to get nature to yield up its fruits – while aristocratic snobbery taught that engaging in labour was inherently degrading. Some places, such as the Kingdom of Naples, had laws which forbade nobles from engaging in gainful employment; others, such as England, relied on social convention. True aristocrats made it clear not only that they weren't contaminated by labour but that they couldn't possibly be: just as Chinese mandarins had long fingernails encased in silver to demonstrate that they could not lift a finger to do anything practical, European aristocrats had clothes that made work impossible – long dresses for women and fine silk breeches for men.

Conspicuous leisure was but one aspect of conspicuous consumption: living nobly meant demonstrating that you had time to waste and money to burn. Nobles employed armies of retainers wherever they went: coachmen to drive them, footmen to tend to them, pages to accompany them, ushers to introduce them, hangers-on to peacock around with them. They built themselves large, sometimes gigantic, houses that required armies of servants to run them and legions of visitors to justify their existence.

For some members of the old aristocracy this prohibition even extended to education, on the grounds that it filled children's minds with nonsense even as it enfeebled their bodies. Richard Pace, Henry VIII's secretary of state, who had studied at Winchester, Padua and Oxford, heard one peer exclaiming, 'I swear by God's body, I'd rather that my son should hang than study letters.' Sir Thomas Elyot complained that 'to a great gentleman it is a notable reproach to be well learned and to be called a great clerk'. Edmund Spenser said that nobles deemed it a 'base thing' 'to be learned'.[26]

As for ambition, a remarkable range of authorities agreed that ambition was a double abomination: a sign of individual depravity and a threat to social cohesion. St Augustine defined ambition as the chief enemy of the good. Machiavelli identified ambition and avarice as 'Furies' that were designed to 'deprive us of peace and to set us at war'.[27] The Calvinists' Genevan translation of the Bible included seventy-seven admonitions against ambition, including the assertions that 'God detesteth ambition' and that Adam was destroyed not by pride but by ambition.[28] Shakespeare's tragedies feature characters who are seized by ambition that drives them upwards beyond the limits prescribed for them by their birth: Richard III is deformed, both outwardly and inwardly, by ambition; Macbeth is a victim of 'vaulting ambition, which o'erleaps itself'. In the *Anatomy of Melancholy* (1628) Robert Burton defined ambition as 'a canker of the soul, an hidden plague ... a secret poison, the father of livor [envy], and mother of hypocrisy, the moth of holiness, and cause of madness, crucifying and disquieting all that it takes hold of'.[29]

How did this society of orders and degrees work in practice? How were privileges passed from generation to generation? How were jobs allocated and opportunities distributed? In order to answer these questions we have to understand that the family was not only the basic *social* unit of pre-modern societies. It was the basic *political* unit as well.

2

Family Power

In *The Communist Manifesto* (1848) Karl Marx and Friedrich Engels declared that 'the history of all hitherto existing societies is the history of class struggles'. It would have been just as true to have said, back then, that 'the history of all hitherto existing societies is the history of family struggles'. Before the mid-nineteenth century the commanding heights of almost all 'hitherto existing societies' were controlled by ruling families. The questions at the heart of domestic politics were family questions. Could the ruling family produce healthy children? Could it hold out against claims to the throne by rival families? Foreign policy was equally dynastic. Royal marriages represented an opportunity to guarantee the social order for future generations by producing an heir: failed successions could lead to bloody civil wars or international conflagrations.

Today we instinctively regard the idea that people should inherit real political power, as opposed to the pantomime variety, as an abomination. The British have turned their royal family into a branch of the entertainment industry: the royals are allowed to live in their gilded cages provided they devote their lives to ceremonial functions (bringing in a Hollywood actress to add more multicultural sparkle proved to be an innovation too far). The moment the royals try to exercise real power, as Prince Charles tried to do with his campaigns on architecture, GM foods and the countryside, they tell them, irritably, to shut up.

We naturally warm to critics of the dynastic principle who have wagged their fingers down the ages, such as Hippocrates, a Greek sage, who warned that 'where there are kings, there must be the greatest cowards. For [here] men's souls are enslaved, and refuse to run

35

risks readily and recklessly to increase the power of somebody else'; or Ibn Khaldun, the great Arabic historian, who argued that dynasties will always degenerate over time because a childhood of luxury corrupts the human spirit.[1] There are only twenty monarchies left in a world that boasts more than 200 sovereign states.

Yet for most of history dynasties have been the rule rather than the exception: today's meritocratic certainties are, in fact, recent innovations which most people in most places would not have understood. People as widely dispersed as the Aztecs and the Chinese have embraced dynasty. The Japanese Yamato dynasty has been on the throne since 660 BC. Dynasties have dominated business as well as politics: Antinoris have produced wine in Tuscany since 1385, Berettas have made guns nearby since 1526 and Rothschilds have played a starring role in banking since the eighteenth century. 'The banker's calling is hereditary,' wrote Walter Bagehot, who followed his father into the banking business and became editor of the *Economist* by dint of marrying the daughter of the magazine's founder as well as possessing unrivalled journalistic talent. 'The credit of the bank descends from father to son; this inherited wealth brings inherited refinement.'

Dynasties have taken different forms in different parts of the world. The West has strongly favoured both monogamy and male primogeniture for a mixture of religious and economic reasons: Christianity forbids even the most powerful rulers from taking more than one wife at a time, while primogeniture prevents the break-up of great estates and limits feuding between rival claimants to the throne. Outside the West, polygamy has been the rule. Powerful men had lots of 'wives', either in the form of legitimate wives in polygamous regimes or concubines in monogamous ones, in part because they could and in part because they wanted to have as many children as possible to maximize their chances of producing that all-important healthy male heir.

Despite these striking differences, dynasties the world over have tended to draw on the same rhetoric and resources. They present themselves as the guarantees of the social order and links between the Earth and Heaven. They act as centrepieces in a wider network of aristocratic families who mix the transfer of power with the transmission of genes. Royals surrounded themselves with other dynasts: Louis XVI decreed that you could not be presented at Court unless you boasted a noble pedigree going back to 1400, which limited the list of candidates to a thousand families.[2] Elite families talked about genealogical links with the same enthusiasm that today's high-flyers talk about their educational credentials.

That said, the relationship between royal families and other aristocratic families was complicated: sometimes royals succeeded in subordinating other dynasties to their will, often by tempting them to abandon their local principalities for life at Court; sometimes aristocratic families succeeded in keeping kings on a tight leash, most obviously in Poland, where they had a right to elect their kings. In aristocratic societies there is usually a battle between the *primus* and the *inter pares*.

Dynasties also went through similar cycles: born out of force or fraud, they eventually clothed raw power in the robes of civilization. Confucius argued that successful emperors rule through moral example. 'He who governs by his moral excellence may be compared to the Pole-star,' *The Analects* has him saying, 'which abides in its place while all the stars bow towards it.' Augustine, Aquinas and Erasmus argued that kings needed to be models of virtue – devout and honest, just and merciful – if they wanted to survive. The populace must submit without question, of course, but the king must play his part by showing grace and benevolence. Dynasties also promoted the same patterns of behaviour: patronage and deference, fawning and intrigue, all follow as inexorably from the dynastic principle as preoccupations with exams and career hierarchies follow from the meritocratic principle.

Dynastic courts were invariably centres of intrigue: whether you examine Turkish sultans or Chinese emperors or European kings, courtiers are always plotting to get the ear of the king or his successor, often to drip in poison about their rivals. Writing about Louis XVI, Britain's ambassador in France argued that intrigue was inescapable:

His Majesty wishes to place Himself out of the Reach of all Intrigue. This, however, is a vain Expectation, and the Chimera of a Young, inexperienced Mind. The throne He fills, far from raising him above Intrigue, places Him in the Centre of it. Great and Eminent Superiority Of Talents might, indeed, crush these Cabals, but as there is no Reason

to believe Him possessed of that Superiority, I think, He will be a prey
to them and find Himself more and more entangled every Day.[3]

Dynasties also had one fundamental thing in common: they minimized the difference between the public and the private, or the
political and the personal: all politics was family politics. Frederick
Pollock and F. W. Maitland got to the heart of the matter in their great
History of English Law (1895): 'Just in so far as the ideal of feudalism
is perfectly realized, all that we call public law is merged in private
law; jurisdiction is property, office is property, the kingship itself is
property.'[4] Countries were essentially family estates: a king inherited
his country in much the same way as a landowner inherited his estate,
and ran it in much the same way. This meant that maps were always
in flux as this or that portion of an inheritance passed from one family
to another. It also meant that alliances could suddenly change as the
owner of one estate fell out with his neighbour or, alternatively, married off his daughter to a neighbour's son. The inhabitants of countries
had no more say in these great affairs of state than the peasants living
on a great estate had in the affairs of a great landowner.

The passage of time weakened Pollock and Maitland's 'perfect feudalism'. In 1419 a French lawyer argued that 'the lordship that the
king has in the kingdom is of a different kind from the lordship of
property that is transmitted through family inheritance'. Even as Louis
XIV declared that 'the state is me', other lawyers distinguished between
the king as a physical person and the king as the embodiment of the
nation state. Even so, dynasties continued to blur the line between
public and private until at least the nineteenth century: they not only
owned large pieces of land personally (as the Queen of England still
does) but also handed out offices of state as if they were personal gifts.

POLITICS AS BIOLOGY

The dynastic principle put the physical person of the monarch at the
heart of power: monarchs led their country's troops into battle at
least until the middle of the eighteenth century and, through the royal
household, provided the nucleus of the state. The closer you were

physically to the king, the closer you were to the centre of power. The oldest offices were all related to the monarch's physical needs – looking after his horse or falcons, guarding his bedchamber – and were all reserved for members of his own family or the most blue-blooded aristocrats. In Britain, the Groom of the Stool, who became one of the most powerful figures in the royal household, originally had the job of supervising the sovereign's bowel movements. In France, the right to present the king's napkin during the dinner was given to the highest-born person present. Post-medieval kings some-times tightened the links between themselves and the upper nobility at the same time as they were building more professional bureaucracies: Louis XIV doubled the number of pages (young nobles of impeccable breeding) who were sent to Versailles in order to learn Latin, dance and horsemanship, from 80 to 160.[5]

Louis XIV – perhaps the most splendid example of the most splendid of European monarchies – demonstrated the importance of putting the physical person of the monarch on display to his leading subjects. Getting dressed in the morning and undressed at night were elaborate ceremonies, known as the *levée* and the *coucher* and lasting about an hour and a half each, which took place before large audiences of the fin-est in the land. Hundreds of people watched him go a-hunting (which he often did several days a week). The king dined in public, with senior aristocrats watching from comfortable seats and lowlier people filing past, sometimes asking for favours as they went. The obvious function of this display was to allow courtiers to beg for favours – which they did morning, noon and night. But it also allowed them to gawp at the royal person – take a measure of his nature and chat about their proximity to the great man to their friends. The king was a pop star to be admired – and even touched – as much as he was a ruler making decisions.[6]

The importance of physical proximity to the king was illustrated at its most brutal by royal deaths. Marie Antoinette's chambermaid described the kerfuffle when news of Louis XV's death arrived: 'A ter-rible noise exactly like thunder was heard in the outer room of his apartments: it was the crowd of courtiers deserting the antechamber of the dead sovereign to come and greet the new power of Louis XVI.' You could never be too early to start grovelling to the new king.

As well as blue bloods, courts contained a variety of hangers-on whose unifying feature was that they existed to satisfy the king's needs, physical, psychological or whatever: fools and minstrels to entertain him; women and boys to titillate or soothe him; bosom buddies to amuse and advise him; writers to sing his virtues; artists to paint his picture and sculpt his form; and huntmasters to prepare for hunting and shooting.

Some monarchs had a weakness for clever companions: Louis XIV brought talented members of the bourgeoisie to Court, including Vauban, Racine, Molière and Mme de Maintenon. Other monarchs deliberately chose weak companions such as dwarfs, exiles or ne'er-do-wells. Henry VII had several mentally defective companions – called 'naturals' or 'innocents' – who accompanied him on his travels around the country.[7] Elizabeth I had a dwarf, Thomasina, whom she showered with gifts such as gowns, gloves and ivory combs.[8] (The Duc de Bourbon's many peculiarities – he was 'very considerably shorter than the shortest men', had livid yellow skin and laboured under the delusion that he was a dog – were put down to the fact that his mother kept a dwarf as a companion.)[9] The Chinese and Turkish courts favoured eunuchs because they couldn't threaten the ruler's bloodline (or ego) by impregnating his concubines, or else challenge his family's claim to the throne by harbouring dynastic ambitions of their own. The Turkish sultans also surrounded themselves with slaves whom they recruited by conquest but then promoted to powerful positions. Many of the most senior officers in the civil service and the military corps started life in bondage.

By putting a monarch on the throne, the dynastic principle also put the facts of biology at the heart of politics. Monarchs might be semi-divine beings to their supporters – the visible links between the earthly and the heavenly orders – but they were also biological beings. The facts of biology could be particularly demanding for European monarchies, reducing the number of legitimate children they could produce and, given high rates of infant mortality, sometimes ensuring that girls or distant relations succeeded to the throne.

The birth of a healthy son was the subject of national as well as familial celebration: when Charles VI of France announced the birth of a male heir on 6 February 1392, Paris exploded with joy, according to one account: church bells rang, the streets filled with revellers carrying lighted torches, and ladies doled out wine and spices from trestle tables.[10] Equally, the failure to produce a son produced trauma. Catherine of Braganza lived a life of misery as she had one miscarriage after another, leaving Charles II without an heir. However unpleasant this was for all concerned, it is understandable in a world where political stability depended on a clear line of succession. Dynastic squabbles could plunge countries into prolonged civil wars or even lead to the collapse of empires. Burgundy disappeared as a separate kingdom after the death of the childless Rudolf III in 1032. Thirty-four years later in 1066 the death of the childless Edward the Confessor led to one of the most profound ruptures in English history, the Norman Conquest.[11]

The importance of male babies turned the most intimate aspects of a monarch's biological make-up into a public issue. Hilary Mantel nicely describes Tudor politics as 'graphically gynaecological' as Henry VIII desperately tried to produce a male heir and his wives suffered a succession of miscarriages, foetal deaths, stillbirths and children's deaths, followed, in two cases, by being beheaded.[12] The same can be said of the politics of pre-Revolutionary France. Louis XVI's failure to consummate his marriage to Marie Antoinette in their first seven years together led to intense speculation from the courts of Europe to the streets of Paris. Was Louis impotent? Was Marie Antoinette frigid? Or a harlot? Her mother, the Empress Maria Theresa, instructed Austria's ambassador to Versailles to persuade Louis to have an operation on his penis to get it working properly. Marie Antoinette's brother Joseph II wrote graphically to their brother Leopold to say that Louis had 'well-conditioned, strong erections and introduced his member, stayed there for two minutes without moving, withdrew without ejaculation, and then, still erect, wished [his wife] good evening'. His solution to this marital conundrum? 'He should be whipped like a donkey to make him discharge in anger.'[13]

Modern historians have added to this gynaecological speculation. Some have argued that Louis had an excessively tight foreskin that made copulation painful. Others have suggested that he had a *bracquemart assez considérable* (an unusually large penis), while Marie Antoinette had an *étroitesse du chemin* (a narrow vagina), which also made copulation painful. Whatever the cause of their problems, the couple eventually overcame them and produced the necessary children.[14]

If infertility could produce sometimes fatal problems for dynasties, fecundity could provide fabulous opportunities. Maria Theresa of Austria secured the survival of the Austro-Hungarian empire by giving birth to sixteen children, seven of whom were married into other European dynasties. The obscure German house of Saxe-Coburg-Gotha transformed itself into the most successful royal dynasty in the world when Prince Albert married the Queen of England, who presided over the world's greatest empire, and sired nine children. Queen Victoria was so successful in marrying her numerous children into the other great houses of Europe that she was known as 'the grandmother of Europe': Elizabeth II and her husband, the Duke of Edinburgh, are themselves both third cousins, as a result of being direct descendants of Queen Victoria, and second cousins once removed, as a result of being directly descended from Christian IX of Denmark.

Still, you could also have too much of a good thing. A large brood of sons might lead to the division of a territory: Charlemagne divided his kingdom between three powerful sons. The arrival of a new son, born to an aged king who had taken on a young wife, could destabilize a family: Charles the Bald, son of the Carolingian emperor Louis the Pious, was born in 823, when the king's other three sons had already been promised parts of the kingdom.

In democracies, you normally have to be in fine physical fettle to earn the right to rule (Franklin Roosevelt escaped this rule partly because the press didn't dwell, as it surely would today, on his polio). In dynastic regimes, you can inherit the throne as an infant and continue to sit on it in your dotage. James VI of Scotland, the 'cradle king', inherited just after his first birthday, when his mother, Mary, Queen of Scots, was forced to abdicate. In France, Louis XIII (1610), Louis XIV (1643) and Louis XV (1715) were all under the age of ten when they succeeded to the throne. Pu Yi was just two when he became the last emperor of China. Minority rule inevitably spelt problems: rule by queen regents, powerful uncles or ambitious courtiers; Court fighting and factionalism; negotiations about future brides for the child ruler; and, after the Reformation, the potential for countries to be torn apart by religious conflict, as when Catholic Spain's Philip II married Henry VIII's eldest daughter, Mary.

Old age also came with its own difficulties. 'Though I am Kinge of men,' the 'cradle king' observed as he whiled away the years as James I of England as well as James VI of Scotland, 'yett I am not Kinge of time, and I growe olde with this.' Senile kings were often captured by scheming advisers. In his later years (he died in 1612), Rudolf II, a Habsburg emperor, became little more than the pawn of a chamber servant who monopolized access to the emperor and sold his influence to the highest bidder, and Rudolf was eventually stripped of all real power by his younger brother. The occasional king presented the problems of both extreme youth and extreme old age: Louis XIV succeeded to the throne at the age of four and then reigned for seventy-two years, to be succeeded by his great-grandson.

Adult heirs could get sick of waiting for their fathers to die, driven to distraction by the old medieval saying 'nothing is more certain than death, but nothing is more uncertain than the hour of death'.[15] Some tried to depose their fathers. Henry II's sons fled to France in the spring of 1173 and joined Louis VII's court, triggering eighteen months of war.[16] The Holy Roman Emperor, Henry IV, was imprisoned by his son Henry V and forced to abdicate.[17] Others contented themselves with establishing rival courts of equally ambitious young courtiers: examples include Joseph, the eldest son of Leopold I; George, the eldest son of George I; and Edward, the eldest son of Queen Victoria, whose long reign became a nightmare for him.

Dynastic rule was particularly complicated for women – and often particularly unpleasant too. A few countries avoided female monarchs entirely: the French crown passed exclusively down the male line from 987 to 1848, when the last king of France was deposed.[18] Those that allowed them viewed their arrival with trepidation. Lonely figures in a man's world, female monarchs had great difficulty in establishing their authority. If they remained virgin queens, like Elizabeth of England or Christina of Sweden, they failed in their job of producing successors, and plunged their countries into a succession crisis when they died; if they married, as most of them did, they lost their independence. Queens could be undermined by rumours of infidelity, however unfounded or, as in the case of Catherine the Great, extravagant. Queen mothers were invariably suspected (not always wrongly) of political scheming.

Daughters also had to be prepared to be used as pieces in the game of thrones, often at startlingly young ages (Isabella of France married Richard II when she was only six).[19] A daughter might be exchanged as part of a peace settlement, even being described as an *obses pacis* or 'pledge of peace'.[20] A king might shore up his power at home by marrying his daughter to a great magnate (though he also risked annoying all the other magnates in doing so. Or he might extend his reach abroad by forming a marriage alliance with a foreign prince.

Foreign alliances could be miserable for the bride in question, who was not only to be married to a man she'd never met but also taken to a country whose language she didn't speak. The heart of the youngest daughter of Edward III, Joan, probably didn't jump for joy when, at the age of eleven, she was told that she was being sent far away to marry the young heir of the king of Castile, later nicknamed Peter the Cruel.[21] But matters of state trumped matters of the heart. Up until the nineteenth century diplomacy was essentially an exercise in dynasty-building: hence what John Roberts describes as 'the monotonous preoccupation of negotiations and treaty-making with the possible consequences of marriages and the careful establishment and scrutiny of lines of succession'.[22]

Monogamy also introduced two shadowy players into the royal drama, mistresses and bastards. Most kings had at least one mistress. Some, such as Augustus II of Poland-Saxony, nicknamed 'the Strong', who reputedly sired 354 children, had a lot more. Mistresses often became the focus of rival factions, and illegitimate children became important members of society, if not powerful political figures in their own right.

The politics of dynasty found their most extreme expression, at least in Europe, in the Habsburg empire. The Habsburgs vaulted themselves from middle-ranking German counts in the twelfth century to rulers of the world's greatest empire in the sixteenth almost entirely by dint of marriage and succession. One branch of the family continued to dominate the Danubian region down to the First World War. Most dynasties eventually decided to link their fates with nation states: for all the claims of their French territories, British kings and queens were primarily kings and queens of the British Isles. The East European Habsburgs remained irreducibly multinational, kings and queens of a conglomeration of territories that were linked by nothing more than Habsburg blood. They had a capital and a territorial base but no common nationality. 'Their instincts were purely proprietary,' Lewis Namier noted. 'The one meaning of an Austrian State to them was that they possessed it; to the outside world, that it existed.'[23] R. J. W. Evans remarked that it was only right that their chosen style was the Baroque – the triumphant reconciliation of opposites in brilliant harmony.[24] German conversation, Spanish ceremony, Italian music: these were the casual background of life in the Court in the world's most multinational empire: a triumph of the power of dynasty over the logic of national identity.

Dynasty ensured that the relationship between social position and personal ability was, at best, arbitrary. Anybody who thinks that abilities are primarily determined by nurture rather than nature should spend a little time studying the history of Europe's royal dynasties. If you happened to have an able ruler, then all well and good, but ability and lineage seldom went hand in hand, and even extreme lack of ability was no barrier to succession. Being the oldest (preferably) male heir was all that mattered. Royal dynasties increasingly loaded the dice against themselves when it came to ability by restricting their choice of mates to fellow members of royal dynasties: by Queen Victoria's reign, the kings of most European countries were all related to each other.

Walter Bagehot argued that 'a royal family will generally have less ability than other families' (and even speculated that in 1802 every hereditary monarch in Europe was insane).[25] There were certainly extreme examples of mental weakness in royal lines. Henry VI of England was mentally incapacitated. George III suffered prolonged bouts of insanity. The Habsburgs were so prone to inbreeding that people joked that they married their cousins and slept with their siblings. The Emperor Charles V had such an extreme case of 'Habsburg jaw' that the upper and lower parts of his mouth didn't mesh (a carriage accident also robbed him of his front teeth). He was always intellectually limited – 'not very interesting', in the words of David Hume – but deteriorated badly in old age and spent his days taking clocks apart and having his servants make them tick in unison.[26] Philip II's eldest son and heir, Prince Carlos, suffered from delusions and dementia, a condition that was not helped by attempts to cure him by forcing him to share his bed with a mummified saint.[27] Charles II of Spain was a mass of genetic problems: his head was too big for his body and his tongue was too big for his mouth, so that he had difficulty speaking and constantly drooled; his first wife complained that he suffered from premature ejaculation and his second wife that he was impotent; on top of all that, he suffered from convulsions.[28] Other leading Habsburgs had evocative names such as Juana the Mad and Twat-Face (*Fotzenpoidl*).

It is easy today to think of the agonies of the Habsburgs as poetic justice: how dare people presume that they should rule just on the basis of inheritance? And what can you expect if you only deign to marry other blue bloods? Looking at the Habsburgs, we can easily conclude that the rule of merit is both natural and inevitable. But are we really as free of dynasties as we like to think? Business dynasties continue to thrive in America and Europe (think of the Murdochs and the Sulzbergers in media alone), while they are also gaining strength in the emerging world. Political dynasties keep popping up not only in India (the Gandhis) but also in Canada (the Trudeaus). Dynasticism is powerful precisely because it appeals to some of the most elemental human motives: the natural desire of humans to favour their children and the willingness of people to bend the knee to well-established families that can advance their interests. In Chapter Fifteen we will look at one of the biggest threats to the meritocratic revolution: the ability of successful families to co-opt the meritocratic principle in pursuit of family power. In the meantime, we will look at the way that dynastic societies went about executing the day-to-day business of governing.

3

Nepotism, Patronage, Venality

How did the old regime of degree, priority and place go about distributing the work of the world? Most people did the same as their fathers and their forefathers: tillers tilled and thatchers thatched. When desirable jobs had to be doled out there were three mechanisms at work: nepotism, patronage and, perhaps even more surprising to the modern sensibility, purchase.

The Italian term *nepotismo* was invented in the fourteenth or fifteenth century to describe the practice of senior clerics giving jobs to their relations – usually their own illegitimate children disguised as nephews.[1] Pope Callixtus III, originally Alfonso de Borgia, made two of his nephews cardinals during his three-year papacy (1455–8). Over the next two and a half centuries the Borgias produced a second pope, eleven more cardinals (including a saint) and numerous princes and potentates. A sixth of Pius II's appointments were given to relatives, one of whom briefly became pope. Paul III appointed two nephews, aged fourteen and sixteen, as cardinals. Sixtus IV made six of his nephews cardinals and, in a fit of avarice, prised the precious stones out of the papal mitre.[2]

The word 'nepotism' thus carried with it a sense of shocked disapproval – senior clerics, after all, were not supposed to sire children, let alone grant them favours. In fact, the practice of securing positions for your children and relations is one of the longest-established habits in the human species and, in many societies, was regarded as a proof of decency rather than of deviance. Most social animals make sacrifices to secure the well-being of their children and hence the survival of their own genetic material. 'Nepotism is the norm for social species,' Mary Maxwell, a biologist, argues. 'I go further: the practice of nepotism *defines* social species.'[3] All healthy societies, starting with the most basic, are organized around the principles of marriage, reproduction and inheritance.

Tribal societies were extended kinship groups that exchanged females both within the group and between groups. The history of the Roman Republic is, at its core, the history of twenty or thirty families that struggled to dominate the spoils of empire and were eventually forced to cede power to one dominant family, the house of Augustus. Augustus solidified his initially precarious position by offering jobs to almost all his relatives, however distant, and by forming marriage alliances with other powerful families.[4] Nepotism was also the hallmark of the earliest family businesses, not just the numerous small companies that advertised themselves under the ampersand '& son' but also multinational behemoths such as the Fugger and Rothschild banks.[5]

Patronage (and indeed nepotism) survives to this day: presidents and prime ministers habitually surround themselves with people they can trust and reward them with coveted positions when they leave office. David Cameron brought a clique of Eton- and Oxford-educated chums with him to Downing Street and gave them baubles when he resigned despite the fact that they lost an unlosable referendum. Donald Trump surrounded himself with members of the Trump organization as well as relatives such as daughter Ivanka and son-in-law Jared Kushner. John F. Kennedy made his brother, Bobby, attorney general, and Bill Clinton gave his wife the job of overhauling America's healthcare system. Yet today's examples of patronage are small compared with the ones we encounter in the pre-modern world. Patronage is usually confined to a narrow range of 'political' offices controlled directly by the prime minister or president. And even here a measure of competence is usually expected – though Trump has stretched this, as well as other conventions, by appointing a previous contestant on *The Apprentice*, Omarosa Manigault Newman, to his White House staff.

In pre-modern societies patronage was pervasive and inescapable. Monarchs devoted their lives to handing out jobs of every size and significance. Courtiers openly begged for favours from the sovereign. And everybody knew that there was 'no damned nonsense about merit' with what was going on, as Lord Melbourne, twice prime minister in the 1830s, said about the Order of the Garter.

The whole system depended on the same notion of property that we encountered in the previous chapter. The king owned the great offices of state much as he owned the royal deer, and he gave them to his courtiers as favours. Landed magnates also had plenty of offices in their pockets – including seats in Parliament. ('May I not do what I please with my own?' was, in essence, the Duke of Newcastle's incredulous retort to parliamentary reformers who wanted to abolish 'pocket boroughs', that is, parliamentary constituencies with tiny electorates that were controlled by local landowners.) And once you'd got a job from a patron you could do anything you wanted: sell it on or hire someone to do the inconvenient work that might be attached to it while you sat at home doing nothing.

Louis XIV was rather like a mother bird who spends her life feeding worms into the mouths of squawking chicks. His Court functioned as a giant jobs market: courtiers had to invest time and money in hanging around the king, but stood to reap substantial rewards if they were in the right place at the right time. It also arguably functioned as a giant reallocation machine of resources from the new world to the old: money that was raised by his loyal bureaucrats through taxes was redistributed to courtiers in the form of salaries, pensions and presents.

Jockeying for jobs never ceased. A common piece of advice on life at Court was 'sit down when you can; piss when you can; and ask for any job going'. People asked Louis XIV for jobs when he was getting up or going to bed, presented him with petitions during his daily promenades or shouted requests as they watched him eating his dinner (various scribes noted down the jobs he gave away during his day, which might be more than a hundred). When someone asked for a dying treasurer's job, he replied, 'The man is not yet dead and sixteen people have asked me for it.' Sometimes petitioners could be remarkably crude: when one petitioner was advised to wait, he drew attention to his missing arm, saying he'd still have two arms, had he waited to enlist. More often they bided their time and lathered on the blandishments. One courtier wrote to his young cousin 'you must have patience there [at Court], ask at the right moment and do not lose heart when you do not at first obtain everything you ask for'.[6]

Some courtiers became powerful job brokers. This was particularly true of women, who were not distracted by fighting wars and duels – and who could exercise their sexual charms on a king who was notably susceptible to them. Maréchale de Noailles was such a successful fixer that her four daughters all married dukes; a corridor was nicknamed the rue de Noailles. People wrote to her from as far away as Spain and Italy to ask for recommendations, favours, pensions and, of course, the currency of any job market, gossip. Mme de Montespan was another skilled fixer who helped to make the career of, among others, Racine, persuading Louis XIV to make him an *historiographe du roi* with a salary of 6,000 livres a year and, eventually, give him an apartment in the palace.[7]

Louis XIV is an extreme example because he did so much to centralize decision-making into his own hands and to turn the French aristocracy into a pack of obedient chihuahuas. But begging great men (and occasionally women) for jobs was a big part of the warp-and-weft of the old regime; as essential as sending out CVs listing your stellar academic credentials is today. One of the first characters we encounter in Leo Tolstoy's *War and Peace* (1869), the aged Princess Drubetskaya, is in nervous agonies as she petitions Prince Vasili to find a job in the Imperial Guard for her son, Boris (she pronounces his name with an accent on the 'o'). The prince carefully weighs her request – he knows that 'influence in the world ... is a capital which has to be used with economy if it is to last', and he worries that if he asks for favours for all and sundry he will never be able to ask for anything for himself – but he eventually gives in because the princess's father had given him his start in life. No sooner does he accede to her request than the princess asks for another favour, to make Boris adjutant to the general![8]

Britain's system of patronage was more complicated than France's during the age of absolutism because there were two centres of power rather than one – the king and Court on the one hand and Parliament on the other. It nevertheless involved the same principles – endless grovelling to patrons and indifference to what we would now call the public good. During the Hanoverian era the Crown sat at the apex of a vast system of patronage, formally controlling not only the great offices of state but also an impressive collection of exotic offices, left over from a previous age, that came with salaries but few duties: the Principality of Wales, the duchies of Lancaster and Cornwall and the Earldom of Chester. Parliament ran a parallel (and sometimes overlapping system). Britain's first prime minister, Sir Robert Walpole, is still unsurpassed among his successors in terms of the art of patronage. The Duke of Newcastle, Walpole's great protégé and secretary of state, spent almost all his time doling out jobs. Sir Lewis Namier describes reading the duke's papers in his great work, *England in the Age of the American Revolution* (1930):

> The three hundred volumes of his papers and correspondence in the British Museum are a monumental dictionary, exhaustive and indiscriminate, of jobs and job-hunters, and of the ways in which places and pensions were solicited, promised, assigned, and obtained. Tide-waiters, riding-officers, surveyors of window lights, postmasters, or parsons, occupied Newcastle's attention as much as those who were to fill high office in the Cabinet and at Court, bishoprics, seats at departmental boards, etc. – they were sand and mortar, pillars and beams for his political edifice.[9]

The great political parties of the eighteenth century were essentially collections of patrons in search of clients to manipulate and clients in search of jobs to gorge upon.

The people who operated the patronage system were the most obvious beneficiaries. 'When we look over this exchequer list,' Edmund Burke noted wryly, 'we find it filled with the descendants of the Walpoles, of the Pelhams, of the Townshends; names to whom this country owes its liberties; and to whom his majesty owes his crown.'[10] Walpole was at least honest about his sticky fingers: he 'frankly owned that while he was in employment, he had endeavoured to serve his friends and relations; than which, in his opinion, nothing was more reasonable, or more just'.[11] (All three of his sons received sinecures in the Exchequer, worth a total of £13,400 a year.) But all of Britain's great landowners were also beneficiaries: forty-nine eighteenth-century peers had at least eight offices, and some had over forty. And the benefits of the system cascaded down to the middle classes and lower. Local landowners controlled a jumble of offices from church livings to wardenships of workhouses to jobs operating toll booths.

The juiciest jobs were pure sinecures which involved no work whatsoever, either because the duties they once entailed had lapsed completely or because the jobs had been transferred elsewhere but the income stream had remained in place. In 1783, a Mrs Margaret Scott was receiving a salary of £200 a year for acting as wet nurse to the Prince of Wales, who was twenty-one at the time.[12] Ancient offices such as the Office of the Pipe, the Pells and the First Fruits were rich sources of functionless jobs. If you couldn't get a pure sinecure, there were always half-sinecures that paid so well that you could hire someone else to do the hard grind. One of the two solicitors on the staff of the Treasury failed to turn up to work for forty years, from 1744 to 1784, until a busybody complained about his poor attendance.[13] Even so, patronage-mongers didn't always bother with the pretence of jobs. Charles II paid £4,700 directly from the post office's coffers to his mistress, the Duchess of Cleveland, while James II paid various sums from the same account to family members and to ministers in the form of 'pensions' that, mysteriously, bore no relation either to age or previous employment.[14]

THE JOBS MARKET

What could be given away in the form of patronage could also be sold: one of the oddities of pre-market societies is that, in many cases, they boasted flourishing markets in jobs. These markets provided benefits for both the seller and the buyer. The sellers (usually governments) got an immediate injection of cash. The buyers got more long-term rewards: access to an income stream in the form of salaries, fees and gratuities; exemption from certain taxes and other 'noble' privileges; and, quite frequently, a combination of the two, with noble titles, for example, providing you with the added benefit of securing a high office in the future. Tax farmers purchased the right to tax subjects (and skim something off the top) in return for an up-front payment. Samuel Pepys's diaries brim with references to bribes that he unabashedly received in the course of doing his job, from silver plates to diamonds to beef tongue.

France's *Ancien Régime* led the way in the sale of offices as much as in the art of patronage. The great job sale began in the sixteenth century, as a stop-gap way of helping the king to pay his bills, and evolved in the seventeenth century into a routine way of raising revenue for the state, and of maintaining a respectable place in society for office purchasers. An up-front payment could pay for a lifetime of respectable vegetation; indeed, more than a lifetime: office holders could hand their office on to their children or sell it on to other people if they needed to raise cash immediately.

Under Louis XVI (r. 17574–993) France boasted about 50,000 venal offices representing a capital value of perhaps a billion livres. Entire divisions of the French state, notably the judiciary, were run by people who had purchased their jobs. The aristocracy was honeycombed with people who had purchased titles along with jobs, with about 3,700 venal offices conferring noble titles. William Doyle, the great chronicler of venality, estimates that during the seventeenth and eighteenth centuries somewhere between 5,500 and 7,500 people left the bourgeoisie for the nobility by this route, perhaps ten times that number if you add in their families. One of the reasons why reformers embraced bureaucracy, a word that came into common currency in the mid-eighteenth century, is that it represented government by 'offices' rather than by 'people', who were thought to be tainted by nepotism and favouritism.

Though Britain didn't go as far down this road as its neighbour across the Channel, office-purchasing was nevertheless rampant. Winston Churchill summed up the situation in the army before the reforms of 1871 in his biography of his ancestor the Duke of Marlborough:

> Every step in the commissioned ranks of the Army, whether gained by seniority or good service, had to be purchased. A captaincy, a majority, a colonelcy, the command of a regiment, of a troop of Life Guards . . . all passed to new recipients of the royal favour at a market price which varied with supply and demand like the membership of the New York Stock Exchange.[15]

The Crown established exact prices for each rank, rather like a real-estate agent selling houses. And as with the housing market, gazumping was rife: in 1832 Lord Brudenell paid more than £35,000 for a lieutenant colonelcy that was advertised at £6,175.[16]

THE VIRTUE OF VICES

It is even harder for us moderns to understand the world of nepotism, patronage and venality than it is to understand the world of dynasties. How can a government do its job if it sells offices to the highest bidder? Why would soldiers want to purchase the privilege of dying in battle? We tend to bundle the whole system together under the general title of 'corruption' and wait with bated breath until the old world is swept aside by revolution (on the continent) or reform (in Britain).

Yet there must have been more to mechanisms that lasted for so long than mere corruption. The system of 'Old Corruption' that lasted roughly between 1660 and 1832 enabled Britain to become the most successful state in the world. Britain had the best navy in the world in the eighteenth century. The British army defeated the French in both the Peninsula and at Waterloo despite massively inferior numbers. The more reform-minded Victorians were in many ways improving on foundations that had been built under Old Corruption. The most interesting question about 'corruption' is the same as it is with dynasticism: not why it collapsed but why it lasted so long.

Patronage provided a rough-and-ready mechanism for identifying raw talent as well as for feeding worms to well-born chicks. Jacky Fisher, a great British admiral, once quipped that 'favouritism is the secret of efficiency' and there are certainly examples of the truth of this in pre-modern administrative history. Thomas Cromwell owed his career to favouritism, first from Thomas Wolsey and then from Henry VIII himself; his first office in government was a pure sinecure, Master of the Jewels;[17] but none of this prevented him from becoming one of great architects of the modern state. Many pre-modern intellectuals owed their careers to great patrons who spotted them while they were young and gave them a start in life. Louis XIV promoted low-born favourites such as Sébastien de Vauban, the great engineer, and Jean Racine, the great dramatist.[18] A Scottish laird, John Stuart, took a shine to a cobbler's son, James Mill, and provided him with an education in exchange for tutoring his daughter (Mill honoured him by naming his eldest son after him). Adam Smith had the leisure to write *The Wealth of Nations* because the Duke of Buccleuch spotted his genius.

Patrons often felt an obligation to recommend competent clients – a complete duffer might prove embarrassing. Equally, clients often felt an obligation to bring credit to their sponsors. 'The Crown and the Executive found in this system guarantees of fidelity and good conduct,' Winston Churchill wrote in his life of Marlborough, 'and no one troubled himself about the obstacles placed in the path of unpropertied ability.'[19]

Samuel Pepys, who owed his career to the patronage of his first cousin once removed, Lord Montagu, is a good example of the working of the patronage system at its best. Though he didn't know the first thing about the navy or indeed administration when he first got his job (and indeed wouldn't have stood a snowball's chance in hell under a more meritocratic system),[20] he became a first-rate chief secretary to the admiralty as well as a diarist of genius (and, incidentally, an MP and a president of the Royal Society). The knowledge that he got his job by favour rather than desert motivated him to work doubly hard, noting in his diary 'how little merit does prevail in the world, but only favour – and that for myself, chance without merit brought me in, and that diligence only keeps me so'.[21] (Montagu, in turn, owed his position to the patronage of Charles II, to whom he offered loyal service after the Restoration.) The fact that he hadn't studied the old ways of naval administration may have made him a more innovative administrator as well as a more diligent one.

Many of the greatest figures in British intellectual and political history owed their careers to patrons who spotted their talent, took a shine to them and helped to advance their careers.

One ingenious economic historian claims that both patronage and purchase were rational solutions to two classic economic problems: information and incentives.[22] In pre-modern societies governments struggled with imperfect information about their agents, particularly those in faraway places: life was too unpredictable, travel links too poor and populations too scattered to be able to keep a careful eye on them. Patronage and purchase provided the best ways to overcome information shortages: patrons like Lord Montagu who vouchsafed for their clients had an incentive to choose honest and loyal men; tax farmers who had purchased the right to raise taxes had an incentive to extract as much as possible from their investments.

This thesis even explains the mystery of the buying and selling of commissions in the army. Men of means purchased commissions in order to enjoy the spoils of war, as Churchill's ancestor the Duke of Marlborough did so spectacularly.[23] The purchase system not only screened out cowards and time-servers who knew they wouldn't be able to recoup their initial investment. It also provided active soldiers with an incentive to maximize their efforts to kill the enemy and plunder his wealth. As an additional bonus, the purchase system even solved one of the thorniest problems for both the state and professional soldiers alike:

pensions. By selling their commissions to the next generation of soldiers, retiring officers could provide themselves with a retirement fund and save the government the expense of supporting them.[24]

The system of patronage and purchase was nevertheless crude. Many members of the establishment felt so entitled to their jobs that they didn't think about honouring their obligations to their patrons (who may have done them a favour several generations back). Pepys's diaries are full of examples of his turning up for a meeting and being informed that the lord had better things to do. 'Up and with Sir W. Pen to White Hall ...' he wrote in his diary for 28 November 1666, 'yet the Duke of York is gone a-hunting. We therefore lost our labours, and so back again ...' ('Lost our labours' is a recurring phrase in Pepys.) And many clients were keen on extracting the maximum rent possible from their good fortune in the world. 'Every little fellow looks after his fees, and gets what he can for everything,' Pepys noted in May 1665;[25] a pattern of pervasive small-time graft that is all too familiar to anybody who has visited emerging countries. Somebody had to pay for this vast superstructure of offices and favours in the form of taxes, fees, bribes and palm grease.

The world of Old Corruption eventually lost its usefulness. A growing number of voices (including those of some of its leading beneficiaries) pointed to its downsides. Burke complained that 'the affairs of the king's kitchen were greatly deranged in consequence of the king's turn-spit being a member of parliament'.[26] Dr Johnson denounced official pensions as 'pay given to a state's hireling for treason to his country'.[27] And the arrival of the toll road, the railroad and the telegram made it possible for governments to keep an eye on their agents without resorting to rough-and-ready devices like patronage and purchase.

The old society was thus ripe for destruction by a coterie of revolutionaries and reformers who wielded the idea of 'merit' as both a critique of what was wrong with the world and a blueprint for how to create a better society. But where did this revolutionary idea come from? And how did it first get a purchase on the human mind? In the next four chapters we will look at the long-term origins of the meritocratic idea in three places – Plato's Republic, China's examination state and the Jewish diaspora – and in the medieval and Early Modern idea of sponsored mobility. We will then chronicle the breakthrough as it occurred in continental Europe, Great Britain and the United States.

PART TWO

Meritocracy before Modernity

4

Plato and the Philosopher Kings

All thinking about meritocracy is a series of footnotes to Plato.[1] In *The Republic* Plato laid out an audacious vision of a society ruled by an intellectual elite and stratified by education. This vision has divided subsequent thinkers. Some regard it as an inspiration: generations of educationalists from Aristotle (who studied under Plato) to Kurt Hahn (who educated Prince Philip and Prince Charles) have tried to create a ruling class capable of living up to Plato's demanding ideals. For others, it is repulsive: Karl Popper denounced Plato as the father of totalitarianism, Aldous Huxley mocked him as the progenitor of the 'Brave New World', and Allan Bloom argued that his position was so extreme, particularly when it came to expelling artists from the *polis*, that he might have been pulling everyone's leg. Still, nobody has seriously disputed Rousseau's verdict on *The Republic*, that it is 'the most beautiful educational treatise ever written'.[2]

THE REPUBLIC

Plato called his Republic an aristocracy ('the rule of the best'), but it was not an aristocracy in the conventional sense: it rested not on inherited wealth and position but on something hitherto unheard of, equality of opportunity. Plato believed that any objective study of the human species revealed that human beings are naturally divided into three types on the basis of their natural abilities: men of gold, men of bronze and men of silver. The men of gold are the rightful guardians of the Republic: the people who, thanks to a combination of natural ability and careful training, have the ability to think more deeply, see more clearly and, as a result, rule more justly than anyone else. The men of silver are the wealth creators, the impresarios of the productive process. The men of bronze are the horny-handed sons of toil who take care of the necessities of life.

But men of gold are not necessarily born to parents of gold, just as men of bronze are not necessarily born to parents of bronze: hence the explosive idea of equality of opportunity. A genetic lottery is at work and society must be readjusted in each generation to make sure that children are assigned to roles suited to their innate natures rather than their parents' ambitions. According to Plato, Greek society was full of examples of the children of great men who had turned out to be nonentities and the children of nonentities who had turned out to be great:

> God as he was fashioning you put gold in those of you who are capable of ruling; hence they are deserving of most reverence. He put silver in the auxiliaries, and iron and copper in the farmers and the other craftsmen. For the most part your children are of the same nature as yourselves, but because you are all akin, sometimes from gold will come a silver offspring, and from silver a gold, and so on all round. Therefore the first and weightiest command of God to the rulers is this – that more than aught else they be good guardians of and watch zealously over their offspring, seeing which of those metals is mixed in their souls; if their own offspring have an admixture of copper or iron, they must show no pity, but giving it the honour proper to its nature, set it among the artisans or the farmers; and if on the other hand in these classes children are born with an admixture of gold and silver, they shall do more honour and appoint the first to be guardians, the second to be auxiliaries. For either is an oracle that the city shall perish when it is guarded by iron or copper.[3]

One of the most remarkable things about the philosopher's vision is that he believed that 'those who are capable of ruling' included women as much as men. Rejecting all the most heartfelt assumptions of his time, he argued that differences between individuals trumped differences between the sexes: 'a good many women are better than a good many men at a good many things'. Society would be damaging itself if it consigned all women, regardless of their abilities, to a subordinate role just because they bear children. His biggest worry about recruiting women to the guardian class was (to us) a somewhat eccentric one: since the guardians will be expected to exercise together, and since exercise is best taken naked, mixing the sexes might prove to be indecorous.

For Plato, the essence of statecraft was making sure that people are given jobs that are suitable to their inner natures: a process that meant re-sorting the population in every generation and carefully adjusting expectations to abilities. This commitment to social mobility explains the most controversial argument in *The Republic*: that potential guardians should be taken from their parents at birth and raised by the community at large. Communal child-rearing performs three functions. It frees women of gold from the burden of childcare. They have better things to do with their talents than humdrum tasks such as feeding babies and wiping bottoms that can just as well be performed by foreign slaves. It makes it easier to provide equal opportunities to children of gold, regardless of their parents' wealth. And it ensures that these men and women of gold put the community before their families. Plato regarded family bonds as a mortal threat to the Republic because they encourage parents to put the interests of their progeny above those of society as a whole, encouraging them to amass private wealth and lobby for family favours. There is no 'I' or 'mine' in Plato's imaginary meritocracy, only 'we' and 'ours'.

Plato laid out an extraordinary training programme for these budding guardians: everything that influences them, from the stories they hear as children to the exercise regime they employ throughout their lives must be subordinated to the business of producing 'hot house saints'.[4] They spend the first eighteen years of their lives in full-time education, with a rigorous regime of physical as well as mental training. They spend two years in military service, learning how to protect the state. After that comes a decade studying mathematics and five years studying philosophy. The philosophical stage is particularly tricky because, if you're not careful, it can easily degenerate into self-indulgent logic-chopping.[5] The guardians are ready for preliminary duties at thirty but are arguably not ready for the most demanding jobs until they are fifty.

This lengthy education is as much moral as intellectual. Plato believed that the soul is subdivided into two parts – reason and the passions – and that the passions are themselves subdivided into two: the cool passions, such as the desire for a good reputation, and the hot passions, such as sexual lust and aggression. In some passages, he imagines that reason is a horseman who rides two powerful steeds pulling in different directions. The point of education is to teach people how to ride those steeds well. Self-control is essential for guardians because they perform the same role for society as a whole that reason does for the individual: preventing the lower orders from giving in to their animal instincts.

If moral training is about teaching the guardians how to ride the stallion of emotion, intellectual training is about teaching them to head towards the light. Education is not about filling children's minds with facts, as you might fill an empty glass with water. It is about persuading them to love wisdom for its own sake. 'After long study and discussion under the guidance of an experienced teacher,' Plato wrote in a sentence that defines the tutorial ideal, 'a spark may suddenly leap, as it were, from mind to mind, and the light of understanding so kindled will then feed on itself.' The aim of all this effort is not just to produce a well-educated civil service, though that is a fine thing; it's to produce a caste of philosopher kings, or intellectual aristocrats, who can lead the Republic towards the light. *The Republic* starts with the question 'what is justice?' Plato's answer in part is that a just society is one in which everybody is in their proper place, ruled over by philosopher kings who know the difference between truth and lies and beauty and ugliness.

This is an austere vision. The lower classes must reconcile themselves to a life of subordination, never questioning the decisions of their superiors. The ruling class must forgo the pleasures of family life and owning property. Anything less will lead to corruption:

> Both the community of property and the community of families ... tend to make them more truly guardians; they will not tear the city in pieces by differing about 'mine' and 'not mine'; each man dragging any acquisition which he has made into a separate house of his own, where he has a separate wife and children and private pleasures and pains; but all will be affected as far as may be by the same pleasures and pains

because they are all of one opinion about what is near and dear to them, and therefore they all tend towards a common end.[6]

Why should gifted people put up with such privations? And why should regular people forgo the dignity of self-rule? The great philosopher answers these questions with yet another extraordinary argument: that the Republic should rest its power on a 'noble lie'. The Republic where truth is king is to be founded on deceit. Just as children are told stories to prevent them from biting their nails or stealing other people's things, budding guardians must be told stories to persuade them to put the common good above private gain. The guardians must be told that they are the children 'of the earth', not of biological parents. The masses must be told that they owe their position to the will of the gods rather than the artifice of men. They must be regaled with tales of oracles – and warned of divine revenge if they step out of line.

If this sounds like an odd way of building a state, Plato argued that the alternatives are worse. His views on oligarchy are correct, if commonplace: rich oligarchs will turn politics into a money-making enterprise. He is far more striking in his discussion of democracy. Democracy is the most attractive of all forms of society, he says, because it combines the maximum opportunity for the regular citizen with the maximum freedom. But these attractions are superficial – democracy is like a 'coat of many colours' that looks good when you see it in the market but turns out to be threadbare after you've worn it a couple of times.

It is threadbare for three reasons. The first is that ordinary people simply don't have enough knowledge, particularly of economics or foreign affairs, to make sensible judgements. They invariably favour the short term over the long term, the exciting to the wise. This means that they enjoy themselves for a while but ultimately end up on the rocks. He drives this point home with the metaphor of a ship's captain: only a fool would put a ship in the charge of a crew who don't know where they're going and are always squabbling among themselves, rather than that of an experienced captain. The second problem is that democracy throws up bad leaders. The most successful vote-getters are demagogues who can weave wonderful fantasies about the state's future but are really nothing more than charlatans, lying their way to power or buying votes with other people's money.[7] Plato was particularly scathing about aristocrat-demagogues who enjoy the advantage of a good education but nevertheless prefer to pander to the mob rather than guide it to the light.

The biggest problem with democracy is that it puts too much emphasis on freedom. While this gives democracy a diversity and variety that is superficially attractive, at least for a while, it also dissolves society's defences against anarchy. Fathers pander to their sons, teachers to their pupils, humans to animals, and 'the minds of the citizens become so sensitive that the least vestige of restraint is resented as intolerable'. Anarchy produces class struggle, as the poor attack the rich and the rich retaliate; class struggle produces war and disorder; and eventually people turn to a dictator who can restore order.

If tyrants are the inevitable consequence of democracy, they are also the antithesis of philosopher kings. They regard power as an end in itself rather than a means to an end. They are also governed by their passions rather than their reason. This leads to the paradox at the heart of tyranny: even though tyrants have absolute power over other people, they have no power over themselves. Slaves to their own passions – 'ill-governed' in their own souls, as Plato puts it – they use their positions to inflict those passions on the entire population. A tyranny is a psycho-drama in which everyone is caught up in the tyrant's raging ego.

THE MAKING OF A MASTERPIECE

The Republic was a contradiction of a book: at the same time an angry critique of contemporary Athenian society written by a disgruntled aristocrat and (as we shall see) a cool meditation on the nature of justice written by a great philosopher. Plato was born in 428/427 BC into a society that was terrified that its best days were behind it, and into an aristocratic class that was convinced it was being robbed of its birthright. His father liked to boast that his family traced their ancestry back to the last king of Athens, a man who almost certainly didn't exist. The Peloponnesian War (which had started some four years before the philosopher's birth) took a terrible toll on the city's resources, both financial and psychological, and ended, after twenty-seven years, in ignominious defeat. The death of Pericles (when Plato was one or two years old) robbed Athens of its greatest statesman. The city practised an extreme form of direct democracy. Admittedly, the city rested on a brutal system of slavery and the franchise was limited to free-born men (making Plato's willingness to contemplate female guardians even more extraordinary). But the minority was expected to take an active part in making decisions rather than just voting every few years. Decision-making power lay with a mass meeting of all voters known as the Assembly. Athens also used the most democratic mechanism possible – the lot – to choose jurors and political officials.

Plato grew up to the sounds of aristocrats in a fury – jeering at the incompetence of the jingo-democrats who filled the Assembly and made the decisions. This led him to two conclusions. The first was that democracy was a distasteful sham: a combination of a spectator sport ('Athens has got talent') and an exercise in bribery. The second was that the only solution to Athens's political crisis lay in philosophy. 'I was forced to the belief that the only hope of finding justice for society or for the individual,' he wrote, 'lay in true philosophy, and that mankind will have no respite from trouble until either real philosophers gain political power, or politicians become by some miracle true philosophers.'

Yet this angry *cri de cœur* was also a cool-headed meditation on the nature of justice. Plato believed in the existence of two worlds – the world of everyday appearances and the world of ideal forms. Ordinary men are like the inhabitants of a cave who watch a shadow-play being projected on to the walls, unaware of the existence of a sunlit world outside, he wrote. Only philosophers have a chance of looking beyond the shadows to the reality above. *The Republic* is thus a collective solution to an epistemological problem: if it is to have any chance of basing its collective decision-making on wisdom rather than illusion, society must laboriously create a class of rulers who can venture beyond the shadows to the world of sunshine. The creation of philosopher kings is a precondition for collective enlightenment.

This contrast between angry polemic and calm meditation was not the end of *The Republic*'s oddities. In some ways, Plato's masterpiece was one of the most apolitical works of politics ever written. Plato had no interest in the practical workings of power. There is nothing in *The Republic* on either restraints on the power of the elite or competition over values. He believed that so long as you put the right people in charge – that is, philosophers – conflicts over values would dissolve and constitutional restraints would be unnecessary.[8] In other ways, it was one of the most practical – a how-to book for creating a ruling class. *The Republic* deals with such a mass of practical questions – including the exact balance between study and exercise – for the simple reason that Plato was in the education business. On returning from a long trip abroad in 386 BC he founded a school for statesmen – called the Academy, after Academus, a mythical Greek hero – and taught there for the rest of his life. This was not the first school of leadership in Athens – Isocrates had been running one for some time, for example – but Plato's Academy tried to distinguish itself by focusing on 'reason' – dialectic, logic and mathematics – rather than, as previous schools had done, on rhetoric. For Plato, it was pointless to teach leaders how to express their thoughts (and persuade their listeners with the beauty of their words) if you didn't teach them how to think in the first place. As ever, the political arts were mere appendages to philosophy.

PLATO AFTER PLATO

Plato's *Republic* is striking in its extremism as well as its poetic beauty, sanctioning removing children from their parents by force; replacing marriage for the guardians with state-sponsored orgies in which they are given the pick of women, chosen for their brains and their beauty; using lies as an instrument of statecraft; and expelling poets from the Republic on the grounds that they are dealers in illusions. Aristotle pointed out that Plato was unable to distinguish between unity and uniformity. 'It is as if one were to reduce harmony to unison or rhythm to a single beat.'[9] Other critics have argued that he was unable to distinguish between heaven and hell. But none of this has stopped his work from exercising an enormous influence which continues to this day. The sun never sets on the master's great book: 'always, someone somewhere is reading the *Republic*'.[10]

Thomas More's *Utopia* (1516) was modelled on *The Republic*. H. G. Wells wrote five utopian novels that featured Platonic guardians, including *A Modern Utopia* (1905), though, given his personal behaviour, Wells was an odd advocate of the virtues of a self-restrained ruling elite. Aldous Huxley created a high-tech version of *The Republic* in *Brave New World* (1932), complete with eugenically bred 'Alphas' and an antenatal regime that does the work of Plato's noble lie: a loudspeaker in a nursery for Beta children inculcates the mantra, while they sleep, that 'Alpha children wear grey. They work much harder then we do. I'm really awfully glad I'm a Beta, because I don't work so hard.'[11]

The Republic's influence was practical as well as theoretical. His Academy was, after all, a real school for statesmen, and during Plato's lifetime Academicians were called upon by at least four cities to compose new laws. But Plato harboured much bigger ambitions than just training constitutional technicians. He believed that there were two ways of giving life to his ideas – turning kings into philosophers or philosophers into kings. Down the ages, people have tried both.

Plato tried his hand at turning a king into a philosopher. When Dionysius I of Syracuse died, Plato's disciple Dion, the state's chief minister, invited him to train his son Dionysius II, who was then twenty-eight, as a philosopher king. The experiment was, at best, a limited success. Dionysius proved a wayward pupil: though he liked Plato's ideas in general, he struggled with them in practice, gagging on the mathematics that Plato force-fed him and eventually kicking his tutor out of the country. (If you're going to train a king, it's better to do it when they're young than when they're in their twenties and already on the throne.) The king tried his hand at implementing his teacher's ideas but failed to distinguish between philosophy and priggishness, driving his subjects so mad with his constant cajoling that they eventually killed him.

A handful of kings modelled themselves on Plato's guardians: Marcus Aurelius, emperor of Rome between 161 and 180, styled himself a philosopher king, and even wrote a Stoic tome, *Meditations*, on how to remain calm in a world that is going mad, a book that bears re-reading today. Matthias Corvinus, King of Hungary and Croatia from 1458 to 1490, became obsessed with Plato, turning Buda into a centre of Renaissance learning and modelling himself on a Platonic guardian. The Enlightened monarchs of the eighteenth century saw themselves as philosopher kings and queens for the Age of Reason.

Predictably enough, the greatest enthusiasts for the idea of philosopher kings were philosophers and their fellow intellectuals. Renaissance humanists focused on shaping a ruling class according to the wisdom of the ancients. If the medieval warrior elite had founded its power on violence, and the medieval clergy had tried to temper violence with faith, the humanists added a third ingredient to the mixture: philosophical wisdom gained from education in classical civilization. The eighteenth-century *philosophes* enthusiastically instructed rulers in the art of reason.

The Victorians took the admiration for the Greeks to new heights. John Stuart Mill said that 'the battle of Marathon, even as an event in English history, is more important than the battle of Hastings'.[12] William Gladstone was so fluent in classical Greek that, in 1858, he gave a speech to the inhabitants of the Ionian Islands (a British protectorate) in the language, blind to the fact that his audience spoke Italian.[13] Plato occupied a particularly honoured place in the Hellenic pantheon. Macaulay defined a scholar as 'one who can read Plato with his feet on the fender'. During his most productive period, in the 1870s, John Ruskin started every day by watching the sunrise and then spending an hour translating Plato 'to build the day on'.[14]

A powerful cadre of educationalists convinced themselves that Plato held the key to creating a responsible ruling class that was capable of putting the long-term interest of society as a whole above the short-term convenience of ruling families. Public-school reformers such as Thomas Arnold, the headmaster of Rugby, adopted many of Plato's signature ideas: that education was as much about shaping character as sharpening intellect; that group loyalty should trump individual self-expression; and that physical education was as important as book learning. They departed from Plato in one respect, however: they were so fixated on teaching the classics (including Plato's writings) that they ignored subjects that Plato himself regarded as crucial to a real education, notably mathematics and science.

Oxbridge colleges added philosophy to this mixture. Benjamin Jowett, the master of Balliol from 1870 until his death in 1893, devoted his life to two great projects: producing a definitive edition of Plato and turning his college into a production line for members of the Victorian ruling class, domestic and imperial, lay and spiritual. Though he failed at his first task – his edition of *The Republic* was completed only after his death, by his friend and biographer Lewis Campbell – he succeeded spectacularly at the second. 'Jowett was Balliol and Balliol was Jowett,' as Leslie Stephen wrote.[15] His pupils included Lord Curzon, a future viceroy of India; Lord Grey, a future foreign secretary; Herbert Asquith, a future prime minister; Cosmo Gordon Lang, a future Archbishop of Canterbury; and Charles Gore, a future bishop, many of whom remained loyal to the cult of Plato. Florence Nightingale, who was one of Jowett's closest friends, wrote to ask him if one young soldier she had met in the Crimea was one of his pupils. 'He talks to his men about Plato tells them they don't do what Plato would have them do, don't realize Plato's ideal of what soldiers ought to be.'[16]

Though Jowett had a well-deserved reputation for sucking up to the products of Britain's great public schools, he also took Plato's injunction to give 'the best education to the best intelligences in every class of society'[17] seriously. He discovered a clever orphan, Frank Fletcher, when he was eleven years old, educated him at his own expense and finally got him into Balliol, where he won the Gaisford Prize for Greek Verse and played cricket and football for Oxfordshire.[18]

The Plato cult arguably intensified as the nineteenth century turned into the twentieth century because Plato appealed to both left-wing Fabians and right-wing empire-builders. Fabians liked his enthusiasm for giving more power to the state over anarchic individualism. The very title of his book made converts of republicans. Imperialists liked the idea of a disciplined intellectual elite bringing Western civilization to what they regarded as benighted parts of the world. Cecil Rhodes created the Rhodes scholarship system to forge an imperial guardian class. Lord Milner created a 'kindergarten' – a group of highly educated Britons, many of them fellows of All Souls, who served in the South African civil service and played a leading role in rebuilding British rule in South Africa in the aftermath of the Boer War.[19]

The American East Coast establishment proceeded down the same route. Late-nineteenth- and early-twentieth-century headmasters such as Endicott Peabody modelled their schools on British public schools, using a combination of God and the classics to train their charges in public service. And Ivy League universities – particularly Yale – became American versions of Oxbridge. The more members of the WASP elite realized that they were taking over from their British cousins as rulers of the waves, the more they looked to Plato to teach them how to navigate. McGeorge (Mac) Bundy, perhaps the quintessential member of the American establishment before it was torn asunder by the Vietnam War, worked on *The Republic* as a junior fellow at Harvard and 'saw himself as one of the guardians, the chosen elite'.[20]

Platonism put up a valiant fight against the incoming tides of democracy and egalitarianism: A. D. Lindsay, master of Balliol from 1924 to 1949 and a staunch supporter of the Labour Party, preserved some of Jowett's spirit, producing a popular Everyman edition of *The Republic* and lecturing to Workers' Education Association classes on the philosopher. But the tradition eventually withered. The intelligentsia progressively turned against the idea of philosopher kings, not just in novels such as *Brave New World* but also in texts of political theory. Richard Crossman, a young Oxford classics don who went on to become one of the most influential figures in the Labour Party, denounced Plato's philosophy, in *Plato Today* (1937), as 'the most savage and most profound attack upon liberal ideas which history can show'. He later played a leading role in turning his party against meritocracy. Karl Popper devoted the entire first volume of his two-volume *The Open Society and Its Enemies* (1945) to denouncing Plato as the intellectual godfather of both fascism and communism. Communists had their own problem with Plato, with Stalinists dismissing him for sins against materialism and, at the height of the Cultural Revolution, Maoists denouncing him as a Western version of Confucius.

From the 1980s onwards public schools have abandoned the time-honoured tradition of classics and cold showers for the children of the elite: today, they focus on science rather than ancient civilization and look more like high-end resorts than austere barracks. The ruling elite no longer subscribes to the doctrine of public duty and private self-denial:

ambitious young people shun politics for money-making, and retired politicians think nothing of cashing in on their expertise by selling knowledge gained in the service of the state to the private sector.

For all his extremism, Plato remains as relevant as ever. He identified the most profound problem with meritocracy: the tension between the natural instinct to look after your children and the meritocratic imperative to provide equality of opportunity. Plato's own solution to this problem – state-sponsored orgies and communal child-rearing – was clearly far-fetched. But more recent attempts to solve the problem have driven policy-makers to adopt controversial policies such as bussing (overriding parents' preferences about where their children are educated and taking them by bus from local schools to distant ones). It has also driven politicians into agonies about how to balance their principles with their urge to do the best for their children. He also identified two of the most revolutionary aspects of meritocracy: the demand for relentless social mobility as children are promoted according to their natural abilities and the rise of women into the knowledge elite.

Plato identified many of the problems inherent in rejecting meritocracy for democracy in its purest form. *The Republic* still provides the best description of the evils of populism. Plato anticipates the great distemper of our times: politics as entertainment; Twitter mobs; the rage against expertise. He also presents the best description available of how the failings of democracy lead to the rise of psychologically challenged tyrants. In the wake of Donald Trump and his fellow strongmen, the world is rediscovering the importance of wise guardians.

For the moment, the Platonic tradition is more honoured in the East than in the West: China talks about a 'guardian discourse' and Singapore selects its rulers early and trains them vigorously. But in the East the ruling class has a tradition of its own to draw upon – the Confucian tradition that goes back just as far as Plato but had a much more direct influence over public policy than the Greek philosopher ever managed.

5

China and the Examination State

In 1601, one of Europe's foremost scholars became the first European to enter China's Forbidden City, the great complex of palaces and temples in Peking that housed the emperor and his staff. Matteo Ricci (1552–1610) had spent two decades preparing for this moment: a year in Macau, a Portuguese island and trading post just off the Chinese mainland, learning classical Chinese; six years in Zhaoqing, a city in southern China, before being expelled by the new viceroy; and a decade moving from place to place in China before finally establishing himself in Peking. Convinced that the best way to advance the Christian faith in China was to present it as a religious philosophy compatible with Confucian teaching, he spent every spare moment during this odyssey burnishing his scholarly credentials, absorbing China's high culture, producing the world's first Chinese–Latin dictionary, translating Confucian classics into Latin, drawing the first map of the Forbidden Kingdom, and telling Chinese mandarins about the West's scientific and mechanical discoveries. He even adopted the traditional robes of a Confucian scholar.

All this effort eventually paid off – but only up to a point. Emperor Wanli, the fourteenth emperor of the Ming dynasty, was so impressed by Ricci's reputation as a master of science – and particularly by the fact that he had correctly predicted the date of a solar eclipse – that he invited him to become an imperial adviser. Ricci never met the reclusive emperor, who spent his days hidden away in the very heart of the palace. Nevertheless, he made many friends among China's imperial elite, earning himself titles such as 'blue-eyed and with a voice like a melodious bell' and 'doctor from the Great West'. Nor did he achieve his dream of using his access to the elite to spark mass conversion. But he is rightly honoured as an extraordinary figure in both the West and the East, an explorer, scholar, polymath and religious giant. The Roman Catholic Church is actively considering making him a saint and the Chinese authorities have buried him in the grounds of the Beijing Administrative College – latterly the Central School of the Communist Party.[1]

Ricci was struck by the similarity between China's mandarin elite and Plato's guardians. In his *History of the Introduction of Christianity to China*, published in Latin in 1615, he noted that, while in the rest of the world the ruling class owed its position to inherited wealth and political favour, in China the elite owed its position to brain-power and scholarship. 'If it is not possible to say of this realm that the philosophers are kings,' he concluded, 'at least one can say with truth that the kings are governed by philosophers.'[2] He helped to bring the word 'mandarin' into common usage in Europe, a word that now means a senior civil servant. He argued ingeniously that the rule of these exemplary scholars somehow heralded the country's conversion to Christianity: just as Greek philosophy had prepared the Roman empire for Christianity, so Confucianism was preparing China for evangelicals like himself.[3] To his mind, Confucianism was a sort of proto-Christianity, complete with a primitive theology, rather like Plato's, a Supreme Being (*Shangdi*) and a heaven (*Tian*).[4]

China's mandarins were selected by the world's most sophisticated examination system: a ladder of success that rose from the lowliest village to the Forbidden City itself. The first level of exams – the *xiucai* – was held every two years in every prefecture in the country. The odds of passing the examination were remote: some 2.5 million Chinese, or 10 per cent of the population, took the first level of examinations in 1,350 examination centres. For the fortunate few, though, the rewards were great: the right to call themselves novice scholars (*shengyuan*), enjoy social privileges reserved for the gentry (special clothes, exemptions from certain taxes and punishments, privileged access to certain officials, and, in some cases, stipends) and put themselves forward for the next level of examinations. The second level was held every three years in seventeen provincial capitals. Candidates passed at a rate of one out of every twenty-five, or one out of every hundred, depending on the quotas that applied at particular times or places. The successful, dubbed 'selected men' or *juren*, were promoted to the upper gentry and deemed eligible for high office, but were nevertheless unlikely to bag a desirable post unless they proceeded to the third level. The third level was held the year after the *juren* in the imperial palace itself. The successful were allowed to call themselves *jinshi* (scholars) and their names were inscribed on stone slabs in order of merit. The *jinshi* were the true national elite who commanded all the great offices of the empire.[5]

Ricci described in detail the examination halls that dotted the country: half palaces, half prisons, and wholly 'monuments to competition', they were surrounded by high walls and contained 4,000 cells, designed to prevent the candidates from communicating with each other (or indeed seeing each other). Guards stood in watchtowers at each end of the building. Invigilators forced candidates to loosen their clothing to make sure they were not smuggling in any texts (candidates tried to outsmart the invigilators by concealing miniature books in the palms of their hands or sewing passages from the classics in their clothes in minuscule lettering). Equipped only with the basic tools of their vocation – pens, paper and a pot of ink – the candidates embarked on a scholarly marathon: the first exam began at nine, the second at twelve, the third at three, and so on, for three days in a row; they slept in the cell, defecated in pots and ate the food that they had brought with them.[6] The examiners went to extraordinary lengths to eliminate favouritism. Professional copyists copied the scripts word for word and gave the candidates numbers to prevent examiners from recognizing any particular individual's handwriting. Candidates with strong personal or regional connections with powerful examiners were forced to sit special examinations.[7]

The ladder of success was the very devil to climb. The examinations were confined to classical learning. The lowest levels of exams required the candidates to demonstrate a command of the Confucian classics and an ability to write so-called 'eight-legged essays' that discussed moral questions according to various elaborate formal rules. The higher-level exams – particularly the palace examination – required them to demonstrate their ability to apply classical knowledge to concrete problems drawn from the country's past.

Classical Chinese is one of the hardest languages to master, and differed markedly from the dozens of vernacular languages spoken across the empire. Would-be mandarins had to memorize thousands of unfamiliar characters and master archaic grammatical forms. This required an early start and unremitting effort. Children began their studies as young as six: childhood was for reciting and memorizing, not for playing. They took their first examinations in their late twenties or even their late thirties. Most candidates failed the first time. Some failed repeatedly – there were examples of candidates in their fifties and sixties still trying to pass the examinations, and even a few cases of octogenarian examinees. Those who failed were allowed to see their papers and learn from the examiners' comments so that they could try all over again. Those who succeeded were whisked into another world.

The cream of the cream moved to Peking to advise the emperor on running the world's biggest empire. The next most successful ran provinces or sub-provinces. Whether they were based in the capital or the provinces, administrators enjoyed succulent perks ranging from stipends to outright bribes. There were also thousands of lesser jobs – as magistrates or lawyers or copyists – or indeed as examiners running the gigantic machine that kept the empire supplied with talent.

Ricci was awestruck by the system. Many mandarins were 'the sons of farmers and artisans who rise to their status because of their studies of letters,' he wrote. But they were treated regardless of their lowly origins like true masters of the universe – carried through the streets on litters 'like the pope' and worshipped by the common people, who fell to their knees before them. For Ricci this was a society in which the rule of the sword and the great estate had been replaced by the rule of wisdom and culture.[8]

THE FIRST INTELLECTUAL
ARISTOCRACY

Francis Bacon, a sixteenth-century English philosopher, remarked that China was responsible for four of the world's great inventions: gunpowder, paper, the compass and the printing press. In fact, these inventions were peripheral to Chinese civilization. Gunpowder was mainly used for fireworks. The Ming dynasty squandered the compass by banning foreign exploration in 1425. Paper and the printing press were just variations on technologies already in use in other parts of the world. China's most important innovation was the mass examination system, the oldest and longest-lived in the world and, until the twentieth century, by far the most ambitious.

The examination system was indirectly inspired by Confucius (551–479 BC), a great philosopher who developed broad principles on how to live a good life and offered politicians advice on how to rule on the basis of those principles. During his lifetime he gathered a devoted following of disciples who recorded his insights in several books, such as the *Five Classics*, *Aphorisms* and *Analects*, which became the foundation of Chinese education. After his death he became the object of quasi-religious reverence, with shrines in almost every town and regular sacrifices to his memory. Confucius was 'the one man by whom all possible personal excellence was exemplified,' James Legge, a nineteenth-century British sinologist observed, 'and by whom all possible lessons of social virtue and political wisdom are taught'.[9]

These Confucian texts contained a complicated theory of meritocracy: a theory that not only explained why society needed a caste of scholar-rulers to provide it with guidance but also how that elite should conduct itself from day to day and hour to hour. Confucius had no time for the idea that scholars should retreat from the world and contemplate the meaning of life. He believed that they had a duty to be power brokers – either by exercising power directly themselves as officials or by exercising it indirectly by acting as teachers of the powerful. And he was astonishingly successful in imprinting his vision on the country's collective psyche: for much of its history, the Chinese empire was jointly managed by the emperors, who inherited their authority by birth, and by professional scholar-officials, who attained their influence through their knowledge of Confucian doctrine.

Confucius focused on three ideas. The first was that the essence of power lay in knowledge rather than armies. 'I got the empire on horseback,' the Emperor Gaozu said in about 195 BC. 'Why should I bother with the *Book of Odes* or the *Book of History*?' 'You got it on horseback,' a Confucian scholar replied. 'But can you rule it from horseback?' The second is a notion of imperial duty. Though Confucius believed firmly in the social hierarchy, with the 'son of heaven' at the summit of the hierarchy, the landed aristocrats next, and so on, down to the farmers and peasants, he also taught that rulers should not act as they liked. A king shouldn't laze around all day and dally with dancing girls all night. He should dedicate himself to the good of the people. 'Encourage the people to work hard by setting an example yourself,' Confucius said on one occasion. 'If you set an example by being correct, who would dare to remain incorrect?' he said on another. Confucianism is a doctrine of constrained rather than absolute authority. The third was the notion of self-cultivation: rulers must develop their characters by immersing themselves in classical culture. Self-cultivation prevents powerful people from being ruined by their power – they spend their time reading and thinking rather than eating and drinking – as well as giving them direction on how to use their power.

More directly, the examination system was inspired by the power struggle between the emperor and China's landed families. The Sui dynasty (581–618) introduced examination by interview in the seventh century in order to centralize control over the civil service. Every local prefecture in the empire nominated three or so men to be presented to the imperial court and examined by high officials. The officials ranked them according to their 'talents and character': top-ranked candidates were given jobs, while lesser-ranked candidates were given more training. The Tang dynasty (618–907) mixed examinations with nepotism. The bulk of imperial jobs, particularly the most important ones, were reserved for either landed aristocrats or the relatives of previous office-holders, but about 10 per cent were awarded by competitive examinations. In 655, the Empress Wu, who ruled as the power behind the throne for eighteen years before seizing power directly, becoming China's only female empress, turned the Court upside down by reserving the top offices for people who passed the examination: towards the end of the Tang dynasty examinations carried such prestige that even people who were eligible for hereditary office tried to pass them.[10] Imagine if Eric Bloodaxe had sat down to take an examination in order to rule over Northumbria rather than relying on gore and pillage and you get a sense of how extraordinary this situation was.

The examination system didn't break the link between class and success: Ricci's vision of a society ruled by the brilliant children of farmers and artisans is far-fetched. More than a third of Tang-era examination candidates, and more than half of the people who eventually bagged the biggest offices, came from the ten most prominent families. Few people could afford the basic tools of scholarship, such as paper and brushes, let alone the years of hard work required for mastering the classics. All the best schools were based in the capital and, even if you managed to scrape together an education elsewhere, you had to travel to the capital to sit the examination. In the early years of the Tang dynasty the examination involved a sort of mating ritual: candidates showed their best work to the examiners and examiners went into battle on behalf of their favourites. In some cases, women were exchanged in marriage. Imperfect though this system was, it nevertheless changed the relationship between the rulers and the magnates. Mandarin scholars were treated as true masters of the universe regardless of their class background. Even the mightiest magnates competed for a chance to turn themselves into mandarins. Over time, the country's centre of gravity shifted from the provinces to the centre and the justification of authority shifted from inheritance to performance in competitive examinations.[11]

Examinations were such an established part of imperial life in the Tang era that a red-light district sprang up near the Directorate for the Education of the Sons of the State, where the candidates studied, and the examination halls, where they met their final fate, and the best courtesans in the city specialized in satisfying the particular needs of examinees. These courtesans developed cultural skills as well as sexual ones: they recited verse (some of which they composed themselves), sang songs and performed elaborate ceremonies. Sometimes successful candidates fell in love with these princesses of the night and took them home as concubines. In a few cases they even married them. In one of the classics of the era, 'The Tale of Li Wa', Li Wa not only nurses an examination candidate back to health after he has fallen in with a bad crowd and got himself beaten up by his own father, she even prepares him for the examinations. After he triumphs in the exams his father forgives him and he marries the reformed prostitute.[12]

The Song emperors (960–1279) established many of the features of the system that survived until the twentieth century. They focused the examinations more exclusively on the intellectual merits of the candidates rather than on their moral character, believing that the possession of intellectual merit was in itself evidence of moral worth, a position later echoed by Macaulay. They established three levels of examination that operated on a three-year cycle. The examination system was briefly challenged by a few interruptions – the arrival of the Yuan dynasty from Mongolia in 1280 and various revolts by disgruntled aristocrats – but the Yuan dynasty reintroduced elements of the system in 1313 and the subsequent Ming and Qing dynasties preserved and improved it.

The curriculum remained remarkably stable, consisting of the same core texts, the Four Books and the Five Classics, works attributed to Confucius and some of his disciples, along with a number of approved commentaries. (China's first examination guide, devised in 1587, when Elizabeth I was on the throne, might still have been of some use in 1905.) It was also a powerful instrument of soft power: the Korean and Vietnamese regimes imitated China's system of elite selection and, in so doing, became satellites of Confucian civilization. You can still see statues of great Confucian scholars who rose to eminence by passing examinations on display in Seoul.

TWO CHEERS FOR THE MANDARINS

The examination system survived for so long because it served vital social purposes. The state used the system to co-opt the provincial elites and empower a caste of scholar-officials. The founder of the Song dynasty, Emperor Taizu (r. 960–76), put it well: 'the country has fastened upon examinations to select scholars, choosing men to become officials. Since picking and ranking men in the public court is preferable to [receiving their] thanks for favours in private halls, this will serve to rectify customs that have been lacking.' To make sure that this 'picking and ranking' was done fairly, the Song dynasty introduced several methods that are still used by examiners today, such as blind grading (copying scripts to eliminate the chance of an examiner recognizing a candidate by their handwriting).

Things didn't always go according to plan: despite his best efforts, the emperor lost touch with the rest of the country and regional elites flexed their muscles. Still, at its best the examination system provided a powerful counterbalance to the centrifugal forces that plagued such a vast country, with its dozens of linguistic and ethnic groups and powerful regional traditions. The examination selected scholars from across the country regardless of their regional roots and forced them to absorb a common classical idiom. The examination system persuaded local elites to focus their energies on proving their intellectual merits to the emperor rather than on establishing independent power bases. It also provided the palace with a self-renewing supply of educated and able people from the length and breadth of the land. Dynasties might rise and fall but there was always a corpus of scholars with the same training and the same mindset to secure continuity.

The examinations provided people from lowly backgrounds with at least a chance of making it into the elite. As early as the tenth century, one commentator, Wang Li, argued that poor people's best chances of achieving justice lay in making the examinations as objective as possible. 'If examination selection is not strict the powerful will struggle to be foremost and the orphans and poor will have difficulty advancing.' A comprehensive study of Chinese social mobility from 1371 to 1904, conducted by scholars at Hong Kong University, found that a third of *jinshi* degree holders came from families that had not produced a single degree-holder over the previous three generations, let alone a holder of a high office; 11.7 per cent came from families that had produced a lower-degree-holder but not a higher-degree holder. The system also did its best to cast a wide geographical as well as social net. Lists of degree-holders feature scholars from the most far-flung regions.

Success in the examination could transform your status in an instant: it was common for elderly people who had only passed the first or second level to prostrate themselves before young scholars who had passed the third examination. Triumphant scholars erected memorial flagpoles or plaques outside their houses to proclaim their achievement to the world.

Examinations persuaded the Chinese collectively to make a substantial investment in education. The millions of people who failed the exams put their learning to good use as schoolteachers, lawyers, notaries and such. The examinations promoted socially conservative virtues such as filial piety and social cohesion, in part because the examinations were focused on Confucian texts that celebrated family loyalty and in part because examinations gave families an incentive to invest in the education of their children, who could then, if successful, return the favour by looking after their parents in old age.

Above all, the examination system put a rich and rigorous philosophy of life at the heart of China's education system for almost 2,500 years, a philosophy that taught the ruling class the most important lesson that any ruling class can learn: self-restraint via self-cultivation. Nobody could claim to be educated or civilized unless they engaged in an intense study of Chinese classical literature and history as defined by Confucius and his followers. And nobody could be considered for a job in the government unless they could prove that they were educated and civilized. Chinese people of all sorts – poor as well as rich, provincial as well as metropolitan, and, crucially, military as well as civilian – recognized classical learning as the proper measure of people's moral and social worth. Those who had absorbed the classics were properly equipped to represent the interests of the Chinese state. Those who hadn't weren't suitable. It was as simple as that.

These Confucian texts contained a sophisticated theory of meritocracy. As well as explaining why society needed an educated elite to provide it with guidance, they also explained how that educated elite should conduct itself. The examinations thus served a double function: they provided tests that only the talented could possibly pass and they provided those talented people with an education in how to conduct themselves if they were among the chosen.

THE MYSTIQUE OF THE MANDARIN

China's examination system had a pronounced impact abroad, with Europeans publishing more than seventy books and articles from 1570 to 1870 describing how the system worked.[13] Ricci was only one of a long list of sages who treated China's mandarins as an indictment of Western decadence. Robert Burton praised Chinese practices in his wonderful *Anatomy of Melancholy*:

Out of their philosophers and Doctors they choose Magistrates; their politick Nobles are taken from such as be *moraliter nobiles, virtuous noble; nobilitas ut olim ab officio, non a natura*, as in Israel of old, and their office was to defend and govern their country, not to hawk, hunt, eat, drink, game alone, as too many do. Their Lausie, Mandarins, Literates, Licentiates, and such as have raised themselves by their worth, are their noble men, only thought fit to govern a state.[14]

Voltaire saw China as a model of enlightened absolutism. 'The human mind certainly cannot imagine a government better than this one where everything is to be decided by the large tribunals, subordinated to each other, of which the members are received only after several severe examinations.' Rousseau, who didn't agree with Voltaire on much, praised China's 'honorable literati' for leading to 'the highest dignity of the state'.[15] François Quesnay, a medical doctor turned economist, argued that 'this vast and magnificent empire, preserved for forty centuries against all the efforts of civilized or barbarous passions, by the sheer power of the philosophic spirit, demonstrates the power and efficacy of *moral* and *political* knowledge'.[16]

Enthusiasm for China, like enthusiasm for ancient Greece, reached its climax in the Victorian era as reformers subjected antiquated institutions to the principle of open competition. Charles Gutzlaff, the first Lutheran missionary to the Far East, summarized a common view of China in his *China Opened* (1838): 'In China, only talent, without the least respect to persons, is promoted . . . The principle is noble, and well worth the adoption of other countries; the application depends upon the state of the country where the experiment is made.'[17] And the East India Company played a central role in importing this 'noble principle' to Britain, not only because it was in constant touch with the Far East but also because it was forever struggling with the problem of selecting able servants to administer a far-flung commercial empire. The company introduced examinations to select and classify its young recruits in feeder colleges such as the East India College in Haileybury, England (now Haileybury School), and the College of Fort William, India.

Enthusiasm for China soon spread beyond the company to the civil service in general. The reformers who introduced open competition into both the Indian and the domestic civil service had China as well as ancient Athens in mind when they designed a system that favoured gentlemen who were educated in history and the classics. Parliamentary debates about these proposed reforms were littered with references to the Celestial Kingdom. In 1853 the Earl of Granville told the House of Lords that, in the words of Têng Ssu-yü, 'one of the principal reasons why a small Tatar dynasty had governed the immense empire of China' so successfully was that it had 'secured the talent of the whole Chinese population by opening every official situation to competition'.[18] The elite civil servants who were produced by the new system were quickly dubbed 'mandarins'.

TOO MUCH OF A GOOD THING?

Yet these successes came at a high cost. The examination cult imposed a terrible strain on its devotees – not just on the young but on all those middle-aged and indeed elderly candidates who continued to put themselves forward. The examination halls that littered the country were widely known as 'examination prisons' and were sometimes subjected to riots and arson. Many of the greatest works of Chinese literature were devoted to demonizing the system. Cao Xueqin wrote *The Dream of the Red Chamber* sometime in the middle of the eighteenth century after his hopes of a civil service career ended in failure. Cao's male characters lived lives punctuated by the triennial menace of the examinations. Pu Songling (1640–1715), a writer and tutor who was born into a poor merchant family, spent forty years trying to pass the *juren* provincial degree and bitterly satirized the 'seven transformations' that affect unsuccessful candidates as they realize that their efforts have been in vain:

> A licentiate taking the provincial examination may be likened to seven things. When entering the examination hall bare-footed and carrying a basket, he is like a beggar. At roll-call time, being shouted at by officials and abused by their subordinates, he is like a prisoner. When writing in his cell, with his head and feet sticking out of the booth, he is like a cold bee late in the autumn. Upon leaving the examination hall, being in a

daze and seeing a changed universe, he is like a sick bird out of a cage. When anticipating the results, he is on pins and needles; one moment he fantasizes success and magnificent mansions are instantly built; another moment he fears failure and his body is reduced to a corpse. At this point he is like a chimpanzee in captivity. Finally, the messengers come on galloping horses and confirm the absence of his name on the list of successful candidates. His complexion becomes ashen and his body stiffens like a poisoned fly no longer able to move.

The cult sometimes debased the very thing it was supposed to be elevating, turning Confucianism into a means to an end (getting a job) rather than an end in itself. Zhang Dai, a seventeenth-century scholar who repeatedly failed the examination, complained that even the finest scholars would 'find no use for their arsenal of talents and knowledge' unless they joined the pack 'submissive in manner, limited in scope, stale in words, poor in attire, with internal feeling rotted away'. Few candidates read Confucius for pleasure. Few successful mandarins used their knowledge of the classics as a spur to their own creativity. Intellectually and culturally, they were as sterile as the Court eunuchs with whom they mixed.

The system may even have been responsible for provoking rebellions. The Taiping Rebellion, which raged from 1850 to 1864 and claimed some 20–30 million lives, was driven, in part, by frustrations with the civil service exam. The rebellion's leader, Hong Houxiu, failed the examination four times before having a mental breakdown. He claimed to be the younger brother of Jesus and pledged to bring down the imperial regime. His earliest followers were village schoolmasters who, like him, had had their hopes of a brilliant future dashed when they failed the second round of the examinations.

The most powerful criticism of all was that the examinations imprisoned China in a gilded cage – and ensured that what had once been the world's most advanced economy fell behind first Europe and then the United States. Even as some Western intellectuals praised the mandarins as philosopher kings, others denounced them as intellectual jailers. For Samuel Taylor Coleridge, 'the immense empire of China' was 'improgressive for thirty centuries'. For Johann Herder, 'the Empire is an embalmed mummy, painted with hieroglyphs and wrapped in silk'.[19] Confucianism was a backward-looking philosophy, based on the assumption that an ancient sage had solved the mystery of the universe, or at least the riddle of civilization, and that the only path to wisdom lay in recapturing his insights. China's mandarins continued to study the same narrow set of texts even as Europe's intellectual life exploded with the scientific revolution of the seventeenth century, the Enlightenment of the eighteenth century, and the rise of the social and biological sciences in the nineteenth century. The Chinese indifference to the new knowledge was captured perfectly when Lord Macartney, a British diplomat, visited the Qing emperor in 1793 and offered him an array of mechanical wonders, including clocks, telescopes and a miniature steam engine, only to be told that 'strange and costly objects do not interest me. We already possess all things. I set no value on objects strange or ingenious, and have no need for your country's manufactures.'[20]

China's mandarins continued to sleep even as neighbouring countries shook themselves awake. Japan began a furious process of modernization shortly after Commodore Matthew Perry sailed his four ships into Tokyo Bay on 8 July 1853. By the beginning of the twentieth century it had one of the world's most formidable navies. China's relationship with the West began much earlier than Japan's, but it didn't begin to modernize seriously until the entire mandarin structure collapsed in the early twentieth century. It was only when the examination system was abolished by imperial edict in 1905 that China could embark on political reform and economic modernization.

FROM HYPER-STASIS TO HYPERLINKS

The two versions of meritocracy we have considered so far both celebrated stability: the Chinese version in particular was about producing a fixed set of rules for governing a large empire. Here dynamism and meritocracy were fundamentally opposed to each other. Our third meritocratic tradition was driven by dynamism and mobility.

6

The Chosen People

The intellectual achievements of the Jewish people are extraordinary: an ethno-religious group that constitutes one third of 1 per cent of the world's population produces intellectual *Wunderkinder* on an industrial scale. It is remarkable enough that the three intellectual giants who defined the modern world – Marx, Freud and Einstein – were all Jews. But if that sounds like a mere curiosity, let's look at some more objective measures of intellectual success. In the first half of the twentieth century, Jews won 14 per cent of Nobel prizes in literature, chemistry, physics and medicine/physiology, despite pervasive discrimination culminating in the Holocaust. In the second half, the proportion rose to 29 per cent.[1] Fifty-one per cent of the Wolf Foundation prizes in physics, 28 per cent of Max Planck medals, 38 per cent of Dirac medals for theoretical physics, 37 per cent of Dannie Heineman prizes for mathematical physics and 53 per cent of Enrico Fermi awards have gone to people of Jewish origin. Since 1880, almost half of all chess grandmasters have been Jewish.

Jews are over-represented in the knowledge professions in vastly different societies. In 2010, 53 per cent of American Jews held professional jobs, compared with 20 per cent of white non-Jewish men. In the same year, a group that represents 2 per cent of the American population won 21 per cent of places at Ivy League universities and 51 per cent of Pulitzer prizes for non-fiction.[2] You could find similar disparities in America's nemesis, Communist Russia. When the Society of Militant Materialist Dialecticians was founded in 1929 to promote the correct interpretation of Marxism, 54 per cent of its members were Jewish. When the Communist Academy held its plenary session a year later, half of its full and corresponding members were Jewish.[3]

This is one subject on which both philosemites and antisemites can see eye to eye. Houston Stewart Chamberlain, one of the fathers of race theory, was worried about the Jews precisely because they were so successful: through innate cleverness and diabolical cunning, he thought, they threatened the rightful dominance of his beloved Teutons.[4] Joseph Jacobs, a prominent Jewish historian, praised Jewish 'thinkers and sages' for their 'eagle vision' and ability, as true aristocrats, to bridge the gulf between the elite and the masses.[5] Antisemitism was rooted in fear of Jewish success rather than, as with most racism, contempt for the vilified group's perceived failure. Under Stalin, as it veered from philosemitism to antisemitism, the Communist Party defined 'the Jewish problem' as a problem of 'excessive success' – and embarked on an elaborate programme of 'normalizing' the Jews by sending them to work on the land and 'normalizing' educational institutions by limiting the number of Jews that were accepted.

Explaining this phenomenon of Jewish intellectual success raises all sorts of fraught questions. What exactly is a Jew, given the incidence of out-marriage? And is it sensible to talk about a Jewish ethnicity when Jews in the Upper West Side in New York live rather different lives from Jews in Baghdad? Nevertheless, the fact that Jews have shone intellectually in so many different times and places suggests that there is something in their culture that favours intellectual achievement. Jews' fate as nomads has forced them to invest in what they carry around in their heads rather than in land. At the same time, their sense of themselves as a special people with a unique relationship with God – a sense that has been massively reinforced by millennia of persecution – has given them the self-confidence, first, to keep themselves to themselves, producing a powerful collective identity, and second, to succeed in their various callings. The two sides of Jewish identity have driven them to make intellectual breakthroughs. Thorstein Veblen argued that the archetypal Jewish intellectual 'becomes a disturber of the intellectual peace, but only at the cost of becoming an intellectual wayfaring man, a wanderer in the intellectual no-man's-land, seeking another place to rest, further along the road, somewhere over the horizon'.[6]

The argument of this chapter is that the Jewish people played a prominent role in developing the meritocratic idea. They didn't develop meritocracy in the narrow sense of selecting people for positions on the basis of their intellectual powers, as Plato did in theory and the Chinese did in practice. But they did so in more indirect ways. They led the world in emphasizing intellectual success as a way of securing the survival of the group. They heaped honour on people who could perform demanding intellectual feats, from rabbis to scholars. They embraced objective measures of intellectual success – particularly examinations – as ways of establishing their credentials and combating anti-Jewish prejudice. Jews played a prominent role in both developing IQ tests and opposing affirmative action: think of Hans Eysenck in the first category and Irving Kristol and Nathan Glazer in the second.[7]

Moreover, Jews embraced a type of mobile meritocracy that has come to the fore in the age of globalization. Both Plato and Confucius were concerned with selecting leaders to rule over particular places – a tiny imaginary city in Plato's case and a real, continent-sized country in Confucius's. Royal houses plucked scholarship boys from obscurity to help them rule their realms. But for most of the history of the Jewish people the Jewish conception of educational excellence was singularly free from the logic of place: Jews might flourish in state administrations, but they always knew they were there on sufferance. Yuri Slezkine, a historian at the University of California, Berkeley, has argued that Jews got to the future first. 'Modernization is about everyone becoming urban, mobile, literate, articulate, intellectually intricate, physically fastidious, and occupationally flexible ... Modernization, in other words, is about everyone becoming Jewish.'[8] Mr Slezkine should have added globally meritocratic to his list.

A DEMANDING FAITH

There are two powerful reasons why Jews embraced intellectual success so early. The first was rooted in the nature of their religion, which demanded a high degree of intellectual commitment from its followers. Mohammed called the Jews 'the people of the book'. Judaism is in fact described in a collection of holy books that provide answers to everything from the most profound theological questions to the most detailed issues of etiquette. The Torah (or teachings) portrays the workings of Abraham's descendants from the creation of the world to the arrival of the Canaan brothers, weary from tribulations, on the borders of the Promised Land. Other sacred texts describe the conquest of Canaan, the destruction and rebuilding of the Temple, and various divine prophesies. Books of etiquette describe what animals the Jewish people could and could not eat, whom they could have sex with, what they should do on specific days, and what sort of haircut they could have (pudding bowls were strictly forbidden). The psalms provide inspiration and the proverbs rules to live by. To this very day, Orthodox Jews spend many hours a day – up to twelve in the case of Haredi men – doing nothing but studying their sacred texts. The catacombs next to the Western Wall in Jerusalem are lined with sacred books, packed in tightly, and bearded rabbis, reading out loud, some of them with bits of sacred text bound to their bodies, the better to absorb God's wisdom.

The Hebrew Bible is one of the most sophisticated products of the human mind – a compilation of great poetry, intricate stories and mind-bogglingly complicated family trees. Jewish law (and lore) is one of the most demanding bodies of reasoning ever produced. God's insistence that Jews must heed the law not only meant that they had to study the law themselves but also that fathers had to teach the law to their children. Though the law was so convoluted that you could spend a lifetime learning it without ever reaching the end, the faithful had no choice but to continue with their search for truth. God had chosen the Jews above all the people in the world. 'For you are a holy people to the Lord your God. You the Lord has chosen to become to him a treasured people among all the peoples that are on the face of the earth.' He had also forged a covenant with the Jews by sending them specific instructions in the form of the Ten Commandments and other detailed laws. Yet Jewish history was defined by tragedy and disaster. So Jews had no choice but to study the precise terms of this covenant in order to see what they were doing wrong and learn how to please the deity that had chosen them.

The Jewish faith gave a leading role to Wise Men who were charged with the twin tasks of making sense of the faith and teaching it to the young. 'The wise man takes precedence over the king,' the Talmud says, 'and a bastard who is a scholar over a high priest who is an ignoramus.' 'A man should sell all he possesses in order to marry the daughter of a scholar, as well as to marry his daughter to a scholar,' it also advises. Jewish society was geared towards producing and harbouring these wise men. Rabbis stood at the centre of religious life: they were designated 'lords' of the Temple and acted as social models for the Jewish people as a whole. Local oligarchs not only supported these rabbis in the demanding work of absorbing and promulgating time-consuming texts. They allowed their daughters to marry the most brilliant students in yeshiva schools, regardless of their social origins.

The Jewish religion also put more emphasis on mass literacy than any other religion until Protestantism. Fathers were required to teach their children to read. Communities were expected to support schools, scholars and, if possible, great libraries (the Oppenheimer family accumulated 7,000 Hebrew books and 1,000 Hebrew manuscripts in the Hamburg ghetto, a collection that now forms the basis of the Bodleian's Hebrew collection).[9] 'Pious Jews saw heaven as a vast library,' Paul Johnson has written in his history of the Jews, referring to the early Middle Ages, 'with the Archangel Metatron as the librarian: the books in the shelves there pressed themselves together to make room for a newcomer.'[10] 'One should sell all he possesses and buy books,' went one popular Jewish saying, 'for as the sages put it, "He who increases books, increases wisdom."' 'If a man has two sons, one of whom dislikes lending his books, while the other is eager, a man should leave his entire library to the second, even if he be younger.' Knowledge is for spreading, not hoarding.

Literacy encouraged the development of broad cognitive abilities. The rabbis in the Talmud are preoccupied not only with the Word but with words – they speak Aramaic on a daily basis, Hebrew on the Sabbath and bits of Greek, Persian, Accadian, Syriac and Latin[11] and spend their every waking hour engaged in intense study. Hebrew is unusually 'rich in expressions for activities demanding qualities of mind', with 'no fewer than eleven words for seeking or researching, thirty-four for distinguishing or separating, and fifteen for combining'.[12] The Torah obliges the faithful to engage in all sorts of complicated calculations about when to perform rituals and when to expect various important religious events.

This respect for learning manifested itself in very different communities in very different eras – in rural Hungary and Poland as well as in cosmopolitan cities such as Budapest and Vienna. In Eastern Europe, the synagogue is still called the Shool (*Schule* or school). 'God help a man against Gentile hands and Jewish brains' was a popular saying among Polish Jews. 'The most valuable individual is the intellectual individual; humanity at its best is intellectuality at its highest' was Werner Sombart's impression of Jewish culture in Germany and Eastern Europe on the verge of the First World War. David Ben-Gurion (1886–1973) recalled that, as a ten-year-old boy growing up in Russian Poland, he heard a rumour that the Messiah had arrived – a 'tall, handsome man, a learned man of Vienna, a doctor no less'.[13] Everywhere it expressed the same insight born of repeated exile: that 'everything that seems solid and valuable is ultimately perishable, while everything that is intangible – knowledge most of all – is potentially everlasting'.[14]

Reverence for learning translated into obsession with passing exams. Exams represented lots of things to Jewish people, especially marginalized ones: not just proof of intellectual success but also a guarantee of acceptance by the official world and, if the official world reneged on its obligations, a portable proof of competence. Isaac Babel's short story on the 1905 pogrom in Odessa, 'The Story of My Dovecot', is a case in point. When the narrator of the story passes the entrance exam to the *Gymnasium*, his Torah teacher, Monsieur Lieberman, gives a toast in which he conflates the fate of the successful scholar with the fate of the Jewish people:

> The old man congratulated my parents in this toast and said that I had vanquished all my enemies at the exam, had vanquished the Russian boys with fat cheeks and the sons of our coarse men of wealth. Thus in ancient times had David, King of Judah, vanquished Goliath, and just as I had triumphed over Goliath, so would our people by the strength of their intellect vanquish the enemies who had encircled us and were thirsting for our blood. Having said this, Monsieur Lieberman began to weep and, while weeping, took another sip of wine and shouted 'Viva!'[15]

Intellectual success was underpinned by an adamantine commitment to the family. God told Noah, after the Flood, to 'Be fruitful and multiply.' He also issued all sorts of instructions on the importance of forming tight family bonds, such as the fifth commandment on honouring your father and mother. Jewish families were often scenes of intense psychic dramas as parents imposed their ambitions on their children and children struggled to realize those ambitions, sometimes crushed under the burden of expectations, sometimes triumphant. Hence the focus on highly sexualized family struggles in great Jewish thinkers such as Freud and Jewish writers such as Philip Roth. Hence the Jewish jokes about over-demanding parents, particularly mothers. (The archetypical Jewish birth announcement supposedly reads: 'Mr and Mrs Marvin Rosenbloom are pleased to announce the birth of their son, Dr Jonathan Rosenbloom.') And hence the extraordinary feats of energy – Mendelssohn could write a symphony in days and Disraeli a novel in weeks. The Jewish family is at once a nexus of mutual obligations and a launching pad for achievement-oriented children.

The second reason why Jews embraced intellectual success so tightly was the fact that, thanks to a mixture of religious exclusivism and social prejudice, they were systematically excluded from the world of degree, priority and place that I described in the first chapter. They were banned from owning land: so they didn't aspire to being feudal aristocrats. They were banned from attending universities, which were then training grounds for Christian priests: so they had more time for unconventional learning, such as science, as well as for their own theological speculations.

The mechanics of 'othering' varied from plain and simple exclusion (being prevented from holding top jobs in guilds and the bureaucracy but allowed to make a living doing things that were forbidden to Christians, such as lending money) to outright persecution. But both types encouraged Jews to specialize in very different skills from those required to run estates and lead men in war: social skills such as forging connections with far-flung trading allies; psychological skills such as creating trust; and, above all, cognitive skills: an ability to work with numbers, to record obligations, to persuade in argument.[16] And both types of exclusion forced them to rely on their own efforts to survive: 'A Jew is like a man with a short arm,' Gustav Mahler liked to say. 'He has to swim harder to reach the shore.'[17]

Cognitive ability and social exclusion reinforced each other. The only way the Jews could preserve their identity in the absence of a state or a homeland was to celebrate their distinctive rituals. This meant giving a leading role to rabbis and cherishing the documents that defined their identity; it meant, in other words, developing a life of the mind to make up for the lack of a fixed place on the Earth. Yet the precise relationship between 'intelligence' and 'exclusion' is complicated – and certainly can't be written simply in terms of a persecuted people reluctantly embracing jobs that were marginal to a feudal society based on landowning and war-making. Jews frequently flourished in their role as insider-outsiders by providing a vital service, money-lending, that was forbidden to Christians, to peasants, tradesmen, knights, courtiers and even monasteries. In 1270, for example, 80 per cent of the 228 adult Jewish males in Perpignan, France, made their living lending money to their Christian neighbours.[18] And European elites frequently courted Jews because they possessed such unique skills. In the early ninth century, for example, a group of Jews who were bound together by elaborate ties of kinship lived in Lucca in northern Italy. They uprooted themselves and moved to the Rhineland and northern France at the invitation of the Emperor Charlemagne, who offered them physical protection and the ability to adjudicate their own legal quarrels, as well as well-paid jobs. (A charter of Henry IV, dated 1090, included the assurance that 'if anyone shall wound a Jew, but not mortally, he shall pay one pound of gold . . . If he is unable to pay the prescribed amount . . . his eyes will be put out and his right hand cut off.')

Whenever Europeans succumbed to the demon of antisemitism and expelled the Jews, they paid a heavy economic price. The expulsion of the Jews from Spain (1492) and from Portugal (1496–7) cost both countries dear in terms of short-term vitality and long-term development. By contrast, the countries and regions who provided a refuge for the persecuted Jews did well as a result. Leghorn in Italy, Hamburg and Frankfurt in Germany, Marseilles, Bordeaux and Rouen in France, Antwerp in the Low Countries, and, above all, Amsterdam, which the Jews dubbed the New Jerusalem, all saw their economic fortunes transformed by the arrival of Jewish émigrés. The same was true of Britain and, particularly, the United States after the Second World War.

THE CHOSEN FEW

In *The Chosen Few* (2012) two academics, Maristella Botticini and Zvi Eckstein, have argued that the relationship between exclusion and specialization was even more nuanced than the above suggests.[19] They maintain that religion provides a better explanation of the Jews' long-standing commitment to education than does persecution: the Jews shifted their focus from farming to urban professions some time before wider society imposed restrictions on Jews owning land. They also point out that there are plenty of examples of persecuted groups, most notably the Romany gypsies, who have done little to invest in education.[20] According to them, the great turning point in Jewish attitudes to education came with the destruction of the Second Temple in AD 70.

Following the Jewish people's Babylonian exile, from the sixth century BC onwards, Judaism had rested on two great pillars: the rituals carried out at the Temple in Jerusalem and the reading of the Torah. A small elite of priests ran the Temple and controlled Torah study. The destruction of the Temple, following the Roman conquest of Jerusalem, quickly switched Judaism's centre of gravity from the priesthood in Jerusalem to a growing community of rabbis and scholars – that is, from *Beit Hamikdash* to *beit hamidrash* (from the Temple to the religious study hall). The only way that Judaism could survive after the destruction of its central institution was to transform itself from a place-based religion into a text-based one. The priests who had fled from the Temple wrote down everything they knew about their ritual; worshippers redoubled their efforts to read what the priests had written, along with the other key texts of the faith; and an education-focused faith was born.

The authors report that Jewish sources from the post-Temple period are filled with words such as 'teachers' salary', 'duties of teachers', 'pupils', 'length of the school day', 'schools', 'books' and 'education tax'.[21] Rabbis and scholars took on a leading role as preservers of the faith and leaders of communities. Worship of God now involved not only prayer but also study, and not only silent study but also social rituals involving reading aloud in the presence of others. Within a century of the high priest Joshua ben Gamla's ordinance of 63–4 AD instructing every Jewish father to send his young son to primary school, the Jews were unique among the world's people in establishing universal male literacy and numeracy.

The literacy requirement created a system of natural selection. Numerous peasants abandoned Judaism for Christianity because investing so much time and energy in learning to read didn't make economic sense in a predominantly agricultural society. On the other hand, people who stuck with Judaism gravitated to more lucrative, urban-based occupations such as crafts, trade and money-lending that allowed them to exploit their hard-earned mental skills: in a largely illiterate society the ability to read and write contracts, business letters and account books turned you into a valuable commodity.

The opening of the Mediterranean and Middle Eastern economies in the eighth to twelfth centuries provided them with further opportunities to specialize and thereby recoup their investment in education. The Jews initially focused on the Muslim world and settled across Yemen, Syria, Egypt and the Maghreb. Between 750 and 900, nearly all the Jews in Mesopotamia and Persia – some three quarters of world Jewry at the time – left farming, moved to the big cities of the Abbasid Caliphate, and began to specialize in educationally demanding professions. This shift from tilling the land to working as educated middlemen took place despite the fact that there was no religious or legal prohibition on Jews owning land. The Jews then shifted in large numbers to Europe, where, despite considerable prejudice against their religious practices, they continued to thrive in their chosen professions.

THE GREAT EMANCIPATION

The final piece of the puzzle of Jewish intellectual success can be found in the progressive emancipation of the Jews from the eighteenth century onwards. Though Jewish society had been designed to produce intellectuals since the destruction of the Second Temple, these were intellectuals of a particular type: religious thinkers who were confined within an introverted society, proudly cut off from the wider world. They thought and debated obsessively – but they thought and debated obsessively within a narrow range of religious orthodoxy. Emancipation took this hyper-intellectual society and plunged it into a wider world of contacts and ideas.[22]

The result was an explosion of intellectual creativity, like dropping molten sodium into a bath of water. Think of Moses Mendelssohn, the polymath, or Heinrich Heine, the poet, or Moses Hess, the philosopher. Many of the children of orthodox parents abandoned orthodoxy as they came into contact with exciting new ideas, particularly enlightened ideas about the supremacy of reason. But even the most irreligious rebels were profoundly shaped by their ancestral religion. This was true of two of the most important thinkers of the modern era. Karl Marx was a descendant of eminent rabbis on both his father's and his mother's side, and he unconsciously preserved old habits of thought in his new philosophy, replacing the Jews with the proletariat as the chosen people and God's will with history as the engine of progress. Sigmund Freud simultaneously dismissed religion as a collective illusion and imitated many of the rules of Talmudic exegesis in his analytic approach.[23]

Emancipation produced brilliant men of the world as well as tortured intellectuals. Mayer Amschel Rothschild, who was such an observant Jew that he employed a man to walk in front of him to clean the doorknobs in order to avoid contamination, built one of the greatest business empires in modern Europe. Benjamin Disraeli, the son of a pious Jew who nevertheless converted to Christianity, dazzled British society as a novelist and socialite and eventually became leader of Britain's establishment party, the Conservative Party, and prime minister of the then most powerful country in the world.

Emancipated Jews pursued two (superficially contradictory) strategies. They espoused liberalism with its emphasis on universal rights and religious choice. Jews gravitated to radical groups, from rationalists to Masons, who wanted to divorce citizenship from loyalty to particular national religions. They also embraced national cultural icons as a substitute for embracing national religious traditions. English Jews became devotees of Shakespeare, German Jews of Goethe, French Jews of Victor Hugo, with baptism in the national canon replacing baptism in the national Church as proof of belonging. While labouring over his great work, *The Jewish State* (1896), Theodor Herzl, the father of Zionism, liked to relax by listening to Wagner, particularly *Tannhäuser*.

WANDERING GENIUS

The Jews are not alone. Other wandering peoples have contributed disproportionately to the development of the meritocratic idea for the same reasons that Werner Sombart outlined in his great book on *The Jews and Capitalism*: rootlessness persuades them to invest heavily in intellectual resources and insecurity gives them an unusual degree of discipline and ambition. They are former outsiders who have succeeded in inserting themselves into the heart of their host societies – particularly in banking, business and intellectual life – and former dissidents who have succeeded in setting the tone of society.

The Parsis are the closest thing to the Jews in southern Asia – 'beneath contempt' in terms of numbers, in Mahatma Gandhi's phrase, but 'beyond compare' in terms of contribution. Followers of the Iranian prophet Zoroaster (or Zarathrustra), the Parsis fled from the advancing Arab tide in Persia in the eighth century, found a home in what is now India, and subsequently thrived by acting as middlemen between European colonialists (first the Portuguese then the British) and the Indian population. Their comparative advantage lay in their rarity: they didn't belong to any of the big ethnic groups that were competing for dominance but instead devoted their energy to protecting their distinctive identity, marrying within their ethnic group and preserving strict religious rituals, but simultaneously forging linkages wherever they could. They are both insiders and outsiders: Indian in their national affiliation; 'British' in their mastery of England's language and habits (every member of the first all-India cricket team was a Parsi, as were all three Indian members of the British parliament); unique in terms of their habits and even gene pools (one 2002 study found that they are genetically closer to Iranians than to their Indian neighbours).[24]

The Parsis quickly became India's most successful businesspeople: by the late nineteenth century they ran most of Bombay's leading banks and businesses, with Jamsetji Tata forging the most successful of them all, the Tata Group. They also became its most enthusiastic supporters of meritocracy: Parsis place a pronounced emphasis on education, including women's education, and Parsi businesses, particularly Tata, pride themselves on their meritocratic habits. Tata's management programme is famous for recruiting people on the basis of open competition and training the company's future elite. Still, they have also paid a price for their habit of keeping themselves aloof: thanks to intermarriage, they have a propensity for certain genetic diseases, particularly Parkinson's disease; thanks to their emphasis on education, particularly female education, they have a very low birth rate. Their numbers have declined from 115,000 in 1941 to some 65,000 today, out of an Indian population of more than a billion.

Similar patterns can be seen among successful ethnic and some-times religious minorities across the world, particularly in old colonial empires. The Jains were even more distinctive than the Parsis: forbidden from killing any living creature, including insects, they avoided agriculture and specialized in money-lending, jewellery-making and, eventually, banking. The overseas Chinese performed a similar middle-man role across South-east Asia. By 2000, ethnic Chinese controlled more than half of the private economies of the Philippines, Malaysia and Thailand, despite representing less than 2 per cent of the populations of each country.

This combination of the book and the compass will become more powerful in the future. Once-mobile groups such as the Jews and the Parsis are set to become more important as globalization continues to transform the modern economy and power continues to shift from national governments to international companies. But they will also become increasingly imperilled as resentment against inequality grows and the backlash against globalization whips up some of the world's most powerful hatreds.

7

The Golden Ladder

The great meritocratic breakthrough took place in the West rather than the East. China's mandarin regime was too fossilized to combine government by a cognitive elite with economic dynamism. By contrast, the West embraced meritocracy at the same time that it embraced science, capitalism and individualism. This chapter looks at three worms that gestated in the belly of the old European society of 'priority, degree and place' and prepared the way for the rise of the meritocracy.

SPONSORED SOCIAL MOBILITY

Sponsored social mobility means, in essence, identifying able people from poorer backgrounds and scooping them up into the elite.[1] It necessarily involves only a tiny proportion of the population – minuscule in the Middle Ages – but also has extraordinary effects not only on the people who are favoured (whose lives are transformed) but also on the wider society (which gets an injection of administrative or intellectual genius). Sponsored mobility started as an ad hoc solution to specific problems: feudal lords identified talented servants who were good at running things or counting things and gave them a leg-up. It later developed into a regulated mechanism: self-conscious sponsors identified talented children, provided them with a privileged education in an elite school and university, and then gave them a position in the elite.

One avenue of social mobility in the early Middle Ages was the aristocratic household. Great households were large administrative undertakings: there were fields to be tilled, servants to be organized, accounts to be kept, retainers to be rewarded. Noble lords could hardly be expected to do all this themselves, particularly if they had several estates in different parts of the country, so they employed supervisors and stewards to do it for them. Many of these supervisors became, over time, honorary members of the ruling elite because they were in daily contact with their betters and intimately involved in many of their most important decisions. 'One phenomenon evident in early medieval sources is the transformation of titles, the tendency for names, which first appear as designations of slaves or servants, to evolve into terms referring to high personages in the aristocracy,' notes a historian of medieval social mobility. 'Knight' derives from a word meaning 'boy' or 'servant', as does the Anglo-Saxon 'thegn'. 'Baron' may derive from a word meaning 'rustic lout'. 'Marshal' originally referred to a servant in charge of horses. This upward drift of language reflects an upward drift of functionaries as they rose up the social hierarchy and added dignity to the names that they bore.[2]

The biggest and most consequential aristocratic household was the royal household. The royal household was originally divided into three departments: the lord steward was responsible for 'upstairs', the lord chamberlain for 'downstairs' and the master of the horse for 'out of doors'. But as the household's focus expanded to include the state of the country as well as the king's personal needs, the number of employees swelled. The king needed clever bureaucrats to raise money, professional soldiers to defend his kingdom and local functionaries to enforce his will, transforming what had once been an entourage into the nucleus of the modern state.

The second avenue was the Church. The Church played an ambivalent role in the old society of 'priority, degree and place' as both a cement and a solvent. On the one hand, it preached unquestioning obedience to the powers that be. On the other hand, it taught revolution. Jesus preached the equality of souls under God – 'There is neither Jew nor Greek, there is neither bond nor free, there is neither male nor female: for ye are all one in Christ Jesus,' as Paul put it in Galatians (3:28). The fatherhood of God means the brotherhood of man. If anything, he leaned towards the sanctity of the poor, devoting his life to outcasts and beggars and teaching that it was harder for a rich man to enter the kingdom of heaven than for a camel to pass through the eye of a needle (Matthew 19:24).

Jesus was as contemptuous of family bonds as he was of social hierarchy. 'If any man come to me, and hate not his father, and mother, and wife, and children, and brethren, and sisters, yea, and his own life also,' he said, 'he cannot be my disciple' (Luke 14:26). Proclaiming that 'I come not to send peace, but a sword,' he added that 'I am come to set a man at variance against his father, and the daughter against her mother, and the daughter in law against her mother in law . . . He that loveth father or mother more than me is not worthy of me . . .' (Matthew 10:34–5, 37) The true believer must be willing to swap his blood relatives for his Christian kin, just as God was willing to sacrifice His only begotten son to demonstrate that we are all His children. 'For whosoever shall do the will of my Father which is in heaven, the same is my brother, and sister, and mother' (Matthew 12:50).

The Church frequently offered direct challenges to the two great buttresses of medieval society: hierarchical bonds and family ties. 'Do not despise these people in their abjection,' St Gregory of Nyssa (c.335–c.395) said of the poor and downtrodden, 'do not think they merit no respect . . . they have taken upon them the person of the saviour'.[3] St Benedict (480–c.547) required monks to wear the same clothes, eat the same food and perform the same tasks, coming to decisions by 'mutual listening' rather than by fiat. St Dominic (1170–1221) told his friars to preach to the poor as well as the rich, and mix preaching with charity. Church lawyers alternated between kowtowing to the secular authorities and insisting that 'natural law' trumped secular law. Driving all these challenges to the old society was the logic of Christian individualism. Unlike previous religions – certainly unlike the animistic religions of the ancient Greeks – Christianity taught the moral equality of individuals. It also gave individuals moral permission to break their communal bonds, including the most intimate bonds of all, with their families, to forge their individual destinies.[4]

By its very nature the Church's ruling caste of celibate intellectuals had to be replenished by recruitment from outside. To be sure, the celibacy obligation was often honoured more in the breach rather than the observance, and the Church produced living refutations of its own doctrine in the form of clerical dynasties. But in the eleventh century clerical reformers made a good job, at least for a while, of outlawing clerical marriages and abolishing clerical dynasties. This meant that one of the most desirable jobs in medieval Europe was open to new men who had an aptitude for scholarship and a faith that was so strong they were willing to renounce the flesh.

The Church produced a long line of low-born men of talent to balance the members of aristocratic dynasties. Pope Gregory VII, who inspired the great eleventh-century reform movement, was the son of a common labourer – a blacksmith or a peasant, according to different sources – who so impressed his teachers at his monastery in Rome that he was given rapid promotion and, in 1073, became one of the few popes elected by acclamation. Abbot Suger of Saint-Denis, who became a close adviser to two French kings, Louis VI and Louis VII, and built one of Europe's first Gothic buildings, was born in obscurity and was handed over to the abbey of Saint-Benoît-sur-Loire to train as a priest. Thereafter he worked his way up the Church hierarchy as secretary to the abbot of Saint-Denis, provost of a couple of abbeys and a delegate to the pope's court, before ending up as an abbot, royal confidant and patron of the arts. Thomas Becket, the Archbishop of Canterbury who stood up to Henry II and paid the ultimate price for his heroism in 1170, was born into a downwardly mobile minor aristocratic family in Cheapside, London.[5] Becket attended a grammar school but didn't fully master Latin, let alone learn canon and civic law, and, after one of his father's financial reverses, ended up working as a clerk. Thomas's great break came when he secured a position in the household of Theobald of Bec, then the Archbishop of Canterbury. Theobald knew talent when he saw it and entrusted Becket with several missions to Rome, sent him to Bologna and Auxerre to study canon law, showered him with important ecclesiastical positions, including Archdeacon of Canterbury, and, in 1155, persuaded Henry II to appoint him Lord Chancellor. Becket was now a fully-fledged member of the elite – Henry II even sent his eldest son to live in his household – and in 1162 was appointed Theobald's successor as Archbishop of Canterbury.

This system of sponsored social mobility was eventually institutionalized in schools and universities. England's greatest public schools were founded to provide free educations for promising but impoverished boys – which is precisely why they were called by the (now confusing) name 'public schools'. William of Wykeham, the Bishop of Winchester, founded Winchester College in 1382, to provide seventy poor scholars with a secondary-school education, and its sister college in Oxford, New College, to provide them with a finishing school. William proclaimed that the school's purpose was 'to hold out helping hands and give the assistance of charity' to

> poor and needy scholars, clerks, present and to come, in order that they may be able to stay or be busy at school, and by the grace of God become more amply and freely proficient in the faculty and science of grammar, and become as is desirable more fit for the sciences or liberal arts, to increase the roll of all the sciences, faculties and liberal arts, and expand as far as in us lies the number of those studying and profiting in them . . .

Henry VI founded Eton College, in 1440, and King's College, Cambridge, in 1441, for the same purpose, insisting, in the charters for both institutions, that the majority of boys come from poor backgrounds. The lucky few usually paid back the cost of their educations by working for either the state or the Church.

Henry Chichele, who founded All Souls College, Oxford, in 1438, was the perfect product of this tradition of sponsored social mobility. Born in relative obscurity in Northamptonshire, he attracted the attention of William of Wykeham because of his obvious intelligence, attended New College, Oxford, embarked on a clerical career specializing in law and diplomacy, and served as Archbishop of Canterbury from 1414 to 1443. Despite his grandness he didn't forget his origins, founding a school in his birthplace, Higham Ferrers, which is now the Henry Chichele Primary School. 'I was pauper born, then to primate raised,' proclaims his gravestone with a certain degree of exaggeration. 'Now I am cut down and served up for worms. Behold my grave.'

Across Europe universities used a system of sliding fees to ease the passage of poorer scholars: noblemen and rich burghers paid more than the statutory fees while the pauper-born paid nothing for their education and were given scholarships, under a system of *privilegium pauperum*. The authorities also provided exemptions for fees because of family circumstances (a death in the family) or social connections (for example, for the children of professors or local princes).[6]

The growth of the state in the Early Modern period expanded the system of sponsored social mobility. Demand for able bureaucrats who could master the government machine grew much faster than the ability of the landed aristocracy to supply them. Thomas Wolsey and Thomas Cromwell effectively ruled England for twenty-five years continuously, despite being, respectively, the son of a wool-seller and the son of a blacksmith. At the same time, demand for knights in shining armour declined: the aristocracy increasingly devoted itself to hanging around the Court and cultivating its manners. Hilary Mantel captures some of this story in her trilogy on Cromwell's life, *Wolf Hall*, *Bring Up the Bodies* and *The Mirror and the Light*. Mantel's aristocrats look down on Thomas Cromwell as they accompany Henry VIII on his hunts and jousts but, while they're away enjoying themselves, he does the real business of statecraft, not just running the country but building the foundations of the modern state.

The Tudor and Stuart period saw a burst of school-building (or rebuilding), as monarchs tried to produce more public servants, businessmen more accountants, churchmen more preachers, and local burghers more functionaries. During his short reign (1547–53) Edward VI created several of Britain's most successful provincial grammar schools, particularly Edward VI Grammar School in Birmingham, a forger of Midlands meritocrats down the ages. When Elizabeth I re-founded Westminster School in 1560 she insisted that at least a third of the intake were chosen on the basis not only of 'teachable-ness', 'goodness of disposition', 'learning' and 'good behaviour' but also of poverty. The mercantile class was also busy scouring the population for talent: John Colet, a humanist scholar and grandson of a merchant, re-founded St Paul's in 1509 to cater for 153 non-fee-paying scholars; various livery companies founded Merchant Taylors (1561) and Charterhouse (1611) for the offspring of the 'poor men'. Shrewsbury, Rugby and Harrow were all founded in the second half of the sixteenth century specifically to provide free educations for local youths.[7]

THE REVIVAL OF THE *POLIS*

City-states introduced a new principle into a Europe dominated by dynasties and their politics: self-government – or at least government by city oligarchies. The greatest of the city-states was Venice, which was both a maritime trading empire and a northern Italian city-state rolled into one. For a long time, the city was part of the Byzantine empire. The emperor sent his war fleets to protect the city whenever the Franks threatened to encroach, and the local representative of Byzantine power was known by the imperial title of *dux* (duke). But in the twelfth and thirteenth centuries Venice gradually detached itself from Byzantium; the *dux* became the doge; and a protectorate became a trading superpower and the richest city in Italy. Venice became a centre of commercial dynamism and innovation – as well as one of the world's most breathtaking cities. Venetian sailors – some 36,000 of them in the fourteenth century – popped up as far away as China. Venetian merchants invented the prototype of today's joint-stock companies in the *commenda*.[8] It also pioneered a new form of self-government, checking the tendency of the doge's office to become hereditary and handing power to a collection of interlocking executive councils. This was far from a proto-democracy: Venice was ruled by an oligarchy of merchant families, but this was an oligarchy that tried both to think in terms of the city-state's long-term interests and to incorporate new men into decision-making.[9] From the late twelfth century onwards, a hundred new members were added every year to the Ducal Council, which in turn kept the doge under tighter control.

Other north Italian city-states asserted their right to self-rule in the eleventh and twelfth centuries, as a glance at their impressive fortifications demonstrates. They created powerful city councils such as Siena's Council of Nine; limited the power of bishops and nobles; played imperial dynasties off against each other; and grouped themselves into a confederacy, the Lombard League, designed to preserve their collective independence. This created some of the world's most complicated and cynical politics but also provided the perfect soil for the Renaissance. Several Northern European cities also flourished by negotiating favourable 'charters' with the king. These charters introduced three radical ideas: they provided cities with corporate rights which limited the rights of dynasts; identified 'citizenship' with the possession of certain civic rights; and empowered city councillors, whether elected or appointed, to govern their cities. This was particularly true of large, rich cities such as Ghent, which had the resources to resist their overlords; but it was also true of small and middle-sized towns in England, France, northern Germany and Sweden.[10] Several of these northern cities eventually produced the Hanseatic League, which escaped from the limits of national or regional politics and created a global trading empire.

PERFORMANCE-RELATED ARISTOCRACY

The concept of 'aristocracy' also acted as a worm in the belly of the old society. We saw in a previous chapter that the feudal aristocracy was the antithesis of a meritocracy: it owed its position to inheritance rather than achievement and its power to land rather than brains. But the term 'aristocracy' also had another meaning: the Greeks contrasted government by the best (aristocracy) with government by the richest and best-connected (oligarchy). Both Plato and Aristotle insisted that the children of the elite needed to be educated to fulfil their high stations in life: even if they inherited their positions through birth they also needed to earn them through performance. Roman sages, particularly Cicero, argued that the nobles had a duty to prevent society from being destroyed by greedy tyrants. Being 'well born' thus implied a duty to work for the good of the republic. This was an attitude perfectly expressed in Goethe's couplet 'Really to own what you inherit/you must first earn it by your merit.'

The Renaissance saw a vigorous reassertion of this classical ideal, a reassertion that began in the Italian city-states (where scholars could draw inspiration from the example of Athenian self-rule as well as from the relics of the Roman empire that lay all about them) but soon spread northwards. The humanists believed that 'aristocracy' wasn't something you inherited regardless of your behaviour. It was a code of conduct you could achieve through education and effort, rooted in the ethereal world of virtue rather than the solid worlds of property or blood. And they restructured elite education from top to bottom in the light of these beliefs, focusing above all on classical civilization on the grounds, first, that the ancient world provided a model to the modern world and, second, that studying ancient philosophers, poets and rhetoricians was the best way to train the moral qualities needed to govern.

Dante provided an early expression of the new doctrine in the fourth book of his unfinished 'Banquet' (1304–7). Nobility could not be the product of ancient wealth, he said, for riches of any kind are inherently base. Nor could it be the product of inheritance, since nothing can guarantee that a distinguished father will sire a distinguished son. The only true nobility is virtue – a personal quality that has nothing to do with families and everything to do with individual success, including individual success in the classroom.

A chorus of other Renaissance thinkers elaborated on the nature of true nobility. They made a radical distinction between real aristocrats and conventional ones while also broadening the notion of public service to include administration as well as fighting. Leonardo of Chios (c.1395–c.1458), a Greek Dominican scholar who taught at both Padua and Genoa, explained that nobility comes in two varieties. One is ostentatious and self-satisfied, and goes along with wealth, ancient lineage, pomposity and hereditary right. The other is quiet and unassuming. True nobility grows from the root of virtue and draws its strength from the 'innate principles of nature' rather than social convention. These nobles of nature are much better suited to governing a republic than nobles by convention.[11] Giovanni Buonaccorso da Montemagno (c.1391–1429) argued that republics don't owe a jot to nobles purely on the basis of their family connections. Only those with learning, wisdom and virtue deserve to rule.

The logical conclusion of this argument was to allocate all positions in the republic, from the highest to the lowest, on the basis of personal abilities. Giovanni Boccaccio (1313–75), the author of *The Decameron*, insisted that natural nobility could be found in all ranks of society, from farmers and craftsmen to the rich and well born. Biondo Flavio (1392–1463), a Florentine historian and one of the first people to divide history into ancient, medieval and modern, argued that ancient Rome's greatness was founded on its willingness to recruit able individuals from outside the old ruling class and even outside Italy. Giovanni Nesi (1456–1506), a Florentine philosopher and follower of Plato, maintained that in any just society 'offices should be determined and ranks conferred in proportion to the merits and virtues of individual citizens'.[12]

The most interesting, as well as the most misunderstood, exponent of this position was Machiavelli (1469–1527), the son of a book-keeper, who enjoyed some success in Florence as a courtier and diplomat, thanks to his intellect, wit and erudition, but eventually fell out of favour, spending his retirement writing political tracts, most notably *The Prince* (1532). Machiavelli thought that the most impor-tant political quality was *virtù*. By this he didn't mean Christian virtue: it was quite possible to be a virtuous person (honest, charitable, decent) while remaining politically irrelevant. Public and private life are governed by different rules.[13] He meant the resolute exercise of one's talents – particularly the resolute exercise of manly talents such as courage, craft and fortitude. *Virtù* derives from the Latin *vir*, for 'man'. For Machiavelli, history is a dance between a female and a male: between *fortuna* (who needs to be tamed and seduced) and *virtù* (who needs to be strong and masterful). The most important manly quality is not the wisdom that lies in the heads of philosopher kings but the hope that lies in the loins of young aristocrats of nature.[14]

Machiavelli believed that *virtù* resides in polities as a whole as well as in the breasts of individual leaders. Great polities, like great lead-ers, are willing to do whatever it takes to master *fortuna* while serving the common good; indeed, the competition between Italy's city-states, which dominated Machiavelli's world, was largely a competition to cultivate *virtù*, both in city government and on the battlefield. Here Machiavelli took a dangerous position for an erstwhile servant of an Italian ruling family: he argued that open republics were much more likely to produce *virtù*-ous leaders than were dynasties.

This is not just because dynasties decay, as weak sons follow strong fathers. It is because *fortuna* is a fickle mistress. The qualities needed to master her change with the times. Open republics allow the public to sack obsolescent leaders and replace them with ones more suited to the times. Hereditary republics are stuck with the leader that they inherit whether that leader is suited to the times or not.[15] Machiavelli illustrated this with the example of how, in its struggle against Han-nibal, republican Rome was able to replace Fabius, who was cautious by nature, with Scipio, a much more aggressive figure:

If Fabius had been king of Rome, he might easily have lost that war because he did not know how to vary his actions to suit the change in the times. But instead he was born into a republic, where there were diverse citizens with diverse talents and approaches, and thus while Rome once had Fabius who was the best leader in times that required sustaining a prolonged war, so it later could turn to Scipio, who was more suited to those times apt for seizing victory.[16]

In Machiavelli's view open republics were more durable than dynasties because they had a free market in talents. They forced politicians to adjust their policies to changing times and, when crisis struck, made it possible to change both leaders and strategies. This posed two practical problems. How do you separate the transmission of power from the dynastic principle that had become so dominant in Europe? And how do you reduce the transfer of power from one leader to another to a matter of routine? Machiavelli answered these questions by sketching out the features of a modern constitutional state. You need a system of universal laws that doesn't privilege some people because of their backgrounds. You need political forums that institutionalize the free exchange of ideas. And you need institutions that are open to merit from whatever corner of society it might come, not only because this increases the supply of talent but also because it persuades regular citizens that their children 'can become the leader of the city' provided they have the right qualities. (In the Roman Republic, he told his readers, with an eye to persuasion more than historical accuracy, 'poverty was not a bar to anyone for any office or for any honour whatsoever, and exceptional talent was sought wherever it happened to be found'.) A modern republic under law will only bestow honours on citizens for good reasons, he argued. A dynastic republic, by contrast, rewards placemen, no matter how corrupt, because of who they are, but also fails to reward good public servants, however valiant and good, because the prince is frightened of stirring up jealousy.[17]

Machiavelli's radical views didn't prevent him from celebrating Italy's great dynasties – he dedicated *The Prince* to Lorenzo de' Medici and fawned over Cesare Borgia. Indeed, most humanists were prudent enough to focus on educating the well born and well connected rather than on re-engineering society from top to bottom. A trio of British statesmen demonstrate the reach of the new philosophy. Sir Thomas Elyot (c.1490–1546), a diplomat, urged that the tongue and the pen could be more effective weapons than the sword and the spear. Sir Thomas Smith (1513–77), a scholar administrator, declared that a kingdom 'is not so much won or kept by the manhood and force of men as it is by wisdom and polity, which is got chiefly by learning'. Sir Francis Bacon (1561–1626), a polymath who served for a while as Lord Chancellor, told the second Earl of Essex that it was not 'martial greatness' that would advance his career but being 'bookish and contemplative'.[18]

Nobody was more important to this humanist revolution than the sage of Rotterdam. Erasmus used his unrivalled classical learning to revive the Christian faith, by producing new Latin and Greek translations of the New Testament, and also to inject classical notions of education into the bloodstream of elite education. In *The Education of a Christian Prince* (1516), written as advice to the young King Charles of Spain, who later became the Habsburg Emperor Charles V, he presented the king as a servant of the people who must rule according to the principles of honour and sincerity. The way to make sure that he ruled according to these high principles was a vigorous education rooted both in the classical world and in Christian principles, focusing on taming the inner beast ('man, unless he has experienced the influence of learning and philosophy, is at the mercy of impulses that are worse than those of a wild beast') and cultivating the habits of gentleness and public service. In *The Prince*, which had been written three years earlier, Machiavelli had argued that it is better for a prince to be feared than loved; Erasmus argued, on the contrary, that it is better for him to be loved than feared, and suggested that the only way to create a lovable prince was to give him the benefit of a well-rounded humanist education.

This new emphasis on learning performed four revolutionary functions. It advanced the idea that admission to the real elite was conditional on your ability to embrace civilization in its widest sense, as a body of knowledge, a type of sensibility, a code of conduct and a set of social obligations. This prepared the way for the doctrine of a natural aristocracy determined by ability and character rather than by parentage, and by state service rather than landed estates. Second, it provided a way of disciplining the behaviour of the old elite or even, at its most extreme, of purifying the noble caste by ejecting people who behaved appallingly. Third, it provided a way of legitimizing the rise of new men who succeeded in commanding aristocratic codes of conduct. And finally, it held out the possibility of creating a trans-national elite of humanist scholars who shared similar training and similar values, and who habitually reinforced their bonds by travelling across Europe.[19] Erasmus, for one, proudly called himself a 'citizen of the world'.[20]

THE DIET OF WORMS

The Protestant Reformation was another great solvent of the bonds of tradition. Martin Luther was driven to break with Rome and launch the Reformation by the world-changing idea that every man is a priest. Who needs a caste of middlemen to interpret God's word – particularly middlemen who extracted such an extravagant and corrupting rent – when you can rely on your own judgement? This view was simultaneously elitist and egalitarian: elitist because it insisted that the spiritual elect had a duty to exercise leadership on Earth before taking up their predestined positions in heaven; egalitarian because it subjected social bonds to the acids of faith. Martin Luther said that 'A Christian man is a perfectly free lord, subject to none.' John Calvin, the founder of a particularly austere version of Protestantism, went further, insisting that the spiritual hierarchy of the elect and the damned bore no necessary relationship with the hierarchy on Earth.[21]

The religious revolution was also an educational revolution. It was no longer enough to gape at the priest mumbling in Latin and performing miracles before the altar. You had to study the Good Book yourself (which had fortunately been made easily available by the new invention of the printing press). It was no longer enough to justify institutions by appealing to tradition. You had to test them in the light of faith. Protestant countries quickly created elite institutions for the spiritual elect. Philip I of Hesse founded the first specifically

Protestant university, the University of Marburg, in 1527, a decade after Luther nailed his Ninety-five Theses on the church door. One of the first things that the Puritans did when they arrived in the New World was to establish Harvard University, in 1636. Protestants also built school systems for the masses: Protestant Holland, for example, created a mass school system long before its sometime overlord Catholic Spain.

The Reformation, particularly in its Calvinist form, also promoted hard work. Max Weber explained the psychological dynamic behind the Protestant work ethic: by holding out the chance of eternal grace but leaving the believer in doubt about his eventual salvation Protestantism encouraged the believer to act as if he is already a member of the elect – sober, earnest and hardworking – but at the same time wracked him with anxiety. Though Weber focused on the way that this anxiety predisposed people to success in business life, it is equally true that it predisposed them to success in intellectual life. What could be a better preparation for the life of a champion examinee than the idea that you should work hard, parcel out your time carefully and act as if you are forever labouring in your great taskmaster's eye?

Where Weber erred was to claim exclusive powers for Protestantism: Martin Luther's greatest contribution to the creation of the modern world was not so much Protestantism as competition. By breaking the Catholic Church's monopoly of faith, the Reformation forced priests of all denominations to improve their performance or lose their market share. The Jesuits, who operated as the shock troops of the Counter-Reformation, recognized that the best weapons against educated Protestants were educated Catholics. They invented the most efficient system of teacher training the world has seen, starting with exhaustive self-education (you can't be a great teacher without being well educated yourself) and involving systematic winnowing of the unfit at every stage of a long apprenticeship.[22] The Jesuits worked hard to find bright children in every corner of society on the grounds that the rich did not have a monopoly of intellectual talent. They developed a curriculum that focused as much on secular subjects as on theology on the grounds that God's wisdom was scattered around the universe rather than contained in a single text. Novices started off by learning Latin and Greek grammar, spent a couple of years studying the great works of classical poetry, history and, most importantly, rhetoric; then they spent three years studying philosophy, beginning with logic and moving on to Aristotle, mathematics and philosophy; and finally they spent four years studying theology. Their pupils included a striking proportion of the intellectual elite of the Early Modern era, from fierce critics of the Church such as Descartes and Voltaire to brilliant defenders such as Matteo Ricci.

The Jesuits were as enthusiastic about examinations as anyone, using them to drive the pedagogic machine and to regulate admission to the Order of Jesus (those who failed their exams, whatever their spiritual virtues, were debarred from the order and encouraged to pursue lower careers as 'temporal coadjutors'). Unlike the Chinese examinations, which took place in private examination cells, the Jesuits liked their grillings to be conducted in public, with a marked emphasis on *viva voces* and the dialectical competition between examiner and examinee. The *Ratio Studiorum* (1599), the official guidelines for Jesuit education, insisted that the philosophy exam in particular should be carried out in public and that 'from this examination, no matter how rigorously it is conducted, usually no Jesuits nor even, if possible, any of our day and boarding students should be excused'.[23]

THE NEW WORLD

Europe's system of sponsored social mobility was a feeble thing compared to China's: the schools and universities were ad hoc responses to local pressures rather than elements in a continent-spanning examination system. The common culture that Erasmus and his fellow humanists had begun to forge was shattered by the Reformation and the Counter-Reformation. The great public schools and universities frequently degenerated into finishing schools for the upper classes.

Nevertheless, Europe had one unassailable advantage over its Eastern rival: it was dynamic. By the seventeenth century, Europe was not only putting in place some of the rungs of the ladder of opportunity that was to transform society, it was putting in place the components of a growth-orientated civilization that was to leave China far behind.

Christianity carried within it the seeds of the liberal belief that all people are equal under the eyes of God but also free to make of their lives what they can. The Puritans put a further emphasis on hard work and self-definition. Lawyers talked of the king being 'under the law' while parliaments, particularly in England, put restraints on royal power. Cities limited the powers of monarchs and nurtured a new commercial class. City charters laid the foundations of social contract theory by defining the rights of citizens, and political theorists such as Hobbes and Locke took this idea further by arguing that a sovereign's power lay in his ability to advance the interests of the citizens – interests being security in Hobbes's case and 'life, liberty and property' in Locke's.

The commercial and scientific revolutions were institutionalized by powerful organizations as well as new patterns of thought. New trading organizations such as the British and Dutch East India Companies explored the world at a time when China banned foreign travel. And Royal Societies sprang up across Europe to advance science and the arts at a time when China remained fatally attached to the Confucian classics. Europe – particularly Northern Europe – thus produced two things that were friendly to the new meritocratic future: an expanding commercial society and an attitude of mind that embraced individual self-assertion as well as obeisance to tradition.

PART THREE

The Rise of the Meritocracy

8

Europe and the Career
Open to Talent

The French Revolution injected the question of meritocracy, like a shot of adrenalin, into the heart of European politics. Article VI of the 'Declaration of the Rights of Man and of the Citizen' (1789) provided the most concise statement of the emerging meritocratic idea:

> Law is the expression of the general will; all citizens have the right to concur personally, or through their representatives, in its formation; it must be the same for all, whether it protects or punishes. All citizens, being equal before it, are equally admissible to all public offices, positions, and employments, according to their capacity, and *without any other distinction than that of virtues and talents* [italics mine].

This contains echoes of the Chinese idea that the mandarin elite should scour the population for potential mandarins or the Platonic idea that embryonic guardians can be found in every class. But it goes further: it suggests that all citizens are equal before the state and can push themselves forward as potential decision-makers. The onus is on individuals to compete for political positions on the basis of their talents and virtues rather than for the state to micromanage things from on high.

The revolutionaries abolished the two great principles at the heart of the old society: the feudal principle that defined the relationship between masters and dependants on the basis of land tenure and the dynastic principle that put a family at the heart of power. Individuals acquired inalienable rights based on their common humanity rather than on their membership of a class or clique or status group. The idea that the royal household forms the nucleus of the state was abolished. This revolutionary philosophy confronted the French with the great questions at the heart of modernity. What does equality mean in practice? Does it mean dispensing with hierarchy altogether? Or does it mean giving people positions according to their abilities and aptitudes? And if it means the latter, what exactly do 'abilities' and 'aptitudes' mean? Are they defined by nature or nurture? And is there a 'natural aristocracy' to replace the artificial aristocracy of the old society?

There were certainly some revolutionaries who favoured the most extreme definition of equality. Maximilien Robespierre and his fellow *sans-culottes* wanted to take an axe to hierarchy in all its dimensions, including superior knowledge. The Constituent Assembly, which sat from 1789 to 1791, rejected the idea of using examinations to determine selection into the officer corps on the grounds that it would create a 'new aristocracy'.[1] But most were drawn to the idea of rule by 'talent' and 'virtue'. One idea floated before the National Assembly (the Constituent Assembly's successor) was that France should create a 'festival of geniuses', a day devoted to celebrating the highest examples of humanity. The festival would honour 'the most precious and lofty attribute of humanity – intelligence – which sets us apart from the rest of creation', argued Fabre d'Églantine, a writer and actor turned politician.[2] Joseph Lakanal, a revolutionary deputy, proclaimed the 'declaration of the rights of genius'. Geniuses took the place of kings and queens on revolutionary playing cards.

No historical subject has been written about more extensively and debated more ferociously than the origins of the French Revolution. For the narrow purposes of this book, however, two things are particularly eye-catching: the Enlightenment philosophers' debate about human nature and the logical contradictions of the absolutist state. The first prepared the ground for the idea that society should be ruled by ability rather than lineage. The second ensured that the government collapsed when it was given a shove.

THE ENLIGHTENMENT AND HUMAN NATURE

The *philosophes* devoted much of their intellectual energy to arguing that the old order was incompatible not just with reason and progress but with human nature itself. Voltaire led the pack. As a young man, he had humiliated a prominent member of the aristocracy in an argument only to find himself flogged by the noble lord's retainers and forced to flee to England. He spent the rest of his life taking revenge for the beating on the *Ancien Régime*'s leading institutions. Aristocrats were pretentious fools (in his great satire, Candide's mother, the sister of a baron, refused to marry his father because, though a noblemen, his escutcheon could prove only seventy-one quarterings). Habits were frozen idiocies. The Catholic Church was *l'infâme*. Hostility to the old order didn't mean support for equality, however. 'We have never claimed to enlighten shoe-makers and servant girls,' Voltaire proclaimed, and frequently used much saltier language in referring to the masses. What the *philosophes* wanted to do was to put society into the hands of people who were born bright rather than just born rich – that is to say, people like themselves rather than people like the aristocrat who had beaten up the young dialectician.

The idea that there is a distinction between the natural aristocracy of talent and the artificial aristocracy of breeding was central to Enlightenment thinking. Even well-born *philosophes* such as the Marquis de Condorcet delighted in this distinction (it meant that they were doubly blessed by both brains and birth). Thinkers from more humble origins seized on it with fervour. One of the most sustained meditations on this subject was produced by an obscure country priest who lived near Bordeaux called Pierre Jaubert. In *Éloge de la roture* (1766) Jaubert indulged in a fiery denunciation of the way that natural talent was being overlooked. The upper classes were full of drones. 'Any titled person who has no merit in his own account, is one of the heaviest burdens that the earth bears,' he said. Yet there were not enough places available to provide opportunities for all the able people in society: 'It is not people of merit who are lacking in the state but often places and employments are lacking for people of merit.'

The worthlessness of titled aristocrats compared with natural meritocrats became a staple of high culture – and found a willing audience among the very aristocrats who were being ridiculed. Figaro, the valet hero of a successful eighteenth-century French comedy which became one of the greatest of all operas, denounced the 'career closed to talents' and jibed that his aristocratic master had done nothing to deserve his privileges beyond going to the trouble of being born. Beaumarchais's *The Marriage of Figaro* (1784) features a blue blood who does all sorts of evil things:

> Because you are a great lord, you think yourself a great genius! ... Nobility, wealth, rank, positions, all this makes you so proud! What have you done for so much? You gave yourself the trouble of being born, that's all. Otherwise, you're pretty ordinary.

This was one of the great hits of the age, selling 6,000 copies in a single day. 'Everyone speaks ill of it, and everyone wants to see it [the play],' wrote an Alsatian noblewoman returning to Paris from a tour of Germany. 'Great lords, it seems to me, were tactless and immoderate in applauding it so; they were slapping themselves in the face; they laughed at their own expense, and what is worse, made others laugh too. They will regret it later ... Beaumarchais has shown them their own caricature, and they have responded: That's it, we are just like that.'[3]

Defining a worthless aristocrat was easy enough. But what made a real, or natural, aristocrat? The *philosophes* were divided between those who argued that natural aristocrats were produced by their environments (nurture) and those who thought that they were born that way (nature). The nurture school had been dominant since at least John Locke, who famously compared the new-born mind to a *tabula rasa* or 'blank slate'. 'Of all the men we meet with,' Locke wrote at the start of his *Some Thoughts Concerning Education* (1693), 'nine parts of ten are what they are, good or evil, useful or not, by their education. 'Tis that which makes the great difference in mankind.' This position enjoyed plenty of support from the *philosophes*. Étienne Bonnot de Condillac suggested that the brain can be filled with experience in much the same way that a container can be filled with liquid. All containers were of roughly the same size, but some were lucky enough to get more 'liquid' (i.e. experience) poured into them.[4] Claude Adrien Helvétius argued that the mind is composed of nothing more than sensations and the associations of sensations. There is no difference between individuals that can't be accounted for by differences in experiences.[5] He believed that there is nothing to prevent the entire population from reaching the same elevated intellectual level, provided that the state is willing to embrace the right policies: 'It is certain that the great men that are now produced by a fortuitous concourse of circumstances, will become the work of the legislature, and that, by leaving it less in the power of chance, an excellent education may infinitely multiply the abilities and virtues of the citizens in great empires.'[6]

The blank-slate theory provoked a lot of spluttering. Diderot couldn't contain his exasperation with Helvétius's position. 'Why does it seem to [Helvétius] to be proven that every man is equally fitted for everything and that his dull-witted janitor has as much intelligence as he himself, potentially at least, when such an assertion seems to me to be the most palpable of absurdities?'[7] Voltaire insisted that 'no one will convince me that all minds are equally suitable to science, and that they differ only in regard to education. Nothing is more false: nothing is demonstrated more false by experience.'[8] Across the Atlantic, John Adams was equally indignant: 'I have never read Reasoning more absurd, Sophistry more gross, in proof of the Athanasian Creed, or Transubstantiation, than the subtle labours of Helvetius and Rousseau to demonstrate the natural Equality of Mankind.'[9]

Adams was unfair to Rousseau: like so many other people at the time, Rousseau was ambivalent on the subject, routinely checking himself if he thought that his assertion of natural equality went too far. Though he opened his *Discourse on the Origin and Foundations of Inequality among Men* (1755) with the striking claim that in the state of nature men are naturally free, independent and equal, he also recognized that some people are naturally stronger, faster and smarter than others. Sweeping away artificial inequalities would quickly allow natural inequalities to assert themselves – he listed differences in aptitude for farming, governing and reasoning – and over time these natural inequalities would lead to social hierarchy. In *Émile* (1762), his treatise on education, he argued that education should be calibrated to suit the natural abilities of individual students: 'Each advances more or less according to his genius, his taste, his needs, his talents, his zeal, and the occasions he has to devote himself to them.' A few geniuses are born leaders as well as born seers, he believed, and, in any reasonable society, the masses would recognize the superiority of the naturally talented and turn to them for guidance.[10]

Indeed, the debate about the origin of talent was liveliest on the subject of geniuses. In his 'Sketch for a Historical Picture of the Progress of the Human Mind' (1795), Condorcet argued that geniuses were the engines of human progress, 'the eternal benefactors of the human race'. Where would science be without Newton or philosophy without Descartes? Marmontel proclaimed that geniuses operate outside the normal constraints of time and space. 'The man of genius has a way of seeing, of feeling, of thinking that is unique to him alone.' The *philosophes* also expanded the empire of genius: starting out by limiting the use of the term to great artists, they progressively extended it to include statesmen and indeed anyone who helped to shape the world. If nobles, at their best, spoke on behalf of local communities, geniuses spoke on behalf of the community of the enlightened.[11]

But where did genius come from? In both the ancient and medieval world, genius had been treated as a gift from the gods. It descends on individuals from heaven, seizes them in its embrace, shakes them around and speaks through them. The *philosophes* thought that this was a cop-out – akin to arguing that man's greatest exemplars were nothing but bagpipes played by a capricious god, in Thomas Hobbes's phrase. So they set about conducting laborious studies of both dead and living geniuses to see what made them tick. They eventually came to the conclusion that they could only be explained by what Immanuel Kant called 'the hand of nature'.[12] Musical geniuses such as Mozart and literary geniuses such as Shakespeare clearly possessed talents that could not have resulted from mere training.[13]

The debate about talent was also driven by statecraft, with both policy-makers and *philosophes* coming to the conclusion that the state's resources included the natural talents of its people as well as its physical resources. A French military reformer argued in 1749 that 'there is not a single person, to the lowest artisan or the crudest villager, who does not possess some precious innate talent'. In an ideal world the king would know them all. 'If the Prince and [his] minister could know the infidel tastes and talents of all his subjects! What great progress would be made in all the professions of society!'[14]

This argument was particularly popular in the German-speaking world. In Austria, a group of political thinkers known as Cameralists treated the state as a machine and judged the constituent parts of the machine on their ability to perform their proper functions.[15] In the German states, leading Enlightenment thinkers discussed talent as a natural resource. Christian Wolff, Germany's leading philosopher between Leibniz and Kant, argued that the key to boosting society's wealth involved more than just encouraging physical commerce and introducing new technology. It involved channelling more of society's intellectual and moral energies into creative and productive activities. One contributor to *Der Teutsche Merkur*, one of the leading periodicals of the German Enlightenment, argued in 1774 that in 'an enlightened age and a sophisticated nation' a citizen's social position should be 'personal' rather than 'hereditary' and 'merited' (*verdienstlich*) rather than 'accidental'. 'The entire hierarchy of ranks and of the various stations should be constituted according to the classification of services, and the relative amount of each capacity and work, and of the value of the thing thereby accomplished, should be the true and actual standard for all civic honour.'

The more influential the *philosophes* became, the more they were drawn to a great political project: using the power of the absolutist state to produce a new social order which matched talent to opportunity and knowledge to power. This was driven by an innovative theory of political legitimacy. In the traditional Christian conception of society, God put everything in its proper place in the great chain of being. In the new enlightened theory of society, God was replaced by nature, and society derived its legitimacy from the distribution of natural endowments and the pairing of talent and reward.[16] Because society frequently got things wrong enlightened intellectuals had to work with enlightened monarchs to restore natural harmony.

This grand vision nevertheless entailed a lot of dirty politics. The *philosophes* shamelessly cultivated their relationships with what Goethe called 'the lords of the earth'. Voltaire sucked up to both Frederick the Great of Prussia, spending time at his Court in Potsdam, helping to popularize the sobriquet *le Grand*, and Catherine the Great of Russia, conducting a long correspondence with her and writing a laudatory biography of Peter the Great. Diderot visited Russia in the winter of 1773–4 and devoted three afternoons a week to holding informal conversations with Catherine, with the philosopher sitting in a chair and the empress on a sofa. (Catherine in turn supported him financially by buying his library and appointing him her librarian.[17]) The philosophes equally shamelessly endorsed the destruction of established institutions, such as churches, guilds and local councils, even if those institutions were relatively popular with the benighted masses. Charles Frederick, the Grand Duke of Baden, pledged to make his subjects 'free, opulent and law-abiding citizens, whether they like it or not', while Turgot, a leading French statesman and philosopher, 'yearned for five years of despotism to set the people free'.[18] The imperative of reordering the world on the basis of natural talent was so overwhelming that you needed a bulldozer, in the form of an enlightened despot, to demolish inconvenient barriers in the form of traditional institutions and benighted peasants.

THE CONTRADICTIONS OF THE ABSOLUTIST STATE

The absolutist state was a contradiction. The state was built on the principle of biological inheritance: absolutist monarchs ruled because of the accident of birth and were intertwined with other great families that owed their position to the same happy accident. The 'lucky sperm club' sat on the thrones of Europe and in its great stately homes. Yet the absolutist state also bent the knee to reason. Threatened by enemies and crushed by debt, the state had no choice but to embrace more scientific methods of waging war, raising revenue and recruiting personnel.

This contradiction can be seen in the development of the aristocracy. The consolidation of the absolutist state on the continent in the eighteenth century significantly increased the demand for able bureaucrats and military commanders. The flashier courts became, the more money they needed to keep up the pomp. And the more sophisticated war became, the more it depended on brains as well as brawn.[19] The state furiously recruited 'new men' – civil servants who understood the mysteries of law, finance and administration and soldiers who could perform demanding tasks such as blowing up fortifications, organizing volley lines and managing supply chains. Yet the state's ultimate goal – indeed, its *raison d'être* – was to defend the old order of inherited privilege. The 'new' men who owed their position to their administrative abilities enthusiastically imitated many of the qualities of the 'old' aristocrats who could satisfy Candide's mother's requirements for ancient lineage. The result was a merger of old and new: old aristocrats became more au fait with modern administrative and military techniques while 'new' aristocrats acquired estates and invented ancient lineages for themselves.

The French state was the prime example of this contradiction. The state revolved around the physical person of a man who owed his position to biological accident (Louis XIV famously declared that *l'état, c'est moi*). Kings spent ever more time cavorting with their fellow blue bloods in Versailles in a whirligig of parties, dinners, balls and sexual liaisons. But the Bourbons were also instruments of rationalization: the only way they could afford to fight their wars and entertain their guests was to rationalize the country's administrative and tax systems. Kings employed a succession of powerful administrators such as Cardinal Richelieu and Jean-Baptiste Colbert who were appointed on the basis of their talents rather than their connections. From the 1620s onwards, monarchs dispatched a corps of efficient bureaucrats from Paris to the provinces to take a scythe to local customs. These *intendants* owed their efficiency to the fact that they were outsiders and held their jobs at the pleasure of the king rather than nobles. Monarchs also established the nucleus of France's formidable technical education system: one of the oldest of the *grandes écoles*, the École Nationale des Ponts et Chaussées, was founded in 1747; France's twelve elite military schools were founded in 1776.

Theorists of absolutism tried to resolve these contradictions by reviving the medieval idea that the king has two bodies, one physical and one artificial. The physical king cavorted with nobles and dispensed favours on a whim. The 'artificial' king ruled according to reason and dispensed his favours with machine-like dispassion, scouring not just his noble friends but the entire population for talent. Richelieu, Louis XIII's leading adviser, believed that, over time, kings would subordinate their physical selves to their artificial selves, setting aside 'distracting interests, pity and compassion, favouritism and importunities of all kinds' and instead govern according to rational principles and the public good. In fact, as we saw in the previous chapter, it is equally arguable that the opposite happened, with Louis XIV distributing a growing proportion of the tax revenue to courtiers on the basis of whim and lobbying. Colbert, the great agent of rationalization, married his three daughters to dukes, saw one of his sons become grand master of ceremonies, and liked to boast that 'the king is much more the father of my children than I am'.[20]

This contradiction produced a tortured debate on the subject of 'merit'. Even before the Enlightenment dawned a chorus of thinkers insisted that it was no longer enough for aristocrats to boast about their noble ancestors in order to prove that they possessed 'merit'. They also had to prove themselves in several ways – by becoming inspired and skilful officers or highly efficient administrators. But two could play at the merit game. Blue bloods were particularly enthusiastic about using the concept of 'merit' to defend their claims to serve in the king's army against moneyed parvenus. In *La Noblesse Commerçante* (1756) the Abbé Coyer argued that France's military might was being undermined by rich playboys who purchased their positions at the top of the army because they liked swaggering about in beautiful uniforms rather than because they possessed a family tradition of martial glory. The government addressed the problem in 1751 by creating a new military school, the École Royale Militaire, which was limited to people who could demonstrate four generations of noble patrilineal descent (there was even a new royal genealogist to enforce the rule) but also provided promotion strictly on the basis of merit.[21] Members of the aspiring military elite, including Napoleon Bonaparte, the scion of a cash-strapped noble family in Corsica, were thus subjected to two examinations: one to check their genealogical histories in order to prove their noble descent and then a succession of examinations to test their educational progress.[22]

Other absolutist states were torn by the same contradictions. In Prussia a succession of strong-minded rulers – the Great Elector Frederick William (r. 1640–88), King Frederick William I of Prussia (r. 1713–40) and Frederick II or Frederick the Great (r. 1740–86) – concentrated power in the hands of the state in general and the military in particular. The Hohenzollerns decided that the only way to remain safe in an unstable neighbourhood was to keep the army on a permanent war footing, drilled to perfection and ready to strike. Standing armies are not cheap, however: in order to keep their men parading around like martinets in their drill yards, Prussia's rulers had to create an efficient tax-raising machine. The civil service reform of 1770 was one of the most ambitious in Europe.

The Hohenzollerns' ultimate aim was to preserve their own power and that of the aristocratic elite to which they belonged. The German-speaking world was famous for its oversupply of snobbish but second-rate aristocrats. Carlyle described the typical German aristocrat as an 'ancient, thirsty, thick-headed, sixteen-quartered baron'. Another visitor complained that 'Germany swarms with princes and dukes of whom three-quarters aren't quite right in the head' or 'competent to rule chickens'.[23] But the Hohenzollerns nevertheless believed that, in the last analysis, the landed aristocracy was the only group of people in Prussia that was capable of putting honour above self-interest and of whipping the vulgar masses into shape. In his 'Political Testament' (1752) Frederick the Great wrote that 'a sovereign should regard it as his duty to protect the nobility, which forms the finest jewel in his crown and the lustre of his army'[24] and he pursued a policy of tough love to put his philosophy into practice. He lent his nobles money so they didn't have to degrade themselves with trade and purged the army of as many commoners as possible ('I will not tolerate non-noble vermin in the officer corps'), so that, by the end of his reign, 90 per cent of the officer corps was titled.[25] He also subjected them to a regime of drills and examinations, some of which he administered himself, and forbade them from marrying without permission.[26]

This aristocratic-driven reform programme worked at first. More than any other aristocracy in Europe, Prussia's landed elite became a bureaucratic elite, a 'partner in autocracy', infused with a powerful spirit of service and state-building.[27] But over time the Prussian state was forced to cast its net wider. Prussia's universities became the best in Europe thanks to the von Humboldt brothers. Its *Gymnasien* transformed themselves from sleepy backwaters into academic training camps. An institution that was supposed to defend the power of the hereditary elite took on a life of its own.

The Habsburg dynasty presented the absolutist contradiction in even starker terms. Both Maria Theresa (r. 1745–65) and her son Joseph II (r. 1765–90) considered themselves to be enlightened monarchs who were in the business of applying the rule of reason to the eccentric conglomeration they had inherited. Maria Theresa embarked on an ambitious programme of school-building. Joseph II challenged many of the prerequisites of rank, abolishing serfdom (which was known as 'the robot' and provided inspiration for the modern word), getting rid of the purchase and inheritance of offices in the civil service, and telling judges to ignore rank in applying criminal justice. Former serfs could choose their own careers and spouses. Academies were opened to the most qualified students, regardless of background, at least in formal terms. Senior civil servants were guaranteed a pension after ten years of service; all civil servants, regardless of rank, were subjected to performance reviews, which required them to fill out a fifteen-item questionnaire every six months stating their qualifications, years of service and accomplishments.[28] He also closed the monasteries and secularized their property, using some of the proceeds to establish educational and charitable foundations.

Yet the only thing that held the empire together was the Habsburg dynasty. Take the emperor or empress away and the conglomeration made no sense. Maria Theresa spent the early years of her reign fighting a war of succession with rival powers which denied her right to the throne. She later revealed the limits of her enthusiasm for searching the population for talent when she said that 'those who are born in boots should not desire to wear shoes'.

Russia did an even worse job of making sense of the contradiction than the Habsburg empire. When he went on his grand tour in 1697–8, Peter the Great (r. 1682–1725) was shocked to discover how far behind the rest of Europe his country had fallen, and returned home determined to drag his subjects kicking and screaming into the modern world. He immediately forced his courtiers to dispense with the most offensive signs of barbarism – long beards: he even shaved the worst offenders himself with a razor – and then embarked on the more laborious work of institutional reform. He started with the military, creating Russia's first navy, for example, and moved on to education and the bureaucracy, founding the Moscow School of Mathematics and Navigation and decreeing that all male children of the nobility should learn mathematics between the ages of ten and fifteen. In 1722 he published an official Table of Ranks, with fourteen ranks, three parallel hierarchies (military, civilian and Court) and titles borrowed from Germany and Japan. Henceforth, service to the state was to be the basis of social distinction: nobles were expected to serve the state as a quid pro quo for their titles and diligent bureaucrats and soldiers were given titles as a reward for their service.[29] Traditional Russian titles such as *boyar* were allowed to die out.

Even so, modernization was inevitably limited: the tsars still theoretically owned the entire country, people as well as land, restricting the development of civil society, and the enthusiasm of the tsars for reform waxed and waned.[30] 'Scratch a Russian and you wound a Tatar.' Count Joseph de Maistre said, lamenting Russia's halting attempts to join the mainstream of European civilization.[31] The upper nobility retained a tight grip on the upper ranks of the Table. Catherine the Great (r. 1762–96) strengthened their position still further by giving special consideration to inheritance.[32] One historian of Catherine the Great's Russia puts her finger on the way that the feudal principle of bondage made a mockery of any attempts at reform:

> the individual was bound to serve a person of, the state; he was bound to a particular community which he could not leave without the permission of the corresponding authority; and he was bound by a system of collective responsibility to the other members of the community he belonged to . . . Russia had thus become a society in which activity did not depend on the free initiative of the individual but on the permission of the government. Everyone was assigned to a particular legal category or status . . . and could only carry out the activities proper to that estate, or enjoy its privileges . . . the one exception to the rule of physical immobility was the estate of the *dvoriane* or nobility.[33]

FROM REVOLUTION TO NAPOLEON

The French Revolution was, among many other things, an attempt to address the contradictions at the heart of the absolutist state. The revolutionaries challenged the tangle of privileges, special immunities and prescriptive rights that the absolutist monarchs could not challenge without challenging the old order itself. They hastened the work of state-building that the Bourbons had begun but couldn't complete without working themselves out of a job. They replaced the spirit of majesty and awe with the spirit of reason and order – for example, they replaced the old currency, based on units in the Carolingian ratios of 1:20:12, with a decimal system, the chaos of old-fashioned weights and measures with a metric system, and the old Christian calendar with a more rational order.

The French Revolution also brought a new urgency to the great debates about human nature: the question of nature versus nurture becomes far more pressing if you are trying to work out whether you have been successful in replacing artificial inequality with natural inequality. Or, if you are designing a school system which made the best use of the available talents. For the most part, as we saw at the beginning of this chapter, the revolutionaries were more likely to talk about 'virtue' and 'talents' than merit. They were also much happier talking about 'virtue', which they could analyse until the cows came home, quoting ancient authorities and Enlightenment luminaries, than they were talking about 'talent'. But as time passed they began to connect 'talents' (usually used in the plural) with more modern ideas about 'abilities', 'capacities' and 'faculties'. Rousseau talked about 'the faculty of self-improvement'. The 1786 edition of the *Dictionnaire de l'Académie française* defined talent as a 'gift of nature, natural disposition or aptitude for certain things, or ability'. Condorcet talked about 'mental capacities'. A few far-seeing people talked about 'intelligence': for example, Charles-Georges Le Roi explained in the *Encyclopédie méthodique* (1795) that this information-processing ability 'produces the different degrees of intelligence that we observe, whether between species or between individuals'.[34]

Whether they believed that the job of the state was to sift society for natural ability (the dominant position) or else pour facts into empty containers (Helvétius's position), the revolutionaries were enthusiastic about education, convinced that it was impossible to build a new world without starting with the schools and universities. In 1794 the government founded the École Polytechnique, to produce military engineers, and the École Normale Supérieure (ENS) to train schoolteachers. Located at the top of the French system, and enveloped with mystery and charisma, these elite institutions exerted a lasting influence over the rest of the educational system, even to this day training the bulk of the country's top bureaucrats and industrialists.

The revolution quickly became a global uprising against the hereditary principle, fuelled by sympathizers around the world such as Thomas Paine (who travelled to France to lend a hand) and William Wordsworth (who contented himself with fine words).[35] In 1792, the revolutionaries declared war on a succession of tyrants, singling out the king of Bohemia and Hungary for particular opprobrium, and for the next twenty years they were on the march, fighting republics as well as kingdoms and empires, venturing as far afield as Egypt, Russia and the Caribbean, and, in general, transforming revolutionary exuberance into imperial expansion.

Napoleon acted as the embodiment of all this reforming and imperial energy – 'world history on horseback', in Hegel's phrase. He created a continental legal code that treated citizens as individuals rather than, as under the old regime, members of exclusive groups defined by class, region or function. He pushed French education in an even more meritocratic direction, defined by examinations and selection. At the same time, he successfully used the principle of merit to control the revolution's more anarchic impulses and to make his peace with the old regime. His famous dictum about every corporal carrying a marshal's baton in his knapsack offered both a promise of mobility and reassurance that ranks are for ever.

At the heart of Napoleon's vision of empire sat his idea of a new service aristocracy: cosmopolitan rather than French and vigorous rather than decadent, defined by merit rather than inheritance – or at least by merit as well as inheritance – and dedicated to the service of the French state. He recruited his marshals from every stratum of society – old-regime nobles such as Louis-Nicolas Davout and Emmanuel de Grouchy rubbed shoulders with plebeians such as Pierre Augereau, the son of a domestic servant, and Jean Lannes, the son of Gascon peasants.[36] He refounded the baccalaureate exam to discover potential public servants and test their exact abilities. He extended the monarchy's work in creating *grandes écoles* charged with producing a meritocratic ruling class. 'I want to create a corporation,' he wrote, 'not of jesuits who have their sovereign in Rome, but of jesuits who have no other ambition than that of being useful, and no other interest but the public interest.'[37]

One of the most important steps towards fusing meritocracy and monarchy was the foundation in 1802 of the Légion d'honneur, an honorific distinction granted to some 6,000 people who had done the Republic some singular service. Napoleon batted aside objections that he was re-creating the old regime by pointing out that honours would be awarded for 'personal merit' rather than birth and to service rather than status:

> The diversity of orders of chivalry and their special rewards sanctified castes, whereas the single decoration of the Legion of Honour, open to all, on the contrary typified *equality*. The one maintained distance among classes, whilst the other was bound to bring on cohesion of citizens ...

The original oath for admission to the Legion required new members to pledge themselves to 'combat by all means ... any measure tending towards re-establishing the feudal order, or bringing back titles and qualities which were part of it'. But as time went by Napoleon came to the conclusion that the only way to preserve social order was to allow people to hand on their property to their children, and he adopted three new policies that merged meritocracy with aristocracy: inviting the old ruling families to return from exile or, if they had stayed, giving them a chance to revive their titles; allowing service families to transmit their titles to their children; and blurring the distinction between the hereditary aristocracy and the service aristocracy.

By now his explicit aim was to meld together the best of the old and the new regimes in order to combine revolutionary zeal with post-revolutionary stability: to make landed aristocrats more useful by encouraging them to provide service to the Republic, and service meritocrats more grounded by giving them a stake in the nation. In exile in Elba, the former revolutionary and scourge of the *Ancien Régime* reproached himself for not having embraced the aristocratic principle earlier.

Napoleon changed his mind on dynasty as well as aristocracy: the greatest self-made man of the eighteenth and nineteenth centuries married into the greatest of the European dynasties, the Habsburgs. He made his son king of Rome, habitually referring to him as 'the little king'. He showered family members with crowns, making his elder brother, Joseph, king of Naples, a younger brother, Louis, king of Holland, and his youngest, and most frivolous brother, Jérôme, king of Westphalia. He also made some of the self-made men around him into hereditary aristocrats. The new emperor was surrounded by a peculiar retinue – members of his own family and his self-made followers, on the one hand, all now turned into royals or aristocrats, and members of the great families of France and the rest of Europe on the other.

Napoleon's plan to shore up his throne by harnessing the power of dynasty and aristocracy failed: Napoleonic rule was followed by the Royal Restoration and the turmoil of the French Revolution by a sharp reaction in favour of legitimacy. The Treaty of Vienna of 1815 declared 'legitimacy' to be the basis of international politics. Liberal Britain, worried as always about the balance of power on the continent, threw in its lot with such conservative powers as Austria and Russia. And the 'legitimate' powers became more conservative as the Enlightenment's legacy slowly faded, with Joseph II's successor, his younger brother Leopold II, embracing empty formalism and the Russian tsars reconciling themselves to backwardness.[38] The spirit of dynasticism arguably grew stronger as the nineteenth century proceeded: European monarchs gave up marrying local nobles and instead married each other, turning Europe's royal houses into a gigantic cousinhood.

The revolution nevertheless marked a global turning point. If Europe's most sophisticated elite could be sent to the guillotine by an angry mob, then nobody was safe. Nobles everywhere rallied behind their rulers to defeat the new scourge of the people in arms. But nobles everywhere also realized that they needed to learn from the spirit of the times if they were to survive. Knowing that they were no longer immortal made them much more cunning.

The restored Bourbon regime led the world in this: it was not so much the Restoration of the old regime as the full flowering of Napoleon's mature vision of the fusion of the service and landed aristocracies. The first draft of the 1814 Constitution declared that 'the former nobility resumes its titles; the new keeps its own by heredity. The legion of honour is retained with its prerogatives.' Napoleon's *grandes écoles* remained at the heart of French society, appealing to the left because they provided the state with a reliable supply of talent, and to the right because they preserved privilege in a democratic and frequently turbulent society. An official report released by a commission set up under the Restoration put it well:

> We live in a time when only the education of the higher classes can ensure the tranquillity of the state, by allowing their members to acquire, through their personal superiority in virtue and intelligence, the influence that they must exercise on others for the peace of all. A happy necessity, if one envisages it with a lofty soul, which leads to the justification of rank by merit and of wealth by talent and virtue . . .[39]

The post-Napoleonic state continued to see education as a way of achieving four of the great aims of statecraft: advancing nation-building (turning 'peasants into Frenchmen', in Eugen Weber's classic phrase); binding society together in the same way that the Catholic Church once had; promoting social control; and boosting material prosperity. Napoleon III expressed all this in the most benevolent terms. The nation with the most schools would be the first nation in the world in its enjoyment of material prosperity, order and liberty, he claimed.[40] Others were less emollient. When François Guizot, the dominant figure in French politics before the 1848 Revolution, passed a law in 1833 requiring that every village should have a primary school, he did so in the belief that 'ignorance renders the masses turbulent and ferocious; it makes them an instrument to be used by factions'. He wanted village teachers to preach the virtues of submission to the authorities in the same way that the village priest once had.[41]

The state's enthusiasm for education was echoed by the larger society, with Zola arguing that 'France will be what the primary teacher makes it,' Comte and Durkheim investing utopian hopes in schools, and the Education League, founded in 1860, becoming one of the most active pressure groups in the country, powered by a belief in the right of humble people to acquire a proper education. The examination system became more demanding as the nineteenth century wore on. In 1820, the École Normale Supérieure started to rank students on a unilineal scale (giving the top student a sense of superiority that would last a lifetime). Soon a similar system was adopted by secondary schools everywhere. In 1865, the state increased the pressure by encouraging the best pupils from across the country to compete against each other in the national *concours généraux*. A senior school inspector wrote in 1879 of his youth that 'the sole preoccupation' of everybody involved in education – headmasters, teachers and pupils – was producing the best exam-performer of the country. The newspapers reported the results of the exam and even published winning essays.[42] (The winners remain much celebrated to this day: in 1994 Emmanuel Macron won the top place in French.)

The result was a national system of education that, more than any other in Europe, was defined by a national curriculum and driven by competition. All secondary-school students studied the same subjects, particularly mathematics, classics and philosophy. All schools subjected their students to a remorseless regime of competition and assessment that measured not just academic success but also values such as punctuality. The most ambitious teachers rated their pupils daily on a composite of academic and character measures, rewarded them weekly with *billets de satisfaction* and published their pupils' precise ranking at the end of each year.

Napoleon's great innovation of the modern baccalaureate remained at the heart of the system. Under the emperor, fewer than a hundred candidates a year took an oral examination based on a single set text. Later, thousands of candidates presented themselves for one of the world's most fiendish written examinations. The restored monarchy turned the 'bac' into an entry requirement for both the civil service and the liberal professions. In 1830, an oral examination became a written one. A new industry developed to cram students for the ordeal. Students groaned under the yoke.

The apex of the educational system was occupied by elite schools, the *grandes écoles* and *écoles d'application*, which controlled access to the state's most desirable jobs. Entrance to the schools was guarded by the country's most demanding examinations. Indeed, it is a measure of the country's preoccupation with examinations that, according to François Guizot, faculty positions were also awarded 'by competitive examinations, where the candidates can exhibit all the newest and most sublime knowledge; no one is restricted from the examination; no idea is prohibited or prescribed, and the public is at the same time judge of [the candidates'] talents and guarantor of their true independence'.[43]

Though they were relative newcomers to the world of elite education, the École Normale Supérieure and the École Polytechnique quickly acquired great prestige, the first as a training ground for high-level teachers in literature, philosophy and science, the second as a supplier of engineers to build the modern nation. They were both residential, so their students developed a powerful *esprit de corps*. They were both much more willing than universities to experiment with innovative approaches to education. The ENS substituted seminars for lectures and encouraged its students to read widely rather than to memorize a few set texts.[44] The École Polytechnique reinforced its *esprit de corps* by dividing its students into groups of eight and getting them to spend most of their time together: the dormitories had eight beds, the studies eight desks and the bathrooms eight washbasins. The school timetable told them what they should be doing every minute of the day.[45] The students were repeatedly examined – often in surprise tests – and were placed in order of merit when they arrived at the school and when they left.

This highly elitist system had many faults.[46] Educationalists questioned the reliability of the marking. Sociologists complained about the uneven quality of local schools. Great men filled their memoirs with stories about the terrors of the bac.[47] In *Education as Homicide* (1867) Victor Laprade described schools as a combination of monasteries, barracks and prisons presided over by a caste of teachers who, because they themselves had done well in examinations, were determined to impose an examination regime on their young charges.[48]

France's elitist and competitive system was nevertheless a highly successful one – successful in practical terms, providing the state with a stream of superbly educated and extremely bright servants, but successful in terms of state legitimacy as well: in a country that ricocheted between monarchy and republicanism and was torn by the competing demands of the revolutionary left and the reactionary right, the meritocratic system remained the best guarantee against anarchy and levelling.

Over the decades, leading educationalists preached that *lycées* made it possible to reconcile elitism with democracy by allowing intelligent boys to climb the educational ladder. In 1871, Émile Boutmy, a pioneering political scientist and founder of Sciences Po, argued that meritocracy was the last best defence against levelling:

> Privilege has gone, democracy cannot be halted. The higher classes, as they call themselves, are obliged to acknowledge the right of the majority, and they can only maintain their political dominance by invoking the right of the most capable. Behind the crumbling ramparts of their prerogatives and of tradition the tide of democracy must encounter a second line of defence, constructed by manifest and useful abilities, of superior qualities whose prestige cannot be gainsaid . . .[49]

In 1895, Georges Perrot, the director of the ENS, argued that 'democracy needs an elite, to represent the only superiority it recognises, that of the mind. It is up to us to recruit this elite, or, to speak more modestly, to work to furnish some of the elements which will constitute it.'[50] In 1943, J. B. Piobetta, the university official in charge of the baccalaureate, declared that 'examinations and competitions are part of our way of life. Some of them are an integral part of our oldest institutions. All of them have become the pivot of our social hierarchy. Careers, public or private, that do not require the possession of a diploma are becoming increasingly rare. Titles and grades, with the official stamp on them, constitute veritable letters of nobility to which rights and prerogatives are attached.'[51] 'One is a *normalien*,' wrote *normalien* and later president of France Georges Pompidou, 'as one is a prince by blood.'[52]

A distinguished group of social theorists put the meritocratic idea at the heart of their thinking. One of these was an aristocrat called Henri de Saint-Simon. During the French Revolution he tried to found a scientific school for social improvement which he hoped to fund by various hare-brained schemes such as buying Notre-Dame Cathedral in order to strip its roof of metal and sell it for scrap. He also became intimately involved in the École Polytechnique when it was founded in 1794.

Saint-Simon's guiding belief was that a properly functioning society should be rooted in the individual merits of its citizens, with those merits determined by their ability to contribute to society's overall productivity.[53] The French Revolution had shaken the old regime to destruction, he argued, because the class structure no longer matched the productive infrastructure. Hereditary rule was based on blood-lines and military prowess at a time when the world demanded scientific knowledge and technical skills. The new society would flourish if people were given jobs based on their natural abilities, which varied enormously, and professional qualifications, which were acquired by prolonged study. Instead of idealizing philosophers, like earlier intellectuals, Saint-Simon worshipped 'knowledge workers', the new class of scientists, managers and bankers who were driving commercial society.

Though there is a Marxian element to this, particularly when it comes to the tension between class structure and productive forces, Saint-Simon saw more deeply than Marx. He realized that modern society would continue to be hierarchical but would be hierarchical in a different way from feudal society. He recognized that the most productive workers were not workers by hand but workers by brain who understood the productivity-raising secrets of science and organization. More controversially, he insisted that examinations on the 'national catechism' should be used to see if people were worthy of citizenship and that idle parasites such as aristocrats and 'metaphysicians' should be deprived of their leadership positions.

Unfortunately, Saint-Simon undermined his own credibility by creating a new version of Christianity, complete with patron saints such as Isaac Newton and a new priestly class of intellectuals, which was intended to do for the meritocratic age what Roman Catholicism had done for the feudal age: reconcile people to their preordained place in the world. For the most part, the masses would accept the rule of people who possessed better qualifications than they did, he argued – nobody but a fool believed that bridges should be designed by the most popular person rather than the best qualified – but if people ever chafed at the bit, then religion could be used to appeal to their poetic and imaginative faculties.

Émile Durkheim, France's greatest sociologist, was equally preoccupied with the nature of talent, the proper distribution of opportunity, and the contribution that the two could make to his holy grail, social solidarity.[54] He believed that the best way to secure both individual happiness and social cohesion was to distribute social functions in accordance with 'the distribution of natural talents'. Or, to put it another way, the surest guarantee of both individual misery and social dysfunction was to distribute social functions according to favouritism.[55]

Durkheim never wavered in his belief in 'the unequal abilities of men'. 'One sort of heredity will always exist,' he wrote, 'that of natural talent. Intelligence, taste, scientific, artistic, literary or industrial ability, courage and manual dexterity are gifts received by each of us at birth.' The adamantine fact of natural inequality had two big social implications. The first is that different people are capable of performing different 'social functions': some can make unique contributions to the advance of civilization while others are relatively 'easy to replace'. The second is that different people are content performing different social roles: a talented painter is only really content when they are painting, a baker when they are baking, and so on. The division of labour is thus, at its best, a system for maximizing not just economic productivity but also human contentment, by allocating individuals to the jobs that can make best use of their talents.[56]

THE GERMAN IDEOLOGY

The French Revolution had a profound influence on France's mighty neighbour, Germany. Carl von Clausewitz pronounced that Napoleon's triumph over Prussia at the battles of Jena and Auerstedt on 14 October 1806 not only ruined the Prussian army 'more completely than any army has ever been ruined on the battlefield',[57] it also ruined the case for resisting promotion on the basis of talent. The most farseeing Prussians recognized that the only way their country could survive in a revolutionary age was to master the forces of the revolution. 'The power of these principles is so great, so universally recognized and widespread,' wrote Karl von Hardenberg, then Prussia's foreign minister, in 1807, 'that a state that does not embrace them must face either their forcible imposition or its own extinction.'[58]

Baron Karl vom Stein, Prussia's first education minister and a man of outstanding intellectual gifts, masterminded a wide-ranging set of reforms designed to do just this. The October Edict of 1807 abolished the legal privileges of the aristocracy, outlawed serfdom, opened civil service posts to commoners, established the principle of careers open to talent in the army and opened new training institutes to give the idea some substance, and, in the process, forced the aristocracy to compete harder for positions than they had under Frederick the Great.[59] Prussia led the rest of Europe in introducing entrance examinations for civil servants and exit examinations for school-leavers. The von Humboldt brothers speeded up reforms, begun even before the Battle of Jena, that turned German universities into world-beaters. Professors took on the role of school inspectors, developing teaching talent and integrating different levels of the school system. German *gymnasien*, once bywords for backwardness, became models of excellence. In the 1810s, Stein talked about the arrival of a new class of 'salaried bookworms'. By the late nineteenth century, Max Weber was worrying that rule by a new caste of mandarins had replaced 'rule by notables'.[60]

The Germans also provided some of the most profound philosophical commentary on the French Revolution. In his 1793 essay 'On the Relationship of Theory to Practice in Political Right', Immanuel Kant argued that modern society was based on two great principles: the 'uniform equality of human beings as subjects of the state', and people's universal rights to 'reach any degree of rank' they could through the exercise of their talent, industry and good fortune. Nobody had a right to hold back a fellow citizen 'by hereditary prerogatives or privileges of rank'. In one particularly striking intellectual move, Kant classified intellectual property as a non-hereditary form of property and argued that the government had a duty to protect people's use of their talents in much the same way as it had a duty to protect their ownership of their physical property. The ability to own and exercise your talents was one of the things that distinguished a citizen with political rights from a mere subject.[61]

Starting in the mid-eighteenth century and with growing self-confidence as the nineteenth century developed, Germans advocated the importance of *Bildung*, a word that means self-cultivation in the broadest possible sense rather than mere book-learning. For its devotees, *Bildung* was simultaneously a badge of honour and a battle standard – a challenge to the old order and a declaration of faith in the educational elite. They marched under the banner of Herder, Goethe and Fichte rather than the Teutonic Knights of old. It also came to define an entire sector of German society: middle-class people who believed that they were exemplars of virtue, worked in the expanding government and educational sectors and prided themselves on their cultivation even more than on their income. While Goethe's Wilhelm Meister had argued that 'universal and personal cultivation is beyond the reach of anyone except a nobleman', advocates of *Bildung* retorted that true noble status is beyond the reach of anyone except a cultivated intellectual.

ROMANTICISM AND THE CAREER OPEN TO TALENT

The French Revolution also unleashed one of the nineteenth century's most powerful intellectual movements, Romanticism. The Romantics questioned most of the tenets of Enlightenment rationalism, asserting the primacy of emotion over reason, tradition over change and, on occasion, the collective over the individual, but they nevertheless celebrated the importance of individual differences, particularly individual differences in creative powers. Rousseau had defined the great theme of the Romantic movement back in the mid-eighteenth century when he announced that 'I am unlike anyone I have ever met . . . I am like no one in the whole world.' And the Romantics spent much of the nineteenth century elaborating on this insight.

The Romantics argued that geniuses are the ultimate lawgivers – the people who tell politicians what to do – because they can distil the essence of the universe in a single insight. Shelley described poets as 'the hierophants of an unapprehended inspiration; the mirrors of the gigantic shadows which futurity casts upon the present . . . the unacknowledged legislators of mankind'.[62] Friedrich Schlegel celebrated them as moral legislators who set the framework in which politicians operated. 'Artists,' he wrote in 1799, 'make humanity into individuals by bringing together past and future in the present. They are the higher organs of the soul, where the spirit of life among public persons meets, and in which the private spirit then works.' Thomas

Carlyle said that writers performed the same function in the modern world that the prophet, priest or divinity performed in the ancient world. Beethoven openly asserted the rights of the new aristocracy of genius over the old aristocracy of position and place. 'Prince! What you are, you are by circumstances of birth,' he said rather cheekily to his patron, Prince Lichnowsky. 'What I am I am through myself. Of princes there have been and will be thousands. Of Beethovens there is only one.'

As the Romantic movement gathered pace, intellectuals extended their focus from artistic geniuses to political geniuses. Napoleon was, naturally, pre-eminent among these. Goethe deemed him a 'genius' whose 'destiny was more brilliant than any the world had seen before him, and perhaps ever would see again'. Byron enraged his classmates at Harrow by keeping a bust of England's number-one enemy in his room.[63] Beethoven (initially, at least) dedicated his Third Symphony to Napoleon, one genius to another. Stendhal felt an almost 'religious sentiment' towards him.[64] Victor Hugo regarded him as a 'Michelangelo of war'. In his *Lectures on the Philosophy of History*, Hegel described the 'world-historical figure' who embodies the will of his age and thereby actualizes his age.[65] Nietzsche, a recovering Romantic, was partly thinking of Napoleon when he said that men of genius 'were like explosives', dangerous but awe-inspiring, primed for creative destruction.[66]

The French Revolution also placed a new principle at the heart of European society: the career open to talent. Paris became one of the most open cities in Europe. New talent-based professions such as journalism and the theatre flourished.[67] Celebrity chefs appeared, with chefs who had once served great aristocrats opening restaurants such as the Café de Paris. Minorities, particularly Jews but also Protestants, embraced the religion of self-improvement.[68] French literature is full of examples of self-made men, such as Balzac's Eugène de Rastignac, who rises ever higher with each new volume of *La Comédie humaine*, or Stendhal's Julian Sorel, who, more tragically, tries to turn his talents into social success but eventually succumbs to his passions. Other European capitals embraced similar values of self-promotion and self-reinvention.

The Industrial Revolution completed the work of the French

Revolution by creating a flourishing middle class across Europe. Captains of business celebrated their ability to reinvent the world. Middle-class businesspeople became leading forces in rising cities such as Manchester and Lyons. A powerful philosophy of liberalism celebrated the importance of both open competition and upward mobility. Thomas Mann expressed the spirit of liberalism in his great novel *Buddenbrooks* (1901). Though the talented son of a harbourmaster is infatuated with one of the members of the socially elevated Buddenbrook clan, he can't help delivering a lecture:

> We, the bourgeoisie – the Third Estate as we have been called – we recognise only that nobility which consists of merit: we refuse to admit any longer the rights of the indolent aristocracy, we repudiate the class distinctions of the present day, we desire that all men should be free and equal, that no person shall be subject to another, but all subject to the law. There shall be no more privileges and arbitrary rule. All shall be sovereign children of the state; and as no middlemen exist any longer between the people and almighty God, so shall the citizen stand in direct relation to the State. We shall have freedom of the press and trade and industry, so that all men, without distinction, shall be able to strive together and receive their reward according to their merit.[69]

The next two chapters will look in some detail at the two countries in which the liberal movement achieved its greatest success: the United Kingdom and the United States.

9
Britain and the Intellectual Aristocracy

Britain's Puritan Revolution of 1640–60 preceded the French Revolution by more than a century. It took an axe to the hereditary principle in the form of the monarchy and the House of Lords and introduced some of the basic elements of meritocratic appointment. Confronting two unprecedented challenges, to defeat a more experienced Royalist army and then to build a revolutionary commonwealth, Oliver Cromwell found the solution in appointing people according to their promise and promoting them according to their ability. This started as an ad hoc solution to pressing problems – John Milton was made Corresponding Secretary of the Commonwealth ('secretary for foreign tongues') because of his demonstrated linguistic ability – but over time it was formalized through tests of future promise. Gerald Aylmer puts it thus in his history of Cromwell's civil service:

> The Commonwealth was a revolutionary regime. It had come to power through civil war and military force, and its legality was not universally recognised in the country. This put a premium on political and ideological reliability, and meant that loyalty to the government was something which patrons needed to stress, and appointing bodies to satisfy themselves about. It also led to a formidable battery of tests and oaths . . . Over and above loyalty and morality, we find emphasis on men's actual fitness for the work in question. It could mean a particular skill in writing, accounting or foreign languages, or a more all-round ability.[1]

The Commonwealth lasted for only eleven years: cheerful Charles II followed gloomy Oliver Cromwell, and the old order of kings and queens, lords and ladies, aristocrats and bishops, resumed its onward march, with the high and mighty once again 'pageanting' themselves about 'among the perpetual bowings and cringings of an abject people', to borrow a phrase from Milton.[2] Patronage and nepotism flourished even more luxuriantly in Jane Austen's England than in Shakespeare's. The lasting break between the pre-meritocratic and meritocratic world came in the late eighteenth and nineteenth centuries.

ASSES FOR LIONS

The second half of the eighteenth century saw a more successful assault on Britain's revived ancient regime. The Industrial Revolution created new wealth. Scotland generated a cult of the common man. And intellectuals – particularly a group of philosophical liberals – produced a new way of looking at the world.

The men who drove the world's first Industrial Revolution were for the most part self-made men who owed little or nothing to the great organs of traditional society, the government, the Church or the ancient universities. John Metcalf – Blind Jack of Knaresborough – was the son of poor parents who lost his sight from smallpox at the age of six and made his living for years as a wrestler. He was one of the great road-builders of his time. James Brindley was the son of a Midland yeoman farmer who was barely able to read or write. He built many of the canals which allowed Manchester and Liverpool to flourish. Richard Arkwright was the son of a tailor. He built the spinning jenny, which helped to power the cotton industry.[3]

These new men thought as radically as they lived. They believed that people derived their worth from what they wrought rather than from what they inherited. And they were instinctively hard on the world: hard on themselves because they needed to wrestle success from the gutter; hard on the aristocracy because they didn't deserve what they had; and hard on their employees because they had risen from poverty themselves. Theirs was a world of profit and loss rather than sentiment and attachment.

Above all, Britain produced a new philosophy for the new world. British liberalism was several things rolled into one. It was a political philosophy rooted in the thinking of Thomas Hobbes and John Locke that saw society as the product of a contract between rights-bearing individuals rather than the product of divine will or the embodiment of a collective spirit; a protest movement against the power of the old ruling elite (particularly when it was rooted in the soil and reinforced by legal privileges); a plea for free trade in all its varieties, not just in goods but also in human talent; and a love song to the power of the human intellect. If conservatives thought that the good society lay in the hierarchical past, and socialists thought that it lay in the fraternal future, liberals thought that it lay in the civilized individual, his brain sharpened by mental exercise and his character formed by a proper education.

The two most important divisions of the liberal army were Utilitarians and economists. The Utilitarians dismissed the idea that it was 'natural' for one class to rule over another. Human society was not an organic entity within which individuals performed quasi-biological roles but a concatenation of individuals who were all striving to maximize their utility. To hell with tradition and sentiment! The Utilitarians argued that the basis of morality was the greatest good of the greatest number – a good that could be calculated with almost mathematical precision by taking a census of people's pleasures and pains.

Adam Smith turned traditional thinking on its head by arguing that the best way to pursue the good of society was to pursue your own self-interest. Despite having once worked as the tutor to the Duke of Buccleuch, he was scathing about the landed aristocracy. 'Being born to greatness discouraged men from aspiring to knowledge, industry, patience, self-denial or virtue,' he complained; and the need to cut a dash in society made things even worse. 'To figure in a ball is his great triumph, and to succeed in an intrigue of gallantry, his highest exploit.' Aristocratic society not only encouraged pointless spending on conspicuous consumption and sanctioned dangerous pastimes such as hunting and duelling. It institutionalized the misallocation of talent: aristocrats usually lacked the ability to make a real contribution to the world, and even on the rare occasions that they possessed it they lacked the motivation to turn it into an achievement. Why go to the trouble of mastering a difficult subject when you could enjoy the deference of everybody around you, simply because of who you are, and all the pleasures of physical life, because of what you own?

A collection of political radicals attacked the principles of hierarchy and deference. Thomas Paine (1737–1809) argued that inheritance was a leading cause of human misery. It was based on a crime and perpetuated by blind obedience: the first kings (such as the loathsome William the Conqueror) were nothing more than the principal ruffians of this or that restless gang.[4] Aristocrats ignored human decency in passing their estates intact to their eldest male children and casting the rest, like orphans, on to the parish, to be provided with sinecures.[5] Nature showed what it felt about the hereditary principle by repeatedly holding it up to ridicule – 'giving mankind an ass for a lion' or allowing kings to continue to rule long after they had become deranged old men.[6]

The hereditary principle rests on an absurd theory of the distribution of abilities, he argued. There is no such thing as a hereditary mathematician or a hereditary poet laureate. Why should there be a hereditary statesman?[7] It also mocks the two sensible justifications of social distinctions: that rewards should encourage effort and recognize real achievement. In Paine's view, Edmund Burke got it upside down when he said that monarchy provides kings with a chance to learn how to rule from an early age: instead it poisons their minds with a sense of self-importance, unearned by individual merit, and ensures that they are ignorant of the condition of their subjects.[8] Worse still: by limiting their potential selection of mates, it condemns ruling families to a cycle of degeneracy. 'The greatest characters the world have known, have risen on the democratic floor. Aristocracy has not been able to keep a proportionate pace with democracy. The artificial noble shrinks into a dwarf before the noble of nature ...'[9]

William Cobbett (1763–1835), a labourer's son who became the most influential journalist of his generation, was equally withering about 'the thing', as he dubbed the British establishment. The establishment existed to support 'tax eaters' at the expense of wealth-creators, and office-holders at the expense of ordinary people: it was thus 'all-corrupting and all-degrading'. The Corn Laws kept the price of food high in order to make life easy for aristocrats. The system of patronage stuffed the administration with bloodsuckers. Cobbett drew up plans to write a play with the memorable title of 'Bastards in High Places' but unfortunately died before he could put pen to paper. Let's hope somebody today takes up both the title and the challenge.[10]

John Wade (1788–1875), a former wool-sorter turned journalist who was inspired by Tom Paine and Joseph Priestley and funded by Jeremy Bentham, provided a full-scale anatomy of these 'bastards in high places' in *The Black Book, or, Corruption Unmasked!* (1820), a laborious account of the abuses of the old Britain, from pluralism in the Church to sinecures in the executive branch to rotten boroughs in the legislature, which sold over 50,000 copies over the years. Wade calculated that Britain paid out more than £1 million a year in pensions and sinecures. The heart of Old Corruption was the royal household, 'the great nursery of indolence, parasites, and courtiers', in Wade's phrase. The royal heart pumped poison through the body politic. The entire political system exhibited 'all the vice, the caprice, and injustice, of aristocratic government: the highest services to the state almost without notice, and the greatest gifts of the Crown lavished on profligacy, servility, and intrigue'. Necessary jobs were left unperformed because they were given to sybarites, he argued. Indolence and luxury devoured the bread for which poverty and application had toiled.[11]

An anonymous poem published in the 1830s captured the mood of zealous disapproval of Old Corruption that this muck-raking provoked:

> What is a peer? A useless thing;
> A costly toy, to please a king;
> A bauble near a throne;
> A lump of animated clay;
> A gaudy pageant of a day;
> An incubus; a drone!
> What is a peer? A nation's curse –
> A pauper on the public purse;
> Corruption's own jackal:
> A haughty, domineering blade;
> A cuckold at a masquerade;
> A dandy at a ball.
> Ye butterflies, whom kings create;
> Ye caterpillars of the state;
> Know that your time is near!
> The moral learn from nature's plan

That in creation God made man;
But never made a peer.[12]

The literature of the period reverberated with similar themes. This was particularly true of Scotland, which had the highest literacy rate in the British Isles, at least in the lowlands, the most advanced universities and the first libraries for the poor.[13] Robert Burns celebrated the virtues of the common man with his great levelling poem of 1795, 'A Man's a Man for A' That': 'What though on hamely [homely] fare we dine,/Wear hoddin grey, an' a that;/Gie [give] fools their silks, and knaves their wine;/A man's a man for a' that'. In Burns's poem you can hear the egalitarian culture of the Scottish kirk and the Scottish marketplace, where an ordinary Scotsman's word was as good as 'yon birkie ca'd [that assertive fool called] a lord' and where an ordinary person's money was as good as a toff's.

English novelists poked fun at the old-fashioned upper classes with their addiction to drinking and hunting and their indifference to the finer things of life. The pioneer of squire-bashing was Henry Fielding with Squire Western in *Tom Jones* (1749). The mid-Victorians hunted backwoodsmen with almost the same enthusiasm that Squire Western hunted foxes: think of the boorish Sir Pitt Crawley in Thackeray's *Vanity Fair* (1848). Even a conservative author such as Trollope cashed in on the fashion with Lord Chiltern in his political novels. Far from setting the tone of society, the aristocratic elite, or the most traditional section of it anyway, was becoming a figure of fun, stuck in the past and unable to drive civilization forward.

Still, it was not enough to delegitimize the old establishment. You also needed to devise a way of identifying men of merit who could take their place. Leading critics of the old regime advanced general arguments in favour of examinations without getting down to the details. Adam Smith suggested vaguely in *The Wealth of Nations* that every man 'undergo an examination or probation in them before he can obtain the freedom in any corporation to be allowed to set up any trade'.[14] Jeremy Bentham was equally vague in his (wonderfully titled) *Official Aptitude Maximized; Expense Minimized* (1830).

The breakthrough was made by Cambridge University, which led the way in introducing written examinations to replace the older tradition of oral examinations, and in linking examination results to substantial rewards in the form of prizes and college fellowships. Trinity, the largest and richest college, introduced entrance examinations in 1744.[15] In 1765, next-door St John's established twice-yearly examinations for its students. (Peterhouse considered a similar suggestion five years later, but rejected it.) In 1786, Trinity began to award fellowships on the basis of competitive examinations. In 1800, the Senate House offered university-wide examinations in mathematics. By the opening decades of the nineteenth century, the University Tripos, as the final examination was called, was the world's most competitive academic examination outside China.[16] Other British universities, such as Oxford, in 1800, and University College London, founded in 1826, had no choice but to follow suit, with the names of successful candidates divided into classes and listed in order of merit.

In Cambridge, candidates gathered in the Senate House for a week-long grilling in either mathematics (arithmetic, geometry, algebra, trigonometry, mechanics, optics, astronomy and Newton's *Principia*) or, after 1824, in classics (candidates who wanted to graduate in classics had first to pass an examination in mathematics, though an exception was made for members of the nobility). Examiners patrolled the room, sometimes distributing printed questions, sometimes dictating questions. Everything was done to stimulate competition. The 'questionists', or candidates, were grouped into brackets at the start of the examination week on the basis of their previous performance. The examiners marked their answers immediately and adjusted the difficulty of the new questions on the basis of their performance: the better they did, the harder the questions became. Once the examinations were finished, the marks were added up – they could run to thousands of points – and the candidates were then arranged in strict order of merit and classified into groups with idiosyncratic names: the Wranglers, as the top examinees were called, had the equivalent of first-class honours, the Senior Optimes had the equivalent of second-class honours and the Junior Optimes the equivalent of thirds. The person who came first was the Senior Wrangler, the person who came last was accorded the Wooden Spoon.

On the principle that the best way to get the English interested in the life of the mind is to turn it into a sporting event, the annual competition had many of the trappings of a horse race. The horses were trained by private tutors rather than university professors, who frequently had little contact with undergraduates, or indeed, in some cases, with the university itself. Students placed bets on the final outcome as the interim results were published and the horses changed their positions in the race. The names of the eventual winners were published in the London papers. These winners were given ample prize money to compensate them for their efforts: the guarantee of a college fellowship that might bring in as much as £250 (£29,500 or $41,000 in today's money) a year for life, so long as you did not get married, and that did not involve much by the way of duties.

Despite all this agitation, the new examination regime did little to elevate the intellectual life of the university as a whole. The runners were a breed apart, who spent most of their time at university locked in their rooms cramming facts into their overstuffed craniums. The vast bulk of students were quite content to pocket a pass degree – or to belong to the Poll (from *polloi* or 'many'), as the university put it – and to spend their time gambling on horses in nearby Newmarket, getting drunk in dining clubs and pubs, brawling with 'townies' and engaging in high-spirited pranks of the sort chronicled by Anthony Trollope in *The Duke's Children* (1880).

The state remained in the hands of placemen. In his *Letter on Administrative Reform* (1855), Matthew Higgins, an Irish journalist, described a world in which Britain was governed by an 'upper ten thousand' who had

> hitherto monopolised every post of honour, trust and emolument under the Crown, from the highest to the lowest. They have taken what they wanted for themselves; they have distributed what they did not want among their relations, connexions and dependents [*sic*]. They have all in turn paid their debts of friendship and of gratitude, they have provided for their younger sons and their worn-out servants with appointments in the public service.[17]

THE INTELLECTUAL ARISTOCRACY

The great breakthrough for the meritocratic idea was the work of one of the most remarkable groups of revolutionaries Europe has produced:

what John Maynard Keynes, one of its leading ornaments, called the 'educated bourgeoisie' and Noel Annan, its most assiduous historian, called the 'intellectual aristocracy'.[18] A list of the surnames of some members of the intellectual elite should be enough to convey their significance: Huxley, Darwin, Butler, Sidgwick, Trevelyan, Fawcett and, of course, Keynes. They owed their positions to their brains and characters rather than their 'friends' and 'connections' (though they certainly relished the friends and connections that their brains brought them). And they tried to reform society so that people like them could rule. This involved providing answers to the riddle at the heart of their ideology: what is merit and how do you go about measuring it? It also involved justifying a peaceful transfer of power from the old aristocracy of land to the new aristocracy of brains. For the most part, the intellectual aristocracy eschewed mounting a full-frontal assault on the old aristocracy in the manner of Thomas Paine. Instead, it put its faith in what the Fabians later called 'permeation' and 'gradualism' – reforming established institutions rather than abolishing them and transforming the aristocratic idea of honour into the modern idea of merit.

The group traced its origins to three religious groups and one secular sect. The religious groups – the Clapham Sect, the Quakers and the Unitarians – were welded together by their common faith in philanthropy as the fruit of God's grace and their common involvement in social reform movements such as prison reform, adult literacy and, above all, the abolition of slavery. The secular sect – the Utilitarians or philosophical radicals – brought to this mix faith in the power of reason and the efficacy of measurement.

The intellectual aristocracy found one of its first spokesmen in perhaps the greatest Victorian historian, Thomas Babington Macaulay. Macaulay's parents were Evangelical Christians who lived near Clapham Common in South London and devoted themselves to the twin callings of saving souls and improving minds. His father, Zachary, worked closely with William Wilberforce in the campaign to abolish slavery, helping to found the Anti-Slavery Society in 1823 and becoming editor of its publication, *The Anti-Slavery Reporter*. He also served on committees that helped to found London University and the Society for the Suppression of Vice.

'Clever Tom', as Macaulay was nicknamed, lived up to his parents' expectations when it came to intellect, learning to write at two and composing a history of the world at seven.[19] When it came to morals, however, the story was more complicated: though he was an inveterate reformer, he abandoned Evangelical Christianity for secular Utilitarianism and the narrow world of Clapham for Whig High Society, paying his way with the proceeds of his prize fellowship at Trinity College, Cambridge, which provided him with a respectable income without making any tedious demands about living in college or producing an academic thesis.

Macaulay was the quintessential Victorian: confident where we are self-doubting and multi-talented where we are specialized. Being a great historian was only part of his CV – indeed his greatness as a historian depended on the fact that he did so much more than just write history. He was a great public intellectual: the mere rumour that Macaulay had produced another essay in the *Edinburgh Review* was enough to set London society alight. He was also a great politician-cum-administrator. One of his earliest essays in the *Edinburgh Review* advocated the abolition of slavery. He championed parliamentary reform as Member of Parliament for Lord Lansdowne's pocket borough of Calne (he understood that you have to enter the system in order to reform it) and later served as both secretary at war and paymaster-general.

India provided Macaulay with a great laboratory for testing his ideas about elite education and open competition. In February 1835 he provided the framework for Indian education in his 'Minute on Indian Education'. Almost twenty years later, in November 1854, he was the chief author of the 'Report on the Indian Civil Service'. His aim was to create an elite class of Indians who might 'be interpreters between us and the millions whom we govern; a class of persons, Indian in blood and colour, but English in taste, in opinions, in morals and in intellect'. This entailed two great reforms. The first was replacing the old system of patronage and connection with a new system of meritocratic appointment: a system that could as well apply to talented Indians as to talented Englishmen. The second was replacing Sanskrit with English as the medium for education for the ruling elite in order to weave the Indian elite into a broader Anglo-Saxon elite.

Macaulay's cocksure certainties arouse fury today, particularly among Indians.[20] Though he spent four years in India, from 1834 to 1838, he never bothered to learn a word of Sanskrit or to immerse himself in classical Indian culture, as some of his English contemporaries did. For him, European civilization was all that mattered. His 'Minute on Indian Education' replaced Sanskrit with English at the heart of Indian education on the grounds that he had never met an Indian scholar 'who could deny that a single shelf of a good European library was worth the whole native literature of India and Arabia'. 'Macaulay's children' was the contemptuous phrase which many Indian nationalists applied to anglicized Indians. Nevertheless, a careful reading of the historian-statesman's various writings, particularly on Indian education, reveals that he also developed a sophisticated theory of meritocracy that challenged not only India's traditional society, with all its virtues and vices, but also Britain's landed elite.

Macaulay's starting point was that people differed in their innate 'talents' and 'diligence'. The great test of a progressive society was to learn how to spot those talents and then deploy them for the common good.[21] This involved distinguishing between 'ability' and 'mere learning'. The job of a well-designed examination, he said, was to 'test the candidate's powers of mind' rather than just 'ascertain the extent of his metaphysical reading'.[22] 'If, instead of learning Greek we learned the Cherokee,' he mused, 'the man who understood the Cherokee best, who made the most correct and melodious Cherokee verses, who comprehended most accurately the effect of the Cherokee particles, would generally be a superior man to him who was destitute of these accomplishments.'[23] (It is tempting to substitute Sanskrit for Cherokee in this sentence.) Anyone who could do best what all the ablest and most ambitious of his contemporaries were trying to do well was guaranteed success; and his peculiar powers of mind, when properly trained and directed, might do notable service to the state.[24] Finally, he believed that examinations provided a good guide to 'what men will prove to be in life',[25] since the qualities required for professional success were precisely those tested in the examination room. As a chaser, he added that examinations provided good tests of moral character as well as general intellectual ability. 'Early superiority in science and literature generally indicates the existence of some qualities which are securities against vice – industry, self-denial, a

taste for pleasures not sensual, a laudable desire of honourable distinction, a still more laudable desire to obtain the approbation of friends
and relations.'[26]

If Macaulay turned India into a laboratory for the meritocratic
idea, Macaulay's brother-in-law, Sir Charles Trevelyan, applied that
idea to the very heart of the British state. Trevelyan was even more of
a prig than 'Clever Tom' himself – 'his mind is full of schemes of
moral and political improvement', Macaulay wrote of his brother-in-
law when they were in India together, 'his topics even in courtship are
steam navigation, the education of the natives, the equalization of
sugar duties'. Despite this, Macaulay used all his influence to get him
appointed assistant secretary to the Treasury in 1840 (one of many
cases of the patronage principle being used to advance the cause of
meritocracy, including Macaulay's own entry into Parliament). In
1853, William Gladstone, then Chancellor of the Exchequer, decided
to make him co-chairman of his inquiry into the state of the civil service along with his own private secretary, Sir Stafford Northcote.

The resulting Northcote–Trevelyan Report (1854) was one of the
central documents in the history of the meritocracy: a devastating
broadside against the old order and a blueprint for a new one – and
all in just twenty-three pages.

The old system of patronage and job security was a festering sore
that was proving more dangerous by the day as the British state
assumed greater responsibilities, the report argued. Britain could not
prosper at home and expand abroad unless it modernized its state
apparatus. The old system attracted the dull, lazy and feeble-bodied
into the civil service – and once you'd given them a job, you couldn't
get rid of them. 'Those whose abilities do not warrant an expectation
that they will succeed in the open professions, where they must
encounter the competition of their contemporaries, and those whom
indolence of temperament, or physical infirmities unfit for active exertions,' the report argued, 'are placed in the Civil Service, where they
may obtain an honourable livelihood with little labour, and with no
risk . . .'[27] The contrast with the private sector was embarrassing: in
the open professions 'the able and energetic rise to the top; the dull
and inefficient remain at the bottom. In the public establishments, on
the contrary, the general rule is that all rise together.'[28]

Their solution to the problem was straightforward: borrow the principle of open competition from the private sector and use it to reinvigorate government: in other words, admit candidates on the basis of merit and promote them on the basis of performance.[29] But how do you inject competition into the civil service? And how do you make sure that competition identifies the most able candidates? The answer, of course, lay in examinations. These examinations needed to be as open and objective as possible. They needed to 'test the intelligence, as well as the mere attainments, of the candidates'.[30] 'The great advantage to be expected from the examinations,' Northcote and Trevelyan argued, 'would be, that they would elicit young men of general ability.'[31] That phrase 'general ability' was to sit at the heart of meritocratic thinking.

Northcote and Trevelyan believed that their principle of open competition would inaugurate a new age of state-making: one that replaced the state as a parasite with the state as a public service. Patronage had allowed the aristocracy to use the public service as a foundling hospital for the waifs and strays of their families: for 'the idle and useless, the fool of the family, the consumptive, the hypochondriac, those who have a tendency to insanity', and for their bastards. Competition, on the other hand, might promote the rule of a Platonic aristocracy of talent, securing 'for the public service those who are, in a true sense aristocrats, the sons of gentlemen, or those who by force of cultivation, good training and good society have acquired the feelings and habits of gentlemen'.[32] These 'natural gentlemen' included two sorts of superior citizens: 'well-educated young men who depend for their advancement upon their own exertions, and not upon their wealth and connexions' and 'well-educated poor men' who are 'notoriously those who throw themselves into their work with the greatest energy and perseverance'.[33]

Open competition was an instrument of moral improvement as well as bureaucratic efficiency.[34] Patronage had promoted the moral disease of dependency.[35] Open competition, on the other hand, promoted the moral virtues of self-reliance. By transforming administrative offices from freeholds, bestowed by patronage, into trusts, awarded for merit, competition would ensure that 'the Government and the governing class would cease to be on the side of corruption'.[36] This would send a powerful signal to the rest of society as well. John Stuart Mill talked about 'the great and salutary moral revolution, descending to the minds of almost the lowest classes, which would follow the knowledge that Government (to people in general the most trusted exponent of the ways of the world) would henceforth bestow its gifts according to merit, and not to favour'.[37]

The report could not have been better timed: the Crimean War, with its futile Charge of the Light Brigade and countless logistical failures, demonstrated that the British state was not up to the new challenges confronting it, and the Indian mutiny shook British imperial rule the year after. Even so, the resistance was fierce. For many traditionalists, it seemed like a crazy attempt to apply the principles of one area of life – the schoolroom – to another area of life that had nothing to do with it, rather like, in contemporary terms, choosing the next governor of the Bank of England on the basis of his or her performance on *Strictly Come Dancing*. Anthony Trollope caricatured Charles Trevelyan as Sir Gregory Hardlines in *The Three Clerks* (1857). Robert Cecil (later Lord Salisbury) worried that civil servants selected by open competition would get above themselves, picking arguments for the sake of arguments and looking down on people whom they were supposed to serve. Walter Bagehot fretted that clever men wouldn't have enough to do in Whitehall – and would spend their time moping, wittering and blaspheming instead.

This opposition succeeded in slowing down the Northcote–Trevelyan revolution. In the first year that they were introduced – 1855 – competitive examinations were used to sift out a pre-selected field of candidates rather than to open up the field to all the talents. The civil service continued to be a byword for sloth: three years after the report, in *Little Dorrit*, Charles Dickens satirized the civil service in his portrait of the Circumlocution Office, staffed by a self-perpetuating oligarchy of interconnected families and their oily dependants and dedicated to the task of preventing British citizens from getting anything done. The reformers nevertheless grasped something important about the working of the state: once unleashed, revolutionary ideas have a tendency to become the new common sense. Northcote–Trevelyan's real achievement was intellectual as much as organizational: it quickly made the old system of patronage impossible to defend.

The reformers also believed that open competition would reinvigorate Britain's education system, which had been warped, from the richest Oxbridge colleges down to the most obscure private schools, by the spirit of patronage and corruption. Fellows and teachers treated their jobs as sinecures. 'Teaching families' passed appointments down the generations. Schoolchildren were allowed to run wild. Scholarships were doled out on the basis of where you came from. A regime of religious tests in universities meant that you couldn't graduate if you refused to sign the Thirty-Nine Articles, a regime that excluded some of the most intellectually dynamic groups in Britain – Nonconformists, Jews and sceptics – from university education.

A few reforming educationalists had already begun to improve Britain's schools in the 1830s. Thomas Arnold galvanized teaching at Rugby through a combination of personal charisma and clever institutional reform, using senior boys to impose order. A group of university reformers such as Benjamin Jowett and Frederick Temple embraced the principle of open competition as a way of reviving the universities and tightening the bonds between the universities and the state. They argued that replacing patronage with open competition would rid the universities of idle drones and send a powerful message to young people (and their parents) that the only way to get ahead was to keep their noses to the grindstone. Macaulay had argued that an annual competition for forty places in the Indian Civil Service – every one of which 'is nothing less than an honourable social position, and a comfortable independence for life' – would turbocharge the British universities.[38] The university reformers believed that adding the enormous riches of Oxford and Cambridge to the pot would have a far bigger impact.[39]

The Royal Commissions on Oxford and Cambridge, which the prime minister, Lord John Russell, established in 1850, provided these reformers with an opportunity to hammer home the case for open competition, providing them with opportunities to hold high-profile public inquiries and then publish agenda-setting reports. The Oxford Commission lamented that only 22 of the university's 542 fellowships were open to real competition: the rest were restricted to candidates from particular districts, schools or families.[40] These restrictions, it argued, damaged both learning and teaching, reducing incentives to effort and populating the colleges with the dull relatives of founders. (Contemporaries commonly used the term 'founder's kin', or 'almost a founder', to mean 'fool'.)[41] Hayward Cox put the point bluntly in his evidence to the commission:

> They crowd the Colleges with inferior men, often without either the power or the inclination to promote the interests of education, withdraw many who might be useful in their appropriate spheres, hold out incentives to indolence, selfishness and self-indulgence, and engage persons in the work of instruction who are without zeal in the pursuit . . .[42]

The restrictions had proved to be so disastrous because they treated educational opportunities as charitable gifts to be conferred on the basis of accident of birth, rather than as just rewards to be offered to those who had proved, through their superior intelligence and outstanding diligence, that they were capable of making good use of them.[43] The solution was simple: abolish restrictions and open fellowships 'to merit, and to merit only'.[44]

The Cambridge Commission found less to complain about. The majority of college fellowships had already been opened up to competition. 'A Student, however friendless and unknown, provided he have the requisite qualifications of character and ability,' the commission purred, 'is as sure of obtaining his Fellowship as another of better family or wealthier connexions.'[45] The commission argued simply that this well-established principle should be universalized, with all fellowships and scholarships 'brought . . . under the one good rule of unfettered and open competition'.[46]

To complete the revolution, the government abolished religious restrictions on the universities. Though the Oxford and Cambridge Universities Act of 1854 and 1856 had removed the requirement that you had to sign the Thirty-Nine Articles in order to enter the universities or take a degree, people who refused to sign were still barred from enjoying the life-blood of meritocracy: higher degrees, college fellowships and university prizes (in 1869, the Senior Wrangler in Cambridge was prevented from taking his distinction on the grounds that he was a Jew). In 1871, Gladstone, perhaps the most profoundly religious prime minister Britain has had, pushed through legislation that abolished religious restrictions at the ancient universities and finally opened the way to the creation of a new ruling class, the secular meritocracy.[47]

The Crimea debacle ensured that the principle of open competition was applied to another arm of the state, the military. Though British soldiers fought with astonishing valour during the two-year campaign, from 1854 to 1856, they were led by buffoons, stupid and stubborn old men who had purchased their commissions and cared more about the rules for circulating port than they did about mastering changes in military science. More than 21,000 died in the war: 2,755 killed in action, 2,019 from wounds and 16,323 of disease. A Royal Commission of 1857 pronounced that the practice of selling commissions was 'repugnant to the public sentiment of the present day, and equally inconsistent with the honour of the military profession'. The system gave 'an undue pre-eminence to wealth', it argued, 'discouraging exertion and depressing merit'; and since a soldier's commission died with him, death-in-battle could prove financially ruinous to the surviving families.

Once again, reform was frustratingly slow: the War Office liked the commission system because it reduced the up-front cost of the army, commission-holders liked it because they paid for their retirement by selling their commissions to younger officers and the commander-in-chief of the army, His Royal Highness Prince George, the Duke of Cambridge, a cantankerous old snob if ever there was one, liked it because it kept out the riff-raff. Edward Cardwell and Sir George Trevelyan, working together and fighting bitter rear-guard resistance from the duke, won the day. After a lengthy debate in the House of Commons, during which Cardwell assured the house that 'if we pass this Bill into a law, its effect will be to attract to the Army the aristocracy of merit and professional talent, which is after all the true aristocracy',[48] the government passed a comprehensive reform of the army which abolished the purchase of commissions, restricted entry into the officer corps to graduates of Sandhurst, and decreed that admission to Sandhurst should be determined by competitive examinations.

The rise of open competition gave examinations a newly prominent role in British life. In *The Three Clerks* Anthony Trollope produces a character, modelled on Benjamin Jowett, who fantasizes about the day when 'every man [/] in England some should . . . be made to pass through "go". The greengrocer's boy should not carry out cabbages unless his fitness for cabbage-carrying had been ascertained.'[49] In Gilbert and Sullivan's *HMS Pinafore* (1878) Sir Joseph Porter sings about wearing clean collars and a brand-new suit for the examination to get into the navy; in *Iolanthe* (1882) the Fairy Queen says that the duke's exalted station was gained by competitive examination.

The newly invigorated universities of Oxford and Cambridge played a leading role in bringing the new cult to the nation's secondary schools. Oxford established a Delegacy of Local Examinations in July 1857 in order to provide schoolchildren with the equivalent of a modern school-leaving certificate, and Cambridge followed suit a year later with its Local Examinations Syndicate. 'Local' meant that candidates could sit external examinations near their homes rather than having to travel up to the universities. Dons arrived by train in full academic regalia, clutching the precious exam papers in locked boxes. The exams lasted for six or seven consecutive days, with separate papers morning, afternoon and in the evening, and often demanded extraordinary feats of memory. Candidates might be asked to draw from memory maps of specified country's coastlines, rivers or mountain ranges, or list the names of kings and queens or recount the main events in a particular period of English history. This inevitably provoked a tense debate: were the exams really testing natural ability? Or were they just looking for extreme (and perhaps unhealthy) feats of memory?

Some historians have questioned the radicalism of this faith in open competition. Surely open competition would only hand more power to people who could afford an expensive education? They can cite the authority of William Gladstone, who wrote a letter to Lord John Russell in January 1845 predicting that a competitive examination which emphasized classics and mathematics would favour the aristocracy:

> I have a strong impression that the aristocracy of this country are even superior in natural gifts, on the average, to the mass: but it is plain that with their acquired advantages, their insensible education, irrespective of book-learning, they have an immense superiority.[50]

Both Gladstone and his latter-day echo chamber miss the point: the most important test of the new system was not whether it promoted social mobility but whether it changed the nature of the state. The old regime was essentially a rent-seeking regime: people saw civil service positions as rents to be enjoyed rather than duties to perform. The new regime was about problem-solving: people held their positions only in so far as they could advance the state's interests rather than line their own pockets.

These examinations forced the old upper class to reform itself from within: effort that once went into lobbying politicians for baubles now went into lobbying schools and universities to improve their performance and urging children to keep their nose to the grindstone. At the same time, the revolution immediately opened opportunities to members of Britain's intellectual aristocracy who had already acquired the wherewithal to compete with their social superiors in education but had repeatedly been excluded from positions of influence by the working of patronage. And in the long run, it opened opportunities to poorer children of talent as the British state began the laborious work of building a ladder of opportunity from the poorest schools to the elite universities. The arch-reactionary Lord Salisbury demonstrated a more acute grasp of what was going on than Gladstone when he described open competition as a mere 'schoolmaster's scheme'. Educational success could never be as certain a guarantee of aristocratic power as patronage and nepotism.

A LIBERAL DILEMMA

The question about how much open competition does to ensure social justice is nevertheless an important one. The first stage of the liberal experiment was relatively simple: all liberals agreed that you needed to open competition to (initially male) talent of all varieties. Once open competition had been established, however, liberals were confronted with a trickier problem. How could you promote the rule of the able when the brilliant children of chimney sweeps left school at eleven and the dullest children of dukes went to Eton? Then again, how could you give the children of chimney sweeps opportunities without breaking with another liberal principle – limited government and low taxation? And how did you know just how much untapped ability there was in the population at large? Debates over these issues divided liberals into several camps.

Some liberals argued that Britain was already making good use of its talent. Samuel Smiles, whose *Self-Help* (1859) was one of the most popular books of the age, selling more than a quarter of a million copies by 1900 and being translated into all the major European and Asian languages, argued that all you needed to do was work hard and opportunity would come along. Industrialization had already replaced a decadent aristocracy of birth with an aristocracy of effort, Britain's new class of 'Industrial Heroes' having, almost without exception, 'sprung from the ranks'. All the young had to do was to work hard and seize their opportunities and they might well become 'industrial heroes' themselves and, even if they didn't rise to such heights, they were guaranteed a good job and a successful life. The only reason that people failed was that they were lazy and self-indulgent. A versifier known to history only as 'E.B.' demonstrated the popularity of Smiles's philosophy in his *Songs for English Workmen to Sing* (1867):

> Work, boys, work and be contented.
> So long as you've enough to buy a meal,
> The man you may rely, will be wealthy by and bye,
> If he'll only put his shoulder to the wheel.

Walter Bagehot argued that beneath the facade of monarchical and aristocratic society the real rulers were professional-class meritocrats – Cabinet ministers and politicians who were selected by a rigorous process of election and parliamentary performance, and senior Whitehall civil servants. Herbert Spencer, one of the founders of Social Darwinism and, for a while, an employee on Bagehot's newspaper, the *Economist*, believed that the fittest had already risen to the top, declaring flatly that the 'superior shall have the good of his superiority and the inferior the evil of his inferiority'.[51]

The problem of wasted opportunity nevertheless troubled even classical liberals. Richard Cobden, normally the gold standard of laissez-faire orthodoxy, conceded that 'government interference is as necessary for education as its non-interference is essential for trade', praising absolutist Prussia as 'the best government in Europe'.[52]

Bagehot argued that the great cause of mid-Victorian England was 'Educate! Educate! Educate!' To this end, the government would have to 'intervene far more widely than as yet thought ere the problem of wide education in a mixed society is solved'.[53] Benjamin Jowett argued that the universities had to do more to search for talent outside the ruling classes. 'It is of the greatest use,' he wrote, 'to awaken in people's minds a sense of the necessity of a liberal education for more than the numbers contained in Harrow, Winchester, Eton etc. The abused grammar-schools and charity foundations supply abundant means.' As the century developed, the case for public education became overwhelming.

J. S. Mill abandoned his support for the 'nightwatchman state' because he could not bear the idea of dunces passing from Eton into the Cabinet while geniuses were left to moulder. Matthew Arnold argued that the state, which represented nothing less than 'the nation in its collective and corporate character', had a duty to provide high-quality education for the middle classes for reasons of both efficiency and culture: if the state held back, Britain would lose out to better-educated nations (such as France and Germany) and society would be consumed by philistinism and selfishness. A group of new liberals eventually embraced a bigger state in the name of opportunity. T. H. Green, who turned Balliol College, Oxford, into the command centre of this new, more interventionist liberalism, argued that liberalism had largely achieved its negative tasks: getting rid of arbitrary power and privilege. The pertinent question for liberal meritocrats was no longer 'Do state and society leave me alone?' but 'Are they doing enough to help me realize my potential?'

An equally fraught issue for liberals was the problem of democracy. They worried that democracy represented a potential threat to the things that they held most dear, notably individual liberty and freedom of thought. John Bright, one of the earliest champions of broadening the franchise, wrote that people who were trapped in 'poverty and dependence' would get in the way of 'intelligent and honest working men'.[54] J. S. Mill worried that 'masses' would advance at the expense of 'individuals', that mediocrities would flourish at the expense of people of real intellectual distinction, and that dissenters would be frozen out of public life while conformists would be loaded with honours, and argued that the educated should be given more votes. Henry Sumner Maine, a great legal historian, worried that democracy would become 'a monarchy inverted'.

Still, most of them realized that resisting democracy was futile, if not counterproductive. A convenient way out of the dilemma was to mix an element of meritocracy in with democracy, either in the form of political meritocracy (reserving more power for the well educated) or cultural meritocracy (spreading high culture as widely as possible). Robert Lowe, one of Gladstone's key lieutenants, told his fellow MPs, after the 1867 Reform Bill extended the franchise, that the country must now 'prevail on our future masters to learn their letters', a phrase subsequently repeated as 'we must educate our masters'. Matthew Arnold argued that a national education system might identify and promote public-spirited meritocrats – '*aliens*', as he called them – 'who are mainly led, not by their class spirit, but by a general *humane* spirit, by the love of human perfection'.[55] These were the true 'apostles of equality' in the modern era.

In the late-Victorian and Edwardian periods two further arguments for meritocratic reform came to the fore, one based on efficiency, the other on compassion. A swelling chorus of intellectuals argued that Britain would not be able to compete with rising powers like Germany if it didn't improve its education system. Karl Pearson, a leading eugenicist, warned that 'you cannot get a strong and effective nation if many of its stomachs are half fed and many of its brains untrained'.[56] More compassionate types worried about all the geniuses who were denied their rightful opportunities by the working of an unequal educational system. One of the great novels of the period, Thomas Hardy's *Jude the Obscure* (1895), tells the story of a brilliant agricultural worker who tries to educate himself, even in the ancient languages, but is frustrated by a mixture of flesh and fate. Sir Robert Morant, the most influential figure at the Board of Education after the turn of the century, and probably the greatest civil servant of his time, mixed all these various arguments for meritocratic mobility in a telling passage:

> the more we develop our Society on democratic lines, without this scrupulous safeguarding of the 'guidance of brains' in each and every sphere of national life, the more surely will the democratic State be beaten, in

the long run, in the international struggle for existence, 'conquered from without by the force of the concentrated directing brain power of competing nations, shattered from within by the centrifugal forces of her own people's unrestrained individualism and disintegrated utterly by the blind impulses of mere numerical majorities'.[57]

THE LADDER OF OPPORTUNITY

The British government responded to these mounting worries about lost talent by building, albeit slowly, a ladder of opportunity that was intended to take able children from the village school to the summit of British life. The Taunton Commissioners (1864–7) argued that no educational system would be complete 'unless it were possible for boys of exceptional talent to rise to the highest education which the country could supply'[58] and pointed out that the grammar schools had traditionally performed this function:

> One great service, which till a very late period was rendered to this country by the grammar schools, was that so many boys of more than ordinary capacity found in them, what they could hardly have found elsewhere, the means of rising to eminence in all professions, and especially in literature.[59]

The Commissioners suggested establishing a system of exhibitions 'open to merit, and to merit only' and designed so that it would be tolerably certain that talent, wherever it was, would be discovered and cherished and enabled to obtain whatever cultivation it required'.[60] This would provide education with 'some connecting thread pervading education of every grade', and 'real ability' with a succession of 'proper openings' that would allow it to express itself.[61] The exhibitions should be open to rich and poor alike, they argued, awarded as prizes rather than charitable gifts. 'The freer the competition the better,' they pointed out. 'Whenever a privilege is to be given as a prize, restrictions are a grievous evil. They damage the value of the prize far more than they benefit those who are thus protected in the competition.'[62] The reason for doing this – and incurring the deadweight cost of giving exhibitions to rich children – was that 'open competition is above partiality, whether personal, social or political; it marks by natural selection those who can profit by an education higher than the rudiments; it puts the free scholar in a place of honour instead of a place of reproach; it stimulates the education without and leavens the mass within; it encourages parents, masters, and scholars.'[63]

Thirty years later the Bryce Commissioners (1893–5) advocated further measures 'to enable children of scanty means and exceptional ability to prolong their education'.[64] They argued that England needed a more generous supply of scholarships if it was to create an educational ladder which would allow 'boys of rare capacity' to pass from elementary schools to the universities.[65] They also took seriously the complaint that the established scholarship system 'discerns, advances and rewards not capacity as such but attainments; and that, as attainments in the earlier years of life largely depend on opportunities and advantages which cost money, students of real promise may be excluded by early poverty from the benefit of endowments upon which they have a just claim',[66] suggesting that the best remedy for the problem was to make sure that scholarship winners were selected '*propter spem* rather than *propter rem*, for promise of general ability rather than for precocity of special attainment'.[67] The examination system should thus be designed to test the 'general intelligence' of the pupils.[68]

The result was the establishment of a radical new principle at the heart of the education system: the principle that children's opportunities should be determined by their general intellectual ability rather than by their ability to pay – that is, by what is in their heads rather than by what is in their parents' bank account. The 1918 Education Act pronounced that children 'shall not be debarred from receiving the benefits of any form of education by which they are capable of profiting through inability to pay fees'. The possession of talent implied a moral claim on the state to provide opportunity and instruction. In 1920 the Departmental Committee on Scholarships and Free Places insisted that scholarship examinations should aim 'as far as possible to test capacity and promise rather than attainments'.[69] The country could not afford 'to miss intelligent children', it warned.[70]

The new principle brought a wealth of fresh talent into the citadels of aristocratic and clerical privilege. The case of Ernest Barker

(1874–1960) is particularly striking. Barker was born in poverty in 1874, the oldest of seven children. His mother had worked in a cotton mill; his father was a miner turned farm labourer with an income of under £50 a year. Ernest won a scholarship to Manchester Grammar School, commuting there daily by train, and attracted the attention of his teachers, one of whom taught him Greek free of charge during vacations; he supplemented his scholarship money with prizes won in open competition; and finally went up to Jowett's college, Balliol, in 1893 with scholarship money from both his school and his college and a loan from his mother's grocer. Though he still didn't have enough to live on he managed to survive by dint of scrimping and saving (he abstained from college dinner two or three nights a week) and winning scholarships such as the Craven.[71] He eventually ended up with firsts in both classics ('Greats') and modern history, a rare double.

Barker paid a heavy price for his success in terms of alienation from his kith and kin: he found himself wrenched away from his family and 'attached to another centre'. When he returned home it was as a stranger, 'with far-away interests, far-away friends, and a separate way of life'.[72] But he succeeded in becoming one of the great academic figures of his generation, far more successful than most of the Etonians and Wykehamists who had been trained in Greek and Latin from the cradle: a fellow of an Oxford college, the principal of King's College, London, professor of political science at Cambridge, and a knight of the realm. His earliest publications, predictably enough, were on Plato.

Barker was a committed liberal, and indeed Liberal, who celebrated the unique role of the voluntary principle in British history in books such as *Britain and the British People* (1942). But the next great push for meritocratic reform came not from liberals who only haltingly embraced the state but from socialists who embraced it with perhaps indecent enthusiasm.

THE MERITOCRATIC TRADITION IN SOCIALIST THOUGHT

Harold Wilson, twice Labour prime minister, quipped that British socialism owed more to Methodism than to Marxism. He could equally well have said, reaching into his own biography, 'meritocracy' rather than 'Methodism'. The meritocratic idea provided an answer to one of the most powerful objections to socialism – that the state is inherently inefficient.[73] Government inefficiency is the result of the capture of the state by the upper classes, socialist meritocrats argued, rather than anything inherent in state power. 'Make the passing of a sufficient examination an indispensable preliminary to entering the executive,' George Bernard Shaw insisted, 'make the executive responsible to the government and the government responsible to the people; and State departments will be provided with all the guarantees for integrity and efficiency that private money-hunting pretends to.'[74] The idea of merit allowed the Fabian left, in its own mind anyway, to appropriate the virtues of capitalism – notably competition and efficiency – while discarding its vices.

The meritocratic idea also provided the working and the middle classes with something that they could unite behind, thereby holding the potentially fissile alliance at the heart of the Labour Party together. It focused on the great emotional question of desert – everybody could agree that the lazy and incompetent should be replaced by the energetic and competent – but also provided practical solutions to practical problems: how do you allocate power in the big organizations that lay at the heart of the socialist project, such as the Coal Board and the London County Council?

The two most sophisticated thinkers about meritocracy on the British left were the husband-and-wife team Sidney and Beatrice Webb, who, among other things, invented Fabian socialism, founded the London School of Economics and persuaded the Labour Party to adopt Clause Four, which committed it to nationalizing the means of production, distribution and exchange. Sidney (1859–1947) and Beatrice (1858–1943) burned with an all-consuming vision of a world that was completely different from the class-ridden society in which they had grown up: a society nurtured by the state, ruled by bureaucrats, guided by science and bent on efficiency. Power was to be transferred not to the masses but to an elite of the able, the expert and the organized – in other words, to the Webbs and their lookalikes. (Sidney had risen into the upper civil service despite his lowly origins and 'tiny tadpole body, unhealthy skin, lack of manner [and] cockney

pronunciation', through outstanding success in examinations; Beatrice regarded herself as 'the cleverest member of one of the cleverest
families in the cleverest class of the cleverest nation in the world'.)
Beatrice Webb outlined their philosophy in her diary entry in December 1894:

> we have little faith in the 'average sensual man'; we do not believe that
> he can do much more than describe his grievances, we do not think that
> he can prescribe the remedies ... We wish to introduce into politics the
> professional expert, to extend the sphere of government by adding to
> its enormous advantages of wholesale and compulsory management,
> the advantage of the most skilled entrepreneur.[75]

Their strongest objection to capitalism was that it rewarded people
not according to their merits but by virtue of their parentage. The idle
and frivolous flourished while the able and studious starved. By living
on inherited wealth, and by divorcing merit from reward, the rich set
an appalling example to society. The Webbs hoped instead that, as
time went by, merit would become the main criterion of social mobility. The able would rise, the dull would sink, and an elite of the able
would gradually supplant the old ruling class. Echoing widespread
worries about national efficiency, they argued that the alternative was
decline and disaster: the government would blunder from confusion
to confusion, the civil service would vacillate and mismanage, the
industrialists would lose their markets, the empire would either disin-
tegrate or fall intact to the Germans, and the population would sink
into poverty, drunkenness and squalor.

The Webbs agreed with Plato that the state's most important function was to identify, train and advance talent, which is the ultimate
engine of economic prosperity. They wanted to 'rescue talented poverty from the shop or plough' and channel it, by way of a scholarship
ladder, leading from the gutter to the universities, into the national
elite. The state should provide a 'national minimum' of education, so
that every child, dull or clever, rich or poor, received the education
requisite for the full development of their faculties. Thereafter, children should be educated according to their varying faculties and
diverging tastes.[76]

The Webbs had no time for what were later to be called comprehensive schools, regarding them as the equivalent of a wholesale product in a differentiated market. 'So infinitely varied is our individuality,' Sidney said, 'that, in matters of social provision as in tailoring, the wholesale supply, when we come more narrowly to scrutinize it, can be nothing better than a series of misfits.'[77] They believed instead in using tests and examinations not just to stream children but to allocate them to different schools suited to their different abilities.

Sidney tried to give life to his vision in the schools of London. He wanted to provide London with 'the greatest capacity-catching-machine that the world has ever yet seen' – to select able children from the lower strata and promote them to their appropriate social positions. He particularly admired the Board of Education's scholarship scheme for working-class children:

> These 2000 scholarships provide for the cleverest children of the London wage-earners a more genuinely accessible ladder than is open to the corresponding class in any American, French, or German city ... Scholarships [/] take the very pick of London's young people to the technical college and the university.[78]

The couple hoped that London University would stand at the summit of the London educational system as a reward for success and a spur to effort. London (and particularly the London School of Economics) would provide what Oxbridge was so clearly failing to provide, a modern and scientific education for the new meritocracy.[79] The university would sink a ladder of opportunity down into the very depths of the London population:

> Wisely organised and adequately endowed, it must dive deep down through every stratum of its seven millions of constituents, selecting by the test of personal ambition and endurance, of talent and 'grit', for all the brain-working professions and for scientific research, every capable recruit that London rears. Hence it must stand ready to enrol in its undergraduate ranks not hundreds a year but thousands.[80]

Though the Webbs were the most devout of the socialist meritocrats, their faith in educated experts and upward mobility was widely accepted across the left. H. G. Wells kept returning to the subject. In *A Modern Utopia* (1905) he envisaged a world state ruled by the samurai – a sort of Platonic elite in Japanese dress. In *The New Machiavelli* (1911), he argued that the prime task of education was to select and train the intellectual elite:

> The prime essential in a progressive civilisation was the establishment of a more effective selective process for the privilege of higher education, and the very highest educational opportunity for the educable. We were too apt to patronise scholarship winners, as though a scholarship was toffee given as a reward for virtue. It wasn't any reward at all; it was an invitation to capacity.[81]

As was his wont, George Bernard Shaw took the same position to the extreme, arguing that 'the overthrow of the aristocrat has created the necessity for the Superman'. Younger left-wing intellectuals sounded similar themes in more modulated tones. In *The Socialist Case*, Douglas Jay, a product of Winchester, New College and All Souls, opined that, 'In the case of nutrition and health, just as in the case of education, the gentleman in Whitehall really does know better what is good for people than the people know themselves.'[82]

Some of 'the people' nevertheless begged to differ: the working class contained large numbers of self-educated people who, thanks to their social backgrounds, didn't get a chance to go to university but nevertheless succeeded in educating themselves. They enrolled in night schools, university extension courses and Workers Educational Association (WEA) lessons. They gobbled up popular editions of classic texts produced by Dent and Co., with working-class readers sticking to the classics, particularly Shakespeare, Milton, Macaulay and Carlyle, for longer than their social superiors in part because the classics were cheap whereas recent publications were full price. A 1906 list of the favourite authors of Labour MPs recalls a lost world of popular learning: Ruskin is number one, followed by Dickens, the Bible and Carlyle, but the list also includes John Stuart Mill, Thomas Macaulay and Adam Smith (Marx doesn't get a look-in).[83]

Sometimes self-education was part of a collective enterprise. Working men's institutes funded prizes for reading and writing and amassed large libraries, particularly in mining communities (Tredegar's was circulating 100,000 volumes a year by the Second World War).[84] Self-help groups formed to circulate books, magazines and, later, gramophone records. More often, it was an individual enterprise that demanded heroic acts of self-sacrifice, starting with choosing the library over the pub. Either way it produced people of astonishing learning: Ramsay MacDonald noted that the intellectual level of many self-educated workers 'is higher than that of many learned university coteries, and incomparably higher than that of wealthy manufacturers' families'.

These autodidacts were often intellectual elitists who enjoyed complicated relationships with their fellow workers. Their passion for books estranged them from their communities – they spent their spare time reading (and sometimes writing) rather than propping up the bar. But at the same time their facility with words and knowledge of facts turned them into natural spokesmen when it came to negotiations. This may explain why Carlyle, with his cult of the hero and disdain for the rabble, was such a popular choice for working-class readers. Keir Hardie, the founder of the Labour Party, said that the real turning point in his life was his discovery of Carlyle's *Sartor Resartus* at the age of sixteen or seventeen.[85] Helen Crawford, a member of the Communist Party's executive committee, read everything by Carlyle that she could get her hands on.

Many leading working-class politicians were self-conscious meritocrats. Herbert Morrison looked forward to a world in which the new middle class and the old working class would combine together to create 'a well-ordered, well-run society in which neither accident of birth nor occupation determines the status of the individual, but only the efficiency of his contribution to the social whole'.[86] Ernest Bevin believed above all in upward mobility for the able – that is, for people like himself. 'If I believed the development of socialism meant the absolute crushing of liberty,' he told some American correspondents in 1947, 'then I would plump for liberty, because the advance of human development depends entirely on the right to think, to speak and to use reason, and allow what I call the upsurge to come from the bottom to reach the top.'[87] Aneurin Bevan, Bevin's great rival, spent his childhood working through as many books as he could in Tredegar's Workmen's Institute library, including F. H. Bradley and Nietzsche, and, when he was at the Central Labour College, he stunned one of his tutors, an Oxford don, with his critique of Kant's categorical imperative.[88] In his pomp he liked to boast that he was one of nature's aristocrats, endowed with peculiar gifts of intellect and imagination. 'I'm not a proletarian or an intellectual,' he once told Richard Crossman. 'I am an aristocrat.'[89] In unbuttoned mood after dinner he liked to hold forth on the inevitability of inequality:

> The duty of a State consists in seeing that all its members are so placed as to be able to seek without favour their own best; in so arranging things as to bring to light each human superiority, wherever it exists. In such wise, after the initial equality, inequality when it comes, will be justified; for it will be sanctioned either by the mysterious powers of nature or the deserving merit of volition.[90]

In the late 1950s and 1960s the British Labour Party turned itself upside down on the subject of meritocracy, embracing first comprehensive schools and then mixed-ability education and preparing the way for Margaret Thatcher to seize the mantle of merit from the left and attach it to the market rather than the state. But in its glory days, culminating in Clement Attlee's 1945 government, when it was on the offensive rather than the defensive, the Labour Party was the party of merit rather than levelling, and opportunity rather than equality.

10

The United States and the Republic of Merit

In 1818, John Adams asked himself what his fellow countrymen meant when they talked about 'the American Revolution'. They meant a lot more than just the War of Independence, he argued. 'The Revolution was effected before the War commenced.' They meant a revolution in the minds and hearts of the people – 'a change in their religious sentiments of their duties and obligations ... This radical change in the principles, opinions, sentiments, and affections of the people was the real American Revolution.'[1]

The real revolution began long before a single shot was fired at Lexington and Concord on 19 April 1775. Little by little, Americans had produced a new theory of society. They rejected the old doctrine of 'degree, priority and place' and embraced instead a society based on individual merit. This revolution did not touch everybody equally: many Americans, including John Adams himself, clung to vestiges of the old order, the South clung to slavery and, even outside the South, blacks were regarded as inferior. But it touched enough people to turn America into a very different sort of place from Europe. Americans 'continually sounded the alarm bell of aristocracy' whenever it looked as if people were getting above themselves.[2] And they instinctively praised people who made their own fortunes and proved their own mettle. Huckleberry Finn was later to capture this spirit with the line that 'all kings is mostly rapscallions'.[3]

America's status as a nation of immigrants predisposed it to believe in self-invention. The settlers who arrived in the new world from the sixteenth century onwards were refugees from Europe's *ancien régimes*: Puritans who wanted to escape from the grip of established Churches; younger sons who wanted to escape from the consequences of primogeniture; sundry adventurers who wanted to escape from a closed society. 'The rich stay in Europe,' wrote the French immigrant J. Hector St John de Crèvecœur, 'it is only the middling and the poor that emigrate.' And America's vast size encouraged mobility. British observers were astonished to see that the colonists were always moving about 'as their avidity and restlessness incite them'. 'They acquire no attachment to place,' said one Briton, 'but wandering about seems engrafted in their nature; and it is a weakness incident to it that they should forever imagine the lands further off are still better than those upon which they are already settled.'[4]

Being on the edge of the civilized world encouraged self-reliance. There were too few official jobs to create a large class of placemen on the European model and with it a culture of fawning and dependence. The few placemen who were carted off to staff the colonial Church and administration were such desperate specimens – the people who were too lazy, stupid or marginal to find jobs in Britain's proliferating patronage system – that the system was condemned, as it were, out of its own mouth. With no chance of climbing to the top of the London-based patronage tree and with official positions at home reserved for England's rejects, colonists had nothing but contempt for what Alexander Hamilton referred to as 'ministerial tools and court sycophants'.[5] Americans instead had to rely on their own talents for survival.

British visitors were struck by America's absence of deference. One noted that 'a spirit of Levellism seems to go through the Country'. A second observed that 'an idea of equality seems generally to prevail, and the inferior order of people pay little but external respect to those who occupy superior stations'.[6] A third, commenting on the Quaker city of Philadelphia, noted that 'there is less distinction between the citizens ... than among those of any civilized city in the world. Riches give none. For every man expects one day to be on a footing with his wealthiest neighbour.'[7] Benjamin Franklin, America's leading example of a self-made man, proclaimed that 'a man who makes boast of his ancestors doth but advertise his own insignificance,' and observed, 'Let our fathers and grandfathers be valued for *their* goodness, ourselves for our own.'[8]

This owed much to the spirit of Puritanism, which did more to shape America than any other country – indeed, America wouldn't exist if it were not for the Reformation.[9] Americans exemplified both the Protestant work ethic – you couldn't conquer a vast continent without being perpetually busy – and the Protestant faith in self-reliance. Edmund Burke contrasted the fear and awe that Englishmen felt towards authority with the 'fierce spirit of liberty' among Americans. Americans, he argued, are Protestants of the kind 'which is the most averse to all implicit submission of mind and opinion. All Protestantism, even the most cold and passive, is a sort of dissent,' he went on. 'But the religion most prevalent in our northern colonies is a refinement on the principle of resistance: it is the dissidence of dissent, and the protestantism of the Protestant religion.'[10]

To the Puritan faith in the spiritual elect Americans added the Enlightenment faith in the rule of reason. The French *philosophes* had railed against the aristocracy and the Church; the British (particularly Scottish) philosophers had emphasized the importance of contract rather than status; and the American revolutionaries put both of these Enlightenment currents together and added another one of their own, an instinctive egalitarianism in personal relations. America thus occupied a confused (and confusing) position: as the greatest product of both the European Enlightenment *and* the European Reformation.

Louis Hartz, a historian, famously argued that America was 'born liberal'.[11] It would be truer to say that it was 'born meritocratic'.

SNIFFING TYRANNY ON EVERY TAINTED BREEZE

The American Revolution strongly reinforced this meritocratic mindset. This began with the fighting itself: British officers were all wealthy gentlemen, whereas in the colonial forces rank meant almost nothing.[12] It then extended to constitution-making. New Hampshire's constitution declared that 'no office or place whatsoever in government shall be hereditary'. Towns stopped assigning pews in churches by age and status and, as befits a commercial republic, began auctioning them off to the highest bidder. The allergy to inheritance was so strong that even the God-like George Washington was not immune: when, in 1783, he agreed to join the Society of Cincinnati, a private society of former army officers with hereditary membership, the out-cry was so fierce, with Samuel Adams calling the order 'as rapid a Stride towards an hereditary Military Nobility as was ever made in so short a time', that he quickly withdrew.

Leading Americans explicitly identified their country as a republic of merit. David Ramsay, a South Carolina historian, celebrated the second anniversary of American Independence by defining what he thought was special about the new country. America was a unique nation in history because 'all offices lie open to men of merit, of whatever rank or condition' and 'the reins of state may be held by the son of the poorest man, if possessed of abilities equal to the important position'.[13] 'In monarchies favour is the source of preferment,' he noted, 'but in our new forms of government, no one can command the suffrages of the people, unless by his superior merit and capacity.'[14] Benjamin Rush believed that the new America was characterized by 'natural distinctions as certain and general as the artificial distinctions of men in Europe'.[15]

Foreigners sounded the same theme. Thomas Paine argued that America was governed by merit, and merit alone. Edmund Burke, Paine's great sparring partner, said that Americans were quick to 'sniff tyranny in every tainted breeze'. Richard Price, a British radical Whig, enthused that America would be able to root out all social evils now that social distinctions were based on 'personal merit'. De Crèvecœur insisted that America was a land where effort could get its just reward, in large part because there were no parasites to suck the rewards of honest labour, 'no aristocratic families, no courts, no kings, no bishops, no ecclesiastical dominion, no invisible power giving to the few a very visible one, no great manufactories employing thousands, no great refinement of luxury'.[16]

America was a beacon to the world because it was engaged in a bold experiment: replacing artificial distinctions with natural distinctions. The great pronouncement at the heart of the Declaration of Independence – that 'all men are created equal' – did not mean that all men are created alike and interchangeable, with the same abilities and virtues. It meant that no artificial differences of class and caste should be piled on top of the natural differences of ability and energy. The aim of the Founding Fathers was to create a republic in which a commercial people could enjoy the fruits of the free exercise of their unique talents.[17] The constitution was designed to leave men with the maximum freedom to exercise their talents while at the same time preventing interest groups from plundering minorities. Individual rights were adumbrated. Interest groups were balanced against interest groups in a 'harmonious system of mutual frustration'. 'They have swept away the privileges of some of their fellow creatures which stood in their way,' de Tocqueville noted in 1840, 'but they have opened the door to universal competition.'

There is, of course, one problem with this happy picture: the problem of black Americans in general and slavery in particular. The men who could 'sniff tyranny on every passing breeze' couldn't smell the stench of human bondage. The men who preached that social distinctions should be based on merit and merit only also enslaved up to five million African-Americans and treated non-enslaved blacks as less than citizens. The majority of the Founding Fathers who dominated America for its first fifty years held slaves: while insisting in the Declaration of Independence that 'all men are created equal', Thomas Jefferson owned 135 slaves, which he had inherited along with his 11,000-acre plantation. These 135 slaves, like the vast majority of black Americans, had arrived in America not in order to exercise their God-given abilities but in the holds of slave ships.

This contradiction sometimes nagged at the consciences of the Founding Fathers, but for the most part they remained blind to it – they talked loftily about the Republic of Merit while ignoring the fact that the people who tilled their fields and put food on their tables were denied not just the opportunity to exercise their talents but the basic right of self-ownership. From its foundation, America was two opposites rolled into one: a great experiment in abolishing ancient privileges (such as primogeniture and the inheritance of offices) and a brutal slave-holding society. This chapter focuses on the first of these because it represented a bold new experiment, whereas slave-holding was the continuation of one of the most ancient of human institutions. But the second clearly distorted the first. Americans remain divided about how reparable that distortion is. Is America's ideal of a republic of merit permanently compromised by the sin of slavery? Or can the meritocratic idea be widened to include all Americans? We will return to this theme in later chapters.

THE NATURAL ARISTOCRACY

Thomas Jefferson (1743–1826) was the most vigorous exponent of the theory of a 'natural aristocracy' among the Founders, so vigorous that he often sounded more like a French Jacobin than a Virginian plantation owner. The 'artificial' aristocracy of old Europe was nothing more than a 'confederacy against the happiness of the mass of the people',[18] he insisted, a collection of plunderers, parasites and ne'er-do-wells. 'Dependence begets subservience and venality,' he wrote in 'Notes on the State of Virginia', 'suffocates the germ of virtue and prepares fit tools for the designs of ambition.'[19] The very last letter he wrote, on 24 June 1826, contained his most memorable denunciation of unearned privilege: 'the general spread of the light of science has already laid open to every view the palpable truth, that the mass of mankind has not been born with saddles on their backs, nor a favoured few booted and spurred, ready to ride them legitimately, by the grace of God'.[20]

Yet Jefferson was no Jacobin. The great aim of revolution was not to create equality of condition or the brotherhood of man. It was to replace the tinsel aristocracy of land and titles with the true aristocracy of virtue and ability. He clarified the distinction between the two types of aristocrats in a letter to John Adams on 28 October 1813:

> I agree with you that there is a natural aristocracy among men. The grounds of this are virtue and talents. Formerly, bodily powers gave place among the aristoi [aristocrats]. But since the invention of gunpowder has armed the weak as well as the strong with missile death, bodily strength, like beauty, good humor, politeness, and other accomplishments, has become but an auxiliary ground of distinction. There is also an artificial aristocracy, founded on wealth and birth, without either virtue or talents; for with these it would belong to the first class. The natural aristocracy I consider as the most precious gift of nature, for the instruction, the trusts, and government of society. And indeed, it would have been inconsistent in creation to have formed man for the social state, and not to have provided virtue and wisdom enough to manage the concerns of the society. May we not even say, that that form of government is the best, which provides the most effectually for

a pure selection of these natural aristoi into the offices of government? The artificial aristocracy is a mischievous ingredient in government, and provision should be made to prevent its ascendency . . . I think the best remedy is exactly that provided by all our constitutions, to leave to the citizens the free election and separation of the aristoi from the pseudo-aristoi.[21]

For Jefferson, as for Plato, finding these aristoi and providing them with an education suitable to their abilities was, after defending itself, the state's most important duty. You could not have a natural aristocracy without some approximation of equality of opportunity, he believed; and you could not have equality of opportunity without energetic state action. To put his ideas into practice he turned to his native state of Virginia. Shortly after writing the Declaration of Independence he left the Continental Congress to join the Virginia legislature, and set to work. He pledged to eradicate 'every fibre' of 'ancient and future aristocracy' in order to ensure the future of republican government. This meant getting rid of primogeniture and entail, disestablishing the Church and, above all, creating a great machine for identifying and promoting natural aristocrats. Jefferson envisioned an educational system that would provide all children with the basics of literacy and numeracy and then provide the most able of these children with access to grammar schools, boarding schools and universities. A generous system of scholarships would ensure that 'the best geniuses' rose to the top and that an 'aristocracy of wealth' would have to make room for 'the aristocracy of virtue and talent, which nature has wisely provided for the direction of the interests of society, & scattered with an equal hand through all its conditions'.[22] 'Worth and genius would thus have been sought out from every condition of life, and completely prepared by education for defeating the competition of wealth and birth for public trusts.'[23]

How could you prevent these natural aristocrats from repeating the errors that equally talented people had made over the centuries – putting on boots and spurs just like the people they were replacing and spending their lives riding on the backs of the little people? Jefferson had two answers: education and agrarianism. 'A nation [that] expects to be ignorant and free,' the great man once said, 'expects what never was and never will be.'[24] The generality of mankind needed to be given enough education to allow them to distinguish between real aristocrats and the tinsel variety. They needed to be arbiters of merit rather than passive recipients of wisdom from on high. At the same time, the geniuses needed to be taught the importance of humility by, among other things, studying the mistakes made by past elites, particularly the fall of Rome. The soil provided a second line of defence. Subject people to the discipline of making their living from the soil and they will choose wise rulers, Jefferson argued. Gather people together in a confined space and tempt them with cheap entertainments, on the other hand, and they are much more likely to elect pseudo-aristocrats who know how to bribe and flatter their way to success. Jefferson's republic, just like Plato's, depended on making a sharp distinction between appearance and reality, but Jefferson thought that the people capable of making that distinction were rural gentlemen, rooted in the land, rather than urban philosopher kings, musing on abstractions.

It is impossible to read Jefferson today without wondering how he reconciled his grand sentiments about how people didn't come into the world divided into two types – those with saddles on their backs and those who were booted and spurred to ride them – with the fact that he owned other human beings. This problem is less urgent with the two other great founding meritocrats, John Adams and Alexander Hamilton.

Adams (1735–1826) had more complicated feelings about the natural aristocracy than his friend, rival and successor as president. Complicated and sometimes incomprehensible: his views not only changed as he grew older but could pull him in different directions in the space of a single letter, with the author not so much expounding a theory as arguing with himself.

He started his career as an archetypical meritocrat. The son of a successful but uneducated farmer, he disliked the Boston upper crust of his day – the Quincys, Winslows, Hutchinsons, Chandlers and the rest of them – on the grounds that 'tis vain and mean to esteem oneself for his Ancestors [sic] Merit'.[25] As an undergraduate at Harvard, Adams stood fourteenth in a class of twenty-four, according to the practice of ranking students by social degrees, but in the top three academically. As a lawyer, he had to deal with law officers who owed their position to patronage.[26]

His first publication, *A Dissertation on the Canon and Feudal Law* (1765), denounced 'all that dark ribaldry of heredity, indefeasible right – the Lord's anointed – the divine, miraculous original of Government, with which the priesthood has enveloped the feudal monarch in clouds and mysteries, from which they have deduced the most mischievous of all doctrines, that of passive obedience and non-resistance'.[27]

Adams's speeches at both the first Continental Congress, in 1774, and the Second Congress, in 1775–81, were full of fiery denunciations of 'connection' and demands that people should be appointed according to merit. The revolution would make 'Capacity, Spirit, and Zeal in the Cause supply the Place of Fortune, Family, and every other consideration which used to have weight with Mankind.'[28] When he was serving as American ambassador to France he received a letter, purportedly from George III, that offered to ennoble all America's leading figures if they pledged allegiance to the Crown. Adams recorded his response in his autobiography: 'An aristocracy of American peers! hereditary peers I suppose were meant, but whether hereditary or for Life, nothing could be more abhorrent to the general Sense of America at that time . . .'[29]

Adams also provided one of the clearest explanations of the distinction between *substantive* and *formal* equality that lies at the heart of the meritocratic creed:

> That all men are born to equal rights is true. Every being has a right to his own, as clear, as moral, as sacred, as any other being has. This is as indubitable as a moral government in the universe. But to teach that all men are born with equal powers and faculties, to equal influence in society, to equal property and advantages, through life, is as gross a fraud, as glaring an imposition on the credulity of the people, as ever was practiced by monks, by Druids, by Brahmins, by priests of the immortal Lama, or by the self-styled philosophers of the French Revolution.[30]

Yet Adams was given to agonizing. In a letter to Benjamin Rush in 1809 he explained that hereditary aristocrats might be bulwarks against political vice:

> I believe there is as much in the breed of men as there is in that of horses. I know you will upon reading this cry out: 'Oh, the Aristocrat!

The advocate for hereditary nobility! For monarchy! and every political evil!' But it is no such thing. I am no advocate of any of these things. As long as sense and virtue remain in a nation in sufficient quantities to enable them [*sic*] to choose their legislatures and magistrates, elective governments are the best in the world. But when nonsense and vice get the ascendancy, command the majority, and possess the whole power of a nation, the history of mankind shows that sense and virtue have been compelled to unite with nonsense and vice in establishing hereditary powers as the only security for life, property, and the miserable liberty that remains.[31]

Four years later he made a similar point to Jefferson, clearly agonized by the contradictions in his position: 'I am for excluding legal hereditary distinctions from the United States as long as possible . . . I only say that mankind have not yet discovered any remedy against irresistible corruption in elections to offices of great power and profit, but making them hereditary.' The tinsel aristocracy of the old world was clearly a terrible thing – and yet equally clearly a born-and-bred political class might prove more of a bulwark against corruption than the nouveau riche.

Adams was sceptical about Jefferson's great project for discovering and training natural aristocrats. The last thing these prodigies needed, he insisted, was a helping hand. 'Pick up the first one hundred men you meet and make a republic,' he challenged his friend. 'Every man will have an equal vote. But when deliberations . . . are opened . . . twenty-five, by their talents, virtues being equal, will be able to carry fifty votes. Every one of these twenty-five is an aristocrat in my sense of the word; whether he obtains his one vote in addition to his own by his birth, fortune, figure, eloquence, science, learning, craft, cunning, or even his character for good fellowship.'

On the contrary, these natural aristocrats needed to be restrained to prevent them from taking over the world. Give them their own way, he worried, and 'they will destroy *all equality and liberty, with the consent and acclamations of the people themselves* [italics in the original]'.[32]

Adams picked other holes in Jefferson's arguments too, first agreeing with Jefferson's general thrust, then raising difficult questions about what they actually meant, and in the process foreshadowing worries that were to dominate the discussion of meritocracy from then on, including those advanced by Michael Young in his classic book in 1958 and extending to today's broadsides about the evils of hyper-meritocracy. He agreed with Jefferson about the existence of 'a natural aristocracy among men, the grounds of which are virtue and talents'. Then he agonized about what 'talents' meant. 'Fashion has introduced an indeterminate use of the word "talents",' he argued.[33] Talents might be good qualities, but they might also be morally neutral ones, like beauty, or even downright reprehensible ones, like craft or cunning. He agreed with Jefferson that 'a body of men which contains the greatest collection of virtues and abilities in a free government is the brightest ornament and glory of the nation'. Then he hastened to add that such a collection is only a blessing if 'it be judiciously managed in the con-stitution. But if it is not, it is always the most dangerous; nay, it may be added, it never fails to be the destruction of the commonwealth.'[34] He welcomed the power of education to elevate the republic. But he also warned that intelligence was not synonymous with virtue, as Jefferson sometimes seemed to think. 'Simple intelligence has no essential asso-ciation with morality. What connection is there between the mechanism of a clock or watch and the feeling of moral good and evil, right and wrong? A faculty or a quality of distinguishing between moral good and evil, as well as physical happiness and misery, that is, pleasure and pain, or, in other words, a *conscience* – an old word almost out of fashion – is essential to morality.'[35]

Adams's most pessimistic reflections on the problem of aristocracy occur in a letter he wrote to Rush in 1810. Here he abandoned entirely the distinction between natural aristocrats (good) and artificial aristo-crats (bad) and argued that all aristocracies represent a threat to the republic. 'I can never too often repeat that aristocracy is the monster to be chained,' he said. 'Yet so chained as not be hurt, for he is a most useful and necessary animal in his place. Nothing can be done with-out him . . . Bind aristocracy then with a double cord. Shut him up in a cage. From which, however, he may be let out to do good but never to do mischief.' By a cage Adams meant a second chamber where the aristocrats could be grouped together and counterbalanced by other elements in the constitution. 'The great secret of liberty is to find means to limit [the aristocrats'] power and control their passions. Rome and Britain have done it best.' Where Jefferson had seen an opportunity in the brute fact of human inequality – select natural aristocrats when they are young and train them appropriately and they will take the republic to new heights – Adams saw a threat. You need to imprison these able and ambitious souls in a gilded cage if the republic is to be prevented from falling victim to their ambitions.[36]

Hamilton (1755 or 1757–1804), the Founding Father who came closest to the ideal type of a self-made man, had none of Adams's convoluted doubts. Hamilton was 'the bastard brat of a Scotch ped-lar', in Adams's phrase, born in the West Indies, the home of the slave trade, brought up in a broken home, forced to make his living for a while as a 'grovelling' shop assistant and, throughout his life, sensitive to 'the most humiliating criticism' about his origins. He arrived in America without a penny in his pocket but rose ever upward by dint of talent and determination, becoming an aide-de-camp to General Washington, then a leading Federalist and finally America's first treas-ury secretary. He was surely thinking of himself when he wrote that, for all their horrors, revolutions 'serve to bring to light, talents and virtues, which might otherwise have languished in obscurity, or only shot forth a few scattered and wandering rays'.[37] Or when he wrote in the 'Federalist Papers' (as Publius) that: 'There are strong minds in every walk of life that will rise superior to the disadvantages of situa-tion, and will command the tribute due to their merit, not only from the classes to which they particularly belong, but from the society in general. The door ought to be equally open to all.'[38]

The notion of talent runs like a thread through Hamilton's writ-ings.[39] He justified the pursuit of liberty in part on the grounds that people should be given the freedom they need to develop their talents. He justified his economic policies in part on the grounds that a more diverse economy, with manufacturing as well as agriculture, cities as well as small towns, would provide an outlet for a wider variety of talents. Suppress liberty or narrow the economy and people's talents would be left to moulder into nothing or explode in frustration. Insti-tutionalize liberty and encourage manufacturing and those talents would find creative expression in every area of life from the economic to the political. In 'Federalist 68', in a phrase that it's hard to read today without wincing, he even foresaw the 'constant probability' of the presidency being occupied by 'characters preeminent for ability and virtue'.[40]

Hamilton believed that the main object of economic life was not just to produce goods and services to satisfy people's wants. It was to allow people to achieve the consummate satisfaction that comes from discovering their talents and turning raw abilities into solid achievements. He argued that 'a more ample and various field of enterprise' would do more than increase the wealth of the nation. It would also allow all 'the diversity of talents and dispositions which discriminate men from each other' to blossom into their fullest excellence. 'When all the different kinds of industry obtain in a community,' he wrote, 'each individual can find his proper element, and can call into activity the whole vigour of his nature.'[41] Men are forever producing new ideas to improve productivity, improvements in productivity are forever freeing men to produce more ideas, and so on and so forth in a virtuous circle of talent begetting improvement and improvement begetting new talent and allowing that talent to flourish. 'Hamilton is most remembered for his praise, in Federalist 70, of "energy in the executive",' George Will says in a lapidary phrase. 'His more fundamental and comprehensive objective, however, was energy in *everybody*.'[42]

FROM JACKSON TO LINCOLN

It was only natural that the founding generation dominated the conversation about meritocracy for several decades after the revolution. These were 'men of merit' par excellence – great thinkers, writers and doers – who first defined America as an opportunity society and then dominated all the senior positions in the new society by the sheer force of their talents.[43] Has any other country produced such a talented group of politicians in a single generation? And has any country fallen further, in the space of 200 years, from Alexander Hamilton to Donald Trump? Yet the new republic was too radical a place – too big and rumbustious and individualistic – for the conversation to be closed down for long. As the founding generation aged and the republic expanded westwards, the debate became more many-sided.

Some worried, much as Adams had done in his later years, that the 'natural aristocracy' was little more than a code word for a self-interested clique who wanted to replace British rule with their own rule. The anti-federalists were particularly suspicious of the new elite: though the Founding Fathers were clearly men of merit, they were also susceptible to self-interest and might be tempted to gang up against the less talented majority and turn themselves into a self-perpetuating ruling class. They conjured up two rival American traditions to challenge the idea of a 'natural aristocracy': individualism and egalitarianism. Aedanus Burke summed up this line of thinking early on in his 1783 polemic against the Society of Cincinnati. The society was a 'deeply planned and closely executed conspiracy' against the new republic, he roared, a 'self-created hereditary order' whose members would soon be 'grasping for everything and rising from one usurpation to another'. Melancton Smith, another vocal anti-federalist, made the same point during the ratification of the constitution in New York five years later: the 'men of merit' all lived in each other's pockets and might easily be tempted to form a cabal against the public interest.[44]

The rise of political parties in the early nineteenth century further complicated the argument by introducing the question of party loyalty. The new party machines quickly became patronage machines: willingness to grovel to party bosses replaced willingness to grovel to kings and queens as the road to riches. In his 1835 biography of Martin Van Buren, William Holland urged his readers to forget about the inconvenient fact that the 'men of splendid talents' were all on the Whig side. The only thing that mattered these days was that Van Buren was a Democrat! The spoils system ensured that many civil service jobs were given to party hacks rather than brilliant mandarins. It also put a question mark over every new government appointee: was the new man being given his job because he really deserved it or because the president had cut a deal with him during his election campaign?[45]

Andrew Jackson (1767–1845), president from 1829 to 1837, was at the heart of the transition from patrician to mass politics. He tried hard to forge two rival prejudices into a governing philosophy: belief in a natural aristocracy on the one hand and suspicion of ruling cliques on the other. In particular, he took Jefferson's aristocratic version of meritocracy (elevating a few geniuses) and gave it a democratic twist (establishing a free-for-all in which the best men came to the fore). In doing so he revised the meritocratic idea for a more rumbustious republic.

The Jacksonian age was an age of opportunity. The frontier was rolling westward. Industry was firing up. America was teeming with 'self-made men' (a phrase that was first used by Henry Clay, a senator from Kentucky, in a Senate debate in 1832) and pulsating with a spirit of individualism. Jackson gave voice to a different South from the South of Virginia's landed estates: the South of traders and small businessmen, of family farms and local shopkeepers; a South that celebrated the spunk of self-made men but also despised the pretensions of the Northern establishment.

Jackson teamed up with Van Buren to create a new political party that united northern workers, southern planters and western farmers against the patrician New England elite. He lost his first election to John Adams's son, John Quincy Adams, but four years later turned the tables, portraying Adams as a symbol of privilege – a man who had never worked an honest day in his life and who despised the common people – while presenting himself as a rugged frontiersman, 'not dandled into consequence by lying in the cradle of state, but inured from infancy to the storms and tempests of life'.

His attack on Adams was part of a broader attack on the collection of great north-eastern families who were becoming accustomed to being 'dandled into consequence by laying in the cradle of state'. He wanted to end life tenure and throw all public jobs open to competition. Public office was not a 'species of property' to be doled out to friends and relations, he said; they were public trusts that should be redistributed as frequently as possible. To Adams's complaint that ending life tenure of public appointments would reduce government to 'a perpetual and unremitting scramble for office', he replied, in effect, bring it on. It was 'rotation of office' that perpetuated American liberty.[46] And it was the scramble for office, however unseemly it might appear, that guaranteed the rule of 'men of intelligence'.

Jackson wanted to extend open competition far and wide. Corporate charters should be given to any businessmen who wanted to create a company rather than be doled out as political favours. The franchise should be as open as possible rather than encumbered with restrictions. The selection of presidential candidates should be handed to party conventions rather than closed caucuses.

For all their anti-elitism, Jackson and his supporters shared Jefferson's belief that men differed widely in their natural abilities. 'Distinction in society will always exist under every just government. Equality of talents, of education, or of wealth cannot be produced by human institutions. In the full enjoyment of the gifts of Heaven and the fruits of superior industry, economy and virtue, every man is equally entitled to protection by law.'[47] Theodore Sedgwick Jr expressed the creed well in 1836: 'Each man should have perfect freedom, unrestrained by monopoly and unjust privilege, to exert his talents and to rise to any height he can.'[48]

The great aim of government was to release human energies while making sure that the successful did not reinforce their positions with artificial privileges and thereby transmit them down the generations:

> when the laws undertake to add to these natural and just advantages artificial distinctions, to grant titles, gratuities, and exclusive privileges, to make the rich richer and the potent more powerful, the humble members of society – the farmers, mechanics, and laborers – who have neither the time nor the means of securing like favours to themselves, have a right to complain of the injustice of their government. There are no necessary evils in Government. Its evils exist only in its abuses. If it would confine itself to equal protection, and, as Heaven does its rains, shower its favors alike on the high and the low, the rich and the poor, it would be an unqualified blessing.[49]

There were blemishes in this vision: not just the Jacksonians' indifference to African-Americans and Native Americans but also their tolerance of political corruption in the form of lobbying and job-buying. Jackson persuaded himself that he earned every success on the basis of unvarnished merit, despite the fact that he was always looking for patronage and preferment. And Jacksonians persuaded themselves that corruption was simply a price for doing business – 'that governments have corruption and inefficiency the way picnics have ants'.[50]

This Jacksonian vision chimed with the idea that economic success is the best measure of individual merit: an idea that had been obscured for a while by Jefferson's agricultural vision of natural aristocracy but which was arguably the default creed of a commercial republic. America was a country of self-made men – 'than which there can be no better in any state of society', as Calvin Cotton said – and the currency of self-made men was money. Horatio Alger's stories of men who had risen by dint of hard work sold in their millions. William Lloyd Garrison, a radical journalist, pronounced that 'the industrious artisan, in a government like ours, will always be held in better estimation than the wealthy idler'.[51] William Gouge, a leading Jacksonian Democrat, argued that 'wealth alone can give permanent distinction' because 'he who is at the top of the political ladder today may be at the bottom tomorrow'. Freeman Hunt, the editor of *Hunt's Merchants' Magazine*, argued that wealth was the most important source of social distinction. 'Aristocracies of talent, education, and refinement' might flourish in irrelevant corners of American life but 'in society at large, graduations of social position are measured by stock certificates, rent rolls, a bank account'.[52]

Mid-century America also saw a fashion for biographical directories of local grandees such as Moses Yale Beach's *Wealth and Biography of the Wealthy Citizens of New York City*, which listed people according to their wealth and made an explicit link between wealth (particularly self-made wealth) and merit. In earlier ages, great men displayed their talents in war and conquest, Beach argued; in modern America, they displayed them in counting houses. These directories of wealth repeatedly celebrated the fact that anybody could make it into one of their pages. 'The laborer of today is the capitalist of tomorrow,' one Massachusetts businessman told a society of mechanics. 'Every man stands on his own merits . . . The fact that he may become a capitalist, is a spur to exertion to the very newsboy in our streets.'[53]

The most acute analysis of Jacksonian America was provided by Alexis de Tocqueville, whose visit there in 1831 coincided with the flowering of Jacksonianism. De Tocqueville saw America as a laboratory of a new sort of society where everybody was on the move, both geographically and socially. 'The first thing that strikes one in the United States is the innumerable multitude of those who seek to emerge from their original condition,' he wrote in one passage.[54] 'Every American is eaten up with longing to rise,' he wrote in another.[55]

We have noted that there was one ghastly exception to this new society: the slave-holding South. 'Exception' is perhaps too weak a word for it. Slavery mocked the very principles of equality and opportunity that America was built on and created a national house that was divided against itself. 'If ever America undergoes great revolutions, they will be brought about by the presence of the black race on the soil of the United States,' de Tocqueville predicted. 'They will owe their origin, not to the equality, but to the inequality of conditions.'[56] Slavery was more than just an overhang from a pre-industrial past: as the Industrial Revolution advanced in the north and across Europe, human bondage was entrenched and extended and enslaved African-Americans were turned into cogs in a vast global cotton economy.[57]

The man who presided over the destruction of slavery, Abraham Lincoln, was a quintessential Yankee: a product of the 'Valley of Democracy', the fresh territory north and west of the Ohio River; a self-made man who liked to play up his obscure origins ('I don't know who my grandfather was,' he once said, 'and I am much more concerned to know what his grandson will be'); an inveterate inventor and tinkerer who lodged a model for a submarine in the US Patent Office; a firm believer in a mobile, opportunity society.

Lincoln saw America as a country in which 'the prudent, penniless beginner in the world, labours for wages awhile, saves a surplus with which to buy tools or land for himself, then labours on his own account another while and at length hires another new beginner to help him.'[58] 'There is no such thing as a freeman being fatally fixed for life in the condition of a hired labourer,' he insisted; and in order to give substance to his vision he supported a range of active government policies such as establishing land-grant universities, giving plots of land to settlers, encouraging railroads to build speculative branches in the west, investing in agricultural research. He believed with every fibre of his being that the constitution was a colour-blind as well as a sacred document. To Stephen Douglas's declaration, during the Lincoln–Douglas debates in 1858, that 'this government was made by our fathers on the white basis. It was made by white men for the benefit of white men and their posterity forever,' he delivered an emphatic rebuttal: 'There is no reason in the world why the Negro is not entitled to all the natural rights enumerated in the Declaration of

Independence, the right to life, liberty and the pursuit of happiness. I hold that he is as much entitled to these as the white man.'[59]

The emancipation of the slaves was an attempt to extend Lincoln's vision of equality of opportunity to all Americans, regardless of race. The emancipation was a success in one way: the alternative vision of American society embodied in the feudal South of the plantations was marginalized and equality before the law was treated as the country's only legitimate ideology. It was a failure in another. Southerners continued to mock equality of opportunity with Jim Crow laws. Economic inequalities rooted in slavery continued to shape the lives of millions of black Americans. The quest to provide substance to Lincoln's vision of an opportunity society continues to this day.

THE RISE OF THE 1 PER CENT

The second half of the nineteenth century saw the birth of a very different America from the egalitarian America of the Jacksonian era. Railroads knitted together isolated hamlets. Rural labourers flooded into the towns. Immigrants flowed into New York and from there across the country. The robber barons created business empires on a scale that had never been seen before, crushing competitors underfoot, employing vast armies of workers and, as a result, reducing the equality of condition that de Tocqueville had celebrated into nothing more than a memory, and thereby confirming the most pessimistic predictions in the more pessimistic second half of *Democracy in America*.[60]

The robber barons who created this new America were embodiments of the meritocratic spirit, self-made men who rose to heights unparalleled before, at least in the private sector. John D. Rockefeller was the son of a snake-oil salesman and bigamist. Andrew Carnegie was an immigrant whose father suffered from long periods of unemployment and who began his career as a telegraph messenger. Edward Henry Harriman liked to say that 'my capital when I began was a pencil and this', tapping his head.[61]

And yet equality of opportunity can sometimes become self-defeating: these apostles of meritocracy were so successful at building business empires from nothing that they eventually became a challenge to America's meritocratic spirit. Henry George complained that 'Capital is piled on capital to the exclusion of men of lesser means and the utter prostration of personal independence and enterprise on the part of the less successful masses.'[62] He might have added that this combination of concentration and displacement was giving America a worryingly 'European' feel. As they grew older the robber barons aped the manners of the Anglophile East Coast elite, competing to get themselves admitted into the *Social Register* (first issued in 1888), joining gentlemen's clubs and country clubs (and, in once-egalitarian Philadelphia, cricket clubs) and sending their children to exclusive schools and universities.

These elite schools and universities prided themselves on their ability to turn the children of billionaires into public-spirited citizens, relying on the English alchemy of daily worship, competitive sports and classical education. The Ivy League universities also continued to admit scholarship boys: in 1900, the year that Franklin Delano Roosevelt went up to Harvard, the position of top feeder school was occupied not by Groton or St Paul's (eighteen students) but by Boston Latin (thirty-eight students).[63] But they were also corrupted by the plutocratic times. The children of privilege increasingly set the tone. Francis Landey Patton, the president of Princeton, boasted that his university was 'the finest country club in America'. The Yale Class of 1905 invented the following ditty. 'Never since the Heavenly Host with all the Titans fought/Saw they a class whose scholarship/Approached so close to naught.' Too often the spirit of the Ivy League was defined by exclusive clubs where the children of the elite made friends for life: the Skull and Bones at Yale, the Hasty Pudding at Harvard and the 'breathlessly aristocratic' Ivy at Princeton, which took in only eleven men a year, one fewer than Jesus Christ.

The threat from the 1 per cent was not confined to the plutocrats: the Jacksonians were right that old families were always in danger of turning into ruling dynasties. The Boston Brahmins were America's version of Britain's intellectual aristocracy: a group of about forty families who relied on the power of their intellects rather than their landholdings (the big difference was that America's intellectual aristocracy was descended from successful businesspeople). They had a commendable history of building educational institutions and opening up opportunities. Harvard University was the Brahmins' proudest creation: for much of the university's history Brahmins dominated the university's governing body, the Harvard Corporation, and provided some of its most distinguished scholars.

But even more than Britain's intellectual aristocrats the Brahmins suffered from the classic problems of introversion and self-interest. They interbred enthusiastically (marrying cousins was a good way of preserving capital in a country that had abolished primogeniture) and identified merit with their own narrow clique. Oliver Wendell Holmes – the man who invented the term 'Boston Brahmins' – admitted as much in his memoir, *The Autocrat of the Breakfast-Table* (1858): 'No, my friends, I go (always other things being equal) for the man who inherits family traditions and the cumulative humanities of at least four or five generations.'[64] They gave people with the right names the benefit of the doubt. When William James presented himself for his examination for his medical degree he was decidedly nervous because he had been abroad for most of his course. But things went surprisingly well. 'The doctor asked the candidate a single question, and when William answered correctly, Holmes . . . said: 'that's enough! If you know *that*, you must know everything. Now tell me – how is your dear old father?'[65] James was a genius, but a similar willingness to give Brahmins the benefit of the doubt cannot always have turned out so well.

Another challenge to the meritocratic idea came from the other end of the intellectual spectrum: the great political machines that dominated America's democratic politics by trading votes for offices. The men who created these machines were the political equivalent of robber barons: self-made men who amassed power (and sometimes money) by a clever business innovation, fusing ethnic patronage with identity politics. They thereby created a cancer at the heart of the American state, ensuring that the parties spent more time on divvying up the spoils of minor office than on addressing social problems.[66] Routine offices were filled with incompetents (the satirist Artemus Ward quipped that the Union Army's retreat after the Battle of Bull Run was caused by a rumour of three vacancies at the New York Custom House). Basic functions were left undone (one investigator, charged with studying government efficiency in New York, found hundreds of sacks of long-neglected mail, including one package clearly addressed to the vice-president, stacked in the corner of the post office). The cancer kept growing: the more people expected offices in return for their votes, the more offices were created in order to buy votes. America had invented a democratic version of the eighteenth-century English patronage system that the revolution was supposed to have ended.

THE RISE OF THE REST

Many of these challenges to the meritocratic idea are familiar today: the consolidation of vast fortunes at the top of society; the growing distance between the professional classes and the masses; and the corruption of politics through money and ethnic voting. Yet Gilded Age America not only preserved its faith in the great trilogy of equality, opportunity and mobility. It pioneered a wide-ranging set of reforms that updated these ideals for new times. Frederick Jackson Turner concluded his classic essay on the closing of the American frontier, which argued that the country's great westward expansion had reached its limits, by warning that it would be 'a rash prophet who would assert that the expansive character of American life has now entirely ceased'. The same could be said of these new impediments to the meritocratic spirit.

Political reformers identified the robber barons as threats to both equality of opportunity and dispersed power. Teddy Roosevelt repeatedly warned of the danger of a new American aristocracy (though it was difficult to discover, from his sprawling rhetoric, whether the threat came from the aristocracy's ability to perpetuate itself from generation to generation or from its progressive enfeeblement by inherited wealth). His solution to the twin threat of dynasty and decadence was to introduce taxes, on both income and inheritance, that would progressively break up great concentrations of wealth and force the ruling classes to rely on their own abilities.

At the same time, the robber barons succeeded in imposing discipline on themselves. They gave away large amounts of wealth, often choosing merit-promoting institutions such as public libraries (Carnegie) and universities (Rockefeller as well as many others). They sent their children to schools that treated them to cold showers, team sports and long sermons. Teddy Roosevelt summed up the new ethic of responsibility when he told Groton students that 'much has been given you. Therefore we have a right to expect much from you.'

The robber barons' biggest contribution to promoting meritocracy was the great American corporation itself: the larger companies became, the more they had to rely on hired hands to do their day-to-day work. The result was the creation of a new class of men – professional managers who measured their lives in terms of their progression up the organizational hierarchy but who owed their service not to the state, like earlier generations of bureaucrats, but to the private sector. America created new institutions to provide these new managers with professional training: the University of Pennsylvania added the Wharton School in 1881 and Harvard the Harvard Business School in 1908. It redesigned its cities to provide them with skyscrapers to work in such as the Metropolitan Life Insurance Building (1928), which was then trumped in its turn by the Empire State Building (1931). Every robber baron's death and every new share issue transferred more power to the professional elite.

The progressive wing of the Boston Brahmins recognized the danger of degenerating into a caste. As president of Harvard, Charles Eliot set himself the task of updating the Founders' ideal of a 'natural aristocracy' for a more democratic and utilitarian age:[67] for example, he introduced professional schools into Harvard in order to make sure that the new professions were dominated by Harvard men but also insisted that these professional schools would provide a broad, liberal education rather than a narrow, technical one. Felix Frankfurter, a Jewish refugee who fled to the United States from Vienna in 1894 aged twelve, confessed that 'I have a quasi-religious feeling about Harvard Law School ... I regard it as the most democratic institution I know anything about.' Dean Acheson, who came from America's top drawer, said that it was only at Harvard Law School that he realized that 'excellence counted – a sloppy try wasn't enough'.[68]

Other captains of learning, including Columbia's Nicholas Murray

Butler, Princeton's Woodrow Wilson, Cornell's Andrew Dickson White and Johns Hopkins's Daniel Gilman, grappled with the same problem of recalibrating America's capacity-catching machine for a more democratic and certificate-obsessed age. Gilman modelled Johns Hopkins on Germany's research university rather than Oxbridge. He wanted to recruit and promote his professors 'on the basis of merit' and drill a hole into society in order to discover 'unusual talent'. For all his reprehensible views on race, Woodrow Wilson waged war on Princeton's culture of social snobbery, embodied in its dining clubs, and intellectual mediocrity, embodied in the cult of the gentleman's 'C'. Undergraduate 'side-shows' – fraternities, secret societies and sports clubs – had 'swallowed up the circus' and reduced those who performed in the main tent to whistling for their audience's amusement, 'discouraged and humiliated'.[69]

While these 'captains of learning' tried to extend the ladder of opportunity downwards, enterprising headmasters tried to extend it upwards. America's big cities created a cadre of highly selective elite schools modelled on the Boston Latin School (founded 1635) but usually more focused on modern subjects. San Francisco's Lowell High School was founded in 1856. Worcester, Massachusetts, opened a citywide secondary programme for children with advanced intellectual abilities in 1901. Cincinnati's Walnut Hills became selective in 1919. The biggest concentration of these schools was in New York City: Stuyvesant on Manhattan's Lower East Side, Brooklyn Tech in Fort Greene, Townsend Harris Hall on the campus of the City College of New York, and Bronx Science in the north-west Bronx.

These schools were hardly lavishly funded: Stuyvesant was obliged to introduce 'double sessions' in 1919 to cope with the surging demand, with one school taking place in the morning and the other in the afternoon. They were so successful because they took pupils of similar academic abilities and stretched them to the full. The Bronx Science School produced five Nobel Prize winners in its first five years of existence. One of the school's first graduates, Roy Glauber, went directly to work on the Manhattan Project, without an intervening spell at college. Townsend Harris routinely condensed four years of high school into three, after which its students automatically gained admission to City College.

An equally inspiring example of the meritocratic idea in practice was provided by the self-improvement movement that developed among African-Americans at the turn of the century. We have seen how leading Americans from the Founding Fathers onwards excluded black people from their 'meritocratic republic'. This exclusion inevitably had psychological as well as economic consequences: slavery and Jim Crow helped to destroy African-Americans' sense of agency and, to some extent, self-worth. The self-help movement tried to restore that sense of agency both on an individual and a collective level. The central figure in this was W. E. B. Du Bois (1886–1963), one of the founding members of the NAACP and one of black America's most prolific authors. The central idea was the notion of the 'talented tenth', an idea that was invented by northern white philanthropists who wanted to create a cadre of black teachers, but popularized by Du Bois.[70]

Du Bois believed that the only way for African-Americans to claim their rightful place in American life was through self-education (he himself was the first African-American to gain a Ph.D. from Harvard). He pioneered large-scale social surveys, interviewing more than 5,000 people for his study *The Philadelphia Negro*, and held a chair in history, sociology and economics at Atlanta University. Education would not only give African-Americans the self-respect that came from improving their minds and toughening their characters, but also allow them to embrace their cultural heritage as proud *African-Americans* rather than just as mistreated Americans. In one memorable passage he said that African-Americans didn't want to have to 'bleach [their] Negro blood in a flood of white Americanism'. They wanted to make it possible for people to be both Negroes and Americans without being 'cursed and spit upon' or 'losing the opportunity of self-development'.[71] The most talented were vital to this process of collective renewal.

'The Talented Tenth', his great 1903 essay, began with a resounding declaration: 'The Negro race, like all races, is going to be saved by its exceptional men. The problem of education, then, among Negroes must first of all deal with the Talented Tenth; it is the problem of developing the Best of this race that they may guide the Mass away from the contamination and death of the Worst, in their own and other races.' Black America should bend every sinew to discover the one in ten African-Americans who had the capacity to become leaders through the power of their minds and the force of their characters. And when it has found them it should make sure that they receive a classical liberal education rather than a narrow vocational one. Du Bois's insistence on the importance of a classical education led to a furious argument with another exponent of self-help, Booker T. Washington. Unlike Washington, he believed that the most important aim of education was not to produce a labour aristocracy that could pile up riches. It was to produce a black intellectual aristocracy that could act as a leadership class – not just leading their fellow blacks in political agitation, though Du Bois put more emphasis on this as he grew older, but also providing broader intellectual leadership. Important in all communities, he argued, the leadership class is particularly important in black America because slavery had robbed black Americans of their best traditions and cast them on to the new continent rootless and alienated. He had no qualms about the idea that reform needed to be not just top down but paternalistic:

> Can the masses of the Negro people be in any possible way more quickly raised than by the effort and example of this aristocracy of talent and character? Was there ever a nation on God's fair earth civilized from the bottom upward? Never; it is, ever was and ever will be from the top downward that culture filters. The Talented Tenth rises and pulls all that are worth the saving up to their vantage ground. This is the history of human progress.

While some progressives were scouring America's minority populations for talent, others were busy dismantling the spoils system. The fight against corruption mobilized thousands, if not millions, of Americans into a reforming crusade that united the old patrician elite with the new professional class and the progressive wing of the Democratic Party with the reforming wing of the Republicans.[72] America's democratic version of Old Corruption suffered a severe blow on 2 July 1881, when a disappointed office-seeker, Charles Guiteau, who thought he should have been appointed consul to France, fatally shot the president, Andrew Garfield, in the waiting room of Washington, DC, railroad station. The Pendleton Act of 1883 established a Civil Service Commission, abolished political tests, ended the requirement that office-holders should hand over a proportion of their salaries to the parties that appointed them, and introduced examinations to test basic competence. The proportion of jobs that were formally governed by what was called the merit system rose from 10.5 per cent in 1883 to 75 per cent in 1930.[73]

The self-styled 'Best Men', who promoted the Pendleton reforms, argued that meritocracy was even more important in an era of assertive nation states than it had been before. In 'The Study of Administration' (1883), Woodrow Wilson called for 'a science of administration which shall seek to straighten the paths of government, to make its business less unbusiness-like, to strengthen and purify its organisation and to crown its duties with dutifulness'.[74] He condemned the old order in phrases reminiscent of William Cobbett's description of Bastards in High Places: 'the poisonous atmosphere of city government, the crooked secrets of state administration, the confusion, sinecures, and corruption ever and again discovered in the bureaux at Washington ...' In his view, America devoted too much effort to limiting government and not enough to energizing it – that is, to making it 'facile, well-ordered and effective'.[75]

Wilson's fellow progressives became more insistent in their demands for a meritocratic administrative elite as time went by. Herbert Croly, who sprang to fame with the publication of *The Promise of American Life* in 1909 (perhaps 'the twentieth century's most influential book on American politics', according to George Will) and co-founded the *New Republic* in 1914 to keep his message alive, proposed the re-creation of Plato's guardian class in the form of councils of experts in law or finance who could 'assist' state governors in drafting laws.[76] Walter Lippmann, an even more famous journalist, suggested that the government should create ten bureaus of intelligence, one for each Cabinet department, which would house a team of intellectuals, appointed for life and provided with regular sabbaticals, whose job it was to gather all the relevant facts relating to the department and explain them to the masses.[77] In the 1930s the intellectuals who flooded into Washington, DC, to help FDR craft the New Deal loved the idea of handing more power to fellow intellectuals who were rigorously chosen by open examinations and allowed to operate at the heart of government regardless of the result of democratic elections.

This highly elitist version of meritocracy was nevertheless kept in check by America's suspicion of centralized power and hoity-toity government officials. Max Weber wrote that, during his American tour in 1904, somebody told him that Americans prefer 'having people in office we can spit upon, rather than a caste of officials who spit upon us, as is the case with you'.[78] This spirit survived progressivism and the New Deal. The Pendleton Act's promoters made a point of arguing that it would not create an 'office-holding aristocracy' because the Act would apply only to lower-level jobs, and use only minimum tests of competence rather than competitive examinations designed to identify the intellectual elite.[79] The purpose of the legislation was to limit party patronage to high policy-makers, rather than to eliminate it entirely, and the reforms hardly scratched the surface of a country that was largely dominated by political machines. Herbert Croly's critics coined the phrase 'Crolier than thou' to mock his elitism.[80]

America's Jacksonian aversion to the elitist view of meritocracy was reinforced by its faith in the bottom-up version of the creed. In Europe, the meritocratic creed was a critique of the old ruling class; in America, it was an appeal to reclaim the founding traditions of the United States from later corruption. In Europe, your position in the status hierarchy was judged on a single linear scale; in America, there were lots of different hierarchies – or, as Suzanne Keller, a Vienna-born sociologist, put it, society was a pack of cards with an ace in each suit. America was honeycombed with educational institutions for every group: Catholic colleges for Catholics, Evangelical colleges for Evangelicals, public universities for the great unwashed. 'Jewish' banks such as Lehman Brothers provided ambitious Jews with the best revenge possible on white-shoe companies like Brown Brothers Harriman that refused to give them jobs – a chance of defeating them. Even in the Gilded Age the American business elite was always different from the European aristocracy: the hallmark of the business elite was not nobility but mobility, and not caste but achievement.

PART FOUR

The March of the Meritocrats

I I

The Measurement of Merit

The years between the two world wars saw perhaps the most remarkable development in the history of the meritocratic idea: the rise of a group of psychologists who claimed to have developed both a scientific theory of merit and a technology for measuring it and who had a transformative influence on public policy. These psychologists were responsible for three big innovations in thinking about meritocracy.

Previous thinkers on the subject had regarded intelligence as one quality among many, such as courage or character: Jefferson and Napoleon talked about 'virtues and talents', for example. The psychologists identified 'merit' with 'mental ability', 'mental ability' with 'intelligence' and, in the case of the most influential group among them, 'intelligence' with a single quality, 'general ability' or 'g'. The great apostles of self-help such as Samuel Smiles looked to individual effort to explain 'merit': successful people owed their success to their ability to work hard and master their impulses. The psychologists placed 'intelligence', and hence merit, firmly in the natural world: people with average natural ability couldn't become geniuses, however hard they worked. Most ambitiously of all, the psychologists claimed to have developed the equivalent of Galileo's telescope: a device for identifying and measuring this invaluable natural ability – the IQ test.

These bold attempts to reinterpret merit as inborn intelligence and to measure innate intelligence with IQ tests encountered fierce opposition. For the arguments were not only breathtakingly bold, they also had revolutionary practical implications for everything from education to the military. Pedagogical conservatives fought intelligence tests on the grounds that they weren't as good at spotting academic merit as traditional examinations. Pedagogical radicals argued that the new breed of psychologists underestimated the power of education to develop ability and unleash talent. All sorts of people objected to the hubris of the testing movement. 'One does not allow the first person who comes along on the pretext that he is a psychologist, to decide in a few minutes whether one is or is not an acceptable sample of humanity,' Albert Challand, a French psychologist, said, 'and to settle definitively the possibilities that one might have for success in one's career.'[1]

Walter Lippmann, the doyen of American columnists, mounted a formidable attack on the new science in a series of articles in the *New Republic* in 1922 that foreshadowed almost all the later criticisms of IQ testing. The concept of intelligence is frustratingly vague, he argued; IQ tests are shoddy measuring sticks; there is no evidence they measure a fixed trait; and 'intelligence', whatever that might be, is only loosely correlated with success in life. He warned that 'if intelligence testing ever really caught on, the people in charge of it would occupy a position of power which no intellectual had held since the collapse of theocracy'.[2] 'I hate the impudence of a claim that in fifty minutes you can judge and classify a human being's predestined fitness in life,' he wrote in a later article in the *Century Magazine*, echoing Challand. 'I hate the pretentiousness of that claim. I hate the abuse of scientific method which it involves. I hate the sense of superiority which it imposes.'[3]

The psychometrists retaliated with a war of propaganda and position: *propaganda* in the sense that they never missed an opportunity to make the case for their new science in the public presses and *position* in the sense that they got themselves appointed to powerful jobs in government, particularly in education departments. They evangelized in favour of the new tests on the grounds that they possessed the power to reveal what was going on inside children's heads. Teachers would be empowered to predict children's future progress. Examiners would be able to replace rule-of-thumb with exact measuring devices. Society would be able to discover geniuses who had previously withered in obscurity. Doctors would be able to identify backward children more humanely. They persuaded a wide range of policy-makers from ministers of education to heads of schools to take their work seriously and, in particular, to use IQ tests to solve the perennial problems of selection, classification and streaming.

FROM MEASURING HEADS TO TESTING IQ

The earliest testers believed that there was a direct relationship between the size and shape of the head and the quantity, quality and variety of intelligence that it contained. Johann Caspar Lavater, a Swiss Protestant minister, argued that you could assess people's mental powers by reading the physiognomy of their faces. Franz Joseph Gall shifted the focus from the physiognomy of the face to the shape of the skull, launching a new discipline which he called 'cranioscopy', and his disciple Johann Caspar Spurzheim redubbed phrenology. Gall argued that different mental faculties such as sensory and moral powers (there were twenty-seven in all) were lodged in different regions of the brain and that you could discover the strength of these faculties by feeling for bumps on the head. Paul Broca, the most celebrated brain anatomist of the nineteenth century, argued that there was a direct relation between the size of the brain and the quantity of intelligence it contained: the brain was generally larger 'in men than in women, in eminent men than in men of mediocre talent, in superior races than in inferior races'.[4]

There is much that is repugnant about these early testers. Their passion for collecting skulls and brains makes them look like deranged proto-Nazis. Samuel Morton collected 6,000 skulls in an attempt to prove two completely crazy theories: that different races could be classified into a hierarchy in terms of their abilities, and that these races had completely independent origins. Gall amassed a collection of skulls and 'brain castes' of 103 notable men, 69 criminals, 67 mental patients, 25 pathological cases and 25 'exotics' (non-Europeans).[5] Broca went further, collecting 7,000 brains and skulls and founding the wonderfully named Society of Mutual Autopsy, in which eminent Frenchmen pledged to leave their heads to science.[6] Indeed, the passion for collecting the skulls of eminent men was so widespread that those of Joseph Haydn, Francisco Goya and Emanuel Swedenborg all ended up in skull collections, and Beethoven's skull was divided into hundreds of squabbled-over pieces.[7]

Moreover, the quest to measure intelligence through head size went nowhere. Reviewing the literature on the subject in 1885, Adolphe Bloch, an anthropologist, came to a devastating conclusion: 'There is no absolute relation between intelligence and the volume of the cranium, because some very intelligent individuals can have a small skull, while very ordinary individuals can have a very large skull. That is known. From another side, in certain races, said to be of little intelligence, one can find a skull or cranial capacity of a relatively considerable size.'[8]

Even at the time, debates about 'large-brained criminals' and 'small-brained men of eminence' raised eyebrows, if not sniggers.[9] Sceptics made merry with questions such as why whales, those leviathans of the deep, were not 'beasts of genius', given their gigantic heads. Broca's followers were embarrassed to discover that Broca's brain weighed in at just 1,424 grams, only slightly above average.

Yet the early stages of any new science can look odd from the lofty heights of modernity: Newton's thinking about the cosmos was tied up with his thinking about alchemy and religion. For all the horrors of some of their thinking, these early phrenologists and craniometrists championed the natural explanation of supposedly spiritual phenomena (Gall was expelled from Vienna by the Roman Catholic Church in 1805 for 'materialism'). They advanced the idea that, far from being bizarre freaks, 'geniuses' and 'idiots' are part of a continuous series of variations.

Alfred Binet (1857–1911) was the first psychologist to come up with a modern intelligence test. In the 1890s, Binet made a name for himself by advocating a new style of psychology, one that was intended to go beyond 'vague notions of man in general' and focused instead on 'precise observations of individuals considered in all the complexity and variety of their aptitudes'.[10] To this end, he produced detailed and fascinating case studies: case studies of intellectual prodigies such as Jacques Inaudi, who was known across Europe for his extraordinary feats of mental calculation, and a portrait of the mental development of his own two daughters, 'L'Étude expérimentale de l'intelligence' (1903). He also experimented with tests of reasoning. In

1904 the Minister of Public Education asked him to devise a reliable means to assess students suffering from mental disabilities, so-called *anormaux*. Working with his assistant, Théodore Simon, he came up with the idea of assigning an age level to a variety of simple intellectual operations, determined by the earliest age at which the average child could complete the task, and ranked children both against their peers and against a normal development curve.[11]

The Binet–Simon test caught on rapidly. It was applied to the rest of the child population, not just subnormal children, and was taken up across Europe and America.[12] William Stern, a German psychologist, invented the notion of intelligence quotients by dividing mental age by chronological age and then multiplying by a hundred to get rid of the decimals. Lewis Terman revised the tests for an American audience, the Stanford–Binet tests, in 1916, and popularized the idea that IQ is a single, fixed quantity that can be measured and expressed in terms of a single number. A testing device that had been invented to provide a way of peering into the minds of educationally disadvantaged children was quickly transformed into a technology for measuring large populations of children (or adults) and ranking them on a single linear scale.

FRANCIS GALTON AND THE STUDY OF INDIVIDUAL DIFFERENCES

The reason why IQ testing became so influential so quickly is that Francis Galton (1822–1911) and his followers had laid the intellectual foundations for an ambitious theory of individual differences over the previous half-century. This theory offered answers to the most urgent questions raised by IQ testing, and indeed mass educational testing in general: How can we tell the difference between people who are merely well taught and those who possess real talent? How do we know if mental tests are merely rewarding the privileged or creating real opportunities for the talented? How is natural ability distributed in the population?

Galton was an archetypical Victorian gentleman-intellectual: he never held a proper job as a scientist but nevertheless made important contributions to statistics, human geography and the study of inheritance.[13] He invented fingerprinting, for example, and coined enduring phrases such as 'nature versus nurture'. He turned to the study of inheritance late in life, after he had established his reputation as an explorer, but, once he had hit upon the subject, he worked upon it with obsessive energy until his death in 1911.

Part of the explanation for his energy is intellectual: the publication of *On the Origin of Species* in 1859 by Galton's cousin Charles Darwin put the subject of inheritance at the heart of Victorian science. Part of the explanation was psychological: his older sister repeatedly told him how precocious he was, he entered Trinity College, Cambridge, with the expectation that he would join the ranks of the Wranglers, perhaps even as a Senior Wrangler, but then cracked under the pressure, suffered a nervous breakdown and left without a degree. This shattering experience had the odd result of persuading Francis not to reject examinations as a lottery but instead to study them compulsively as the ideal way of proving people's mental worth. And part lies in pure snobbery: he loved to trace the manner in which abilities ran in families like his own and to speculate how much better the world would be if only these families would produce more children.[14]

Galton's methods were deficient by the standards of modern science. He defined his key term, 'natural ability', vaguely, as a mixture of intellect and character, and used it interchangeably with the even vaguer term 'civic worth'. He gleaned evidence of 'natural ability' from studying biographical data on hundreds of eminent Britons and foreigners. The result was often a circular argument: people's achievements were proof of their 'natural ability' and 'natural ability' was the explanation for their achievements.[15] His arguments were also warped by his passion for eugenics. In 1865, this childless university failure proposed a scheme for radical social reform: the most talented men and women would be selected by examination, married in a great ceremony in Westminster Abbey in the presence of the Queen, and then given a prize of £5,000 to start their lives as prodigious breeders.

Galton nevertheless used these rough-and-ready methods to produce some influential ideas. One was that abilities are distributed in the population according to a normal distribution curve: geniuses, whom he regarded as the engines of civilizational progress, are simply the far end of a normal curve and crop up roughly in a ratio of 1:4,000. The second was that ability was inherited rather than acquired. Galton had no time for the idea that ability is just a matter of working hard, a view endorsed by both philosophers such as John Stuart Mill and moralists such as Samuel Smiles:

> I have no patience with the hypothesis occasionally expressed, and often implied, especially in tales written to teach children to be good, that babies are born pretty much alike, and that the sole agencies in creating differences between boy and boy, and man and man, are steady application and moral effort ... The experiences of the nursery, the school, the University, and of professional careers, are a chain of proofs to the contrary.[16]

The range of mental powers between the cleverest and the dullest was enormous, he argued, 'reaching from one knows not what height, and descending to one can hardly say what depth', and no amount of social engineering could change this adamantine fact.[17]

Galton devoted most of his life to fleshing out these ideas. In *Hereditary Genius* (1869), he analysed the pedigrees of 977 eminent members of the English establishment, distributed among 300 families. This persuaded him that 'characteristics cling to families' and ability goes 'by descent'.[18] In the 1870s, he studied generations of sweet peas in order to understand the process of descent more clearly.[19] In 1884, he established an anthropometric laboratory at the Science Museum in South Kensington and set about measuring some 9,000 people, including both parents and children, for a variety of physical characteristics.[20] He published his results, duly processed by his pet statistical techniques, in his most influential book, *Natural Inheritance* (1889), in which he discussed one of the central problems of evolutionary theory, how given characteristics are transmitted from one generation to another.

Galton's influence on the burgeoning sciences of human biology, psychology and statistics was enormous. University College, London, founded the Galton professorship of eugenics in his honour in 1911. Karl Pearson, the first holder of the professorship, more or less single-handedly established the modern discipline of mathematical statistics, including making breakthroughs in correlation theory.[21] R. A. Fisher laid the foundations for the science of population genetics.[22] The most important protégé from the point of view of the development of the theory of meritocracy was a young army officer turned psychologist called Charles Spearman. Spearman fleshed out his insights about 'civic worth' in his seminal article '"General Intelligence", Objectively Determined and Measured' (1904).[23] Poring over the results of mental tests that he had applied to a large group of children on the isle of Guernsey, he came to the conclusion that 'all the mental powers' were correlated with each other. This led him to reject a number of common explanations of mental abilities – that the mind is divided into a number of compartmentalized faculties (the mere existence of positive correlations between different tests dispensed with this idea) or that abilities are clustered into several distinct groups – and to suggest instead that all abilities are primarily manifestations of one underlying general ability. The result of every IQ test could be divided into a 'general factor' (g), which is the same for every mental operation, and a 'specific factor' (s), which varies with different types of ability.[24] Spearman believed that he had provided psychology with its holy grail: a central fund of mental energy, fixed by inheritance, common to all mental acts, varying from person to person, open to scientific definition, and capable, when measured, of ranking the entire population in a single hierarchy.

Galton's influence was also seen in the enormous popularity of eugenics, a term he invented from the Greek roots for 'good' and 'heredity'. It's impossible today to hear the word 'eugenics' without thinking of Hitler's doctrine of racial superiority. But it's important to bear two things in mind. The first is that Galton and his followers were mostly interested in individual differences rather than group differences: indeed, during the 1930s, the British Eugenics Society fought a vigorous battle against what they regarded as the corruption of Galton's legacy by the Nazis. The second is that the doctrine of eugenics was embraced right across the political spectrum from the right to the left. Indeed, it was arguably even more popular with the left than it was with the right because it was identified with progressive ideas such as family planning and state intervention.

In Britain, the roll call of leading eugenicists in the first forty years of the twentieth century includes all the most illustrious names in the progressive world: writers such as H. G. Wells and George Bernard Shaw, political activists such as Sidney and Beatrice Webb, birth-control campaigners such as Marie Stopes. Shaw believed that 'the only fundamental and possible Socialism is the socialisation of the selective breeding of Man'.[25] Bertrand Russell argued that the state should provide everyone with coloured 'procreation tickets' and impose a heavy fine on people who chose to reproduce with the possessors of incompatible tickets.[26] Harold Laski, one of the Labour Party's most outspoken intellectuals, and sometime tutor of John F. Kennedy, founded the Galton Club when he was an undergraduate at Oxford just before the First World War.[27] During his long life supporting left-wing causes, J. B. S. Haldane, the biologist, was proud to contribute his name, money and sperm to the cause. As the *New Statesman* explained in July 1931, 'the legitimate claims of eugenics are not inherently incompatible with the outlook of the collectivist movement. On the contrary, they would be expected to find their most intransigent opponents amongst those who cling to the individualistic views of parenthood and family economics.'[28] The most outspoken opponent of eugenics was the proud Catholic reactionary G. K. Chesterton, who disliked eugenics for the same reason that he disliked birth control, because it represented human arrogance in interfering with the natural order of things.

HITTING THE BIG TIME

IQ testing got its great practical breakthrough with America's entry into the First World War in 1917. The army commissioned a group of psychologists, most notably Lewis Terman and Robert Yerkes, to classify more than 1.7 million soldiers; and the psychologists quickly devised two sorts of mass tests, alpha tests for people who were literate in English, and beta tests for those who were not. They were soon processing more than 10,000 examinees a day – an extraordinary achievement for a new and controversial technique. Unit commanders paid increasing attention to the results of the tests in deciding which soldiers to keep and which to try to pass on to other companies: some 7,700 recommendations for discharge and 28,000 for transfer were forwarded to army discharge boards on the basis of the tests.[29] The tests might not be able to provide a direct measure of bravery or the power of command, Yerkes admitted, but then added, on the basis of no clear evidence, that these qualities 'are far more likely to be found in men of superior intelligence'.[30]

After the war psychologists consolidated their success by turning to education and vocational guidance. Terman and Yerkes adapted their army tests for schoolchildren. A phalanx of private companies – the Psychological Corporation, the C. H. Stoelting Company, Houghton Mifflin and the World Book Company – not only modified but also commodified intelligence tests for the mass market.[31] By the mid-1920s, more than 80 per cent of cities were using IQ tests in schools to classify their students into ability groups. The federal government devised 'mentality tests' for civil servants. Big cities applied them not just to bureaucrats but also to police (particularly detectives) and trainee drivers ('Court seeks curb on moron drivers,' pronounced *The New York Times*).[32]

The British army didn't embrace IQ tests with the same enthusiasm as the American army, but British educationalists nevertheless warmed to the new technique. The London County Council used psychological tests in order first to identify backward children and then to supplement academic questions in scholastic examinations. The British Board of Education – the equivalent of today's Department for Education – published an influential report on *Psychological Tests of Educable Capacity* in 1924.

IQ tests caught the optimistic mood of the times: the combination of beliefs in democracy tempered by elitism, opportunity tempered by realism about human inequality, and science powered by technology. In 1912 Henry Holmes of Harvard University's Graduate School of Education summed up the mood in a concise paragraph:

> As a movement for social justice democracy must make real the vision of Lincoln – 'a fair chance and an unfettered start in life for every child'; must keep open 'the road to talent', which seemed to Napoleon the essence of the matter; must provide genuine equality of opportunity

so that every man may be able, in the spirit of that superior definition which President Eliot [of Harvard] likes to quote from Louis Pasteur, 'to make the most of himself for the common good'.[33]

In America, progressives updated Thomas Jefferson's vision of a 'natural aristocracy' of talents in terms of an 'aristocracy of brains' selected by scientific tests and promoted via a national education system. In Britain, they updated the intellectual aristocracy's vision of a peaceful transfer of power from the old landed elite to a new aristocracy of talent. IQ tests were the instruments of a silent and bloodless revolution. Everywhere, practical-minded people sensed that the basis of civilization was changing from strength to intelligence. 'Sheer brawn, youth, quickness no longer count for all,' Elizabeth Frazer, an American journalist, opined. 'It all needs something else to get by. And that something is grey matter. Brains.'[34]

The tests also caught a darker side of progressive thinking: worry about the degeneration of the race thanks to the fact that poorer people were having more children than richer people. The most widely reported result of the army tests was that the average American soldier had a mental age of thirteen. A couple of big books on the tests – Clarence Yoakum and Robert Yerkes's *Army Mental Tests* (1920) and Carl Brigham's *A Study of American Intelligence* (1923) – claimed to provide incontrovertible proof that, first, Northern Europeans were brighter than other groups and, second, that a worrying number of Americans were feeble-minded. In *Is America Safe for Democracy?* (1921), William McDougall, a Harvard psychologist, used tests to buttress his case that democracy was doomed. In *The Revolt against Civilisation* (1922), Lothrop Stoddard, a Boston lawyer, used the tests to reinforce his case that the 'thin red line' of 'rich, untainted blood which stands between us and barbarism and chaos' was even thinner than people had imagined. In 1924 the United States passed an act limiting immigration, and in 1927, in *Buck v. Bell*, the Supreme Court upheld enforced sterilization of the feeble-minded, with Oliver Wendell Holmes, one of the lions of liberalism, proclaiming that 'three generations of imbeciles are enough'. The same worries were echoed in Britain – though in more moderate form and without the result of state-sanctioned sterilization.

The best way to understand the strange mixture of ideas at the heart of intelligence testing – the dream of an intellectual aristocracy on the one hand but also the willingness to harbour dark thoughts about the less able on the other – is to examine the careers of three great exponents of standardized testing: Cyril Burt in the United Kingdom, and Lewis Terman, and, slightly outside the IQ school but giving a massive boost to standardized testing, James Conant in the United States.

CYRIL BURT AND THE 11-PLUS

Cyril Burt (1883–1971) was the most influential British psychologist of the twentieth century. He did more than anyone to apply psychometric theory to educational practice, particularly to the practice of educational selection. He was the chief psychologist of the London County Council from 1913 to 1932, and, having been initially appointed to select backward children for special schools, he broadened his remit to include selecting bright children for scholarships and studying children of all varieties, gifted as well as backward and delinquent. He acted as an adviser to the Board of Education between the wars, producing a cycle of influential reports on educational testing, selection and the education of children through every stage of childhood and adolescence. It's misleading to call him the 'inventor of the 11-plus': the examination evolved over time and depended on a wide variety of tests, academic as well as IQ. But he nevertheless profoundly shaped the life-changing examination and provided vigorous theoretical support for educational selection, acting as the leading advocate of testing when the ladder of opportunity was under construction from the 1920s onwards and the most ferocious defender when the 11-plus was under assault from the late 1950s.

Burt is made all the more intriguing by the fact that his death was followed by a furious debate about the solidity of his work. His critics accused him of a long litany of sins: fabricating research on identical twins; inventing collaborators in order to add weight to his fabrications; and filling the *British Journal of Statistical Psychology*, a journal which he edited for decades, with articles that he wrote under pseudonyms. His defenders also fought back: two closely written and carefully argued books anatomized the anatomizers and concluded that, even if he was guilty of writing too much too quickly, Burt was innocent of the major charges levelled against him.[35]

Burt revered Francis Galton as the 'father of British psychology' – the man who had made 'the first attempt to turn the study of individuals into a reputable branch of science' – and devoted his life to refining and reinforcing his three main arguments: that general intelligence exists; that it can be isolated and measured; and that it is inherited rather than acquired. One of his first scientific papers, published in 1909, concluded with the triumphant statement that: 'Parental intelligence ... may be inherited, individual intelligence measured, and general intelligence analysed; and they can be analysed, measured and inherited to a degree which few psychologists have hitherto legitimately ventured to maintain.'[36] Sixty years later, his last, and posthumously published paper, was devoted to proving that 'the hypothesis of a general factor entering into every type of cognitive process' and 'the contention that differences in this general factor depend largely on the individual's genetic constitution' were 'wholly consistent with the empirical facts' and thus 'beyond all question'.[37]

'Beyond all question'? In reality, Burt's arguments were subjected to probing criticism throughout his life. His most perceptive critic was a fellow English psychologist, Godfrey Thomson. In 1916, Thomson demonstrated that the hierarchical arrangement of correlation coefficients could be explained by the laws of chance.[38] He managed to produce a hierarchy from the results of a set of imitation 'mental tests' which can't have had a common factor, since they were the throws of dice. The implication was that tests measured statistical abstractions rather than concrete entities.[39] Leading American psychologists were equally sceptical about the idea of 'g'. In 1928, T. L. Kelly argued for the existence of several powerful group factors, such as verbal, numerical and spatial ability. In 1938, L. L. Thurstone, of the University of Chicago, claimed that 'intelligence' consists of eight primary mental abilities. Rather than resembling a pyramid with 'g' sitting like a monarch at the top, intelligence consists of a house with many mansions.[40] Burt hit back at all these critics with his monumental study, *The*

Factors of the Mind, published just as the world was descending into war, which argued that, although group factors might exist, they were far less important than the general factor, or 'g'.

These arguments might sound abstruse, but they had powerful practical implications: if 'g' mattered more than anything else, then it was reasonable to classify people according to a single unilineal scale of abilities; but if group factors mattered more, then children who excelled in, say, literature might lag in mathematics, and a unilineal scale was not simply wrong but harmful, while the theory that specific factors were all important meant that all attempts at classification were foolish. Spearman had unconsciously exposed the political implications of his theory in his ground-breaking paper back in 1904: the theory that 'g' was all important was 'monarchical', the theory that group factors mattered more was 'oligarchical' and the theory that specific factors ('s') were what mattered was 'anarchic'.

Burt was also at the heart of a great debate about the relationship between intelligence and social mobility. In his Huxley Lecture of 1901 Galton had suggested that social classes possessed different levels of 'civic worth', or natural ability, with professionals and employers at the top, the respectable working class bunched around the mean, and criminals and paupers at the bottom.[41] Galton suggested that regression to the mean both explained social mobility and set strict limits on it. The children of the gifted would seldom be as talented as their parents, and must expect to sink in the occupational hierarchy in consequence. Yet substantial promotion from the manual classes would be so rare as to constitute a statistical freak.[42] This was very much a view of society from the professional upper middle class. The overall social structure was accepted as a reflection of the inflexible laws of nature; the classes were ranked in terms of their possession of professional qualities, such as intelligence and zeal, with the paupers and thieves lumped together in the bottom of the statistical range, but society was not static: there was a constant circulation of elites as talented individuals competed for the top slots.

This argument was sketchy, to put it mildly. But it was soon given new life by both Charles Spearman, with his notion of 'g', and R. A. Fisher, a geneticist who clarified Galton's assumptions about regression in his path-breaking paper of 1918 on 'The Correlation between Relatives on the Supposition of Mendelian Inheritance'.[43] Burt's work on occupation and ability was a sophisticated synthesis of Spearman and Fisher. Civic worth became IQ; regression became a Mendelian process; and social mobility within a stratified occupational hierarchy became the product of the working of genetic laws.

Critics have predictably presented Burt's work on social mobility as a biological justification of the status quo. Yet, in reality, it is a justification for meritocratic mobility rather than aristocratic stasis. Given that the correlation between the IQs of fathers and sons was only 0.5, there had to be considerable social mobility for IQ distribution by class to persist. In a 1961 paper he emphasized that the link between occupation and ability was only proximate: only 55 per cent of the population could be regarded as correctly placed if intelligence were the only criterion of allocation: nearly 23 per cent were in a class too high and, with a perfect scheme of vocational guidance, ought to be moved down, while 22 per cent were in a class too low and ought to be moved up. In the lowest class, unskilled workers, some of the brightest members were more intelligent than the dullest members of the 'lower professional class' – a vast waste of human resources and a standing condemnation of existing social policy.

Two of Burt's central ideas were inimical to the status quo. The first was Mendel's notion that 'the chance re-combinations of a definite number of unalterable factors will yield, as a consequence of sexual reproduction, a wide variety of patterns in the ensuing generation, as dissimilar as the figures formed by shaking the coloured chips in a child's kaleidoscope'. The second was the law of regression to the mean. Burt's organizing belief came straight out of the pages of Plato's *Republic*, which he had studied as a classicist at Oxford: that the government's most important job, other than defending the state, was to discover talented children in whatever social class they were born into and give them an education appropriate to their abilities. The big difference was that the prodigies he sought were not primarily Plato's 'men of gold' who could guide the republic in the right direction, though they mattered. They were the scientific geniuses who could produce ideas and innovations that could improve the lives of the broad mass of humanity.

Burt thus presented the 11-plus (for all its practical imperfections, rooted in tradition and geographical inequality) as the best expression Britain had of the meritocratic idea: a way of testing the entire population for their IQ and then redistributing opportunities on the basis of innate abilities rather than social privilege. Far from being a defence of the status quo, it was an attempt to readjust society in every generation in accordance with the laws of genetics; and far from being a defence of the old establishment, it was part of a broader attempt to replace the old, decadent establishment with a new progressive and scientific one.

LEWIS TERMAN AND THE RISE OF SILICON VALLEY

Lewis Terman (1877–1956) came from a different world from Cyril Burt: he was the son of a struggling farmer in Indiana, while Burt was the son of a comfortably off doctor; and he attended local public schools, while Burt was educated at a public school (albeit one for swots rather than nobs, Christ's Hospital). He nevertheless shared the same intellectual influences and passions. 'Of the founders of modern psychology,' he once wrote, 'my greatest admiration is for Galton. My favourite of all psychologists is Binet, not because of his intelligence test, which was only a by-product of his life work, but because of his originality, insight, and open-mindedness, and because of the rare charm of personality that shines through all his writings.'[44] That could easily have been Burt talking.

Terman devoted his life to perfecting Binet's tests in order to carry out Galton's research programme. He adapted Binet's tests for a mass American audience and produced several revisions during his lifetime (a fifth revision of the tests is currently in use). He popularized the idea that IQ is a fixed quality that can be expressed by a single all-important number. 'The feeble-minded remain feeble-minded, the dull remain dull, the average remain average, and the superior remain superior. There is nothing in one's equipment, with the exception of character, which rivals IQ in importance.'[45] He had the same virtues as Burt – he believed in providing more opportunities for bright children from the lower classes and engaged in the detailed study of individual subjects, particularly children, rather than just collecting quantitative data on entire populations – but also had the same vices, and more so. Burt's enthusiasm for eugenics was never contaminated with racial prejudice. The same cannot be said for Terman.

While Burt focused on the backward and delinquent, Terman focused on geniuses. Hitherto, researchers had examined geniuses only retrospectively: they took great men and women and traced their genius back into their childhoods. Terman believed that, thanks to IQ tests, they could now look forward by identifying gifted children and following them through their careers in order to understand 'genius in the making', and he devoted much of his career to studying a group of gifted children – dubbed the 'Termites' – and recording the results of his study in a monumental five-volume work, *Genetic Studies of Genius* (1925–59).

Genetic Studies was conceived on the sort of grand scale that was appropriate to the California of the interwar years, the country's biggest state and one that was then entering its golden age. Terman asked teachers from across the state to nominate the brightest students from their classes and then gave the chosen ones IQ tests with a cut-off point of 140. He ended up with 643 prodigies, a number that later grew to more than a thousand, initially calling them 'geniuses' but later preferring the more modest term 'gifted'. Two thirds of them were WASPs; a tenth were Jewish; very few were black or Hispanic; and none were Chinese, despite the significant presence of Chinese-Americans in the Californian population, particularly in the Bay area. Terman was a man of terrier-like persistence as well as grand vision, barraging his 'Termites', along with their parents, with questions for decades to come. The fifth volume, produced thirty-five years after the first, examined the children in mid-life, even pursuing one serving soldier to a foxhole.

Terman's study was far from foolproof. He passed over two future Nobel Prize winners in physics, Luis Alvarez and William Shockley, something that rankled with the IQ-obsessed Shockley for the rest of his life. He broke some of the basic rules of objective research with a nonchalance that now strikes us as astonishing: he regularly had affairs with his female graduate students who were helping him on the project; he was infatuated with 'my gifted children', as he called them, lobbying teachers and employers on their behalf; he chose his own son and daughter as his subjects.

A study of Terman's geniuses, *Terman's Kids* (1992), by Joel Shurkin, reveals that 'nurture' imposed far more barriers to 'nature' than Terman acknowledged. Terman did little to comb minority-heavy schools for 'hidden Einsteins'. The most successful family in his sample – two sons and three daughters of a Japanese father and an American mother – were hounded by a former US senator, who complained to Stanford about their inclusion in the sample.

The study also veered into eccentricity. The entire second volume, which was written by Catharine Morris Cox under Terman's over-enthusiastic supervision, was devoted to measuring the IQs of famous dead people. Terman established the field of administering IQ tests to corpses in a 1917 paper on Francis Galton: 'From the evidence given,' he concluded, referring to a smattering of reports on Galton's childhood activities, pastimes and accomplishments, 'one is justified in concluding that between the ages of three and eight years . . . Francis Galton must have had an intelligence quotient not far from 200.'[46] Cox applied the same methods to 301 notable figures up to 1850. John Stuart Mill topped the charts with an IQ of 190, putting him in spitting distance of Galton. Goethe, Leibniz and Grotius followed closely at 185. Voltaire recorded a respectable 170, but Newton (130), Napoleon (135) and Beethoven (135) scored so badly that, had they been around in California between the wars, they would not have made it into the ranks of the Termites.[47]

Odd though it was, *Genetic Studies of Genius* nevertheless had merits. It reinforced the idea that genius could be studied alongside other natural phenomena. It exploded popular stereotypes of gifted children that had their roots in the Romantic idea of mad geniuses. Far from being small and sickly, Terman discovered, they were taller and fitter than average; far from being scrofulous misfits, they were better adjusted than average. The Termites went on to have highly successful careers, earning higher salaries and better professional rewards than a control group.

Terman's fixation on 'natural genius' was driven in part by his autobiography – he was one of ten children, suffered from tuberculosis as a child, attended a one-room schoolhouse and spent his summers working on the farm – and in part by his enthusiasm for national efficiency, a fashionable idea when he was growing up. 'Whether civilization moves on and up,' he argued, 'depends most on the advances made by creative thinkers and leaders in science, politics, art, morality, and religion. Moderate ability can follow or imitate, but genius must show the way.'[48] Geniuses might not be the stunted freaks of popular lore, but if you put them in classes that failed to stretch their abilities they might well become misfits and rebels.

Whatever its origins, Terman's preoccupation with genius had revolutionary consequences: he has as good a claim as anybody to be considered the grandfather of Silicon Valley, and thus of today's tech economy. He persuaded Stanford to be a pioneer in using IQ tests 'as a partial basis for selection of candidates for admission to the University'. He introduced an advanced programme for exceptionally gifted children to California schools. His son (and subject), Frederick, was one of Stanford's greatest institution builders: as dean of engineering, he turned the engineering department into a world-beater and, as provost, he secured a grant from the Ford Foundation that aimed at turning it into a West Coast challenger to Harvard. He also encouraged the development of a large number of high-tech companies around the campus. *Si monumentum requiris*, try googling his name – or indeed anything.

JAMES CONANT AND THE JEFFERSONIAN TRADITION

James Conant (1893–1978), Harvard's president from 1933 to 1953, was the most impressive of an impressive cohort of 'captains of learning': a man who thought as deeply as anyone about the nature of merit and who then applied his thinking to America's most famous institution of higher education. Conant came from a much humbler background than the two Brahmins who preceded him as president of Harvard, Charles Eliot and Lawrence Lowell. He grew up in middle-class Dorchester, Massachusetts. He studied chemistry, obtained a Ph.D., and, as a young academic, published an indecent number of scholarly articles. But his elevation to the presidency of Harvard turned him, in the words of a *Newsweek* cover story, into 'the number one man in American education'.

One of his first acts as president was to establish a programme of National Scholarships that were intended to bring a wider range of candidates to the university. 'We should be able to say that any man with remarkable talents may obtain his education at Harvard,' he wrote in his first president's report, 'whether he be rich or penniless, whether he comes from Boston or San Francisco.'[49] He insisted that scholarships should be awarded on the basis of academic merit – 'potential for success in college work' – rather than fluffy qualities such as leadership skills or irrelevant ones such as athletic ability.[50] Conant's remarks about national scholarships contained both a rebuke of the old Harvard that had nurtured him and a vision of the future. The old Harvard had been too much of a finishing school for the children of the north-east WASP elite, children who were not conspicuous for their industry or, in all too many cases, for their grey matter. Conant's new Harvard was to be a training ground for a new meritocracy selected on the basis of intellectual merit and drawn from every corner of the country: new brains rather than old blood.

How do you identify 'potential for success in college work'? Conant thought that the answer lay in the SAT – a device that was developed by Carl Brigham, a psychologist at Princeton, and embraced by two of Conant's closest lieutenants, Henry Chauncey, assistant dean at Harvard from 1928 to 1945 and president of the Educational Testing Service from its inception in 1948 to 1970, and Wilbur Bender, dean of admissions from 1952 to 1960. Conant's enthusiasm for using the SAT to identify National Scholars proved to be contagious. In 1937, thirteen elite universities asked the College Entrance Examination Board to develop a one-day version of the SAT to serve as a scholarship examination for all scholarship candidates. On 14 December 1941, just a week after the Japanese bombed Pearl Harbor, Harvard together with a group of other private colleges introduced SATs for all applicants, not just scholarship candidates, thereby laying the foundations for the test-based meritocracy that arose after the war.

Conant's guiding educational philosophy was that great private universities like his own had a duty to fulfil Jefferson's vision: that is, to 'cull from every condition of our people' the natural aristocracy of talents and virtue and prepare it by education at the public expense for public concerns. Only by actively searching for children of merit in the whole of society could great universities succeed in preserving excellence in a democratic age; and only by educating those children to their full potential could they contribute to national efficiency. He laid out this vision in a succession of widely discussed works.

In 'Education for a Classless Society', published in *Atlantic Monthly* in 1940 as America debated the case for going to war with Hitler, Conant explained his reasons for thinking that America's survival as a free society depended on the ability of its educational system to break the barriers of hereditary privilege. America was unique among the great powers in that it was both free and classless – Russia was classless but not free, he claimed, Britain was free but not classless, and Germany was neither free nor classless. Still, this unique position was more precarious by the day: since the Gilded Age, America had become less successful at redistributing power and privilege with each new generation. Inequality had widened and caste behaviour had put down roots. What was needed was not 'a radical equalisation of wealth' – that would be counterproductive – but a 'more equitable distribution of opportunity': only if each generation believed that it could start life afresh and that hard work and high ability would find their just rewards would America remain immune to the twin European afflictions of class consciousness and political extremism.

In 'Public Education and the Structure of American Society', a lecture delivered in 1945, Conant elaborated his ideas further. Capitalist society is subject to an inherent tension between legal equality on the one hand and inequality of reward on the other. One of the most important jobs of the education system is to prevent these tensions from exploding into revolution. Conant added a new argument to the Jeffersonian one: do everything you can to minimize the visibility of social stratification while at the same time increasing its complexity. Europeans tended to play up status differences. Americans were much wiser to play them down, even while allowing for inequalities of reward – in effect, encouraging billionaires to wear beanies rather than top hats.

Conant had nothing but contempt for the popular idea that human beings are all basically equal: 'only in matters connected with organised sport does the average American think clearly about the significance of innate ability,' he wrote, 'yet when it comes to studies, parents often expect the school and college to accomplish the equivalent of turning a cripple into a football player'.[51] His solution to the problem of combining meritocracy with democracy lay in selection by stealth: accept the necessity of comprehensive high schools but divide those schools into grammar schools and secondary moderns under a single roof by internal differentiation. Selection by stealth would not only avoid the political problems that were to doom the British grammar-school system, it would also make it easier for schools to correct mistakes by moving children from one track to another.

Conant didn't always live up to his fine words: the man who denounced privilege in theory frequently went out of his way to preserve Harvard's links with the Protestant upper class in practice.[52] He insisted that Harvard should pay attention to 'character', 'leadership' and 'athletic ability' in choosing its students. The university did not want to become an asylum for autistic bookworms. Most disgracefully, he continued with his predecessor's policy of setting a ceiling on Jewish enrolment for at least a decade after his appointment.[53] In 1951, eighteen years after Conant had taken over the presidency, Harvard was still admitting 94 per cent of legacies (students related to alumni) and discouraging bright Jews from applying.[54] Conant was clearly a very pragmatic president who went out of his way to keep all Harvard's various constituencies, not least the WASP elite, happy. He was acutely aware that a great research university is an expensive undertaking that depends on attracting a large number of 'paying guests' not only for tuition but for donations.[55] He nevertheless pushed relentlessly, both rhetorically and practically, in the meritocratic direction. His decision to impose an up-or-out system on the faculty dramatically changed the character of the governing body as the gentlemen gave way to the players. Conant's system of National Scholarships brought some of the best minds in America to Harvard: James Tobin, who reached Harvard's class of 1939 from a modest background in Champaign, Illinois, went on to be one of the earliest winners of the Nobel Prize in economics.

Conant's lieutenant at Harvard, Henry Chauncey, played a leading role in taking testing national. Chauncey was more upper class than

Conant – his forebears came to America on the *Mayflower* and he was educated at Groton and Harvard – but his gentlemanly exterior concealed a fanatical zeal for social justice in the form of meritocracy. He left Harvard to establish the Educational Testing Service (ETS) in a comfortable campus near Princeton. The ETS was a strange beast: a private organization that performed the semi-public function of choosing students for university places and a research organization that was also in the business of selling tests.[56] Despite these contradictions, it succeeded in inserting itself into the very heart of America's higher education system – and hence into the heart of American society.

THE POLITICS OF IQ TESTING

Few groups of intellectuals have been subjected to such a concerted attack on their reputations as the proponents of standardized testing in general and IQ testing in particular. Stephen Jay Gould dismissed IQ testing as the latest, and most audacious, example of the mismeasure of man, a way of blaming social inequalities on Mother Nature and thereby delegitimizing righteous social reform.[57] Liam Hudson accused IQ testers of providing 'ammunition for all those people – racists, political reactionaries, elitists – who are preoccupied with the belief that some of us are inherently inferior to others'.[58] Leon Kamin claimed that 'the IQ test has served as an instrument of oppression against the poor – dressed in the trappings of science, rather than politics'.

This argument is an exercise in anachronistic sermonizing rather than serious historical understanding, which at its best is an exercise in grasping the intricacies of context rather than projecting our own prejudices backwards. Set the proponents of IQ testing in the world they inhabited and a very different pattern emerges. It is also an exercise in shoddy thinking: there is no reason why commitment to biological explanations of inequality should make people conservative or belief in sociological explanations should make them liberal. Sensible conservatives are happier resting their conservativism on social conventions (which can be passed from one generation to another) than on the facts of biology (which are subject to a genetic lottery).

Until the 1960s, mental measurement found its most passionate supporters on the left and its most serious critics on the right. Ralph Waldo Emerson, one of the founders of the American transcendentalist movement, advocated the creation of an 'anthropometer' that could gauge everybody's innate merit. 'I should like to see that appraisal applied to every man, and every man made acquainted with the true number and weight of every adult citizen, and that he then be placed where he belongs, with so much power confided to him as he could carry and use.'[59] J. B. S. Haldane, a leading member of the British Communist Party and an editor of the party's mouthpiece, *The Daily Worker*, dismissed 'the curious dogma of the equality of man'.[60] 'We are not born equal, far from it. The best community is that which contains the fewest square pegs in round holes, bricklayers who might have been musicians, company directors who, by their own abilities, would never have risen above the rank of clerk.'[61] Haldane believed that, if anything, supporters of grammar schools didn't go far enough: 'the most important experiment, to my mind, would be to start a school whose membership was confined to really intelligent children. Such children could easily reach the standards of the average university graduate at eighteen.'[62]

In Russia, the early Bolsheviks were devotees not just of IQ testing but of craniometry. In 1923, as Lenin lay dying, Trotsky told the Party that 'Lenin was a genius, a genius is born once a century, and the history of the world knows only two geniuses as leaders of the working class: Marx and Lenin', and to prove the general point (soon dissociated from 'the traitor Trotsky'), the Party invited a German neurologist, Oskar Vogt, to come to Moscow in 1925 to study their recently deceased leader's brain to understand why he was so exceptional. Vogt dissected the brain into more than 30,000 pieces, analysed the pieces in all sorts of ways and, after months of deliberation, came to the conclusion that Lenin was indeed a 'mental athlete' (*Assoziationsathlet*). Vogt secured Stalin's support to establish the V. I. Lenin Institute for Brain Research in a lavish mansion expropriated from an American businessman: the institute served as a research centre, studying the brains of Lenin and other leading revolutionaries, and housed a Pantheon of Brains, comprising a large collection of the brains of prominent Soviet intellectuals. It still exists but remains closed to foreign scholars.[63]

By contrast, many conservatives regarded mental measurement as the devil's work. Lord Percy of Newcastle, the Conservative president of the Board of Education under Stanley Baldwin and a younger son of the 7th Duke of Northumberland, the grandest grandee in northern England, felt that those psychologists who held that children inherited a fixed IQ had fallen 'easy victims to the calvinistic nightmare of predestination'.[64] T. S. Eliot argued that 'an educational system which would automatically sort out everyone according to his native capacities' would 'disorganise society and debase education'.[65] Edward Welbourne, the reactionary master of Emmanuel College, Cambridge, dismissed IQ tests as 'devices invented by Jews for the advancement of Jews'.[66]

The best way to expose the foolishness of the Gould–Kamin school of thought is to set the IQ testers in their historical context: reconstruct the social structures and social attitudes of the first half of the twentieth century and it's impossible not to be struck by the radicalism of the IQ testing movement. The champions of mental measurement were advocating nothing less than a reconstruction of the established social order and the replacement of a ruling class based on lineage and tradition with one based on ability and achievement. 'Reactionaries' have never come in such a revolutionary form.

Joseph Schumpeter, the great economist, noted that European society remained profoundly 'old-fashioned' until well into the twentieth century: topped by 'divinely ordained' monarchs and their courts (in Schumpeter's Austria, only nobles with a direct link to the Habsburg family going back fourteen generations were admitted to the highest functions) and buttressed by the landed nobility and the Church (which was often staffed by nobles). Prior to the Great War, in France, 40–45 per cent of the active population, producing 30–35 per cent of national income, were employed on the land. Even in fast-industrializing Germany the relevant figures were 40 per cent of the labour force and 20 per cent of national income.[67] Germany's largest landowner, Prince Hohenzollern, owned almost a quarter of a million acres.[68] Austria-Hungary had more than two dozen landowners who could match him acre for acre. Great tracts of Great Britain were owned by aristocratic landowners who, at least until the tax revolution of the First World War and, in some cases, well beyond, continued to live in grand style in their country palaces. Europe was very far from being what Pareto, one of the founders of elite theory, dubbed a 'graveyard of aristocracies'.

This is not to say that the great meritocratic reforms from the mid-nineteenth century onwards had made no difference: they had succeeded in forcing the old elites both to reform themselves along meritocratic lines and to build a ladder of educational opportunity which could take the exceptionally able from the village school to the top of the state and academia. But it's nevertheless important to bear two things in mind: the first is that pre-meritocratic attitudes continued to survive, particularly given that the meritocratic revolution was so partial, and second, far from simply fading, old attitudes frequently fought back, corrupting the very meritocrats who were supposed to be crushing them. Pause with the meritocratic revolution for a moment and you start going backwards.

The old European ruling class continued to set the tone of the state apparatus as well as wider 'society'. The rising bourgeoisie aped the manners of established elites, purchasing country estates, sending their children to ancient schools where they learned Latin and Greek, agitating to get them into exclusive fraternities, particularly in Germany, where a duelling scar was a mark that you had made it into society. The French liked to put the particle *de* in the middle of their names and the Germans the prefix *von*. The Italians liked to triple or quadruple their surnames by adding the names of their mothers and grandmothers.[69]

The same pattern was repeated in the headquarters of the Industrial Revolution. 'A duke is always a personage with us, always a personage, independent of brains or conduct,' Matthew Arnold told Andrew Carnegie. 'We are all snobs. Hundreds of years have made us so, all snobs. We can't help it. It is in the blood.'[70] Even if they didn't own any land, many Britons 'felt that they were landowners in the sight of God and kept up a semi-aristocratic outlook by going into the professions and the fighting services rather than into trade'.[71]

Many establishment types continued to value sound character above intelligence and effort, with 'too clever by half' acting as a common put-down. Daisy Brooke, Prince Edward's mistress, said that his set had difficulty in accepting Jews because 'they had brains and understood finance. As a class we did not like brains.'[72] Cyril Connolly felt that, at Eton, 'Intelligence was a deformity which must be concealed; a public school taught one to conceal it as a good tailor hides a paunch or a hump.'[73] George Orwell, Connolly's Eton contemporary, pointed out that 'millions of English people willingly accept as their national emblem the bulldog, an animal noted for its obstinacy, ugliness and impenetrable stupidity'.[74]

British politics continued to be heavily influenced by aristocrats until well into the twentieth century. Bonar Law's Cabinet included eight members of the aristocracy, both Baldwin's Cabinets included nine, and Chamberlain's Cabinet included eight. In 1938, no fewer than nine members of the Cabinet were related to each other. A landed estate could bring a seat in the House of Lords – which is why W. S. Gilbert, in *Iolanthe*, called landed aristocrats not just 'pillars of the British nation' but also 'paragons of legislation'. It could also bring you a chance of getting an early start in the people's house: Lord Winterton was elected to the House of Commons while still an undergraduate at Oxford.

Some elements in the civil service continued to resist the new regime of open competition for a remarkably long time. Until 1918, recruits to the Diplomatic Service had to guarantee a private income of at least £400 a year for their first two years, and had to be personally acquainted with the secretary of state into the bargain. The Colonial Service retained straightforward patronage until 1931, and then introduced a system not of competitive examinations but of competitive interviews. The more meritocratic Home Civil Service was still dominated by products of the public schools, with state-educated entrants increasing from 6 per cent before the First World War to 29 per cent before the Second.

The two ancient universities preserved two streams: a scholarship stream for the able and a C-stream for the rest. You could become a 'gentleman commoner' without having to take the rigorous entrance exam reserved for scholars. A good family and an ability to pay your fees were all that was required. And you could sail your way to a gentleman's pass without darkening the doors of a college library, let alone the university library, the Bodleian. In the mid-1930s a quarter of undergraduates only bothered to take pass degrees – admittedly an improvement on the 40 per cent before the First World War, but hardly evidence that Britain was waking up to the urgency of the times.[75]

As for the United States, the republic of merit contained powerful anti-meritocratic counter-currents. America possessed a collection of hidden aristocracies that dominated various regions: most obviously, the Southern planter elite, which survived the abolition of slavery, but also the Proper Philadelphians, the Nob Hill set in San Francisco. The period after the First World War saw America buffeted by powerful anti-meritocratic currents. America's elite universities competed with Oxford and Cambridge in their anti-intellectual snobbery. The *beau idéal* of the Ivy League boy was the all-rounder – the golden boy who shines on the sports field, is elected to all the right social clubs, who joins in with jolly japes but is nevertheless a natural leader. Owen Johnson's *Stover at Yale* (1912) celebrated the all-rounder who gets elected to Skull and Bones, Yale's most socially exclusive secret society, and pours scorn on the bookworm: 'Wookey, the little freshman from a mountain village of Maine, the shadow of a grind, whom no one knew in his class, and who would never know any one'.[76] The prejudice in favour of the all-round man also extended to the faculty: the Yale faculty lounge was dominated by Episcopalians with triple-barrelled names (Chauncey Brewster Tinker, William Lyon Phelps, Samuel Flagg Bemis and Norman Holmes Pearson) and recruitment was more a matter of clubability than academic merit. More than half the professors were old Yalees.[77]

The prejudice against 'swots' and 'grinds' became stronger in the 1920s thanks to the growing cult of the WASP. F. Scott Fitzgerald idealized Princeton as a place populated by willowy young men strolling from luncheon to tea without ever taking a detour to the library. Others were openly antisemitic in their vituperation against 'greasy grinds' who wasted their university years in study. In 1926, Yale produced a new admissions policy that was intended to put *more* emphasis on character. The student-run *Yale Daily News* praised the policy on the grounds that it would prevent the university from being overrun by 'abnormal brain specimens' but suggested that the admission tutors go further: candidates should be required to submit photographs of their fathers along with their applications.[78]

These prejudices led to fixed quotas on Jewish students, who were regarded as the archetypes of 'greasy grinds'. Harvard's president, Robert Lowell, fought a long battle, starting in the early 1920s, to reduce the intake of Jews to 12 per cent. Union College in New York State limited Jewish entry to 8–10 per cent of the body in 1930, a restriction that remained in place until the 1960s. Deans of admissions merrily rejected bright Jews, just as they currently reject bright Asians, on the vague grounds that their 'general bearing' was off-putting or their educational outlook 'too narrow'.

These general attitudes lasted well into the 1950s. In 1952, Wilbur Bender, the dean of admissions, wrote to a scholarship committee warning that Harvard had to make sure that it did not acquire a reputation of being 'full of long-haired esthetics [sic], of pansies and poets and various la-de-da types' as well as 'parlour pinks, communists, fellow travellers etc.'[79] But he worried that it was too late: the pass had been sold and Harvard had already become what he most feared: 'a place only for grinds … a big-city college full of muckers and public-school boys and meatballs', a place sadly bereft of 'virile, masculine, red-blooded he-men'.[80]

The meritocratic idea may well have its faults. So may the psychologists who tried to turn it into a reality. But they are not quite the faults that Stephen Jay Gould and his allies imagined: they are the faults (if so they be) of mobility rather than immobility and revolutionary change rather than defence of the status quo.

12

The Meritocratic Revolution

The Second World War turbocharged the meritocratic revolution. Mass mobilization demonstrated how much talent had been wasted in the past. The post-war expansion of the welfare state increased ordinary people's opportunities. And the shift from a manufacturing to a knowledge-based economy increased the rewards for brainpower.

Britain provided a vivid example of this transformation. The demands of total war tested the bonds of a class-based society to breaking point.[1] The military had no choice but to promote brilliant proletarians over Colonel Blimps.[2] Factories experimented with scientific management. Soldiers demanded social justice as a quid pro quo for military sacrifice. Policy-makers, from William Beveridge down, promised a future in which ordinary people were no longer 'employed below their capacity' while toffs were promoted beyond their abilities.[3] 'The Stock Exchange will be pulled down,' George Orwell predicted in *The Lion and the Unicorn*, in 1941, 'the horse plough will give way to the tractor, the country houses will be turned into children's holiday camps, the Eton and Harrow match will be forgotten . . .' Even Winston Churchill, a proud Old Harrovian, concluded that the public schools could survive only if they embraced the spirit of meritocracy: he argued that they should be obliged to give 60–70 per cent of their places to poor scholars on bursaries and added that 'the great cities would be proud to search for able youths to send to Haileybury, to Harrow and to Eton'.[4]

The election of the 1945 Labour government ushered in the age of the common man, breaking, for a while, the dangerous spell that the aristocracy had exercised over the country. Denis Healey might have gone over the top at the Labour Party Conference in May 1945 when he declared – still in uniform – that 'the upper classes in every country are selfish, depraved, dissolute and decadent'.[5] They certainly looked increasingly like fish out of water – too privileged to thrive in the age of the common man but too drab to thrive in the age of Hollywood glamour. Bertie Wooster does not appear in P. G. Wodehouse's *Ring for Jeeves* (1953) because he has gone to a school designed to teach aristocrats to fend for themselves (i.e. learn how to darn their own socks), lest 'the social revolution should set in with greater severity'.[6] Even the legal system belatedly conceded the idea that all men are equal before the law: in 1948 peers finally lost their right to be tried before their fellows in the Lords.[7]

At the same time, the war reinforced the cult of education and science that had sprung up during the Great Depression. Scientists had invented the world's most powerful weapon, the atomic bomb. Boffins had broken the Germans' codes in Bletchley Park. Maynard Keynes had invented a way of saving the economy from depression. Academics moved in and out of Whitehall in the form of the 'great and the good', a development celebrated in C. P. Snow's meritocrat-worshipping 'Strangers and Brothers' novels. Ensconced in romantic Oxford and Cambridge colleges, gifted with elegant prose styles, linked by friendship and even marriage to fashionable society, post-war intellectuals such as A. J. P. Taylor, A. J. Ayer and Hugh Trevor-Roper became egghead celebrities, inspiring thousands of schoolchildren with the dream of winning scholarships to Oxbridge.

The 1944 Education Act was universally celebrated as a pillar of the opportunity society. The fact that it was designed by a Tory, R. A. B. Butler, implemented by a Labour government and preserved by later Conservative governments, underlined that the new vision was beyond class politics, an integral part of the new 'Butskellite' consensus. Consider two books published simultaneously by Penguin in 1947, John Parker's *Labour Marches On* and Quintin Hogg's *The Case for Conservatism*. Parker argued that 'By Social Democracy I mean so-called "Equality of Opportunity" – and a basic minimum for all those who are handicapped in the battle of life … To each man and woman, rich and poor, must be offered an opportunity limited only by his capacity, skill and energy.'[8] While Hogg insisted that 'The vast majority of our fellow countrymen … wish to see equal opportunity and social security; they desire to see industrial policy subordinated to national will and made the subject of a conscious plan. But they do not desire equality of income.'[9]

The new meritocracy had a decidedly technocratic flavour. The 1945 Percy Report on Higher Technological Education and the 1946 Barlow Report on Scientific Manpower recommended a sharp increase in the number of scientists and technologists going to university. The University Grants Committee summarized the new consensus: 'If this country is to maintain its place in the world it cannot afford to fall behind in the pursuit and application of new knowledge.'[10] In 1959, the year of C. P. Snow's broadside on the 'two cultures', 55 per cent of A-level passes were in the sciences.[11]

Revolutions inevitably produce counter-revolutions, and the aristocratic spirit underwent a striking revival during the 1950s with the Churchill–Macmillan–Eden administrations and the Coronation of Elizabeth II. 'Most of Macmillan's ministers exhaled an upper-class Oxbridge fragrance,' according to Noel Annan, whose nose for such fragrances was second to none, 'and after his notorious 1962 reshuffle nearly half the cabinet were Etonians.'[12] But the 1940s revolution resumed with a vengeance in the 1960s. Grammar-school products made it into Downing Street in the form of Harold Wilson and Ted Heath. Eldon Griffiths, a rising young Tory MP, told the House that 'the people who have been variously described as the technocrats, the meritocracy or the salariat ... they are the fulcrum of British politics. They are neither to the Left nor to the Right; and as they go so goes the nation'.[13] Satirists such as Peter Cook and Dudley Moore and the *Private Eye* crowd mercilessly satirized the old Establishment, despite (or perhaps because of) the fact that most of them had been educated at public schools themselves. Harold Nicolson complained in 1961 that 'today, it is as difficult for an aristocrat to enter the foreign service as it would be for a camel to pass through the eye of a needle'.[14]

The post-war expansion of the grammar schools provided a growing number of bright children from middle- and working-class backgrounds with a chance to get an elite education. In *Education and Leadership* (1951), Eric James, the High Master of Manchester Grammar School, the most selective of direct grant schools, proclaimed that 'every child from Bricktown Secondary School who secures a commission, or a position in the administrative civil service, or a controlling place in industry or commerce, is a portent of an immense social change, the slow creation of an elite of merit, a transfer of power to those whose qualification for wielding it is neither birth nor wealth, but talent'.[15] Plenty of Labour activists were happy to give James's view a loud hurrah: surveying the 1953 Labour Party Conference, Richard Crossman saw the fruits of the grammar-school revolution wherever he looked: 'nearly all the delegates were at grammar school or have their children at grammar school, and are not quite so susceptible to the romantic socialism of the 1920s'.[16]

As grammar schools boomed, public schools entered a prolonged crisis. In the immediate aftermath of the Second World War, they looked as if they might become casualties of Britain's 'meritocratic moment'.[17] In his penultimate annual report to the Warden and Fellows of Winchester College in 1945, Canon Spencer Leeson, the school's headmaster, asked how many 'parents of the "Winchester type" ' would continue to be willing and able to pay the high cost of prep school, Winchester and university 'when they can get State-aided education of a rapidly improving quality . . . for nothing or next to nothing'. And in the coming decades they struggled hard to keep up with the grammar schools. In 1956, Sir Harold Webbe, a Tory MP, warned the Independent Schools Association that private schools might be unable to compete with the 'quite fantastic' level of facilities in local state schools. In 1960, a group of Eton dignitaries put their names on a letter to the Provost complaining about the 'high rate of failure at A-levels' (which the school had initially refused to recognize) and 'the quality of some of the masters'. In 1963, an internal paper at Westminster School revealed that average marks in English, biology, geography and even Greek were below the national average. A year later, a survey of seventy-five public schools for *The Times* found that Eton, Harrow and Charterhouse fell into the 'high fees' 'low A-levels' category.

The great public schools rested on a rickety foundation of prep schools that were frequently run by what might politely be called oddballs. Jeremy Paxman's prep school in the early 1960s was fairly typical of the breed: 'Our teachers were the usual collection of eccentrics, drunks and no-hopers. Latin masters whose threadbare jackets rattled with matchboxes filled with pinched-out fag-ends, their ciga-rette fingers stained the colour of mahogany ... One retired colonel who taught French was fired in front of the school over breakfast for failing to pass the marmalade to the headmaster's wife.'[18]

Such incompetence tested the loyalty of even the loyalist parents: the proportion of children attending public schools in England and Wales declined from 6.7 per cent in 1955 to 4.5 per cent in 1978. Eric Anderson, one of the great public-school headmasters of the post-war era, speculated that 'sixty per cent of the public schools would have gone under if the grammar schools had remained'.[19]

George Orwell famously compared England to a family in which the wrong people were in charge. In post-war Britain it looked as if, largely thanks to the grammar schools, the family was beginning to sort things out.

PEOPLE OF PLENTY

Post-war America saw many of the same developments as post-war Britain: the growing conviction that, in Churchill's phrase, 'the empires of the future will be empires of the mind'; the commitment to an expanded welfare state, albeit a welfare state with American char-acteristics; and, above all, the quest for a fairer post-war order. The same themes were nevertheless woven together in rather different pat-terns. America had the benefit of more variety than Britain: meritocratic educational initiatives were sponsored by companies and think tanks as well as governments, meritocratic government reforms were spear-headed by think tanks, particularly the Rand Corporation, as well as government departments. America did not suffer from the same agonies of class guilt as Britain (though it suffered from worse agonies of racial guilt, agonies that were suppressed during the 1950s but transformed politics in the 1960s). In post-war America the merito-cratic revolution was all about delivering the promise of American life, as codified in the Declaration of Independence and the constitu-tion, rather than overturning an unjust social order.

The great harbinger of the meritocratic revolution was the GI Bill. More than 1.6 million veterans enrolled in college in 1947 alone, a number equivalent to the total college population in 1940, and more than 60 per cent of them studied science and engineering. Post-war America was much more inclined to romanticize the scientific hot-houses such as Berkeley's Lawrence Livermore Laboratory that had produced the nuclear scientists who had done so much to win the war than it was to look back at F. Scott's Fitzgerald's Princeton.

Some Americans also began to reject the racial prejudices that had been so open in pre-war America. Harry Truman took a much tougher line on civil rights than his predecessor: the President's Commission on Civil Rights published the landmark 'To Secure These Rights' (1947), which argued that the federal government had a duty to secure rights as well as just to prevent abuses, while the Commission on Higher Education published the equally forthright 'Higher Education for American Democracy' (1947), which described quotas directed against Jews and Negroes as 'un-American', while *Gentleman's Agreement* (1947), a film starring Gregory Peck, won an Oscar for its devastating portrayal of gentlemanly antisemitism. Carey McWilliams's *Mask for Privilege* (1948) detailed just how widespread the prejudice remained. By 1952, public opinion polls began to show a marked decline in antisemitism.[20]

America embraced IQ tests and their various offspring, such as SAT tests, with an even greater enthusiasm than the British, though they preferred to use them to stream children rather than to separate them out into sheep and goats at eleven. The Truman Commission rested its case for expanding college enrolments on the results of the Army General Classification Test (AGCT), which had been administered to 10 million recruits during the Second World War and which revealed a lake of untapped ability in the population at large: 49 per cent of the population had the brains to complete fourteen years of schooling and 32 per cent had the brains to complete college.[21] Stanley Kaplan developed a successful business training people to take tests, which soon included tests for professional schools, such as LSATs for law schools, as well as SATs.

Policy-makers emphasized the importance of 'superior talent'. The Educational Policies Commission published a rousing report on *Education of the Gifted* (1950), which called on Americans to 'invest a larger proportion of their economic resources in the education of individuals of superior talent'.[22] The Early Admissions and Advanced Placement (AP) programmes tried to liberate bright children from the lock-step uniformity of the average high-school. The National Merit Scholarship Corporation, which was established in 1955, tried to raise public respect for intellectual excellence. On the principle that the best way to get people interested in intellectual excellence is to make it as much like sport as possible, the corporation turned competition for the scholarships into what the corporation's president, John Stalnaker, called a 'scholarama', complete with public ceremonies and 'letters of recognition'.

A chorus of American intellectuals argued that the meritocratic revolution that had followed the Second World War needed to be pushed further still. William H. Whyte portrayed 'organization man' (in his 1956 book of that title) as an intellectual lightweight who selected trainees on the basis of personality tests that were designed to eliminate non-conformity. C. Wright Mills denounced 'the power elite' (as his 1956 book was called) for its lack of 'meritorious ability'.[23] Members of the elite might look good on paper – Groton followed by Yale followed by Harvard Law School – but they all moved in the same narrow circles, drinking in the same clubs, putting on the same greens and swapping the same anecdotes. The future icon of the New Left called for the establishment of an 'administrative corps' of elite civil servants who could outlast America's ever-changing and inevitably short-sighted administrations.[24]

A cadre of indefatigable government reformers continued to try to establish a British-style elite civil service at the heart of American government: that is, alpha civil servants who were recruited on the basis of their general ability and expected to spend their careers moving from one job to another. Though Eisenhower and Nixon successfully led a Jacksonian resistance to this Jeffersonian scheme to create a 'natural aristocracy', a new generation of reformers came up with a clever idea to get around their objections: simply ignore the federal government and start again. The government established 'think factories' such as the RAND (short for Research and Development) Corporation that could recruit the best talent in the federal service without jumping through civil service hoops and then put that talent to work on the most pressing problems of the time.

If the meritocratic revolution was started by the GI Bill, it was put into overdrive by the launch of *Sputnik* on 4 October 1957. The success of the Russian satellite raised a possibility that few Americans, in the flush of their post-war boom, had dared to contemplate: that they were losing the brain race with the Soviet empire. The response was swift. Congress declared 'an educational emergency'. A year later the federal government passed the National Defense Education Act to increase the supply of brainpower and established the National Aeronautics and Space Administration (NASA) to reassert America's mastery of the heavens. Funding for the National Science Foundation more than tripled in a single year from $40 million to $134 million.[25] In *Excellence* (1961), John Gardner, the president of the Carnegie Corporation of New York and a future secretary of health, education and welfare under Lyndon Johnson argued that the pressure of technological competition had finally tipped the balance in favour of an educated elite. American life had always had an egalitarian tone, he argued: no sooner did elites emerge than populists tried to snuff them out. But the meritocrats were finally on the advance not because they were well organized but because they were in the vanguard of scientific change. Gifted children who had once been treated with 'an almost savage rejection' were now being feted as agents of national survival.[26]

The Ivy League universities broke the aristocratic embrace and threw in their lot with James Conant's meritocratic vision. The change in Yale, Harvard's great rival, was particularly striking. In the mid-1950s, Yale's president, the magnificently named Alfred Whitney Griswold, proclaimed that he would not allow Yale man to become 'a beetle-browed, highly specialised intellectual'.[27] When Griswold died in 1963 Yale appointed a president of a very different kidney, Kingman Brewster. Brewster briskly declared that he didn't 'intend to preside over a finishing school on Long Island Sound' and, aided by his own equivalent of Henry Chauncey, R. Inslee 'Inky' Clark, as dean of admissions, he set about rebuilding the student body, and indeed the faculty, along meritocratic lines, putting Groton and the rest on notice that Yale would no longer accept mediocre students just because they came from 'Yale families' and reaching out to public schools. Yale's class of 1970 contained 50 per cent more public-school graduates than the class of 1969, many of them, presumably, 'beetle-browed intellectuals'.[28]

LA FRANCE MÉRITOCRATIQUE

France was even more in need of reconstruction after the Second World War than Britain: the country had been in decline since at least 1871, with a grim record of military defeat, colonial retreat and domestic instability, and that decline had culminated in collapse before the Nazis and the humiliation of the Vichy regime. The French decided that the key to reconstruction lay in reaching back into the country's meritocratic tradition and updating it for a new age of European integration and technological innovation.

The overall architect of this rebirth was General de Gaulle, who combined a profound belief in France's ancestral 'grandeur' with a commitment to technocratic reform. Far more than either Churchill or Macmillan, he succeeded in combining nostalgia for his country's past with a commitment to embracing a very different future, believing, as he wrote in his youthful treatise on military reform, *The Army of the Future*, that 'nothing lasts unless it is incessantly renewed'.[29] The self-styled representative of *la France profonde* was also a believer in scientific management. The poetic exponent of 'a certain idea of France' was also a sworn enemy of 'feudalities' that stood in the way of progress and reform.[30]

France could also call upon a cohort of civil servants – most of them in their early thirties in 1945 – who came to power after the Second World War and remained at the centre of power even as de Gaulle himself came and went. These *hauts fonctionnaires* inherited France's established cult of the disinterested public servant working for the quasi-sacred state but added to it the glamour of Keynesian economics and scientific management. They knew in their bones that the only way France could overcome the economic weaknesses that had led to the defeat in 1940 was to renew the economy by investing in infrastructure and science. They believed in the broad creed of 'modernization' – using the power of the state to invest in infrastructure (particularly railways) and new technology (particularly atomic power) – and loathed with equal intensity both Anglo-Saxon liberals (who left everything to what they regarded as the anarchic market) and French reactionaries (who looked back to the world of feudal lords and happy peasants). They liked to think of themselves as 'conspirators of modernization' who were engaged in a behind-the-scenes battle against France's more conservative bureaucrats, but they were also 'very public conspirators' who spread their ideas through public lectures and articles in the press.[31]

These *hauts fonctionnaires* rode to de Gaulle's aid twice: first, during the immediate post-war reconstruction, when they established much of the technocratic infrastructure of the new France; second, during de Gaulle's presidency, from 1959 onwards, when they staffed the administrative machine of the Fifth Republic and dominated the government commissions and quasi-governmental organizations that de Gaulle favoured. A central member of this group was de Gaulle's fellow resistance fighter Michel Debré. Debré played a prominent role in creating Gaullism by drafting the new constitution that established the Fifth Republic and acting as the great man's first prime minister. But his most important contribution to the new French meritocracy was the creation of the École Nationale d'Administration (ENA) in 1945, which, as de Gaulle wrote in his memoirs 'came all prepared from the brain and the work of Michel Debré'.[32]

Admission to the ENA was through a rigorous and gruelling set of examinations. The candidates needed to take five written exams (in public law, economy, general knowledge, a summary of documents in either European law and policies or social law and policies, and a fifth exam, to be chosen from subjects ranging from maths to languages). The candidates with the highest marks then took five oral exams, including a forty-five-minute public trial in which any question could be asked. In a gesture to the Platonic ideal of the guardian fit in body as well as mind, the exam included a test of sporting fitness.

From the first, the ENA admitted just forty to eighty candidates a year, far less than Harvard College, which currently admits 1,600, or Oxford (3,200). The chosen few were treated to two years of ultra-competitive education and training at the ENA and then ranked numerically according to academic performance. They were also infused with a sense of the dignity of their calling. 'The training – one need not hide this – also has a moral objective,' wrote Debré. 'It is not one of the missions of the school to play politics or to impose a particular doctrine. But the School must also teach its future civil servants "le sens de l'État", it must make them understand the responsibilities of the Administration, make them taste the grandeur and accept the servitudes of the *métier*.'[33] Students were treated as civil servants as soon as they were offered a place, including being paid salaries, and were guaranteed top jobs. The top fifteen almost always chose to enter one of three administrative corps – the Conseil d'État, the Inspection des Finances or the Cour des Comptes. Civil servants were also given much more freedom to move about than their equivalents in Britain: they could move not only between politics and administration but also between the public sector and the private sector. The French thus took the Northcote–Trevelyan belief in 'general ability' to a new level, arguing that, if you had sufficient brainpower, you should not be confined by bureaucratic rails but should be free to apply it in any area where you saw fit.

De Gaulle's new creation provided France with a regular supply of high-quality Platonic guardians, including presidents (Valéry Giscard d'Estaing, Jacques Chirac, François Hollande and now Emmanuel Macron), prime ministers (Laurent Fabius, Michel Rocard, Édouard Balladur, Alain Juppé, Lionel Jospin and Dominique de Villepin) and leading civil servants and businesspeople. Typically, between a third and a half of every French Cabinet since the 1960s has been composed of ENA alumni (the Sarkozy administration was a deliberate exception).

France's new meritocratic machinery did exactly what de Gaulle had hoped, revitalizing a great French tradition, injecting some dynamism into a previously sclerotic country and restoring pride in the French state. France enjoyed thirty glorious years of sustained economic growth led by a combination of powerful government departments and successful private companies. In 1945–55 the growth rate hit a remarkable 4.5 per cent a year.

The meritocratic revolution transformed society so thoroughly after the Second World War that it's impossible to describe it without trying the reader's patience beyond endurance. So I've decided to tell the story through three snapshots: the success of (mainly working-class) grammar-school boys in post-war Britain; the rise of research universities in America; and the new cult of intelligence in business. The first shows how meritocracy opened up elite positions to a new class of people – and what this meant in human as well as social terms. The second shows how the revolution placed the elite research university at the heart of the knowledge economy. The third shows how business was transformed by the new meritocratic spirit. The three taken together are designed to demonstrate just how wide-ranging the revolution was: there was almost no aspect of post-war society that wasn't transformed by the new revolutionary spirit.

THE USES OF SCHOLARSHIPS

Alan Bennett's *The History Boys* is one of the best fictional portraits of the promise and pain of high-stakes examinations. The play, which premiered in 2004 and was turned into a film in 2006, deals with a group of boys from a modest grammar school in Sheffield who, having got unusually good results in their A-levels, are asked to stay on at school to take the scholarship examination for Oxford. The main theme of the play is the struggle to master a demanding subject and impress the Oxford examiners. An important subtheme is adolescent self-discovery and homosexuality. It is all very touching – particularly for those of us who went to obscure grammar schools and then won places to read history at Oxford.

The work has an anachronistic feel: though it's set in 1983, when Britain was polarized by Thatcherism, and shaken by punk rock, the history boys don't discuss politics, listen to pop music or find it odd that they are attending a grammar school when the rest of the state education system has gone comprehensive. The reason for the anachronism is simple: what Bennett is really writing about is the England of the late 1940s and early 1950s, when he himself went to Leeds Modern School and then won a scholarship to Exeter College, Oxford, to read history, eventually getting a first and spending time studying for a doctorate with the legendary medievalist Bruce McFarlane before flying, moth-like, to the bright lights of London.

Mr Bennett's fellow grammar-school products mounted a remarkably successful assault on Britain's clubby establishment. The public schools' share of Oxbridge places declined from 55 per cent in 1959 to 38 per cent in 1967 with the difference made almost entirely by grammar schools.[34] The proportion of eldest sons of peers who gained admission to the two ancient universities declined from nearly 50 per cent in the 1950s to 20 per cent in the late 1960s.[35]

As teddy-bear-toting aristocrats disappeared, grammar-school swots acquired a new swagger. Noel Annan recalled that 'the manners of the grammar school boys became ascendant and the public school boys found themselves at a disadvantage'. 'The grammar school boy was freer, more successful with girls, more self-confident and streetwise.'[36] William Waldegrave, who went up to Corpus Christi College, Oxford, from Eton in the mid-1960s, made a similar point. The tone of the university was being set by the products of grammar schools rather than public schools:

> My friends and competitors were as likely – possibly more likely – to come from the great Lancashire and Midlands grammar schools as from my old school or Winchester or Harrow. They were confident, clever and at least as widely cultured as we were ... A surge of new, meritocratic ability refreshed Britain, even if a disconcerting number of the new television iconoclasts at whom we laughed turned out to have attended Shrewsbury or Charterhouse.[37]

Grammar-school boys seemed cooler than their public-school counterparts: both Mick Jagger and John Lennon had been to grammar schools. They also seemed more serious: at Cambridge, for example, they made a cult of high-minded scholars such as F. R. Leavis and Geoffrey Elton. Grammar-school-educated writers broadened the range of British fiction from the drawing rooms and country-house parties of Evelyn Waugh and Anthony Powell to the cramped living rooms of two-up two-down houses in the Midlands and the North. Grammar-school-educated scientists and technicians stoked the white heat of the technological revolution.

The products of grammar schools revolutionized first the Labour Party and then the Conservative Party. Harold Wilson, the son of a self-educated textile chemist, climbed the educational ladder from his local council school, via Wirral Grammar School, to Oxford, won a clutch of university prizes, including the Gladstone Memorial Prize, took an outstanding first in Politics, Philosophy and Economics (PPE) (legend has it that he got alphas on all his papers except moral philosophy), was awarded a research fellowship on graduation, and became President of the Board of Trade at the age of thirty-one.

The Labour Party presented the 1964 general election as a conflict between the fourteenth Mr Wilson with his white laboratory coat and the fourteenth Earl of Home with his three-piece tweed suit. 'For the commanding heights of British industry to be controlled today by men whose only claim is their aristocratic connections or the power of inherited wealth or speculative finance,' Wilson told the 1963 Labour conference, 'is as irrelevant to the twentieth century as would be the continued purchase of commissions in the armed forces by lordly amateurs. At the very time that even the MCC has abolished the distinction between amateurs and professionals, in science and industry we are content to remain a nation of Gentlemen in a world of Players.'[38]

The Conservative Party retaliated by appointing a scholarship boy of their own, in the form of Edward Heath, a product of Chatham House Grammar School, Ramsgate and Balliol College, Oxford. (It is proof of how unaccustomed the parliamentary party was to dealing with grammar-school types that it chose such an unappetizing representative of the breed, mistaking boorish bad temper for proof of grammar-school authenticity.) Throughout his career, Heath emphasized his humble background and his Balliol scholarship and, at one point, presented himself as the representative of capitalist meritocracy as against trade-union-dominated collectivism.

The success of the grammar schools even produced a weird debate about whether Britain suffered from *too much* social mobility. Sociologists based at the Institute of Community Studies, an urban studies think tank founded by Michael Young in 1954, examined the way that grammar schools broke down the bonds of solidarity that held working-class communities together. Working-class intellectuals made names for themselves by decrying their educational opportunities. Dennis Marsden, a member of Young's Institute who had made it to Cambridge from the provincial working class, described the loneliness of the scholarship winner. 'I knew what a mountaineer feels on an exposed climb.'[39] Richard Hoggart, a working-class boy who went from Leeds city schools to Leeds University, described scholarship winners as 'the uprooted and anxious' in his best-selling *The Uses of Literacy* (1957).[40] They spent their childhoods at the friction point between 'middle-class' grammar schools and their working-class homes, cut off from their own communities and learning to use a pair of accents and adopt a dual set of characters and values.

It is impossible to read Marsden and Hoggart these days without a sense of surprise: would that we had similar problems today! Would that working-class boys and girls could complain about being whisked too quickly up the social system rather than about being left to rot at the bottom! For all their regrets, Williams and Hoggart were members of one of the luckiest generations in British history, not just in material terms but also in spiritual terms: their schools and universities introduced them to the glories of civilization and allowed them to exercise their intellectual powers to the full.

The number of people who went to university was still small by modern standards: as late as 1968 the British admitted only 8 per cent of the age group to university. The conveyor belt was nevertheless expanding. The fortunate few were also presented, at public expense, with a golden ticket to post-war prosperity. They were given full scholarships rather than loaded down with debt. On arriving at university they were treated as if they were no different from the sprigs of the upper class who had hitherto dominated such institutions – at Oxford and Cambridge everybody had servants (called scouts at Oxford and bedders at Cambridge) to look after them. On coming down they were guaranteed a secure place in the apparatus of post-war affluence, teaching in universities, administering cities, staffing hospitals and, if they had a political flare, performing in Parliament.

There were history boys across the rich world in this era: the children (particularly male children) of coal miners and dock workers who were suddenly given a chance, thanks to the expanded welfare state and booming economy, to rise up the social system on the basis of pure brains and effort. The Italians doubled the number of children in full-time education in 1959–69 (though Italy did not raise its school-leaving age to fourteen until 1962). The French quintupled the number of high-school graduates from 1950 to 1970.[41]

Though it is easy to focus, as so many sociologists have done, on the incompleteness of the scholarship system, the post-war expansion of educational opportunity nevertheless marked a stark break with the past. Hitherto, the grammar schools, *lycées* and *Gymnasien* of Europe had been overwhelmingly the preserve of the ruling elite. They reinforced rather than conferred status. In the post-war era they were sometimes dominated, both numerically and culturally, by a new class of strivers. This opened a breach between the scholarship winners and their parents. It also opened a breach between a world where educational opportunity was determined by class background and one in which it was determined by intellectual ability

THE RISE OF THE ACADEMIC MERITOCRACY

No book is more redolent of the optimism of the post-war academic boom than Clark Kerr's *The Uses of the University* (1963). *Uses* is best remembered for introducing the concept of the 'multiversity': the idea that the university's job was to meet multiple social needs from the economic (providing engines of growth) to the cultural (acting as centres of cultural life) and to serve multiple constituencies. Kerr (1911–2003) was partly drawn to this idea for marketing reasons: when he wrote the book he was president of the University of California, the country's biggest and best public university, with 40,000 employees and parking spaces reserved for Nobel Prize winners, and his appetite for money was limitless. He also meant what he said: the university bureaucrat burned with a vision of a new social role for universities. The multiversity was a machine for delivering Kerr's ideal of research-based meritocracy.

The book was most obviously a riposte to John Henry Newman's *The Idea of a University* (1852). Newman had argued, in some of the finest prose written in a century of fine prose, that the purpose of a university was to turn students into cultivated gentlemen. Kerr retorted, in rather flatter prose, that the university had lots of purposes rather than one but that those purposes included turning out accomplished technocrats. At the same time, it was a gloss on Thomas Jefferson's writings about the natural aristocracy. Though Kerr shared Jefferson's enthusiasm for identifying natural ability and providing it with the opportunities that it deserved, he believed that 'natural aristocrats' ought to be rigorous professional scholars selected on the quality of their published work rather than the extent to which they exemplified civilized values. They needed to be given the time and resources to produce substantial works of research, with light teaching loads, fawning research assistants, generous grants to attend international conferences and carefully chosen graduate students. Kerr was unashamed of his academic elitism: 'The great university is of necessity elitist – the elite of merit – but it operates in an environment dedicated to an egalitarian philosophy. How may the contribution of the elite be made clear to the egalitarians, and how may an aristocracy of intellect justify itself to a democracy of all men?'[42]

Kerr's answer to this question was that first-rate research makes the world richer as well as wiser. Great scientists can turn atoms into atomic energy; great social scientists can solve problems like poverty; great scholar-administrators can extend the rule of reason. Kerr held that leading research universities ought to be temples to the mind – but he conceived of the mind not as pure reason, divorced from the world, but as a problem-solving machine, immersed in the world. The role of the scholar was not just to understand the world but to change it for the common good.

This vision of the research scholar as the meritocrat-in-chief was rooted in his autobiography. Kerr's father held a master's degree from the University of Berlin and spoke five languages. Kerr was encouraged to apply to Swarthmore College, a selective liberal arts college, after he got the second-highest IQ score in his school, Reading High School, Pennsylvania. He flourished at Swarthmore partly because he was assigned to the school's intensive honours programme and partly because he embraced the school's Quakerism (which meant social activism as much as spirituality). Kerr moved to the West Coast to pursue his interest in social justice but soon gravitated back to academia, taking a Ph.D. in economics at Berkeley, joining the faculty in 1945, becoming an iron-bottomed committee man, and, as a reward for shuffling all that paper, being appointed president of the University of California in 1958. A quintessential scholar-administrator who spent much of his time jetting from one conference to another, Clark nevertheless made sure that he spent his spare time mastering slices of artistic or literary history, lest he should become, like so many of his kind, a bureaucrat pure and simple.

Uses was much more of a practical blueprint than Newman's work had been. Before publishing his book, Kerr had spent years putting into place his 'masterplan' for the University of California. The 'masterplan' was designed to produce a new kind of university, less snobbish than the Ivy League universities of the East Coast but more heavyweight than the old-fashioned state universities. It was also designed to produce a living paradox, an institution that was simultaneously open to everybody but also at the cutting edge of scientific research. Kerr thought that he could resolve this paradox by making judicious use of differentiation and concentration. He drew a bright line between the University of California (which was allowed to give Ph.D.s) and state colleges (which focused on teaching). He also reinforced the hierarchy within the University of California, with Berkeley at the top and other campuses, including two new campuses at Irvine and Santa Cruz, lower down. Research funding was ruthlessly focused on a small collection of institutions and professors (most of them at Berkeley) whose job was to explore the frontiers of knowledge. Kerr was so highly regarded as a reformer in his day that his face, like Conant's before him, graced the cover of *Time* magazine.

Clark Kerr was unusual in the breadth of his vision and the rigour of his thinking. For most academics the post-war meritocratic revolution was a more prosaic affair: an opportunity to turn themselves into professionals and pluck the fruits of their professional status in the form of sabbaticals and conferences in comfortable places. Gone were the days when academics were gentlemen first and scholars second. The large group of researchers who flooded into academia after the Second World War were professionals who measured their lives in terms of Ph.D.s earned and articles accepted.

Yet even as academics became more obsessed with producing professional articles, universities became more important in controlling entry into the professional life, including business life.

BUSINESS INTELLIGENCE

In Chapter Ten we noted that American business played a significant part in nurturing the meritocratic spirit. Giant businesses such as the railroads required specialized middle-managers to keep the trains running on time, and great universities such as the University of Pennsylvania and Harvard established business schools to produce them. The advance of the business meritocracy was nevertheless patchy before the Second World War. Much of the business world remained resolutely anti-intellectual. Sinclair Lewis's *Babbitt* (1922) is a merciless portrait of American business at the beginning of the roaring twenties. George F. Babbitt, the eponymous hero, is the very model of a solid citizen: an estate agent by profession, 'nimble in the calling of selling houses for more than people could afford to pay', and a conformist by temperament, proudly devoid of original ideas or intellectual curiosity. He surrounds himself with clever gadgets like alarm clocks and electric toasters that symbolize the power of technology. He wears a booster's club button to signify his loyalty to his local town, Zenith, and his willingness to praise it on all occasions, however overwhelming the evidence to the contrary. His friends, such as Joseph K. Pumphrey, owner of the Riteway Business College and 'instructor in Public Speaking, Business English, Scenario Writing, and Commercial Law', are all exactly like him, boosters and conformists. The book gave the English language a word, 'Babbitt' – meaning a 'person and especially a business or professional man who conforms unthinkingly to prevailing middle-class standards' – and a George Gershwin song, 'The Babbitt and the Bromide'.

Babbitt was typical of many American businessmen in his contempt for 'book learning' and his admiration for 'common sense'. In 1924 an anonymous businessman wrote an article in an American magazine under the title 'Why I Never Hire Brilliant Men'. Brilliance is invariably associated with intemperance and irresponsibility; it's far safer to rely on 'hard-headed' and 'hard-muscled' types.[43] The great entrepreneurs were usually self-made men who had succeeded without the benefit of higher learning or careful breeding (in 1900, fewer than one in five business leaders had completed a university degree).

Henry Ford combined a genius for car-making with buffoonish, and frequently contemptible, views on foreign policy and politics. H. L. Mencken thought that the average American businessman belonged to the species 'Boobus americanus'.

Business schools started life as crosses between trade schools and rotary clubs: students picked up a smattering of trade craft and a collection of friends for life but didn't engage with the big ideas that were transforming economics. Consultancies focused on forging lasting relations with big companies rather than selling ideas. Marvin Bower, McKinsey's guiding spirit, was so determined that McKinsey men should look the part that he insisted, until 1963, that they wore a hat when they went out in public. Many company men preferred to acquire their knowledge on the job rather than in universities, with the most successful companies, such as IBM, General Electric and Kodak, offering lifetime employment and sending promising company men (and a few women) to their own internal training schools.

The great American sociologists of the 1950s portrayed businessmen as anti-intellectual conformists. In *Organization Man* (1956), William Whyte described the typical businessman as an affable type who puts fitting in above everything else – pleasant, easy to get along with, but hardly rocket scientists. He entitled one chapter 'The Fight against Genius'.[44] In *The Pyramid Climbers*, Vance Packard described successful executives as 'polished, cool, handsome, adaptable, highly energized, soft-spoken, over-integrated, non-oddball power players. Often they also have demonstrated during their rise a conspicuous ability to keep their heads down and their noses clean.'[45] The command centres of the business world were rotary clubs and golf clubs rather than faculty lounges and laboratories.

The first sign that the relationship between business and trained intelligence was changing was provided by the arrival of the whizz-kids after the Second World War. The whizz-kids were a group of highly educated Air Force officers, including Robert McNamara and Tex Thornton, who persuaded Henry Ford II to give them all a job at the end of the war. They then succeeded in rescuing the ailing company from disaster not by producing better products – they didn't really know that much about motor cars – but by producing better companies, largely by imposing tight financial and managerial controls.

They then applied the same techniques to a range of other companies and institutions outside the automobile sector: Thornton created Litton Industries, America's first major conglomerate, and McNamara moved to the Pentagon, where he tried to win the Vietnam War by escalating kill rates, and then the World Bank.[46]

The two institutions that cemented the relationship between business and trained intelligence were business schools and consultancies. In 1966, the Carnegie and Ford foundations combined to publish a searing report that argued that business schools needed to justify their place in universities by producing more original research. Thereafter, the schools embraced both the publish-or-perish mentality and the intellectual star system that prevailed in the rest of academia. Business schools hatched professors who were notable not just for their knowledge of particular businesses but for their ability to produce intellectual models: strategists such as Michael Porter and finance theorists such as Michael Jensen, who tried to bring the rigour of economics to the study of business. They also mass-produced MBAs who had little time for the post-war business establishment, with its clubby culture and three-Martini lunches, and who wanted instead to force American business to sit up and shape up – by pursuing shareholder value if they were disciples of Jensen or by examining the operation of the 'five forces' if they were Porterites.

The same cult of 'smarts' gripped management consultancies. Bruce Henderson, the founder of the Boston Consulting Group (BCG), believed that the company's only chance of challenging McKinsey lay in out-thinking it rather than out-networking it. To that end, he produced a series of elegant intellectual models such as the 'experience curve', which taught companies that they could reduce their costs as they expanded their market share, thanks to the accumulation of knowhow, and the 'growth share matrix', which encouraged companies to view themselves not as an undifferentiated whole but as a portfolio of businesses that make different contributions to the bottom line ('cash cows' vs 'dogs', for example). McKinsey hit back by producing business gurus of its own such as Tom Peters and Robert Waterman, the authors of *In Search of Excellence* (1982), and Richard Pascale, the author of *The Art of Japanese Management* (1981).[47]

A good example of the growing influence of business theory is

provided by the Romney dynasty. George Romney, who didn't graduate from university, worked in the manufacturing sector for twenty-three
years, running the American Motors Corporation for eight of them
and becoming 'a folk hero of the American auto industry'. Mitt Romney graduated in the top 5 per cent in his class at Harvard Business
School before joining three IQ-obsessed consultancies, first BCG in
1975, then Bain and Company two years later and, finally, as CEO,
Bain Capital, which married strategic consultancy with the shareholder-
value revolution by investing money in the firms it advised. Under
Romney's direction Bain Capital 're-engineered' more than 150 companies in a bewildering variety of industries and made the future
Republican presidential candidate and US senator an estimated fortune of $200 million.[48]

The new meritocrats thus transformed everything that they touched
in post-war society: schools became avenues of mobility, universities
became research institutions-cum-professional training schools; business became more preoccupied with the brainpower of its employees.
All this inevitably provoked a backlash – first from the left and then
from the right – as students baulked at relentless competition and
employees wearied of being messed around by corporate whizz-kids.
Before looking at the backlash we need to go back and tell our story
once again from the female perspective. For the rise of the meritocracy was as much as anything else the rise of women.

13

Girly Swots

In the summer of 1947, a young woman from the Midlands graduated from Oxford University with a good second-class degree in
chemistry. Margaret Roberts encountered plenty of gender-based discrimination as an undergraduate. The grandest colleges, with their
dreaming spires and magnificent gardens, were reserved for men while
women had to make do with pokier places on the edge of town.
Women weren't admitted to the Oxford Union, the debating society
where Edward Heath, Denis Healey and Tony Benn forged their political careers. Roberts encountered plenty more restrictions as she tried
to combine a high-flying career with marriage and motherhood. As a
young chemist fresh from university, she was given an uninspiring job
on the grounds that she would soon marry and have children. On
being shortlisted for a North London parliamentary seat, she worried
that 'the usual prejudice against women will prevail and that I shall
probably come the inevitable "close second"'.[1] When she first entered
Parliament, she found herself in a clubby world where only about 3
per cent of MPs were female and where many decisions were made in
male-only dining clubs. Women were provided with a special room in
the basement equipped with a chaise longue and an ironing board.
There were no female lavatories in the division lobbies until 1997,
when the election of 120 women, many of them quickly dubbed
'Blair's Babes', took the proportion of female MPs above 10 per cent
for the first time.

Roberts nevertheless found that every door opened if you gave it a
shove. Her selection for a safe Tory seat at the age of thirty-two made
her the youngest MP. ('The Conservatives of Finchley have armed
themselves with a new weapon,' the *Finchley Press* declared, 'a clever

woman.')[2] She rose up the ranks swiftly, becoming education secretary in 1970, leader of the opposition in 1975 and prime minister in 1979. Mrs Thatcher's eleven-year premiership was one of the most consequential in twentieth-century British history, with the radical policies she pioneered catching fire across the world.

Mrs Thatcher was the consummate example of an upwardly mobile grammar-school type who believed that barriers were for overcoming rather than agonizing over. Her first surviving letter discusses her exam performance.[3] She disliked the languid public-school types who believed that government was about managing decline almost as much as she loathed the leftists who manned the picket lines demanding higher pay for less work. She made no secret of the fact that she thought that many of the men in her Cabinet were indecisive wafflers: (*Spitting Image*, a satirical comedy show, did a famous sketch about her going out to dinner with her Cabinet. 'Steak or fish?' asks the waiter. 'Steak, of course,' she replies. 'What about the vegetables?' Surveying the room imperiously, she replies, 'They'll have the same.')

Though Margaret Thatcher's story was an extraordinary one, it also echoed many of the themes of post-war Britain. Institutional prejudices against women were so entrenched that, in *The Rise of the Meritocracy*, Michael Young envisioned women staying at home to devote themselves to rearing male meritocrats. Yet Thatcher's generation of females found restrictions collapsing all around them: the first female prime minister coincided with hundreds of other female firsts who, in their turn, blazed a trail for younger women who found even fewer prejudices and even greater opportunities.

The story of the rise of women has often been written in terms of collective struggle and heroic political gestures. Women agitated for the vote in their millions. Suffragettes chained themselves to railings, starved themselves almost to death and threw themselves in front of the king's horses. Yet there is another story behind the public one: one that is meritocratic rather than egalitarian and individualistic rather than collectivist. Lonely scholars burned the midnight oil to prove that they were just as good as men, if not better. Bureaucrats and lawyers extended the principle of open competition to the other half of humanity. The same forces were at work with the 'second sex' as with the first: a meritocratic idea that emphasizes the importance of open competition and level playing fields; an intellectual aristocracy that tries to wrest power from the old landed elite; a cadre of psychologists who discovered that differences between individuals are far bigger than differences between groups; and an expanding state that was forced, by a combination of logic and necessity, to look for talent wherever it could find it.

Let's cast our minds back to the glory days of the meritocratic revolution, in the mid-nineteenth century, when liberals were doing battle against place- and class-based restrictions in the name of open competition, and re-examine it again from a woman's perspective. How did the ancient distinction between the sexes finally fall victim to the logic of meritocracy?

THE SUBJECTION OF WOMEN

When Macaulay and Co. were singing the praises of open competition for their fellow men, women suffered from restrictions on their lives that now strike us as astonishing. They couldn't vote, let alone sit in Parliament. In Westminster, women who wanted to watch parliamentary debates not only had to sit in a special ladies' gallery but also behind a metal grille so that MPs couldn't see their distracting female forms.[4] Women spent their lives subject to men, obeying their fathers before they got married and their husbands afterwards. On marriage, they even had to surrender their property to their husbands in a process that the eighteenth-century jurist Sir William Blackstone dubbed 'coverture' ('husband and wife . . . are one person in law, so that the very being and existence of the woman is suspended during the coverture, or entirely merged and incorporated in that of the husband').[5] The commitment to keeping women under control extended to dress: middle-class women were forced to dress in corsets – the Western equivalent of Chinese foot-binding – and women in service were expected to dress in uniforms. Queen Victoria was the only Victorian woman who didn't suffer from legal restrictions on her rights based on her sex – as Queen, she enjoyed exactly the same rights, down to the letter, as her predecessor as monarch, her uncle, William IV – but even Her Majesty was expected to wear corsets.

These second-class citizens were invariably subjected to double standards: men could divorce their wives if they found that they were guilty of adultery, but women couldn't do the same. Men will be men, after all. They were sometimes treated with shocking brutality: Britain's Contagious Diseases Act of 1864 gave the supposedly nightwatchman state the right to arrest women, subject them to humiliating examinations and hold them against their will in state hospitals.

This treatment of women depended on two articles of faith. The first was the doctrine of 'separate spheres', which held that men and women held sway in different areas of life, each of which had its own distinctive functions and regulations: women ruled in the 'private sphere', which was focused on home-making and child-rearing, while men ruled in the public sphere, which was devoted to competition and money-making. 'Their vocation is to make life endurable,' a Tory MP told the Commons. The two spheres complemented each other: the home was a necessary counterbalance to the capitalist world of self-seeking. One American advice manual, *A Voice to the Married* (1841), told wives in no uncertain terms that they had a duty to provide their husbands with a haven in a heartless world: 'an Elysium to which he can flee and find rest from the sorry strife of a selfish world'.[6] Without the 'haven', administered by what Coventry Patmore dubbed, in 1854, 'the angel in the house', the world would be too heartless to be endured, but without the heartless capitalist doing battle in the marketplace there would be no money to sustain civilization.

The second was the idea that women are the 'weaker sex', at once frailer and finer than men. This started with a simple physiological observation – that women are, on average, shorter and physically weaker than men – and then proceeded to construct a mighty skyscraper of prejudice on this foundation. Women are slaves to their body's menstrual rhythms, which can render them moody and distracted. They are more intellectually and physically fragile than men – 'Frailty, thy name is woman,' as Shakespeare has it in *Hamlet*. On the other hand, they are closer to heavenly things – like a 'milk-white lamb that bleats for man's protection', as Keats put it. Expose them to horrible sights and they will fall apart. Subject them to hard thinking and they will become deranged. Women are like beautiful flowers which make the world more splendid but wither and die in harsh conditions.

These beliefs were reinforced by men's ignorance of women, an ignorance that easily tipped into misogyny. Most men in the Anglo-American upper class grew up in a homosocial world. They moved from all-male schools to all-male colleges to all-male professions, expending their surplus energy on all-male games and relaxing in all-male dining societies, and they rather liked their world 'clean of the clash of sex', as Kenneth Grahame wrote of his masterpiece, *The Wind in the Willows* (1908).

Both doctrines strengthened as capitalism advanced: the more cut-throat society became, as old-fashioned paternalistic relations collapsed in the face of industry and finance, the more the authorities felt the need to protect women from the marketplace and put them back in the home. It was as if the Victorians realized that it was impossible to construct a society that consisted of nothing more than rights-bearing rational individuals bent on maximizing their utility: in order for half of society to operate according to such unforgiving principles, the other half had to operate according to the principles of the hearth and home.

These twin notions of separate spheres and female frailty shaped women's education, such as it was. Upper- and middle-class women were educated in the domestic arts of stitching, sewing and other female 'accomplishments' in all-girl schools, many of them no better than Miss Pinkerton's Academy, so ably caricatured by Thackeray in *Vanity Fair* (1848). Whenever the idea of improving women's education popped up, the second argument about female weakness came into play: educating women would either test their brains to destruction or else turn them into unnatural bluestockings who would never find the real happiness of married life. In *Sex in Education; or, A Fair Chance for the Girls* (1873), based on a study of seven Vassar College students, Dr Edward Clarke argued that women who were subjected to the same demanding course of advanced education as men developed 'neuralgia, uterine disease, hysteria and other derangements of the nervous system'.[7]

At the high point of Social Darwinism, in the late-Victorian and Edwardian eras, these two ideas were reinforced by a third, that women were lower down the evolutionary scale than men. Charles Darwin set the ball rolling in *The Descent of Man* (1871), arguing that, across the natural world, full-grown females are more backward than full-grown males. Gustave Le Bon, the author of *The Psychology of Crowds* (1895), ran with the ball: women 'represent the most inferior forms of human evolution ... they are closer to children and savages than to an adult, civilized man. They excel in fickleness, inconstancy, absence of thought and logic, and incapacity to reason.' He dealt with the problem of female geniuses such as George Eliot with a chilling aside: 'Without doubt there exist some distinguished women, very superior to the average man, but they are as exceptional as the birth of any monstrosity, as, for example, of a gorilla with two heads; consequently, we may neglect them entirely.'[8]

To prove his case, Le Bon went around measuring women's heads, along with the heads of 'savages', 'geniuses', and so on, even inventing a portable cephalometer which he could whip out whenever the mood took him. The result was clear to him: women have smaller heads than men, mediocre men have smaller heads than talented men and 'inferior races' have smaller heads than 'superior races'. He also employed (somewhat random) archaeological evidence to prove that these differences had become greater over time, as the differential pressure of evolution made men more 'dominant' and women more 'passive'.

Sociobiologists believed that, if evolution was allowed to work its magic, this process of differentiation would become more marked in the future. 'An adult white woman differs far more from a white man than a negress or pygmy woman from her equivalent male,' H. G. Wells, an enthusiastic popularizer of biology, insisted.[9] But there was a great threat to this natural process: if women were allowed to free themselves from the tyranny of biology, they would doom the human race to destruction, first through a decline in quality (the educated were the first to limit their fertility) and then through a decline in quantity.

The meritocratic idea played a central role in exploding these cultural and intellectual barriers to women's progress. By putting the question of open competition at the heart of politics, it raised the question of why women weren't included in that competition; by elevating the importance of intellectual ability over all other attributes, particularly physical strength and courage, it made it much easier for women to compete head to head with men.

The American Revolution had inevitably raised an important gender-related question, not just in America itself but in any country that took the liberal cause seriously: why weren't women included in the phrase 'all men are created equal'? Abigail Adams raised the question gently in a letter to her husband, John, pleading that the men who were making a new set of laws to govern the new nation should 'remember the ladies'. Other women raised the question less gently when they argued that the new republic had no choice, if it was to avoid making a mockery of its founding principles, but to extend the principle of equality to women. The first Woman's Rights Convention, in Seneca Falls, New York, in 1848 adopted a Declaration of Sentiments which repeatedly echoed the Declaration of Independence. The declaration began with the resounding assertion that it's 'self-evident that all men and women are created equal', before producing a catalogue of 'injuries and usurpations' of men towards women that were all designed to establish men's 'absolute tyranny': men had forced women to obey laws that they had no role in making; had monopolized profitable employment; and had 'created a false sentiment by giving the world a different code of morals for men and for women'.[10]

The centenary of the Declaration of Independence in 1876 gave women's leaders a chance to publish a Declaration of Rights pointing to the illogic of excluding women from the full benefits of the constitution. This document, like most feminist writings of the era, sounded a thoroughly individualistic tone: women, as individuals, should be put on the same footing as men, as individuals, because they possessed the same rights and abilities. They should be judged according to universal principles rather than treated as a separate class of beings, whether being treated as a separate class meant being discriminated against or protected and pampered.

The case in favour of equality, particularly equality of voting rights, was given a further boost by the anti-slavery movement. The movement trained thousands of women in political activism: the National Loyal Women's League, which was organized by Elizabeth Cady

Stanton and Susan B. Anthony, raised 400,000 signatures in favour of the Thirteenth Amendment to abolish slavery, a formidable accomplishment in the pre-internet age.[11] It also raised the question of comparative disadvantage: if black men deserved certain rights based on their common humanity, why didn't women deserve the same rights? In 1837, Sarah Grimké wrote to the president of the Boston Female Anti-Slavery Society making an explicit connection between men and slave-owners and women and slaves:

> All history attests that man has subjugated woman to his will, used her as a means to promote his selfish gratification, to minister to his sensual pleasures, to be instrumental in promoting his comfort; but never has he desired to elevate her to that rank which she was created to fill. He has done all he could to debase and enslave her mind; and now he looks triumphantly on the ruin he has wrought, and says, the being he has thus deeply injured is his inferior.[12]

There was a pronounced class element to this argument: in the aftermath of the Civil War many women were furious that, as affluent, educated Anglo-Saxons, they were being denied rights that were being extended to newly freed blacks and newly arrived immigrants. In 1902, Elizabeth Stanton said that she was prepared to accept a general restriction on suffrage, with poorly educated people of both sexes denied the vote, so long as well-educated women were given the vote. Four years later, Florence Kelley told a women's suffrage rally that she had 'rarely heard a ringing suffrage speech which did not refer to the "ignorant and degraded men" or "ignorant immigrants" as our masters. This is habitually spoken with more or less bitterness.'[13] This repeated emphasis of the early feminists on education and ability is striking.

FROM SPANIELS TO BLUESTOCKINGS

Two books were seminal in making the case that relations between the genders needed to be rethought in the light of the new doctrines of open competition and equality of opportunity. Mary Wollstonecraft's *A Vindication of the Rights of Woman* (1792) argued that the rights of man so conspicuously advanced by the French Revolution necessarily entailed the rights of woman. Wollstonecraft (1759–97) was an example of a social type that was to become increasingly important in coming years: a woman who came from a relatively humble social background but who was convinced that her intellectual gifts entitled her to something better. Women were just as able as men, she said. But they had been reduced to the level of mere fripperies – 'toys' or 'spaniels' – because men had deliberately denied them a proper education. 'Taught from their infancy that beauty is woman's sceptre, the mind shapes itself to the body, and roaming round its gilt cage, only seeks to adorn its prison.' The only solution to this would be a 'REVOLUTION' (her capitals). Girls and boys should go to school together and learn the same things. This would not only teach men and women to respect each other in later life. It would prepare women to act as proper companions to men – helpmates in mind as well as body.

Wollstonecraft's harshest words were reserved not for defenders of the old order – they were beyond redemption – but for her fellow radicals, who should have known better. Top of the list was Rousseau, who had argued in *Émile* that women's lives should be deliberately planned in relation to men's needs and desires – 'to please men, to be useful to them, to win their love and respect, to raise them as children, to care for them as adults, correct and console them, make their lives sweet and pleasant . . .' This was a battle that was still being fought by feminists with their fellow radicals in the 1970s!

John Stuart Mill took the feminist argument further in *The Subjection of Women* (1869). During his extraordinary middle years, Mill not only questioned the Utilitarian creed that he had grown up in, under the impact of Coleridge and de Tocqueville, but also patriarchy, under the influence of Harriet Taylor, the wife of a friend. His friendship with the brilliant Mrs Taylor quickly persuaded him that women can be just as intelligent as men. Then, as friendship turned into a love affair, it forced him to question Victorian conventions about divorce, domesticity and marriage. The proper counterbalance to a competitive society, he concluded, was not a domestic goddess but a fellow intellectual.

Mill argued that the denial of equal opportunity to women was not only 'wrong in itself' – a denial of their basic rights as human beings – but also an impediment to human progress in general: 'The principle of the modern movement in morals and politics, is that conduct, and conduct alone, entitles to respect: that not what men are, but what they do, constitutes their claim to deference; that, above all, merit, and not birth, is the only rightful claim to power and authority.'[14]

In progressive societies, human beings are no longer born in their place in life and kept there by adamantine chains. They are freed from bondage and allowed to exercise their faculties and advance themselves in the world. This has been good for society because it allows society to make the best use of the talents of its citizens, and good for those citizens because it allows them to develop their God-given abilities. Freeze people in their pre-ordained places and you impoverish society, by preventing economic growth, and immiserate individuals because you force talented people to waste their abilities.

In 'improved countries' there was one glaring exception to this general pattern of progress, Mill argued: laws and institutions continue to tell women that, simply because they are women, they will 'never in all their lives be allowed to compete for certain things'.[15] (Mill was blind to similar problems suffered by blacks or Indians.) They are like medieval serfs, subject to rules imposed on them by their feudal overlords, vassals in an age that is supposed to be defined by freedom. 'Marriage is the only actual bondage known to our law,' he wrote acidly.[16] They are even forced to submit to so-called conjugal rights – 'the lowest degradation of a human being, that of being made the instrument of an animal function contrary to her inclinations'.[17]

The preservation of these quasi-feudal arrangements encourages men as a class to have an unjustified sense of their own abilities:

> The self-worship of the monarch, or of the feudal superior, is matched by the self-worship of the male. Human beings do not grow up from childhood in the possession of unearned distinctions, without pluming themselves upon them. Those whom privileges not acquired by their merit, and which they feel to be disproportioned to it, inspire with additional humility, are always the few, and the best few. The rest are only inspired with pride, and the worst sort of pride, that which values itself upon accidental advantages, not of its own achieving.[18]

Mill dismissed the idea that women are inferior to men in their natural capacities as twaddle twice over: twaddle because it rests on an equation between physical ability and mental ability, despite the fact that women's relative physical weakness tells us nothing about their mental abilities; and twaddle because it depends on the ludicrous assertion that 'the most eminent women are inferior in mental faculties to the most mediocre of men'. There was already ample evidence that queens can be just as good at their jobs as kings, if not better, he says: compare Queen Elizabeth I with her successor, James I. Why not apply the same tests to the rest of society? The only way to test whether women can in fact succeed in the great learned professions is to open positions in those professions to women and see how they perform in practice. 'What is natural to the two sexes can only be found out by allowing both to develop and use their faculties freely.'

Here Mill deployed an argument based on the interaction of nurture with nature. Equality of opportunity would do more than provide society with access to talents that had previously been ignored. It would develop those talents as never before. Under current social conventions women are encouraged to be weak and dependent – spaniels, in Wollstonecraft's phrase. In a world of equal opportunities, they would have the same incentives as men to develop their brainpower and stiffen their characters. Simpering – or frustrated – dependants would be transformed into intellectual equals.[19]

Mill's arguments were reinforced by growing evidence of the enormous talent of the subjugated sex. A remarkable number of women had overcome social prejudice and poor educations to achieve distinction: Jane Austen, Mary Shelley and George Eliot in literature (though, significantly, Eliot had thought it expedient to adopt a man's name); Mary Somerville in astronomy; Elizabeth Elstob in the study of Anglo-Saxon and the early Teutonic languages; Ada Lovelace in mathematics and computing; Florence Nightingale in nursing; and, towards the end of the century, Beatrice Webb in social policy.

Victorian literature is full of accounts of women who almost went mad through lack of an outlet for their talents. Perhaps the greatest English novel of the nineteenth century, George Eliot's *Middlemarch* (1872), is a novel about frustration. The heroine, Dorothea Brooke, is a highly intelligent woman who falls for a local clergyman, Edward Casaubon, because she takes him for a great scholar when he is, in fact, an addle-pated antiquarian. Rather than discovering 'large vistas and wide fresh air' in her husband's mind, as she so desperately hopes, she discovers 'anterooms and winding passages which seemed to lead nowhither'.

Mill's arguments also received some unexpected support from one of the principal targets of his barbs, the cult of domesticity. A growing number of women reasoned that the only way to preserve the purity of the home was to venture forth into the hostile world and do battle against the various pollutants, prime among them alehouses and whore-houses, that threatened that purity. The more they ventured out into the world, the more they discovered their talents for public life. This raised intriguing questions which first befuddled purity campaigners and then radicalized many of them: why shouldn't women be able to apply their talents to public life as well as charitable life? Why shouldn't they be able to shape laws as well as mores? If they were such peculiarly moral beings, as their masters were always telling them, then surely the public world would be purified by their active presence. Mary Lease, a tem-perance campaigner, declared that 'man is man' but 'woman is superwoman'.[20] Frances Willard, another campaigner, argued in favour of women's suffrage so 'that Woman, who is truest to God and our country by instinct and education, should have a voice at the polls where the Sabbath and the Bible are now attacked by the infidel foreign population of our country'.[21] The first party to declare itself in favour of women's suffrage was the heavily female Prohibition Party.

In Britain, the intellectual aristocracy played a leading role in driving these arguments home, much as it did in advancing open com-petition in the first place. Intellectual aristocrats weren't bound by the same rules as landed aristocrats: intellectual patrimonies weren't diluted in the same way as landed patrimonies if you didn't entail them to your eldest sons; you didn't cheat your sons if you invested in your daughters. Intellectual aristocrats also married other intellectual aristocrats in an early example of the assortative mating that has done so much to shape our own times. So they were surrounded by broods of clever children, girls as well as boys and, increasingly, the girls weren't willing to play second fiddle to their brothers, or reconcile themselves to a life as baby-machines.

Henry Sidgwick, a Cambridge philosopher, married Eleanor Balfour, niece of Lord Salisbury (prime minister 1885–6, 1886–92, 1895–1902) and elder sister of Arthur Balfour (prime minister 1902–5) and a formidable figure in her own right who eventually became principal of Newnham College, Cambridge (1892–1910). Graham Wallas, a leading political scientist and Fabian intellectual, married Ada Radford, a Cambridge-educated mathematician and friend of Eleanor Marx. Ada even tried to do for clever women what Macaulay had done for clever men and provide them with an intellectual genealogy in the form of *Before the Bluestockings*, a study of learned ladies in the seventeenth and eighteenth centuries.[22] John Neville Keynes, a future registrary of Cambridge University, married Florence Ada Brown, another product of Newnham, a woman who not only gave birth to Maynard, Margaret and Geoffrey but also became president of the National Council of Women.

These intellectual aristocrats spearheaded the advance of female education. The North London Collegiate School and Cheltenham Ladies College were both founded in the 1850s. Oxford and Cambridge established women-only colleges in the 1870s and 1880s, decades which also saw the creation of Wellesley (1875), Smith (1875), Spelman (1881), Bryn Mawr (1885) and Barnard (1889) in the United States. The University of London allowed women to graduate in 1878, Scottish universities followed suit in 1889 and Trinity College Dublin in 1904, while the new civic redbricks such as Birmingham and Liverpool admitted women on equal terms with men from the very beginning.

Women were determined to prove that they could do just as well at school and university as men. And what better way to do this than by acing examinations, which, as well as being free from the taint of subjectivity, were also tests of toughness as much as ability? Women's colleges did their utmost to prepare their most promising students for these intellectual trials of strength, feeding them delicacies, making sure that they got the right mixture of sleep and exercise, boosting their morale and making heroines of their most successful pupils such Charlotte Scott, at Girton, Cambridge, who was informally bracketed as Eighth Wrangler in mathematics in 1880, and the same college's Agnata Ramsay, who was the only candidate of either sex who was deemed fit to occupy the first division of the first class in Part Two of the Classical Tripos in 1887.[23] Gilbert and Sullivan satirized the fashion for rigorous female education in their 1884 operetta, *Princess Ida*, whose eponymous heroine founds a female-only university in which women are taught that they are superior to men.

One of the seminal moments in the advance of women came when the daughter of two leading members of the intellectual aristocracy sat England's most gruelling examination. Henry Fawcett was one of the most impressive figures of his generation, ranking Seventh Wrangler in mathematics in 1856, bagging a fellowship of his college, Trinity Hall, in the same year, and, despite being blinded in both eyes in a shooting accident two years later, becoming the professor of political economy at Cambridge in 1863, a member of parliament in 1865 and postmaster general in 1880. He was also one of the most consistent advocates of open competition: in 1869, he moved a resolution demanding that all civil service posts should be open to competition, and in 1880 he took his beliefs to their logical conclusion, opening clerkships in the post office to women as well as men and freeing postmistresses who married from the ancient obligation to re-register their premises in their husband's name.[24] In 1867, he married into one of the first families of the burgeoning feminist movement, first asking Elizabeth Garrett, a pioneering doctor, to marry him and then, when she declined, turning successfully to her younger sister, Millicent. (Today's Fawcett Society, a charity devoted to women's rights, is named after Millicent.)

The couple determined to give every opportunity to their only child, Philippa, who proved to be a mathematical prodigy. Before going up to Cambridge, Philippa was given special coaching by Karl Pearson. At Newnham, she was groomed by Mary Ellen Rickett, the college's most successful performer in the mathematics Tripos to date, as well as by the university's top male coaches. In 1890, she scored the highest marks in Part One of the Tripos, the intellectual equivalent of winning the Grand National. Because women weren't formally allowed to take degrees at Cambridge, she couldn't be given her rightful place as Senior Wrangler. So she was instead given the idiosyncratic – and rather glorious – rank of 'above the Senior Wrangler'. (Her former tutor, Pearson, had only managed third place.) This inevitably created a sensation in Cambridge: when Philippa's name was read out, the Senate House erupted in pandemonium and she proceeded in triumph back to Newnham, where she was feted with bonfires, dancing, feasting and a victory ode:

Hail the triumph of the corset
Hail the fair Philippa Fawcett
Victress in the fray
Crown her queen of hydrostatics
And the other Mathematics
Wreathe her brow in bay.[25]

The news went global: the *Daily Telegraph* proclaimed that 'once again has woman demonstrated her superiority in the face of an incredulous and somewhat unsympathetic world . . . And now the last trench has been carried by Amazonian assault, and the whole citadel of learning lies open and defenceless before the victorious students of Newnham and Girton. There is no longer any field of learning in which the lady student does not excel.'

The triumph of women was far from complete in institutional terms: the Senior Wrangler that Philippa was bracketed above went on to become a life-long fellow of Emmanuel College, with a university appointment, whereas Philippa had to content herself with a temporary college lectureship.[26] Another member of the intellectual aristocracy, Virginia Woolf, drew a striking sketch of the way that men continued to occupy the best positions in 'the citadel of learning' in *A Room of One's Own* (1929). A men's college she visits is the product of 'an unending stream of gold and silver' that has poured forth over the centuries. A women's college is like a boarding house.[27] The Fawcett incident nonetheless marked a turning point: henceforth it was impossible to argue that women lacked the mental ability to beat men in the hardest subject available or the mental fortitude to survive the most testing examination known to man – or woman.

Though the number of university women was small – and the number of female Wranglers vanishingly small – these stories of intellectual prowess changed popular perceptions of women's abilities. Cartoonists made hay with images of educated women riding bicycles in bloomers, or sitting in their studies, pince-nez perched on their noses, surrounded by piles of books and papers. In 1894, *Punch* magazine derided 'New Women' for living on 'nothing but foolscap and ink'.[28] Novelists turned 'graduate girls', many of them educated at Girton, into stock characters: Grant Allen's *The Woman Who Did* (1895) was a 'Girton Girl';

McDonnell Bodkin's lady detective, Dora Myrl, was, improbably, both 'a Cambridge Wrangler and a Doctor of Medicine'.[29]

Mental tests provided some of the most solid evidence for women's intellectual ability. Psychometricians exploded claims made by earlier sociobiologists that women were naturally inferior to men because they had smaller brains or because they were designed by nature to look after children. They demonstrated instead that individual differences were far more important than group differences: whatever tiny differences there might be in the average IQ of women and men (a much-disputed possibility), they paled into insignificance compared with the vast individual differences. They also discovered that, in so far as there were any significant group differences, it was that girls matured earlier than boys. Psychometricians found that they had to rig the all-important 11-plus exams to make sure that the same number of boys passed as girls. Though giving boys extra points because they were late developers might make sense because boys would eventually catch up with the girls, it made it doubly difficult to argue that girls are second-class citizens.

Women also found themselves at the cutting edge of the Victorian version of the information revolution. The almost simultaneous development of two new information machines – the typewriter and the telegram – boosted demand for women, who were not just cheaper than men (you could pay them a fraction of the male wage and sack them when they got married) but were also supposedly more dextrous too (employers were struck by the similarity between typewriters and sewing machines). Writers celebrated the liberating effects of the information revolution on young women in works such as Grant Allen's *The Type-writer Girl* (1897), written under the pen name of Olive Pratt Rayner, Tom Gallon's *The Girl behind the Keys* (1903) and J. M. Barrie's one-act play *The Twelve-Pound Look* (1910).[30]

In Britain, women's skills with telegrams provided them with their first ladder of opportunity in the civil service. The great meritocratic machine that Macaulay and Trevelyan constructed at the heart of the British government had initially been reserved for men. But in the 1860s the post office – by far the government's largest department and the one at the heart of the information revolution – took over the country's private telegraph companies and with them 3,300 female employees.[31]

Being for the most part better educated than their male counterparts and from more advantaged social backgrounds, these female telegraph operators frequently outshone them: in an informal race between the sexes in the Central Telegraph Station to send out the queen's opening speech to Parliament, the women won easily.[32]

The logic of examinations eventually completed the revolution that the telegraph had begun, as clever women did as well as clever men in the civil service entrance examination and then went on to shine just as brightly. In 1936, for example, Jenifer Williams came third out of 493 candidates. Williams later left the civil service to become an academic – she married H. L. A. Hart, a first-rate legal philosopher, and was a close friend of Isaiah Berlin and other academic luminaries – but she retained an academic interest in the rise of the meritocracy as one of the first historians to recognize that the Northcote–Trevelyan reforms were a subject worthy of academic interest.

'EQUAL AS WE ARE'

The First World War transformed the position of women. Woodrow Wilson's declaration that America's mission in the First World War was to 'make the world safe for democracy' had the benign side-effect of forcing him to abandon his opposition to female suffrage. American women were given the vote in 1920 and British women in 1928. The Second World War provided women another big push. In America, Rosie the Riveter became a symbol of women's can-do spirit as they took the place of men in factories. In Britain, some 8,000 women, making up 80 per cent of the workforce, worked at Bletchley Park, Britain's code-breaking headquarters, operating the cipher machines that, according to some historians, shortened the war by two years.[33] Some of the women were recruited in fairly conventional ways, by asking Oxbridge tutors to nominate their brightest students, but some were recruited more imaginatively, by getting women to complete cryptic crosswords at high speed.

Women's forward march after the Second World War was not straightforward. They retreated into the domestic sphere in the late 1940s and 1950s to take care of the babies that arrived in vast numbers when the troops returned. Their return to the public realm was slow and tentative. In *The Power Elite* (1956), C. Wright Mills did not even mention the absence of women from the corporate and military elite: it was simply taken for granted. Kennedy's 'New Frontier' Cabinet did not contain a single woman. In the early 1960s, the Senate contained only two women, one of whom had inherited her job from her husband, and Princeton, Yale and Harvard had only one full female professor between them, at Harvard.

As women became more ambitious, they also encountered strong opposition. Women were routinely subjected to casual sexism – as *Mad Men*, a television drama about advertising executives in the 1960s, demonstrates painfully. As late as 1969, F. Skiddy von Stade, Harvard's dean of freshmen, said that

> when I see bright, well-educated, but relatively dull housewives who attended the Seven Sisters [female-only colleges], I honestly shudder at the thought of changing the balance of males versus females at Harvard . . . Quite simply, I do not see highly educated women making startling strides in contributing to our society in the foreseeable future. They are not, in my opinion, going to stop getting married and/or having children. They will fail in their present role as women if they do.[34]

Nor did the opposition come only from men. One of the most talented Republican women of her generation, Phyllis Schlafly, led a successful campaign against the Equal Rights Amendment (ERA), intended to enshrine women's rights in the constitution, on the grounds that it would disadvantage homemakers.

Still, their advance quickly built up a remarkable momentum. Starting in the 1980s, a higher proportion of women than men obtained college degrees and voted in elections. And by the second decade of the twenty-first century, women made up more than half the professional workforce in the United States and Great Britain and sat in the top jobs in such corporate giants as General Motors, IBM, PepsiCo, Lockheed Martin and DuPont. Today the appetite for female labour is probably greater than the appetite for male labour: the US Bureau of Labor Statistics calculates that women make up more than two thirds of employees in ten of the fifteen job categories likely to grow fastest in the next few years.

THE GREAT ACCELERATION

The great acceleration from the 1950s onwards was driven by a combination of powerful economic and political forces. The decline in manufacturing and the rise of the knowledge and service economies levelled the gender playing field or even tilted it towards women. (The landmark book in the rise of feminism was arguably not Betty Friedan's *The Feminine Mystique* (1963) but Daniel Bell's *The Coming of Post-Industrial Society* (1973).) Household appliances such as vacuum cleaners, washing machines and the rest reduced the amount of time women had to spend on housework. Improved contraception, particularly the contraceptive pill, increased women's control over their fertility and revolutionized their incentives: women now had much more reason to invest time and effort in acquiring skills, particularly slow-burning skills that are hard to learn and take many years to pay off, because they are much less likely to have to drop out of university or law school to have an unplanned baby. The logic of the Cold War drove the West to make better use of female brainpower. In 1957, shocked by *Sputnik*, Eisenhower's Commission on Scientists and Engineers denounced the 'long established prejudices against women in engineering and science'.[35] A year later Congress passed the first major piece of federal legislation to enshrine the principle that men and women should receive equal funding in education, the National Defense Education Act.

With feminism draped in the stars and stripes, the rest of the government joined in. In 1961, John F. Kennedy appointed a Commission on the Status of Women. Three years later Congress added gender to other forms of discrimination in the 1964 Civil Rights Bill. At the same time, talented lawyers such as Ruth Bader Ginsburg repeatedly demonstrated that gender discrimination was incompatible with the protections provided by the US constitution. In the wake of all these pressures, a growing number of institutions felt that they had no choice but to remove barriers to women's opportunity – and women poured through the breaches in the walls.

The logic of meritocracy also proved self-reinforcing. Elite universities and colleges made a cold calculation in the 1970s that they would lose market share if they remained single sex while their competitors admitted women. In America, universities that held out against admitting women, notably Princeton, saw their 'yield rate' (their ability to convert offers into acceptances) decline precipitously compared with other elite colleges that had chosen to go co-educational.[36] By contrast, co-educational institutions found that their average performance increased sharply because they had the pick of the best from both sexes. In Oxford and Cambridge, male colleges all rushed to admit women at the same time because they worried that other male colleges would steal a march on them. ('A College that creams off the girls/will (ergo) cream the boys' went a bit of doggerel at the time.)[37] The biggest losers were ironically women-only institutions like Philippa Fawcett's Newnham and Margaret Thatcher's Somerville, which had pioneered the cause of female education for decades but which saw the best girls snaffled up by previously all-male institutions which had better grounds and longer histories.

The expansion of higher education boosted women's job prospects more than men's, not only improving their value in the job market but also shifting their role models from stay-at-home mothers to successful professional women. The best-educated women have always been more likely than other women to work, even after having children. In 1963, 62 per cent of college-educated women in the United States were in the labour force, compared with 46 per cent of those with only a high-school diploma. In 2014, 80 per cent of American women with a college education were in the labour force, compared with 67 per cent of those with only a high-school diploma and 47 per cent of those without one. Women also chose to study more lucrative subjects at university. In 1966, 40 per cent of American women who received a BA specialized in education; 2 per cent specialized in business and management. The figures are now 12 per cent and 50 per cent.

MERITOCRACY VERSUS THE FAMILY

The advance of women across the rich world from 1950 onwards was one of the most remarkable revolutions of the past fifty years. Remarkable because of the extent of the change: millions of people who were once dependent on men took control of their own economic fates. Remarkable also because of the lack of friction: a change that affects the most intimate aspects of people's identities – and which broke with centuries' worth of inherited practice – was widely welcomed by men as well as women. Revolutionary social change has seldom taken such a benign form.

Yet even the most benevolent revolutions entail disappointments as well as triumphs and costs as well as benefits. Aspirations have outpaced achievements: women have been encouraged to climb on to the occupational ladder only to discover that the middle rungs are dominated by men and the upper rungs are out of reach. Only 2 per cent of the bosses of *Fortune* 500 companies and 5 per cent of those in the FTSE 100 stock market index are women, for example. Social arrangements have failed to evolve as rapidly as economic changes. Many women have found that they often have to make a choice between motherhood and careers. Childless women in corporate America earn almost as much as men. Mothers with partners earn less, and single mothers a lot less. Children have sometimes paid a price for the rise of the two-income household. Even well-off parents often feel that they spend too little time with their children, thanks to crowded schedules and the ever-buzzing smartphone. For poorer parents, things can seem impossible: child-care costs eat up a terrifying proportion of the family budget, and many childminders are untrained. The empowerment of women may be contributing to inequality as high-powered women marry high-powered men, leaving less successful women to marry less successful men.

The ascent of women thus helped to promote the two great backlashes against meritocracy that will dominate much of the rest of our story: worries that women were being held back by structural constraints on their opportunities helped to drive the politics of the left in the 1960s; and worries that high-income couples were drawing away from the rest of society helped to drive the populist revolt on the right against meritocracy in the 2010s.

PART FIVE

The Crisis of the Meritocracy

14
Against Meritocracy: The Revolt on the Left

We have seen that the meritocratic revolution was largely driven by the left: by left-wing political parties that wanted to open up opportunities to members of the working class; by left-wing intellectuals who wanted to introduce a scientific method for allocating social positions; and by feminists, who wanted to extend opportunities to girls as well as boys. Yet from the 1930s onwards the left gradually turned against its intellectual offspring. The anti-meritocratic revolution came in three waves: first, academics questioned the idea that you can measure merit with any precision; second, public intellectuals questioned the idea that meritocracy is worth having at all; and, third, progressives embraced the alternative values of 'equality' and 'community'. The revolt against meritocracy had a profound influence on social policy across the rich world: the British abolished grammar schools and introduced mixed-ability teaching; the Americans introduced affirmative action and waged war on elite secondary schools; several continental countries went further still and introduced open admission to universities.

THE MEASUREMENT OF MERIT ANATOMIZED

The trial of the meritocracy began in the 1930s in the halls of academe. The first witnesses for the prosecution had a pedigree that looks strange today: they were sociobiologists who were concerned with the way that biology determines individual destiny and eugenicists who were preoccupied by the genetic fitness of the population. They were soon joined by more familiar figures: sociologists who studied the way that society limited opportunities, and public intellectuals who were worried about the impact of educational selection on the tenor of daily life. Though these witnesses spoke in a somewhat obscure academic language, their work had big practical consequences, tipping the consensus against psychologists such as Cyril Burt and Lewis Terman and preparing the ground for the dismantling of academic selection, at least in the form of the 11-plus and other forms of high-stakes selection for high schools.

The most stinging criticism came, surprisingly, from the heart of the British eugenics movement. The mastermind of these criticisms was C. P. Blacker, a brilliant medical psychiatrist who pioneered the study of shell shock (post-traumatic stress disorder) during the First World War and was appointed general secretary of the Eugenics Society in 1931. Blacker was determined to prevent Francis Galton's legacy from degenerating into a sterile and reactionary orthodoxy. Though he shared the founder's commitment to using contraception to improve 'the quality of the population', he also believed that eugenics needed to be revised in the light of new knowledge, particularly knowledge about the role of the environment in determining opportunities. Above all, he wanted to disassociate British eugenics from Nazi 'racial science'.[1] He found allies (not all of them entirely congenial) among a wide range of biologists, sociobiologists and medical scientists.

Lancelot Hogben, one of Britain's most distinguished biologists and a communist fellow traveller, was a particularly painful thorn in the IQ testers' side. In 1930, he was appointed head of the department of social biology at the London School of Economics, a new department that was established to bridge the gap between the natural and social sciences, and he quickly turned the department into a base for a guerrilla operation.[2] Hogben sounded many of the criticisms which were to dog intelligence testing in coming decades: that IQ tests reflected environmental as much as genetic factors, such as the uterine environment, the condition of the home, the availability of food, sunlight, sleep and exercise, the social traditions of the family, and the protracted period of development which preceded formal schooling. He was particularly withering on the idea that different occupational groups had different average IQs, on the grounds that such groups live in very different environments:

A human society may be crudely compared to a badly managed laboratory in which there are many cages each containing a pair of rats and
their offspring. The rats are of different breeds. The cages are at different distances from the window. Different cages receive different rations.
Rats in the same cage cannot all get to the feeding trough together. So
some get more food or light than others.[3]

Richard Titmuss, one of the leading thinkers on the welfare state,
who was also based at the LSE, added his weight to these arguments.
His main focus was on inequalities in health and nutrition between the
rich and the poor: for example, he insisted that, whereas 'we still have
no conclusive proof of the simple inheritance of intelligence', there
could be 'little doubt that sustained vitamin and mineral deficiencies
have a harmful effect on mental ability'. 'Many a child classed as dull
or backward should have been recorded as deficient in vitamin A.'[4]

Lionel Penrose, the leading English expert on the genetics of mental
backwardness, focused his fire not just on intelligence tests ('tests
resembling parlour games')[5] but also on the great God of the intelligence testing movement, the bell curve. There were many different
types of retarded minds, as different from each other as they were
from normal minds, he argued. The more severe cases of defect could
no more be regarded as the tail of a normal distribution than could
congenitally short people, who were vastly more frequent than they
should have been on the basis of the normal distribution of statures.[6]
He even accused the Galtonians of ignoring the Darwinian truth that
variations within the species were favourable to long-term survival:
'the genes carried by the fertile scholastically retarded may be just as
valuable to the human race, in the long run, as those carried by people
of high intellectual capacity'.[7] When Penrose was appointed Galton
Professor of Eugenics at University College, London, he chafed at the
title and eventually, though only in 1963, got it changed to Galton
Professor of Human Heredity.

In the heady days after the Second World War the British Communist Party also generated many of the arguments against IQ tests that
were to dominate left-wing thinking in the future. Brian Simon, the
Party's leading spokesman on education, produced a flood of polem-
ical books and articles arguing that selective education was perverting

the 1944 Education Act from an instrument of opportunity to an excuse for repression. Simon, the son of a wealthy Manchester industrialist, who had been educated at Trinity College, Cambridge, argued that the 'real' function of IQ tests was economic rather than educational: having first made their appearance with the 'advent of imperialism',[8] they provided 'an apparently scientific foundation for social, and in particular, educational policies of an extremely reactionary nature which militated against the working class'.[9] He looked forward to a future of non-streamed schools presided over by an elite of psychologists and educationalists thoroughly versed in the 'laws of dialectical materialism'.

By far the most important post-war critics of mental measurement, however, were sociologists, who enjoyed a remarkable boom in both intellectual esteem and job prospects after the Second World War.[10] For the most part these sociologists were focused on one big subject: what impact was the welfare state having on Britain's class composition? Was it equalizing opportunities, as its architects hoped? Or was it proving to be an expensive disappointment? The more they looked, the more worried they became.

In *Social Class and Educational Opportunity* (1956), J. E. Floud, A. H. Halsey and F. M. Martin conducted a detailed survey of the impact of the 1944 Education Act on the social composition of grammar schools in two local education authorities. They noted that grammar-school places were overwhelmingly taken by middle-class children – who, thanks to the Act, no longer had to pay fees. The significant increase in the absolute number of working-class children concealed very small increases in their relative chances of getting a place. They noted that the crude economic factors that had governed selection in the past – most importantly, the cost of secondary-school education – were being replaced by more subtle influences such as the size of families and the absence of a tradition of education in working-class homes.

Scholars from related disciplines produced similar conclusions. In *The Home and the School* (1964) and *All Our Future* (1968; co-authored with J. M. Ross and H. R. Simpson), J. W. B. Douglas, director of the Medical Research Unit at the LSE, examined the ways in which environmental and health factors explained 'educational wastage' among working-class children who scored well on IQ tests when they were young but then gradually deteriorated over the years.[11]

The result of all this research was a cross-disciplinary consensus: the unprecedented expansion of the educational system had done little or nothing to improve the relative life chances of disadvantaged children. Middle-class pupils retained almost intact their historical advantages over their working-class contemporaries. Instead of determining social stratification, education continued to validate distinctions which had their origins in social inequality.

The simultaneous debate in the United States was even more bad-tempered than the one in Britain. This was partly because America's eugenics movement had been more extreme than Britain's: thanks to Oliver Wendell Holmes's harsh words, in the 1927 Supreme Court ruling *Buck v. Bell* ('three generations of imbeciles are enough'), hundreds of Americans had been forcibly sterilized. It was also partly because the problem of race is so poisonous in the United States. Many proponents of IQ tests seemed to take delight in the idea that the relatively poor performance of African-Americans in national tests proved that they were genetically inferior as a group rather than the victims of terrible circumstances.

The most searching criticism of IQ tests came from cultural anthropologists. Franz Boas, a professor at Columbia University who was widely regarded as 'the father of American anthropology', made a powerful case that 'nurture' rather than 'nature' explained the difference in average IQs between broad ethnic groups.[12] He even demonstrated, through a series of studies of head size and skeletal anatomy, that both the shape and size of human skulls were highly malleable, depending on environmental factors such as health and nutrition. Otto Klineberg, a Boas pupil who eventually became a key witness in *Brown v Board of Education*, the 1954 Supreme Court case about school segregation in the South, demonstrated that the average IQ of blacks in the North was higher than the average IQ of blacks in the South, a difference, he argued, that could only be explained by differences in educational opportunities.[13]

In 1930, confronted with all this evidence, Carl Brigham dramatically recanted his 1923 *A Study of American Intelligence*, in which he had argued for the existence of a biological hierarchy of European races (Nordic then Alpine then Mediterranean).[14] Margaret Mead, another Boas pupil who, thanks to her studies of *Coming of Age in Samoa* (1928) and *Sex and Temperament in Three Primitive Societies* (1935), became one of the twentieth century's great celebrity intellectuals, went so far as to argue that 'we are forced to conclude that human nature is almost unbelievably malleable, responding accurately and contrastingly to contrasting cultural conditions'.[15]

There was one area in which the backlash against IQ testing was more measured in America than in Britain, however: the area of educational selection and classification. America was free from the all-or-nothing 11-plus examination that was such a cause of anxiety in Britain. It also sent a far higher proportion of its school-leavers to college than its European counterparts: at the outbreak of the Second World War, 14.6 per cent of eighteen- to twenty-one-year-olds enrolled in university, compared with 3.6 per cent of Britons, 3.9 per cent of Germans and 2.6 per cent of French. America was also much better at providing second chances than Europe, with its tradition of dividing sheep from goats. While the British used tests to make once-in-a-lifetime decisions about whether children would go to high-status grammar schools or to secondary moderns, the Americans were preoccupied with second chances.[16]

Americans echoed many of the themes of British social scientists, particularly the role of nurture in explaining why middle-class children continued to outperform working-class children even as opportunities expanded after the war. In the 1940s and 1950s sociologists such as W. Lloyd Warner, of the University of Chicago, invoked 'social forces' as the ultimate explanation of social mobility. Likening the educational system to 'an enormous complicated machine for sorting and tracking and routing children through life', Warner argued that the operation of the machine was determined by the prejudices of the people who operated it rather than the selfless pursuit of talent: for example, if middle-class teachers found working-class children studying Latin, they immediately moved them to vocational classes.

So far, most social scientists had discussed the question of social mobility within a meritocratic framework. They might emphasize the role of the home environment in determining IQ. They might argue that advanced societies were wasting a gigantic amount of working-class talent. But they nevertheless accepted the meritocratic calculus: that individuals differed in their innate abilities and that the role of the state, in a just society, was to discover ability, wherever it occurred in society, and to give it the opportunities that it demanded. Jean Floud summed up the consensus as well as anyone when she argued that the 'fundamental' challenge of education is to reduce differences in educational performance to differences of natural endowment:

> Some pupils will always do better than others, but it is desirable that the order of inequality should be, as it were, a natural one, unmarred by fictitious and irrelevant social differences. No matter that such an objective is 'only an ideal' and must in practice remain for ever unattainable; the important thing is that it should guide policy and that we should actively seek to approach it.[17]

They were reacting against the severity and suddenness of the 11-plus – which inevitably made mistakes that might blight children's lives for ever – rather than against the process of sifting and sorting per se. What they wanted was a humane and efficient meritocracy rather than a brutal and sometimes arbitrary one.

This general meritocratic prejudice was shared by leading black social scientists such as Horace Mann Bond, Charles Johnson, Howard Hale Long and J. St Clair Price, who had provided such a convincing demolition of Carl Brigham's work on group differences. They firmly believed that nature mattered just as much as nurture: hence all those bright black children raised in poverty and those dull white children raised on the Upper East Side. They also regarded IQ tests as a way of protecting blacks against the cruder forms of prejudice, embodied in segregation and quotas, that were based on an attempt to ignore the importance of individual differences. 'It is not with Intelligence Tests that we have any quarrel,' Bond observed. 'In many ways they do represent a fundamental advance in the methodology of the century. It is solely with certain methods of interpreting the results of these tests that we, as scientific investigators, must differ.'[18]

From the late 1950s, however, a growing number of intellectuals began to turn against the meritocratic idea as such, concluding that the problem with meritocracy lay not in the poor implementation of a good idea but in the idea itself. Meritocracy was a false god – a dystopia masquerading as a utopia and an unjust society masquerading as the embodiment of justice. A convenient way to look at the revolt against the meritocratic idea is to examine three books that were the products of very different intellectual traditions – sociology, investigative journalism and philosophy – but which collectively mounted a powerful case against meritocracy.

AGAINST THE MERITOCRATIC IDEA

In 1958, Michael Young (1915–2002) published the book that gave 'meritocracy' its name.[19] Many readers took the book to be a celebration of the meritocratic idea: after all, Young was a leading intellectual ornament of a Labour Party that prided itself on having opened up an oligarchical society to outside talent, the co-author of the 1945 Labour Manifesto and serial founder of left-wing think tanks and pressure groups. But Young was a maverick as well as a genius: he liked to see the world from the point of view of ordinary people rather than 'the gentleman in Whitehall' (he helped to inspire the consumer movement, as a co-founder of *Which?* magazine) and he was becoming increasingly disillusioned with the legacy of Fabianism. *The Rise of the Meritocracy* was a no-holds-barred denunciation not just of meritocratic practice but of the meritocratic idea itself.[20]

The book's construction is eccentric and sometimes confusing: it purports to be a thesis written by a graduate student in 2034 to explain the rise of the meritocratic society. Much of it is a history of meritocratic breakthroughs such as the Northcote–Trevelyan Report of 1854 and the Butler Education Act of 1944. Some of it is futurology: the book is purportedly written against the background of a growing revolt against the meritocracy and it ends with the death of the graduate student who is writing the thesis. All this is designed to hammer home a simple point: that the meritocratic idea is the opposite of the real socialist ideal of equality because it smuggles competition and inequality into the heart of socialism by substituting equality of opportunity for equality of outcome, and economic efficiency for social compassion.

Young was unsparing in his condemnation of his party's creation. Meritocracy offers upward mobility for the few at the expense of the continued degradation of the many. It strengthens the ruling class by allowing them to co-opt the brightest workers, while weakening the working class by depriving them of their natural leaders. Psychologically, meritocracy is devastating for the winners and losers alike – for the rulers because it persuades them that they owe their positions to their own talents alone, rather than to the luck of their birth; for the lower classes because it persuaded them, in turn, that they have nobody to blame for their failures but themselves. Young felt that this terrible knowledge 'may condemn to helpless despair the many who have no merit, and do so all the more surely because the person so condemned, having too little wit to make his protest against society, may turn his anger against, and so cripple, himself'. Hence the dramatic ending of the book: an anti-meritocratic spring in which the unmeritorious many rise up against the smug elite.

The Rise of the Meritocracy represented a sharp change of direction in the public debate. Most of Young's fellow socialists criticized the Britain of the late 1950s because it was run by a 'magic circle' of Old Etonians led by that great conjuror Harold Macmillan, the prime minister. Young criticized it for being *too meritocratic*. Most of Young's fellow sociologists worried that IQ tests were inaccurate, measuring cultural advantage rather than native ability. Young worried that the tests were *too accurate* – and that they allowed the ruling class to identify talented children and kidnap them, as it were, from the working class.

This sharp change of direction may help to explain why Young had so much difficulty finding a home for his brainchild. Young's manuscript was rejected by eleven publishers – and only made it into print because of a chance meeting on a beach in North Wales with an old friend, Walter Neurath, who happened to have founded a publishing house, Thames and Hudson.[21] Young's reviews were also mixed. Sir Eric Ashby, an educational grandee, grasped what Young was getting at:

> Dr Young has written an admirable tract on latter-day Platonism. He has shown how social inventions, like technological inventions, can turn and bite the inventor. It is not many years since horticulturists discovered that DDT was not an unmixed blessing ... Dr Young's fantasy is a discovery that the Education Act, too, is not an unmixed blessing. In saving Britain's intellect, it may destroy Britain's soul.[22]

But many other reviews were uncomprehending or dismissive. Alan Fox, an Oxford sociologist, asked 'was there ever such a society as ours ... for projecting nightmare visions of its own future?' The *Economist* was vitriolic.[23] The book nevertheless became a bestseller in a succession of Pelican editions – and its popularity grew as the 1960s wore on and people began to warm to its real argument.

The Rise and its 'nightmare vision' were part of a bigger debate on the left about the merits of educational selection. The Fabian Society's *New Fabian Essays* (1952) is an interesting case in point not only because it contained contributions by so many Labour luminaries but also because the Old Fabians had been such unbending meritocrats. Richard Crossman characterized the managerial society created by Clement Attlee as a betrayal of the socialist idea and a veiled form of totalitarianism in which remote elites manipulated a passive and alienated population in the name of efficiency:

> The impression was given that socialism was an affair for the Cabinet acting through the existing Civil Service. The rest of the nation was to carry on as before, while benefits were bestowed from above upon some, and taken from others. Thus the first stage of socialism was executed primarily by anti-socialist managers and neutral Civil Servants.[24]

For New Fabians, managerialism and meritocracy were tied hip and thigh. Meritocratic allocation brought efficiency at the cost of division and alienation. In particular, it forced the failures to feel a sense of personal worthlessness which could not be mitigated by blaming the system.[25] Selective education perpetuated class resentment and the segregation of elites from the rest of society.[26] Sharp inequalities of wealth and power were repugnant – even if wealth and power were distributed as fairly and as efficiently as possible.[27]

The New Fabians also anticipated Michael Young's argument that selective education was working all too well. Roy Jenkins warned that bright working-class children who, had they been born in an earlier generation, might have become Bevins, were being sifted by an increasingly efficient educational sieve and turned into 'middle-class intellectuals' – the comfortable and complacent citizens of the opportunity society. Soon the trade union movement would lack people with the ability to challenge the existing distribution of wealth or allocation of power.[28]

Anthony Crosland echoed similar themes in *The Future of Socialism* (1956), insisting not only that the 11-plus was unjust but that equality of opportunity, as opposed to equality of outcome, was an unworthy goal for the socialist movement. Taken as an end in itself, equality of opportunity promoted 'insecurity and ferocious competition'; threatened to 'replace one remote elite (based on lineage) by a new one (based on ability and intelligence)'; induced a total sense of inferiority in those who failed, since they could no longer blame the system; and robbed the labour movement of their natural leaders, raising the possibility that 'the Trade Unions will be led by the indifferent residue, and the Labour Party entirely by Old Etonians'. 'When socialists speak of "equal opportunity" in terms of a narrow ladder up which only a few exceptional individuals, hauled out of their class by society's talent-scouts, can ever climb,' he added in *The Conservative Enemy* (1962), 'they concede the narrow, reactionary interpretation of their opponents.'[29]

The second book, David Halberstam's *The Best and the Brightest*, was written against a far more fraught background than Young's: the America of the Vietnam War, where eighteen-year-olds dreaded being called up, the anti-war movement was tearing the country apart, and the most powerful country on earth looked as if it was going to be humiliated by a poorly armed insurgency.

The book's main insight was that the Vietnam War was not the product of Republican knuckleheads, as the Democrats liked to pretend, but of Democratic intellectuals, particularly the gilded Harvard types who formed the inner circle of John F. Kennedy's Camelot. It was a professor's war rather than a soldier's war. The father of the Vietnam War was arguably the personification of meritocracy, McGeorge Bundy: first in his class at Groton, where he also ran the school newspaper and debating society; the first candidate for Yale University to get three perfect scores on his college entrance exams; a fellow of the Harvard Society of Fellows, where, as we have seen, he worked on Plato; an intelligence officer during the Second World War; the youngest-ever dean of Harvard College, committed to turning Harvard into a merit-based university; and National Security Advisor to JFK and then LBJ. He deployed his combination of intellectual skills and Ivy League aura to change the direction of American foreign policy in East Asia: if America didn't act quickly, then Vietnam would be the first of a series of Asian countries that would fall to communism in what he dubbed a 'domino effect'.

Bundy was the central figure in a constellation of supposedly brilliant policy intellectuals. 'If those years had any central theme,' Halberstam noted, 'if there was anything that bound the men, their followers and their subordinates together, it was the belief that sheer intelligence and rationality could answer and solve anything.' Even the formidable Lyndon Johnson, the prickly product of Southwest Texas State University, was mesmerized by the intellectual wattage of the Kennedy Cabinet. Having attended his first Cabinet meeting as vice-president, he delivered a glowing account to his friend and mentor, the House Speaker, Samuel Rayburn. 'Well, Lyndon,' Rayburn replied, 'you may be right and they may be every bit as intelligent as you say, but I'd feel a whole lot better about them if just one of them had run for sheriff once.'[30]

Rayburn turned out to be right: a dose of common sense (as opposed to educated intelligence) would have suggested that fighting a war against 'Communism' half a world away might turn into a quagmire; that the Vietkong might be able to co-opt the mighty force of Vietnamese nationalism; that guerrilla fighters defending their back yard can outperform foreign fighters who are thousands of miles from home; that people who have nothing to lose are impossible to defeat without using methods which democracies are unwilling to sanction. Officials at the Department of Defense repeatedly made the case for common sense. But the intellectuals overruled them, aided by their intellectual glamour and personal ties with the president, and when their ideas collided with reality they simply demanded that the war machine try harder. Thanks to Halberstam, the phrase 'the best and the brightest' now comes with an exasperated sneer.

If Halberstam's *The Best and the Brightest* attacked one of meritocracy's most cherished claims, that it produces ruthless efficiency, John Rawls's *A Theory of Justice* (1971) attacked the other, that it produces justice. Rawls, a professor of philosophy at Harvard University and one of the most influential intellectuals of his time, wanted to ban 'merit' from any calculus of distributive justice. He argued that inequalities in wealth or authority were justifiable only in so far as they benefited everyone in society and, in particular, the 'least amongst them', a principle established by using the 'veil of ignorance', behind which people are supposed to think about the design of a fair society without knowledge of their own particular talents, class or sex. Rawls argued that even a system of 'fair' equality of opportunity – one which adequately compensated for class differences – would not make for a just society. People no more deserved their success because they were blessed with high IQs than they did because they had rich parents. Differences in talent are as morally arbitrary as differences of class. To quote Rawls himself: his theory of justice 'nullifies the accidents of natural endowment and the contingencies of social circumstances as counters in the quest for political and economic advantage'.[31] Rawls's strictures applied as much to effort as to IQ: hard work did not make you any more deserving of superior reward, because the propensity to work hard was also inherited.

Rawls didn't conclude from this that people who are lucky enough to be talented should be forcibly held back – required to wear elaborate encumbrances (as in Kurt Vonnegut's short story 'Harrison Bergeron') or obliged to keep their abilities a secret (as in the *Incredibles* cartoons). He argued that the winners should be forced to share their winnings with people who are less fortunate than themselves through progressive taxation. Rawls dubbed this approach 'the difference principle'. The difference principle represented an agreement to regard the distribution of natural talents as a common asset – a nationalized industry, as it were – and to share in the benefits of this distribution whatever it turned out to be. Those who had been favoured by nature, whoever they were, could gain from their good fortune only on terms that improved the situation of those who had lost out.

A Theory of Justice was a landmark in political thinking: professional philosophers approach the text in much the same spirit that medieval scholastics approached the works of Thomas Aquinas, and philosophy students learn about Rawls's 'veil of ignorance' alongside Plato's Ring of Gyges, which allowed its wearer to become invisible, as one of the great intellectual breakthroughs in philosophical reasoning. This is as it should be: the veil of ignorance is a powerful conceit that forces you to think about the world in fresh ways. In many ways, it is a strikingly radical book. Rawls broke with the old-fashioned American faith in both hard work and individual achievement. The main theme of American radicalism from Jacksonian campaigns against monopolies to feminist campaigns in favour of equal reward for equal pay has been the desire for distributive justice. This faith burns particularly brightly among John Rawls's own tribe of New Englanders. Rawls, by contrast, was interested in limiting inequality rather than opening up opportunities. Yet *A Theory of Justice* doesn't look forward to our current era of campaigns for racial justice: the volume doesn't contain any reference to race, despite the fact that, when it was written, America was being shaken up by the civil rights movement and traumatized by civil unrest in its great cities, including Boston.

These books all had a big impact outside the academy and the salon. Young's influence was the most complicated. Though many Labour politicians understood exactly what he was trying to say – Anthony Crosland was a close friend and interlocutor – the most important of the lot, Tony Blair, got the argument upside down. At the height of New Labour's success, Young even wrote an article in the *Guardian* taking the Labour leader to task and remaking his case with renewed urgency.[32] *The Best and the Brightest* stayed on the *New York Times* bestseller list for thirty-six weeks and influenced a whole generation of young activists, who graduated from protesting against the Vietnam War to becoming Democratic Party stalwarts. His book also exercised influence in a surprising quarter: Steve Bannon, Donald Trump's chief strategist and one of the heroes of the global populist right, was spotted reading it in February 2017.[33] *A Theory of Justice* became required reading not only in philosophy departments but also in law schools across the world, not least in Harvard Law School, which has educated a disproportionate number of America's senior judges. On the other hand, Rawls's thinking was vigorously rejected by conservative jurists who currently have the upper hand in the Supreme Court.[34] Antonin Scalia, in particular, enjoyed making references to sports precisely because the results of sporting competitions were by their nature ruthlessly unequal.

EQUALITY AND COMMUNITY VERSUS MERIT

The critique of meritocracy gathered momentum so quickly because it could draw on two ideas that have always exercised a fascination for intellectuals: equality (in the sense of equality of results rather than equality of opportunity) and community.

Egalitarian arguments come in two distinct forms: *factual* arguments about the nature of individual differences and *normative* arguments about the desirability of an egalitarian society. These arguments reinforce each other: for the most part (though Rawls was a notable exception), people who believe that individual differences are rooted in nurture rather than nature also believe that society should be more equal.

We have seen that the idea that humans are equal in the state of nature has always aroused scepticism from people like John Adams, who looked at the world and saw irrefutable evidence of natural differences in ability. It also suffered a major intellectual reversal with the publication of Charles Darwin's *On the Origin of Species* in 1859, which situated man in the natural world and thereby stimulated the scientific study of natural variations in human populations. Yet the 1960s saw a revival of the 'blank slate' theory of human nature as sociologists argued that what Peter Berger and Thomas Luckmann dubbed 'the social construction of reality' applied to everything from educational failure to criminality.[35] In Britain, Basil Bernstein, a professor of the sociology of education at the London Institute of Education, Britain's leading training institution for schoolteachers, argued that working-class children perform less well on verbal tests than middle-class children because they are confined to a 'restricted linguistic code', whereas middle-class children have access to an 'elaborated linguistic code'.[36] Working-class people are so entwined with each other's lives that they can convey their meaning with slight shifts of pitch, stress and gesture. Middle-class people, on the other hand, are so distant from each other that they tend to use much more abstract language. In France, Pierre Bourdieu developed the notion of 'cultural capital' to explain educational differences. Cultural capital allows the privileged to control access to prestigious positions in government, business and the professions and then to reinforce their position by persuading the poor that they deserved to remain at the bottom of society. For Bourdieu, the 'real' function of schooling is not to enhance society's productive power or allocate ability to opportunity. It is to persuade the winners that they deserve to win and the losers that they deserve to lose.[37]

These supposedly factual arguments were reinforced by normative ones. From the 1960s onwards, left-wingers increasingly rejected the idea that social justice is about providing equal opportunities to become unequal and instead embraced the opposite idea: reducing differences in pecuniary reward, by paying the poor more and taxing the rich, and abolishing a world in which differences in health, security and esteem were linked to differences in background.

The egalitarian revolt against the meritocracy took place against a background of growing disillusionment as evidence mounted not only that middle-class children continued to do better than poor children in the educational race (and upper-class children continued to do better than middle-class children) but also that the middle classes were better at securing state benefits.[38] This suggested that the only way to promote social justice was to take a more aggressive view of the concept of equality and eliminate the causes of poverty and disadvantage. It also took place against the background of a cultural revolution: the 1960s was all about challenging inherited hierarchies and encouraging people to do their own thing, even if the established hierarchies seemed the most natural things in the world and the cost of letting it all hang out looked steep. R. D. Laing, a British psychoanalyst, became a celebrity by arguing that schizophrenia is a rational response to an irrational society. Ken Kesey's *One Flew over the Cuckoo's Nest* (1962) argued that the people who run lunatic asylums are crazier and more dangerous than the people they lock up. Michel Foucault produced a succession of zeitgeist-shaping books that tried to reverse the Enlightenment's belief in the rule of reason: for him 'modernity' is synonymous with inventing classificatory regimes and institutions that are designed to marginalize groups such as homosexuals and non-conformists and indeed restrain the human psyche itself.

The second line of attack was the communitarian one: that the individualism at the heart of the meritocracy atomizes communities and immiserates the individuals who constitute them. Many of the earliest communitarian critics of meritocracy were conservatives who looked for inspiration in (idealized) communities of the past rather than the utilitarian calculus of the present, particularly in the Middle Ages, when, as they saw it, everybody had known their place ('the rich man in his castle/the poor man at his gate') but had been happily bound to each other by mutual obligations.

Conservatives argued that this happy state of affairs had been ended by the twin tragedies of the Enlightenment and market capitalism. The Enlightenment had alienated men from God. Capitalism had put the cash nexus at the heart of society. Both had dissolved common aims in the acid of individual egoism. Edmund Burke complained that 'the age of chivalry is gone. That of sophisters, economists, and calculators has succeeded; and the glory of Europe is extinguished forever.'[39] Both Tolstoy and Dostoevsky noted that the road to hell is paved with pleas for moral autonomy. T. S. Eliot, a self-proclaimed royalist, Anglo-Catholic and classicist, denounced meritocracy as a formula for disorganizing society and debasing education.

The left also boasted several powerful communitarian divisions. William Morris wanted to rebuild old communities in order to address the growing problem of alienation ('fellowship is heaven, and lack of fellowship is hell,' he liked to say) and to rediscover old ways of doing things in order to address the all-enveloping problem of ugliness.[40] Guild Socialists argued that people needed to submerge their identity into a communal whole rather than obsessing about differences.[41] R. H. Tawney insisted, in a dig at the Fabians, that a socialist society was not 'a herd of tame, well-nourished animals, with wise keepers in command' but a community of responsible men and women working in comradeship for common ends.[42]

Romantic socialists had always agreed with romantic conservatives that society needed to be treated as an organic whole rather than an efficiency-maximizing calculating machine. But their vision differed in two important ways. They replaced the conservatives' faith in intellectual elites with a faith in the working class (or later other marginalized groups), and the conservatives' belief in reviving a communitarian past with a belief in creating a communitarian future, sometimes by freeing oppressed groups from the rule of 'instrumental rationality' but more often by creating a future based on different principles.

After the war, the communitarian left succeeded in turning their rather vague philosophy into a concrete policy: getting rid of educational selection in the name of comprehensive schools. The 11-plus was the very embodiment of an atomizing philosophy which broke up communities in the name of efficiency and wrenched working-class scholarship winners from the bosoms of their families. The Institute of Community Studies, a think tank that Michael Young and Peter Willmott founded in Bethnal Green in 1954,[43] produced several best-selling books that emphasized the tension between organic communities and the atomizing state: *Family and Kinship in East London* (1957), presented working-class Bethnal Green as a closely knit community, based on extended family ties, distinguished by intense sociability, bound together by an ethic of mutual aid, that was engaged in a long-running battle with a welfare state that offered social benefits at the expense of breaking traditional bonds.[44] For the institute, grammar schools were not avenues of opportunity but agencies of disruption. The schools tried to inculcate alien middle-class values in their pupils – and working-class children naturally reacted defensively by refusing to compete with their neighbours and imposing fierce sanctions on those pupils who went to grammar school. ('Grammar-bugs stinking slugs, dirty little humbugs', 'grammar school slops', 'grammar school spivs', 'grammar school sissies', 'filthy twerps' were just some of the anti-grammar-school taunts that Iona and Peter Opie collected in *The Lore and Language of Schoolchildren* (1959).)[45]

These communitarian arguments were even more extravagant on the American left. C. Wright Mills not only coined the term 'new left' but also anticipated its preoccupation with alienation. 'The uneasiness, the malaise of our time,' he argued, in an astonishingly broad-brush statement, 'is due to this root fact: in our politics and economy, in family life and religion – in practically every sphere of our existence – the certainties of the eighteenth and nineteenth centuries have disintegrated or been destroyed and, at the same time, no new sanctions or justifications for the new routines we live, and must live, have taken hold.' This agony is particularly acute for the archetypical figure of our time, the white-collar worker: 'For security's sake, he must strain to attach himself somewhere, but no communities or organizations seem to be thoroughly his.'[46]

In the 1960s, the new left built the quest for community into the heart of its politics. Mario Savio, the Berkeley student who sparked the free speech movement, decried the impersonal nature of Clark Kerr's mega-university: 'There is a time when the operation of the machine becomes so odious, makes you so sick at heart, that you can't take part.'[47] This was in many ways a response from below to Clark Kerr's vision of the meritocratic multiversity. Kerr had emphasized the importance of supporting world-class scholars who could push forward the bounds of knowledge. Savio accused his university of short-changing its students and treating them merely as tiny cogs in a vast bureaucratic machine.

The Port Huron Statement, published by Students for a Democratic Society (SDS) in 1962 and largely written by Tom Hayden, a University of Michigan student who was radicalized by the anti-war movement, was one of the era's most important polemics against alienation. The statement was a rambling 25,000 words, sometimes eloquent, more often self-indulgent ('we are people of this generation, bred in at least modest comfort, housed now in universities, looking uncomfortably to the world we inherit ... if we appear to seek the unattainable, then let it be known that we do so to avoid the unimaginable'),[48] but united by a common communitarian yearning for a world of participatory democracy and enhanced belonging.

The most striking political expression of the left's growing concern with equality and community was enthusiasm for group rights. The old left had focused on questions of race and gender because they were ancient barriers that prevented individuals from achieving their potential simply because of the accident of skin colour or gender. Martin Luther King famously insisted in his 'I have a dream' speech in 1963 that people should be judged by the content of their character rather than the colour of their skin. Appearing on behalf of the American Civil Liberties Union, Ruth Bader Ginsburg told the (all-male) Supreme Court ten years later that 'I ask no favour for my sex. All I ask of our brethren is that they take their feet off our necks.'[49] But what did treating minorities like everyone else mean? Was it enough simply to ignore the colour of people's skin when blacks had suffered from disadvantages for centuries, including slavery? Was it enough to introduce gender-blind hiring when women continued to bear the greater burden of child-rearing? Radicals increasingly questioned the logic of the pure meritocratic calculus as applied to people who had been subjected to slavery and discrimination and argued that *collective* wrongs, imposed on people because of their sex, race or sexuality, required *collective* solutions.

Radical literature emphasized the importance both of group identity and group solutions: second-wave feminist literature such as Robin Morgan's *Sisterhood is Powerful*, Germaine Greer's *The Female Eunuch* and Kate Millet's *Sexual Politics* (all 1970); black power literature such as James Baldwin's *The Fire Next Time* (1963) and Stokely Carmichael and Charles V. Hamilton's *Black Power: The Politics of Liberation in America* (1967); and gay rights literature such as Gore Vidal's novels and Paul Goodman's *The Politics of Being Queer* (1969). Carmichael and Hamilton argued in *Black Power* that 'black people have not suffered as individuals but as members of a group; therefore, their liberation lies in group action'. Carol Hanisch made the same point regarding feminism in her 1968 article 'The Personal is Political': 'there are no personal solutions at this time. There is only collective action for a collective solution.'[50]

Universities institutionalized many of these radical ideas in new academic disciplines as well as in new approaches to established disciplines. The first black studies department was founded at San Francisco State University in 1969 and the first women's studies department at San Diego State University in 1970. These departments then swept the country, along with Chicano studies and sexuality and gender studies. Activists also laid the foundations for what is now called intersectionality by emphasizing the common interests of marginalized groups. In 1965, Casey Hayden and Mary King equated the 'racial caste system' with the 'sexual caste system'. Goodman, a white man, began his 1969 essay by declaring that 'in essential ways, my homosexual needs have made me a nigger'.[51] In an open letter written in 1970, Huey Newton, a Black Panther, made the case for a grand alliance between black revolutionaries and 'the Women's Liberation and Gay Liberation Movements'.

Catharine MacKinnon, a leading feminist theorist at the University of California, Berkeley, argued in favour of group consciousness as well as group rights. 'The white man's standard for equality is: are you equal to *him*?' she argued. 'That is hardly a neutral standard. It is a racist, sexist standard ... But if you present yourself as affirmatively and self-respectingly a member of your own culture or sex ... if you insist that *your* cultural diversity be affirmatively accommodated and recognised in ways equal to the ways *theirs* has been, that's not seen as an equality challenge at all.'[52]

IDEAS HAVE CONSEQUENCES

One striking example of the practical impact of the revolt against the meritocracy was the abolition of the grammar schools in Britain in the 1960s and 1970s. The Labour Party initially embraced comprehensives as a way of getting rid of the crudeness of the 11-plus. Harold Wilson nicely described comprehensives as 'grammar schools for all'. Anthony Crosland insisted that, if Britain wanted to avoid the low academic standards of American high schools, 'division into streams, according to ability, remains essential'.[53] But as time went by, the Party became more egalitarian. Crosland, who was appointed minister of education in 1965, became a bitter opponent of grammar schools – he once told his wife, Susan, that 'if it's the last thing I do I'm going to destroy every fucking grammar school in England. And Wales. And Northern Ireland'[54] – and an increasingly warm supporter of progressive education. He was heavily influenced by prominent sociologists such as Michael Young, Jean Floud and, particularly, A. H. Halsey, who accepted a job as his adviser at the Department of Education despite disapproving of Crosland's louche personal style ('a profligate drinker and philanderer ... alcohol, cigars, women, even opera were avidly consumed').[55]

Progressive educationalists broadened their target from selection at eleven to streaming by ability. How could you rely on tests to divide children into different ability streams if you couldn't rely on them to divide children into different schools? they asked. And why would you want to do so anyway, if 'ability' was the result of circumstances rather than raw capacity?[56] Comprehensive schools should be 'equality machines', not grammar schools by other means or training camps for the workforce.

At the same time, the Labour elite neglected the problem of the public schools, which were far more responsible than grammar schools for perpetuating Britain's class divisions. In *The Future of Socialism* Crosland had argued that it would be 'absurd' to abolish the grammar schools while leaving the public schools intact,[57] a position vigorously shared by Hugh Gaitskell.[58] But he later rejected the idea of absorbing public schools into the state sector by forcing them to give scholarships to bright children who couldn't afford the fees, on the grounds that 'Dr Young's dreaded "meritocrats" would then finally have their fingers at our throats.'[59] And as secretary of state for education and science, in 1965–7, he forgot his own warning about absurdity.

There were many reasons for this. The Labour Party didn't want to get into a row about preventing people from spending their own money on education. The Department of Education was worried about the cost of absorbing millions of public-school pupils into the state system (public-school parents subsidized the state system by paying, through their taxes, for places that they didn't take up). The Wilson government had its hands full with the fight over abolishing grammar schools. Whatever the reason, the consequences were divisive, as we will see in the next chapter: the Party effectively destroyed one set of elite schools which provided a ladder of opportunity for the middle classes and, to a lesser extent, the working classes, while leaving another set of even more elite schools, which catered for much richer parents, intact. The only elite which has succeeded in rivalling the public-school elite's grip on British society was abolished.

THE AMERICAN JOURNEY

America followed a similar arc to Britain: policy-makers initially focused on removing formal barriers to upward mobility – most notably, overt racial discrimination – but were eventually drawn in more radical directions. There were lots of reasons why the American debate differed from Britain's. The American educational system is far more decentralized than the British one. The Department of Education accounts for only about 6 per cent of educational spending and schools are supported by local property taxes, so inequality of funding is much more marked. The courts are also far more powerful in America than in Britain: Supreme Court rulings having the power to guide the behaviour of institutions across the land and Americans, as a consequence, have a tendency to debate public policy in terms of abstract legal principles rather than in terms of the 'art of the possible'. The debate about the meaning of equality of educational opportunity frequently took place in the courtroom rather than the policy seminar.

In the wake of Kennedy's assassination in 1963, Lyndon Johnson mounted a determined push to address America's many social problems in the name of building a 'great society'. The Great Society programme was in many ways a thoroughly meritocratic one (indeed, the phrase was borrowed from one of the leading Edwardian Fabians, Graham Wallas). LBJ tried to address overt discrimination with the Civil Rights Act (1964) and the Voting Rights Act (1965), which guaranteed basic civil and voting rights. He also tried to address more structural barriers to inequality.

In a speech in Independence Hall, Philadelphia, on 22 February 1861, Abraham Lincoln had declared that the Declaration of Independence's affirmation of equality 'gave promise that in due time the weights would be lifted from the shoulders of all men, and that all should have an equal chance'.[60] LBJ believed that Lincoln's 'due time' had finally come. In a landmark speech at Howard University on 4 June 1965, he declared that 'freedom is not enough. You do not take a person who for years has been hobbled by chains and liberate him, bring him to the starting line and then say, "you are free to compete with all the others" and still justly believe that you have been completely fair. Thus it is not enough just to open the gates of opportunity. All our citizens must have the ability to walk through those gates.' Daniel Patrick Moynihan, who was then assistant secretary of labor, spelled out the vision in more detail: 'It is not enough that all individuals start out on even terms if the members of one group almost invariably end up well to the fore, and those of another far to the rear.'

Addressing the deepest American problem proved more difficult than anyone – and certainly more than the ever-optimistic Johnson – had expected. The optimism of the Great Society dissolved into a firestorm of assassinations, race riots, campus sit-ins and violent protests. The urban riots of the late 1960s spooked white America ('Is Civil War Next?' asked *US News and World Report*). A government report into civil disobedience – which was released on 29 February 1968, and quickly became known as the Kerner Report after its chairman Otto Kerner – concluded that America was moving 'towards two societies, one black, one white – separate and unequal'. The blame for the nation's social troubles rested squarely with white America, the report argued. 'What white Americans have never fully understood – but what the Negro can never forget – is that white society is deeply implicated in the ghetto. White institutions created it, white institutions maintain it, and white society condones it.'

The earliest intellectual blow to Johnson's vision of solving America's oldest problem came with the so-called Coleman Report: a massive study of educational spending in 4,000 schools with nearly 600,000 students produced in 1966 by a sociologist, James Coleman. Coleman concluded, much to his own surprise as well as everyone else's, that there was little difference between white-majority and black-majority schools when it came to physical plant, curricula or teacher characteristics. There were certainly big differences in performance – differences that continued to widen as children spent more time in school – but these differences could not be explained in terms of how much was spent on schools. The one school characteristic that did show a relationship to scores in achievement tests was the presence of affluent families.

The conclusion of the report was shocking to a country that believed that problems could be fixed by spending money on well-intentioned social reforms. You couldn't solve the problem of minority poverty simply by improving the quality of the physical plant. You had to go deeper into the structure of society – perhaps challenging America's wide inequalities of reward, as the left argued, or perhaps looking at problems of the black family structure, which had been shattered by slavery, as the right, and particularly a new school of former Democrats known as neoconservatives, argued. The report was so shocking that the Johnson administration considered not releasing it, and eventually did the next best thing, releasing it on the Friday of a fourth of July weekend.

Every attempt that America made to address the problem of racial disparities proved to be more frustrating than it had imagined. The most ambitious attempt was affirmative action, which was intended to compensate for past injustices and present inequalities by providing members of minorities – particularly African-Americans – with a leg-up in the form of preferential treatment in admission to universities and some jobs. Affirmative action certainly changed the face of elite America, as universities and companies enrolled or employed more minorities. It also produced a good deal of unease. A majority of the American public consistently opposed the idea that some ethnic groups should be held to different standards than others. And the courts progressively narrowed the scope of affirmative action over the years: in *Regents of the University of California v. Bakke* (1978) the Supreme Court established that race could be considered in admissions decisions but only so long as 'fixed quotas' were not used. Other rulings, such as *Hopwood v. State of Texas* (1996), made it harder to take race into consideration.

The practice of affirmative action also left much to be desired. Affirmative action had always been intended to be part of a wide range of programmes that universities used to address the problems of non-traditional students, such as mentoring and coaching. But many universities simply treated it as a mechanical formula and, having recruited them, left affirmative-action students to sink or swim without any additional guidance. Affirmative action had initially been a short-term solution to a specific problem: Sandra Day O'Connor, a Supreme Court justice, made it clear that she was only supporting it in the hope that in the long term it would become unnecessary. But again, it became a bureaucratic formula that was indiscriminately applied to all sorts of groups (such as recent immigrants) that had not been victims of the institution of slavery.

Another solution to the problem of racial integration – bussing – was even more unpopular than affirmative action. The bitterest fight took place on the Democrats' home turf of Boston. Judge W. Arthur Garrity, a graduate of Harvard Law School and close friend of the Kennedy clan, decided to mix two schools together – South Boston High, in the heart of Irish 'Southie', and Roxbury High, in the heart of the black ghetto. The result was a social explosion, pitting race against race and the working class against the mandarins. State troopers were mobilized. Parents punched each other. Whites fled the school system: soon there were just 400 pupils attending South Boston High – guarded by 500 police.[61] Racial hostility was reinforced: one study of the long-term impact of bussing on racial attitudes concluded, coolly but devastatingly, that 'the data suggest that, under the circumstances obtaining in these studies, integration heightens racial identity and consciousness, enhances ideologies that promote racial segregation, and reduces opportunities for actual contact between the races'.[62] Class hostility was added to racial hostility: Judge Garrity lived in genteel Wellesley, where the children were unaffected, and Michael Dukakis, the Massachusetts governor who sent in the troops, lived in equally genteel Brookline. This was clearly a case of the ruling class imposing their elevated principles on everybody's children but their own. Bussing caused mayhem but did nothing to improve educational results: in 1974, Roxbury High and South Boston High had been the two worst-performing schools in Boston; a decade later, they were even worse.

A final controversial solution to racial discrimination was the attempt to dismantle elite academic schools. America's selective high schools had been created in the big cities in the late nineteenth and early twentieth centuries and had been celebrated for their ability to offer first-class opportunities to the gifted children of poor immigrants. 'It seems naive today,' Gene Lichtenstein, a 1948 Bronx Science graduate, told *The New York Times* magazine in 1978, 'but Science was perceived then by parents and teachers as the embodiment of the American Dream, meritocracy at work ... For those accepted, the future could be open and unlimited, despite income and family origins. It was all dependent on performance.'

The mood changed sharply in the 1960s – hence Lichtenstein's comments about naivety – largely because educational administrators worried that the schools admitted too few African-Americans. The critics lambasted the schools for basing admission on standardized tests (which usually lasted two and a half hours) and argued instead that they should take into account a broader range of criteria such as background and race. In 1975, a federal judge imposed racial quotas on Boston Latin School. In 1983, another federal judge pronounced that San Francisco's Lowell High School contained too many Asians and ordered it to apply different admission standards to different racial groups. Activists made repeated attempts to dissolve New York's elite high schools, or to dilute the role that tests take in determining admission, despite the fact that they are popular (with more than ten applicants per place), successful (with nine Nobel Prize winners among their alumni and a roster of leading academics and businesspeople) and, certainly in terms of the social backgrounds of their students, diverse (a third of the students at Stuyvesant are eligible for free or reduced-cost school meals).

The campaign against elite schools continues to this day. Bill de Blasio, New York City's mayor, has kept up a guerrilla war against elite schools. San Francisco's school board has decided that adjusting test results doesn't go far enough and forced Lowell High School to abandon tests completely and admit students on the basis of a random lottery, initially for an experimental period of a year but, in reality, probably in perpetuity. This followed an angry debate in which protesters had criticized the school for having too few black students, while defenders had praised it for practising colour-blind meritocracy (more than half the school's students are Asian).

THE CURSE OF GOOD INTENTIONS

There are good reasons why the meritocratic dream lost its lustre as the golden age of the post-war era faded. The welfare state failed to deliver a full measure of equality of opportunity – particularly where race was concerned in the United States. The welfare state often seemed distant and arrogant – particularly with the remorseless working of the 11-plus in the United Kingdom. And groups that had been subjected to collective injustices naturally clung together in order to seek collective redress. Nevertheless, the revolt against meritocracy often proved too short-sighted and self-indulgent. The deep roots of inequality (such as America's system of funding schools through local taxes) remained in place. Policy-makers railed against elite state schools while elite private schools flourished. And radical dreams of creating participative communities often turned out to be nothing but hot air. The next chapter will show just how counterproductive the left-wing revolt against the meritocracy proved to be.

15

The Corruption of the Meritocracy

The egalitarianism of the 1960s and 1970s was followed by the festival of capitalism of the 1980s and 1990s. The pro-market revolution gave birth to a new elite that soon acquired a plethora of names: 'the new class' (Irving Kristol), the 'creative class' (Richard Florida), 'bourgeois bohemians' (David Brooks), the 'anywheres' (David Goodhart), the 'Brahmins' (Thomas Piketty), 'Davos Man' (Samuel Huntington) or the 'cognitive elite' (various). This new elite regarded itself as the meritocratic spirit made frequent-flying flesh. It was significantly bigger than the old meritocracy: high-IQ jobs expanded rapidly in these years, in both the public and the private sectors, and universities expanded even more rapidly in order to (over) supply the new market for academic talent. It was also significantly different in its attitude to money. The old elite had been primarily a professional elite that despised new money; the new elite regarded money as a measure of success.

The new elite was fashioned by three powerful forces: the marriage of merit and money as the new rich found clever ways of buying educational privileges for their children while the old rich embraced meritocracy; the globalization of the elite as surging flows of goods, information and, above all, money tied the world together; and the decline in overall levels of social mobility, as the destruction of old avenues of upward mobility, particularly selective education, triggered by the left-wing assault on meritocracy, made it more difficult for poorer children to make it to the top. Medieval historians sometimes refer to 'bastard feudalism' to distinguish the feudalism of the late Middle Ages from the purer feudalism of earlier years.[1] It is arguable that the 1980s saw the birth of a 'bastard meritocracy' which preserved the form of meritocracy (people increasingly thought that they got what they deserved) but lacked the mechanisms of social mobility which rendered meritocracy inclusive and dynamic.

MARRYING MERIT AND MONEY

The decades after 1980 saw the marriage of meritocracy and plutocracy. The new meritocratic elite learned how to transmit their privileges to the next generation, either by sending their children to private schools or moving to gilded suburbs with first-rate state schools. At the same time, the old rich started to ape the meritocrats by putting more emphasis on academic credentials. The result was social closure: in America, thirty-eight elite colleges now have more students from the top 1 per cent of the population than from the bottom 60 per cent and the average parental income of students at Harvard College is $450,000 a year. In Britain, about half the places in Oxbridge go to pupils who were educated at private schools that cater for 7 per cent of the population. An ideal that had been created to open opportunities and promote social mobility is being turned upside down, an excuse for social stasis and inherited privilege.

The new rich come from IQ-heavy areas such as finance, law, corporate engineering and, above all, technology. A 2014 calculation found that by far the biggest group of billionaires under forty – 40 per cent – made their money in technology (the next-largest group, with 16 per cent, made it in hotels and retail).[2] High-IQ types have also revolutionized old-fashioned industries such as manufacturing thanks to their ability to subject production processes to the icy discipline of numbers.

The new rich put a high value on raw brainpower. They like to socialize at ideas-rich conferences such as the World Economic Forum's annual meeting in Davos, in Switzerland, in the winter; at the Aspen Institute's Ideas Festival in Colorado in the summer; and at various meetings of TED throughout the year; indeed, they mark the passing of the seasons with conferences in the way that the old rich used to mark them out with horse races and regattas. They count big thinkers such as Thomas Friedman and David Brooks among their friends.

They subscribe to ideas-led magazines such as *Foreign Affairs* and the *New Yorker*. They are the *Economist* rich rather than the *Tatler* rich.

Peter Thiel, a venture capitalist who founded PayPal and was one of the first investors in Facebook, likes to fly provocative intellectuals to have dinner with him in San Francisco to discuss their latest books (he has also written a rather good book of his own, *Zero to One*).[3] Mark Zuckerberg hosts an online book club. Reid Hoffman, the founder of LinkedIn, toyed, as a young man, with becoming a public intellectual and still likes to reminisce about his time studying philosophy at Oxford. Eric Schmidt, a former chairman of Google, is the author of a lengthening list of books and a fixture on the ideas-conference circuit. (A jocular dictionary of Silicon Valley-speak defines a 'thought leader' as an 'unemployed rich person'.)[4] Bill Gates issues a recommended summer reading list every year. The most fashionable companies sponsor ideas conferences of their own: Google holds an annual 'camp' or 'meeting of minds' where billionaires mix with big thinkers. In 2019, the issue was climate change and the guests showed how seriously they took the subject by using 114 private planes and a fleet of superyachts to get to the conference on time.

At the same time, the old rich have embraced meritocratic values. The days when Bertie Wooster could float through Eton and Oxford without breaking the spine of a book and then devote his adult years to propping up the bar of the Drones Club are gone. The sprigs of established families now spend their childhood passing exams and learning how to hold their own with serious people. Business schools such as INSEAD and IMD are Europe's new finishing schools and marriage market. One of the biggest hits at the 2019 Google Camp was Prince Harry, who gave a lecture on climate change in his bare feet.

Elite institutions are becoming much more exam-focused as competition for places intensifies. Fifty years ago, America's most prestigious universities admitted 30 per cent of their applicants and reserved places for 'all-rounders' who were never expected to shine academically but provided the rowing club with willing muscles and the social clubs with thirsty mouths. Today, they admit fewer than 10 per cent of students and Stanford admits fewer than 4 per cent. The 'happy bottom half' is a distant memory.[5]

This is nevertheless a meritocracy marinated in money: the more money that you have, the more likely you are to be trained to pass those all-important examinations and emerge with that vital diploma. It is also a meritocracy that apes many of the exclusionary habits of the old aristocracy, from intermarriage to nepotism. Thomas Piketty is over-optimistic when he calls the current world 'hyper-meritocratic'. It would be much more accurate to call it 'pluto-meritocratic' – an uneasy marriage between meritocracy and plutocracy.

There is no better example of the merger of merit and money than the transformation of British public schools in the decades after 1980. We saw earlier that for the three decades after 1945 the public schools looked as if they might become casualties of the meritocratic revolution, stuck in the past and unable to compete with grammar schools. Today, once-mouldering institutions have reinvented themselves as gleaming merit-factories that mix the offspring of the British establishment with the children of the new global elite. The proportion of public-school graduates who proceed to university has increased from 48 per cent in 1979 to 90.1 per cent today (though the number of universities has also increased). More than a third of boarders in British public schools come from abroad (in 2014, 9,085 came from Hong Kong and China). Public schools have established campuses across the world: Kazakhstan (Haileybury), Dubai (Repton) and Bangkok (Harrow). Dulwich has three campuses in China, one in South Korea and one in Singapore. Westminster, one of the hottest of these hothouses, plans to build six branches in China over the next ten years, giving it the ability to educate twenty times as many children in China as it does in Britain.[6]

Public schools are trouncing state schools in academic subjects. Half of all A and A* grades at A level in the UK are regularly secured by the 7 per cent of students who are privately educated. Four private schools and one highly selective state sixth-form college send more children to Oxbridge than do 2,000 other secondary schools. One study ranked the success of schools, over a five-year period, at getting their pupils into Oxbridge. There were twenty-seven private schools in the top thirty; forty-three in the top fifty and seventy-eight in the top hundred. Westminster came top, with a 50 per cent hit rate. Privately educated children are five times more likely than the national average to be offered a place at one of the Russell Group universities, the top twenty out of more than a hundred universities.

The public schools' success extends beyond the narrowly academic to other areas that can count in your favour when it comes to getting university places and elite jobs. In 2019, 37 per cent of rugby internationals and 43 per cent of members of the England cricket team were privately educated.[7] This dominance is particularly marked in sports that require expensive equipment, such as rowing, horse-riding or cycling: an Old Etonian has won a medal in 'sitting down sports' in every Olympic Games since 1992. A remarkable number of Britain's most successful actors were educated at Eton (Damian Lewis, Eddie Redmayne, Dominic West and Tom Hiddleston) with Old Harrovian Benedict Cumberbatch providing a bit of diversity.

The transformation of the public schools is particularly striking in the education these schools provide for scientists and girls. Once upon a time, these schools treated both scientists and bluestockings as freaks. Today, they excel at producing both. In 2011, public schools accounted for 14.3 per cent of all A-level entries but 41.9 per cent of A*s in further maths, 36.6 per cent in physics, 33.7 per cent in chemistry and 32.8 per cent in biology. More than 90 per cent of public-school-educated girls go on to university.

The public schools have achieved this spectacular success through a combination of money and good management. They have raised their fees threefold since 1980, putting them out of the price range of many families of the 'public-school type', such as journalists and clergymen, and populating them with the children of bankers, CEOs and entrepreneurs. They have also spent lavishly on hiring the best teachers and providing the best facilities: schools such as Eton and Marlborough boast Olympic-sized swimming pools, brand-new laboratories, professional-quality theatres, Mandarin teachers and learning-disabilities specialists. During the pandemic several public schools purchased £35,000 Covid-19 testing machines so that they could continue with elite-preparation as normal.

They pour some of these additional resources into gaming the system. They are more successful than state schools in gaining additional time in exams for their pupils to compensate for dyslexia and other learning difficulties. They spend liberally on challenging exam marks (figures from the Scottish Qualifications Authority for 2017 showed that private schools are almost three times more likely to challenge the marks their pupils receive in national exams). They offer valuable advice on applying for universities abroad, particularly in the United States, where it is easy for ingénus to fall at the first hurdle.

This marriage of merit and money represents a distortion of the mission of institutions which were founded to educate poor children and still enjoy tax-exempt status as charities. The Independent Schools Council reported in 2019 that just 1 per cent of private school pupils had all their fees paid for by their schools and just 4 per cent had more than half their fees covered.[8] The pupils (and indeed their parents) are obsessed by the rat race. 'Tom Brown's School-days' have been replaced by 'Tom Brown's Porsche Days', as John Rae, a former headmaster of Westminster once put it, with pupils bent on getting the right grades and forging the right contacts so that they can eventually buy that red Porsche and a house in the south of France.[9]

ASSORTATIVE MATING

The marriage of money and merit is being driven by two of humanity's most basic instincts: our tendency to marry people like ourselves (assortative mating) and our desire to do the best for our children. We may continue to read our children stories about Cinderella marrying a prince, but in the real world university graduates marry other university graduates and high-school dropouts marry other high-school dropouts. Throw young adults together in the hothouse atmosphere of residential universities and there is a reasonable chance that they will mate. And if by some chance they don't, there are always elite dating sites that can make up for lost time: the League, a dating service for Ivy League students, is informally dubbed 'Tinder for the elites'. (Facebook itself started life as a dating site that was restricted first to Harvard and then to the Ivy League.) The proportion of men with university degrees who married women with university degrees nearly doubled between 1960 and 2005, from 25 per cent to 48 per cent, and the change may well have accelerated since then, helped in part by dating apps, which makes it easier for potential partners to screen each other for education.[10]

The past few decades have seen the multiplication of meritocratic power couples as elite universities and colleges have gone co-educational and women have enjoyed growing professional success. In America, Bill and Hillary Clinton, for decades the first couple of the Democratic Party, met at Yale University. In Britain, Ed Balls and Yvette Cooper, the golden couple of New Labour, met at Oxford, where they both read PPE. In France, François Hollande, a former French president, was in a long-term relationship with Ségolène Royal, who challenged him for the leadership of the Socialist Party. A glance at the annual Record of Balliol College, Oxford, with its litany of 'all Balliol' marriages and 'all Balliol' babies, shows that the old adage that 'at the top of the tree in every profession you will find an arboreal slum of Balliol men' needs to be modified to include 'Balliol women and babies'.

Assortative mating acts as a mighty multiplier of inequality: two married lawyers are substantially richer than two married shelf-stackers. It also has a much bigger impact on the overall tenor of society than the existence of a handful of billionaires somewhere in the stratosphere. One academic study of the United States shows that in 1960 a couple of high-school graduates who married each other earned about 103 per cent of the average household income. In 2005, a similar couple earned about 83 per cent of the average. At the other end of the spectrum, a couple in which both partners had done post-graduate work earned about 176 per cent of the mean household income in 1960 but 219 per cent in 2005. If people married each other at random, the overall level of inequality would be much as it was in 1960.[11]

Assortative mating is reinforced by geographical self-segregation. The super-rich have always gathered together in areas such as Palm Beach, the better to soak up the sun and have affairs. Over recent decades, the highly educated have started gathering in a handful of highly educated cities (London, Paris, New York, San Francisco, etc.) and in a handful of rich neighbourhoods within those cities (Islington in London, Manhattan and Brooklyn in New York, Palo Alto in Northern California). The property prices in these cities are now so inflated that middle-class families are leaving: San Francisco, a once-proud blue-collar city, is inhabited by a mixture of digital millionaires and analogue street beggars.

Once they have dated and mated, high-IQ couples engage in a joint project – the 'concerted cultivation' of their children.[12] This is at its most striking in the advanced country where inequality is most glaring, the United States. By the time they are three, they have an average vocabulary of 1,116 words, compared with 749 words for working-class children and 525 words for welfare children. By the age of four, the children of professional parents have heard some 45 million words addressed to them, compared with only 26 million for the children of working-class parents and 13 million for the children of parents on welfare.[13] Elite parents then devote their combined resources of IQ, money and organizational flair to get their children the best educations available. If they stay in the public sector, they move to gilded zip codes, where, thanks to the school funding system, public schools are private schools in disguise (the Scarsdale Union Free School District in New York recently spent $27,000 per student while Barbourville Independent School District in Kentucky spent $8,000). They also raise extra money for their schools whenever it's needed (school fund-raising is so much part of the woof and weft of American life that a hit TV series, *Big Little Lies*, revolves around a murder at a particularly extravagant fundraiser for a junior school). A quarter of parents who make more than $200,000 a year now send their children to private schools, a significantly higher proportion than in Britain, and a remarkable development in the land of the 'common school'.

Competition among the rich for school places can be vicious, and starts with kindergartens. Fieldston, a pre-kindergarten in New York City, charges $50,000 a year, but admits only 5 per cent of applicants.[14] Jennifer Brozost of PEAS, an educational consultancy, recommends that parents apply to eight to ten kindergartens, write 'love letters' to their top three, and bone up on how to make a good impression on the school principal.[15] The late Christopher Hitchens told me that one of the banes of his life was having to write letters of recommendation for friends for Washington's favourite pre-schools.

Parents are so worried about giving their children a leg-up that there is now a literature devoted to the problem of 'helicopter parents' who hover over their children's lives, ferrying them from piano lessons to algebra camps to coding clubs in order to squeeze the maximum value out of their every waking hour, helping them with their homework to the point of actually doing it for them. Many

American schools have a 'parent portal' that allows parents to see whether their children turned up for class and what grade they got.

Helicopter parenting can extend to the student years. Some British universities have complained that they have so many parents coming to their open days that there is not enough room for potential students. American parents have been found sleeping in their dorms along with their student-children. Graduate programmes are rife with stories of parents accompanying their graduate-student offspring to interviews. Parents have even been known to accompany their adult children to job interviews.

One step up from helicopter parenting is tiger parenting. Amy Chua, a Yale law professor, caused a stir in 2011 with her semi-autobiographical the *Battle Hymn of the Tiger Mother*. Her argument, summed up in an article in the *Wall Street Journal*, went like this:

> A lot of people wonder how Chinese parents raise such stereotypically successful kids ... Well, I can tell them, because I've done it. Here are some things my daughters, Sophia and Louisa, were never allowed to do: attend a sleepover; have a playdate; be in a school play; complain about not being in a school play; watch TV or play computer games; choose their own extracurricular activities; get any grade less than an A; not be the No. student in every subject except gym and drama; play any instrument other than the piano or violin; not play the piano or violin.[16]

Though Ms Chua's book provoked a mixture of horror and anxiety among her fellow parents, all she was really doing was taking elite parenting to its logical extreme.

Rich parents can also game the system by employing professionals – dubbed 'Ivy Whisperers' in the United States – to prepare their children for tests or give them a hand in writing 'personal statements'. The Independent Educational Consultants Association (IECA), in Fairfax, Virginia, calculates that the United States has more than 8,000 full-time professionals who are employed to help get children into elite universities, as well as thousands more who moonlight from their day jobs as admissions officers or guidance counsellors. One consultancy, Ivy Coach, sells a $1.5 million 'full-service package' that guides children over five years. Starting in the eighth grade, students are steered towards picking the right mix of classes and extracurricular activities. Then comes the intensive coaching for the SATs and other standardized exams, careful editing of college essays and, never to be forgotten, fine-tuning of those personal statements. Several national chains of tutors/advisers, such as Kumon and Kaplan, are trying to turn the art of child-preparation into a science.

Some rich parents are so desperate to get their children into their chosen schools that they have resorted to corruption. In 2018, the FBI launched an investigation called 'Varsity Blues'. It discovered that in 2011–18 one particularly flamboyant college counsellor, William 'Rick' Singer, had earned $25 million for helping the children of the rich and powerful to cheat their way into elite universities such as Stanford and Yale. Mr Singer's clients included Felicity Huffman, a star of *Desperate Housewives*; Gordon Caplan, the co-chairman of an international law firm; and William McGlashan, a Silicon Valley private-equity executive who champions ethical investing. His methods included bribing proctors of admissions exams to fake scores, concocting false diagnoses of learning disabilities, forging athletic records, complete with altered photos showing the students playing sports that they had little interest in or aptitude for, and then bribing athletics officials to accept those concoctions. According to prosecutors, Mr Caplan faked a diagnosis of learning disability for his daughter and paid $75,000 for a boosted admission score, and Lori Loughlin, an actor and producer, paid $500,000 to get her daughters, who are both minor celebrities and Instagram influencers in their own right, designated as recruits to the University of Southern California's rowing team, despite the fact that neither of them knew one end of an oar from the other. In the case of one daughter, she even used a photoshopped image showing her rowing.[17]

In one recorded call to a client, Mr Singer argued that there are three 'doors' into elite colleges. There is the 'front door', 'which means you get in on your own'. The creation of that front door over the decades has been the subject of this book. There is the 'back door', which you can enter only if you make multibillion-dollar donations to universities. Putting an egalitarian gloss on his scam, Mr Singer claimed to have discovered a side door which allows millionaires to gain the same privileges for their children that billionaire children get for theirs: you bribe your way in by massaging test scores and greasing palms.

Mr Singer's scam provoked outraged headlines. But the real disgrace is not the isolated scam (which resulted in legal action) but the lucky breaks that tilt the system in favour of the rich. Commentators have understandably focused on the fact that Ivy League universities unashamedly practise affirmative action for children of alumni, or 'legacies'. In elite colleges, the children of alumni are more than six times more likely to gain admission than regular applicants. Every year, about a third of Harvard's new class consists of relatives of people who've been to Harvard. But there are lots of other forms of 'affirmative action' for the rich. Athletics is a popular one, as the Singer scandal revealed: at one elite college, Williams, in New England, a third of each class consists of athletic recruits. Elite universities regularly give preferences to people who participate not just in any old sport but in exotic sports such as rowing, golf and lacrosse: the University of Virginia has scholarships for polo players, relatively few of whom come from the inner cities.

In what often amounts to institutionalized venality, elite universities go to extraordinary lengths to admit the children of the seriously rich and famous. Harvard has something called a 'Z' list – a list of applicants who are given a place after a year's deferment to catch up – that is dominated by the children of rich alumni. Duke University's admissions director visited Steven Spielberg's house to interview his stepdaughter. Princeton found a place for Lauren Bush – the president's niece and a top fashion model – despite the fact that she missed the application deadline by a month. The father of Trump's son-in-law, Jared Kushner, reportedly pledged $2.5 million to Harvard just as young Jared was applying. The young man gained admission to the great temple of meritocracy despite mediocre grades. Donald Trump, the self-styled hillbilly billionaire, may have donated over the years $1.5 million to his alma mater, the University of Pennsylvania's Wharton School, the destination of two of his children, Donald Jr and Ivanka.[18]

Rich children benefit from all sorts of 'lucky breaks' in addition to expensive preparation. The proportion of places in elite universities that are 'unhooked' – i.e. rewarded on merit, rather than because of ties to rich parents or sporting prowess, is as low as 40 per cent.[19] Students who make it to elite universities against all the odds – true aristocrats, in Jefferson's terms – can often find themselves acting as domestic servants to those who got there thanks to a combination of privilege and 'hooks' in order to pay their way.[20] One student was confronted with a fellow student's excrement. 'The most disgusting thing was the faeces all over the toilet. It was hard to clean. There was just so much stuff on the floor; we had to move their underwear out of the way. I don't know how they could go in there and use the bathroom every day.'[21] Another faced a sea of used condoms: 'One room, the floor was covered in used condoms. It was the lacrosse team. It was nasty, but it was more just how dismissive people were.'[22]

This institutionalized prejudice in favour of the rich is often combined with a prejudice against certain categories of regular people, most notably Asian-Americans. It seems that striving too hard is as much a sin as playing lacrosse is a virtue. *The Gatekeepers* (2002), a study of the admissions system at Wesleyan, an elite liberal arts college in Middletown, Connecticut, by Jacques Steinberg, a veteran education correspondent at *The New York Times*, makes for both fascinating and infuriating reading. Mr Steinberg shows that, as well as valuing clout and connections, admissions officers frequently give free play to their ideological and ethnic prejudices. One candidate, Tiffany Wang, was a Chinese immigrant student whose SAT scores were more than a hundred points above the Wesleyan average, despite the fact that English wasn't her first language. She was also a National Merit Scholarship semi-finalist, putting her in the top 0.5 per cent of high-school students. The admission officer rejected her application but later admitted that she might have changed her mind if she'd realized how much time and effort Tiffany put into campaigning against the death penalty.[23]

You might expect academics to object to this system of favouritism and patronage, particularly in disciplines that make a fuss about social justice. But they have remained remarkably quiet, partly because they are happy to subcontract admissions to professional bureaucrats so that they can concentrate on their own scholarship and partly because they benefit from the system of 'hooks' themselves. They are not only excused tuition fees if they can get their children into the universities where they teach. They get easier admission as well. Boston University accepted 91 per cent of 'faculty brats' in 2003, at a cost of about $9 million. Notre Dame accepts about 70 per cent of the children of university employees, compared with 19 per cent of 'unhooked' applicants, despite markedly lower average SAT scores.

Elite employers such as consultancies, investment banks and big law firms add lucky breaks of their own. A study by Lauren Rivera, of Northwestern University's Kellogg School of Management, documents the sundry ways in which elite employers screen for class privilege as well as 'smarts'.[24] They favour people who have filled their leisure time doing 'upper-class things' like playing tennis or going skiing. They put heavy emphasis on subjective things like 'fit', rather than objective tests. A lot of what they do is simply the old-fashioned notion of whether somebody is a 'good chap' dressed up in modern language. One consultant interviewed by Ms Rivera put it perfectly: 'We like to interview at schools like Harvard and Yale, but people who have 4.0s and are in the engineering department but, you know, don't have any friends, have huge glasses, read their textbooks all day, those people have no chance here … I have always said [my firm] is like a fraternity of smart people.'[25]

THE NEW NEPOTISM

The new meritocracy is further disfigured by a modern version of nepotism. The new nepotism is more sophisticated than the old: you can't inherit a top political job directly or hand an office to a relative in the way that you once could. The Bush dynasty is not the Saxe-Coburg dynasty. You have to accumulate respectable qualifications: George W. Bush went to both Yale and Harvard Business School. Leading families nevertheless continue to cling to high offices by cultivating contacts and connections. They whisper a word in the right ear, make that conviction for drunk driving disappear, put a thumb on the scale at just the right moment.

Family privilege is particularly disturbing in politics because democratic politicians are supposed to represent ordinary people, not a self-perpetuating clique. In America, politics is, to a remarkable degree, a game played by elite families. A Bush or a Clinton took part in every presidential race from 1980 to 2004. There is some evidence that the dynastic principle is actually getting stronger. The 2000 contest was the first race to involve two sons of leading politicians and the first since 1912 to involve two Ivy League candidates. George W. Bush was the first presidential son to end up in the White House since 1824 (and the first one ever to do so as a member of the same party as his father). Donald Trump gave senior jobs to close members of his family, not least his daughter, Ivanka, and her husband, Jared Kushner. George P. Bush, Jeb Bush's eldest son, is already climbing up the greasy poll as Commissioner of the Texas General Land Office and is a growing voice in the national Republican Party (the 'P' stands for Prescott, the name of his grandfather, a US senator).

The Bushes and the Clintons are the tip of a vast iceberg of nepotistic political families: think of Andrew Cuomo, the governor of New York and son of Mario; Jerry Brown, the former governor of California and son of Pat, another governor of California; and sundry Kennedys, including Caroline Kennedy. Mitt Romney, the Republicans' 2012 candidate, was the son of a governor of Michigan and sometime presidential candidate George Romney. 'Reciprocal nepotism' is now a commonplace on Capitol Hill, with Congress people giving jobs to the children of friends in return for their friends giving jobs to their children. Hunter Biden traded on his father's famous name in order to get seats on various boards, particularly in Eastern Europe. 'Members of Congress basically are profit centres for their entire families,' says Melanie Sloan, of Citizens for Responsibility and Ethics in Washington. 'Some people can get by solely on talent, but talent and connections is a much better combination – and if you have to have one or the other, it's probably the connections.'

The new nepotism suffers from many of the same problems as the old. The nepotists are cut off from the people that they presume to govern by a wall of privilege that is obvious to everyone except the people who are protected by it. (Mrs Clinton was serious when she said that she and her husband were 'poor' when they left the White House in 2000 because she had got so used to moving in the world of the super-rich that she had lost any sense of what the word 'poor' actually means.) But in one important way it is worse: the new nepotists are losing the sense of guilt that used to be the saving grace of their predecessors. Jim Hightower's quip about George H. W. Bush – 'he was born on third base and thinks he hit a triple' – is true of the vast majority of new nepotists because, in their own minds, they made it through the educational system on the basis of their own merits.

The new nepotists have reinvented aristocratic connections for a democratic-cum-meritocratic age. Being the child of a dynast increases your chances of winning a place in an elite university, a job in a brand-name company or think tank, and a spell carrying a bag for an established politician. This is particularly important in a world where growth is slow and rents are high: dynasts can always stay with their parents, do some unpaid volunteer work and hang around until something comes up. They have also reinvented aristocratic connections for the age of globalization: the pluto- – and often pseudo- – meritocrats are not only cut off from the wider society by the fact that they marry each other and socialize with each other. They are cut off from the wider society by the fact that they pursue global careers in global institutions. David Miliband, who abandoned British Labour politics for a very well-paid job running the International Rescue Committee in New York City, once tweeted a photograph of a very scenic-looking Aspen, proclaiming that it was a perfect place to discuss refugees.

THE COSMOS CLUB

The idea of 'a global elite' selected by merit and interlinked by institutional affiliation has been the dream of some uber-meritocrats for centuries. Cecil Rhodes established a Rhodes Scholarship to select the most promising candidates from across the English-speaking nations to spend time at Oxford University. David Rockefeller worked tirelessly to support or build global organizations such as the Bilderberg Group and the Trilateral Commission. Karl Schwab arguably topped both of them by creating the World Economic Forum. The WEF is famous for its annual jamboree in Davos, a Swiss village, where some 1,300 people descend every January to forge global connections and generally 'pageant themselves about'. But that is not the half of it: the Geneva-based organization also publishes reports, selects 'global leaders' and holds other, smaller meetings all around the world.

Mr Schwab got his timing exactly right. The 1,300 men and women who travel to Davos every winter are the leading members of a proliferating global class: the people who fill the business-class lounges of international airports and provide the officer class of the world's companies and global institutions and, through their incessant travelling, networking and management-book reading, make the world a smaller place.

The most ambitious members of the global elite no longer content themselves with running national institutions. They crave the global stage. The further people rise up their professional pyramids, the more they interact with their peers around the world, forging, in the process, a common global class, selected and promoted by achievement and linked by an ever-thicker web of connections: university and business-school ties; membership of the boards not just of companies but also of charities and arts organizations; business deals and investment flows; all of which are marinated in a common set of attitudes and assumptions.

The primary engines of the global meritocracy are global companies. During the golden age of globalization from 1980 to the global financial crisis, leading companies embraced globalization with wide-eyed enthusiasm, first by establishing subsidiaries in lots of countries, then by trying to manage themselves as integrated operations. Most continue to embrace it today, although more nervously. Many of the prophets of globalization believed that global competition would lead to the 'demise of size' as small companies learned how to take advantage of a borderless world. In fact, the opposite has happened: the biggest global companies have consolidated their hold over the world economy. An annual list of the world's top multinationals produced by the United Nations Conference on Trade and Development (UNCTAD) shows that, judged by measures such as sales and employment, such companies have all become substantially bigger since the mid-1990s. Big companies have reaped enormous efficiencies by creating supply chains that stretch around the world and involve hundreds of partners, ranging from wholly owned subsidiaries to outside contractors.[26]

These big global companies have put great effort into producing a global 'leadership class', recruiting employees from around the world through broadly meritocratic processes and then providing them with a global career. Henkel, a German chemical-maker, insists that executives live in at least two different countries before being considered for promotion. Nestlé, a Swiss food company, boasts executive board members from eight different countries. Procter & Gamble subjects high-flyers to 'accelerator experiences' and 'crucible roles' in different parts of the world.

Management consultancies are in the vanguard of global meritocracy. Every year, McKinsey screens 50,000 résumés and undertakes tens of thousands of interviews, many of them involving senior partners, in order to hire 500 new associates. The consultancies then devote an impressive amount of time to drilling their tyros in the language and techniques of management theory. Consultancies allow their members to amass a far broader range of experience than regular business executives have by setting them to work in a variety of countries and industries. They also keep their people on the move, switching them from posting to posting, lending them to other offices for short-term stays and obliging them to fly hither and thither for specialized meetings (though the flying was sharply reduced by Covid).

The result is that former consultants are beginning to form a quasi-Masonic elite at the summit of modern business – and this elite regards the global life as a precondition for success. The frenetic pace of the business is such that junior consultants seldom see anybody outside work and thus form bonds that last long after they have moved on. Just in case these informal bonds are not enough, McKinsey has produced an alumni directory, complete with contact numbers, which means that products of the firm can be sure of finding others of their kind in whatever city they happen to touch down. McKinsey's 5,000 alumni form an international network running a significant proportion of the world's top companies.

Business schools are the boot camps of the global meritocracy. In the old days, Oxford and Cambridge selected and trained a national elite often by teaching them English history and literature, or a distinctively English style of analytical philosophy. Today, business schools select and train a global elite by teaching them about supply-chain management and globalization. Harvard Business School requires its students to spend time in emerging countries. INSEAD calls itself 'the business school for the world' and has campuses in Singapore and Abu Dhabi as well as Fontainebleau, France. Fuqua School of Business at Duke University boasts that it is 'the world's first legitimately global business school'; it has campuses in six countries. All leading business schools make sure that their alumni keep touch with each other for the rest of their careers.

Globalization exaggerates both meritocracy's best tendencies and its worst. Older elites usually owed their wealth to property, which, by its nature, bound them to particular places; global meritocrats, by contrast, usually owe their positions to information and expertise, which strives to be placeless. Their loyalties are international rather than local, and calculating rather than emotional: they are far more concerned with the smooth operation of the system as a whole than with the health of any particular part of it. They like transnational institutions such as the European Union and the United Nations and worry about nation states, which they regard at best as hold-overs from a more primitive age and at worst as potential bearers of destructive nationalism.

Globalization reinforces the winner-takes-all effect not just by multiplying the rewards for winning but also by allowing global companies to game the tax system. Companies buy foreign companies in order to move their nominal headquarters and thereby minimize their tax obligations ('inversion'). They also charge affiliates for using intangible assets, such as brands, intellectual property or business services, in order to shift profits around ('transfer pricing'). Not that long ago, only the most buccaneering companies made extensive use of tax havens. Now, leading companies such as Google do. Google achieved an effective tax rate of 2.4 per cent on its non-American profits in 2007–9 by routing profits to Bermuda, via Ireland and the Netherlands, an arrangement known as a double Irish. Thanks to the application of so much brainpower to tax minimization, about 30 per cent of all the world's foreign direct investment now flows through tax loopholes.[27]

THE WIDENING DIVIDE

What makes the marriage of merit and money particularly dangerous is that it's taking place at a time when merit and democracy are getting divorced.

The engines of upward mobility have been silting up for decades. In the United States, inner-city public schools are being pulverized by social problems. In Britain, comprehensive schools are less effective at producing scholarship boys and girls than grammar schools once were. Those working-class children who make it through school and university face a lengthening ladder, containing post-graduate degrees, internships and study periods abroad, which it is hard to climb without money, connections and somewhere to stay, rent free, in expensive global cities. The more social mobility depends on endurance rather than on being spotted early by the elite and given a scholarship, the bigger the advantage of people who have abundant resources.[28]

Powerful cultural forces are also pulling society in different directions: the merito-plutocratic elite has become more conservative when it comes to family values even as the working class has become more bohemian. The best evidence for this cultural division, and what it means for the next generation, can be found in the United States, in part because the problem is most advanced there, and in part because American social scientists, on both the left and the right, have treated the problem with the seriousness it deserves.

Americans are dividing into two classes when it comes to family formation: planners and drifters.[29] Planners wait to get married before having children and treat child-bearing as part of a carefully crafted life-plan involving having a career and accumulating wealth. Drifters have children early, don't bother to get married and drift from partner to partner in much the same way as they drift from job to job.

The educational divide between the cognitive elite and the rest is also an illegitimacy divide. The proportion of American children born to single mothers has grown from 10 per cent in 1969 to 41 per cent today, while the proportion of children living with two married parents fell from 77 per cent in 1980 to 65 per cent in 2011. But the growth is concentrated among the less educated. Sixty per cent of births to women with only a high-school certificate occur out of wedlock, compared with only 10 per cent to women with a university degree. The rate of unplanned births for young unmarried women living below the poverty line is six times the rate for more well-off young unmarried women. The rate of single parenting is the most significant predictor of social immobility in the country.

The same applies to the divorce divide. Marriage break-up rates soared across the board in the 1960s and 1970s. For women who got married for the first time in 1970–74, the share whose marriage failed within ten years stood at 24.3 per cent for degree-holders and 33.7 per cent for the rest. But since the 1970s, divorce rates have fallen significantly among the highly educated while remaining stubbornly high for everyone else. Only 16.7 per cent of women with at least a college degree got divorced within ten years of their first marriage in 1990–94 – a 30 per cent drop from twenty years earlier. For women without high-school degrees, the marriage break-up rate was 35.7 per cent – 6 per cent higher than twenty years earlier.[30]

Health provides a vivid demonstration of this growing social divide. The life expectancy of members of the elite continues to increase, while that of members of the working class has started to stagnate or even decline. 'Deaths of despair' are taking their toll as the number of poor people who commit suicide or drink-or-drug themselves to death grows.[31] Poorer Americans are much more likely to be obese than richer Americans (having a sculpted body is a sign of social status as well as good health) and therefore to suffer from obesity-related problems such as diabetes and heart disease. Predictably, unhealthy adults are more likely to bring up unhealthy children just as healthy adults are more likely to bring up healthy children.

The divide inevitably has a racial dimension. Black households earn 60 per cent of what white households earn; over 30 per cent of black children grow up in poverty, a rate three times that of white children. One in three black men born in 2001 can expect to spend some time in prison, compared with one in seventeen white men. Seven in ten African-American babies are born out of wedlock, a figure that is higher than for any other ethnic group, even if you control for education and poverty, and their parents are overwhelmingly likely to have broken up five years after their birth. Black children are three times more likely to have high levels of lead in their blood, which is associated with lower IQ and higher levels of violence in adulthood. They are one and a half times more likely than white children to have asthma.[32]

Nevertheless, talk of white privilege oversimplifies things. White America is being torn apart by a growing class divide. Poor whites often have more in common with poor blacks than with affluent whites. J. D. Vance provides some personal insights into the way that a significant section of white America is falling behind the rest of the country in his memoir of growing up in Kentucky and Ohio, *Hillbilly*

Elegy (2016). A bright and articulate boy, the young Vance nevertheless constantly flirted with failure at school. His mother's addiction to
drugs and unsuitable boyfriends left him with a pervasive sense of
anxiety. He couldn't concentrate on his schoolwork because a simple
question such as 'have you got any brothers or sisters?' tied him up in
knots. ('The answer was "complicated".')[33] He couldn't do his homework because his mother might be stoned on the couch or rowing
with her boyfriend. He couldn't reach for the stars because everything
he saw told him that he was destined for the gutter: that life meant
little more than a series of casual jobs and casual hook-ups; that being
a man meant little more than drinking beer and screaming at a woman
when she screamed at him; and that nobody ever made it out of the
Hillbilly Nation.[34] 'The constant moving and fighting, the seemingly
endless carousel of new people I had to meet, learn to love, and then
forget – this, and not my subpar public school, was the real barrier to
opportunity.'[35]

Vance was held back for a year in kindergarten because his behaviour was so atrocious that his teacher contemplated leaving the
profession.[36] He almost failed his first year in high school, earning Ds
and Fs and complaints about poor attendance. He grew fat on a diet
of McDonald's and Kentucky Fried Chicken and experimented with
drugs and alcohol. Chaos begat chaos and disaster disaster. The sheer
imperative of surviving trumped the desire to do well in school.

The young tearaway eventually graduated from one of America's
leading factories of the meritocracy, Yale Law School, thanks to a
lucky combination of trump cards – the support of his grandparents,
a spell in the army and his natural abilities. But millions of young
Americans, their intellects cramped and their souls shrivelled by dys-
functional families, remain trapped in a swamp of low achievement
and low expectations.

The widening meritocracy gap can also be seen right across Europe,
in Germany and Scandinavia as well as Spain and Greece, but the
closest European equivalent is America's fellow Anglo-Saxon country,
the United Kingdom. Poorer children suffer from a cascade of disadvantages. Half of pre-school children from low-income families live
with only one parent, a problem that is particularly pronounced in
the white working class.[37] Vocational education is poorly funded and

badly organized: only one in ten British adults has a technical qualification, compared with more than one in five in Germany. The number of 'deaths of despair' has jumped from thirty per 100,000 in the early 1990s to fifty in 2020. These problems are magnified by regional and racial disparities. Londoners enjoy twice as much spending per capita on transport as, say, Mancunians. Only 29.5 per cent of white students go on to university when they leave school, compared to more than 41.2 per cent of black students, 46.7 per cent of Asian students and 66.3 per cent of Chinese students. The growing meritocratic gap is, to some extent, a gap between an increasingly multicultural cognitive elite that comes from stable families (particularly in London) and a white working class (particularly in the North) that is suffering from multiple signs of social disintegration. This gap is a recipe for race-fuelled populism if ever there was one.

Darren McGarvey has written a chronicle for his British tribe in much the same way as Vance has done for his American one. Born to a drug- and alcohol-addicted single mother in Pollok, a troubled housing estate in south Glasgow, McGarvey forged a more unconventional path to success than Vance: rather than the Marines and Yale, he chose rapping (under the name Loki) and journalism, becoming, for a while, rapper-in-residence at Police Scotland's Violence Reduction Unit. His book *Poverty Safari* (2017) echoes many of Vance's themes: that the biggest threat to educational success is not physical poverty (though that's certainly a problem) but family dysfunction; that the worst sort of family dysfunction is created by women hooking up with a succession of unsuitable men; and that the divide between the cognitive elite and the poor is tearing society apart, not just because the poor are angry and alienated but because the state employees who are supposed to look after them are so disconnected from their lives.

Poverty Safari chronicles the ways in which poor people are deprived of many of the things that regular people take for granted. They live in constant fear of violence or bizarre behaviour. They are surrounded by noise: the noise of their own chaotic families but also, thanks to paper-thin walls, the noise of their neighbours arguing, flushing toilets, watching the TV, playing loud music and having sex.[38] They can't bring friends home without a sense of dread (on one occasion McGarvey brought two friends home only to find most of the contents of his flat laid out in the front garden, incinerated).[39] They act out in various ways – numbing the pain with drink, drugs and junk food, taunting authority figures, joining gangs, engaging in random acts of violence. McGarvey notes that educational failure and sudden bursts of violence are self-reinforcing: people strike out because they're terrified that they're 'not smart enough', but striking out means that they're thrown out of school.

In left-behind Britain, only a handful of institutions continue to appeal to people's better natures: for example, public libraries offer both a haven from the noise, a break from the constant pressure to spend money, a place where people who are trying to better themselves can meet each other. 'Particularly in communities characterised by poor education, low opportunity and high levels of stress,' he writes, 'the library is an engine room of social mobility where people go to complete college and job applications, get help filling out forms to access benefits and bursaries as well as accessing the internet and books to learn new skills or find information'.[40] Yet these institutions are being threatened by cuts in public services and crowded out by dozens of institutions that appeal to people's inner devils, from gambling emporiums to corner shops selling cheap booze. The links between the meritocratic Britain that the elite occupies and the rest of the country are becoming more tenuous by the day: the problem with reigniting social mobility is not just that the ladder of educational opportunity has lost many of its rungs but also that the working-class culture of self-help and self-improvement has shrunk and in some areas disappeared entirely.

PROMISE BETRAYED

In his classic *The Promise of American Life* (1909), Herbert Croly noted that 'a democracy, no less than a monarchy or an aristocracy, must recognize political, economic, and social discriminations, but it must also manage to withdraw its consent whenever these discriminations show any tendency to excessive endurance'. With the gap between the meritocratic elite and the struggling masses widening and a growing number of people trapped at the bottom of society, 'democracy' is doing exactly what Croly predicted and withdrawing its consent.

16

Against Meritocracy: The Revolt on the Right

The revolt against the meritocratic-cum-plutocratic elite reshaped global politics in the second decade of the twenty-first century. On 23 June 2016, the British shook the establishment to its core by voting, by a narrow but decisive majority of 52 per cent to 48 per cent, to leave the European Union. Five months later, on 8 November, the Americans produced an even bigger earthquake by voting, by an even narrower margin, to elect Donald Trump, a quixotic real-estate tycoon who had never stood for office before, over Hillary Clinton, one of the most experienced politicians in the country. (Mrs Clinton admits in her memoirs that, when Trump declared his candidacy, she thought it was a joke; it turned out 'the joke was on us'.)[1] In Hungary and Poland, voters chose 'blood and soil' nationalists over technocrats. In Mexico and Brazil, they chose Trump-style charismatic leaders. A chaotic election in Italy led to a coalition government composed of the right-wing populist Northern League and the anti-establishment Five Star Movement. Nations that are bywords for stability, such as Sweden, Denmark and Germany, have seen insurgent populist parties enter their parliaments. Vilfredo Pareto, echoing Machiavelli, said that there are two types of rulers, foxes who are defined by their intelligence and lions who are defined by their strength. The 2010s was a decade of lions.

These political upsets were driven by many things: the revolt of the provinces against the capitals; of the workers against the bosses; of traditionalists (particularly older people) against bohemians; of outsiders against the self-dealing establishment; of native-born populations against immigrants; of 'somewheres', who feel rooted in particular places, against 'anywheres', who are always on the move, in David

Goodhart's phrase. Though these revolts all play their part, they are overshadowed by a bigger revolt: the revolt of the masses against the meritocrats, of workers by hand against workers by brain, of merit-ocracy's losers against meritocracy's winners. Michael Young's revolt against the meritocracy had come a decade earlier than he predicted.

The groups that are driving the rise of populism have disparate and sometimes clashing material interests, consisting of a mish-mash of blue-collar workers, Main Street businesspeople such as real-estate agents and old-line manufacturers, and older voters who came of age before the great university expansion of the 1960s. The British joke that Brexit was driven by an alliance of the housing estates and the landed estates. But they have a common cognitive interest: they are united by their shared opposition to the meritocratic elite with its cosmopolitan values and habit of privileging intellectual achievement over tangible skills and traditional values.

The democratic divide is becoming a diploma divide. In Britain's EU referendum, 72 per cent of people with no educational qualifications voted to leave, compared with only 35 per cent of those with a univer-sity degree.[2] In America, Donald Trump won whites without college degrees by a 36 per cent margin, while Hillary Clinton won whites with college degrees by a 17 per cent margin. The first female presiden-tial candidate for a major party lost white women without a degree by twenty-seven points. It turns out that the average waitress doesn't care that much about 'breaking the glass ceiling' if it means getting more women on to the boards of *Fortune* 500 companies.

One reason why the Leave vote proved such a surprise for pollsters in Britain was that it was driven by a surge in turn-out among less edu-cated people who had almost lost the habit of voting. Areas with large numbers of people with no educational qualifications witnessed a larger increase in turnout (8.4 points) than areas with large numbers of middle-class graduates (6.6 points). Frank Field, who was Labour MP for Birkenhead from 1979 to 2019, says that he saw people queueing up to vote whom he'd never seen voting about anything before. The estimated participation gap between highly educated professionals (who largely voted Remain) and people with lower levels of education (who usually voted Leave) was reduced from 39 per cent in the 2015 general election to only 20 per cent in the 2016 referendum.[3] If the gap hadn't narrowed, Britain would still be in the EU, and years of political turmoil would have been avoided.

The electoral map is becoming a map of educational institutions. In Britain, the Remainers won by big margins in knowledge-intensive cities such as London and in college towns such as Oxford and Cambridge. The Leavers won in the provinces and in smaller towns. In America, the Democrats win in places where colleges are thick on the ground – the coasts, the cities and the university towns – while the Republicans win in places where Wal-Marts jumble up against Applebee's and Cracker Barrels. That divide got bigger in the era of Trump: in 2012, Obama won the fifty most-educated counties in the country by seventeen percentage points, whereas in 2016 Clinton won them by twenty-six points. Trump won the fifty least-educated counties in 2016 by nearly thirty-one points, compared with ten points for Mitt Romney in 2012. Nearly three fifths of Republican voters believe that universities are bad for their country.[4]

In Britain, the clash between the meritocrats and the masses is also a clash between London and the provinces. London is home to Britain's financial services industry, including about 250 overseas banks, its most powerful cultural institutions, including the BBC, and its largest collection of universities (with Oxford and Cambridge only an hour away by train). It is also home to Britain's highly centralized and intrusive government. Britain's revolt against the EU was arguably just as much a revolt against London and the type of pro-globalization policies that the London-based elite has supported as it was a revolt against Brussels. Dominic Cummings, the architect of the Leave campaign, cut his teeth as a political organizer in the North, running campaigns against Britain joining the Euro and against establishing an elected regional assembly in the North-east. The Conservative Party's pledge to 'get Brexit done' was key to its success in winning a swathe of Northern seats from Labour in the 2019 general election.

Then there is the question of the sort of campaigns the parties fight. In America, Republicans now tout their hostility to the cognitive elite, while Democratic candidates tout their intellectual credentials. This began long before Trump. George W. Bush and Al Gore had roughly the same educational qualifications – indeed, Bush had rather higher SAT scores than Gore. But, aided by his family's long-standing problems with the English language, Bush successfully presented himself as a Texas yokel, while Gore couldn't resist displaying his intellectual credentials. Donald Trump happily admitted that he never read books (while also emphasizing that he possessed a stratospheric IQ). He wanted to prove that his ability was 'natural' rather than the product of swotting. Hillary Clinton said, in an aside that did as much as anything to doom her campaign, that 'you could put half of Trump's supporters into what I call the basket of deplorables'. By contrast, Trump declared that 'I love the poorly educated – I am your voice.' 'The forgotten men and women of our country will be forgotten no longer,' he declared in his victory speech on 9 November 2016. One of the reasons why Joe Biden proved such a difficult candidate for Trump to demonize in 2020 was that he is a genuine product of blue-collar America who was educated at the University of Delaware rather than the Ivy League.

The revolt against the meritocrats is producing a rolling political realignment, starting with the United States and Great Britain but quickly spreading elsewhere. Since the Second World War, the main political division has been over class and state activism. Parties of the left have based their support on the working class, particularly the trade unions, and favoured more state activism to stabilize the economy and redistribute wealth. Parties of the right have tried to temper state activism and redistribution while also moving with the times. This is changing fast: increasingly, the key division is not class but education, and not your relationship to the means of production but your relationship to the machinery of meritocracy. This is because the great meritocratic machine determines not just how much you earn but also how much status you command.

This revolution is also reconfiguring the relationship between the masses and the political elite – by which I mean not just the politicians but also the upper bureaucracy that shapes and administers the politicians' decisions and the media that reports on them. In the Brexit vote, the entire political establishment – starting with the government, with its formidable resources, including both the main political parties and the majority of the opinion-forming classes, and extending to such figures as the Pope, the President of the United States, the heads of the EU and its constituent countries – urged the British to vote to remain in the EU. In America, the entire political establishment, Republican as well as Democratic, believed that Trump was a no-hoper. Many remained unreconciled after his victory, becoming 'never Trumpers' and campaigning for Joe Biden in 2020. In Italy, Beppe Grillo, the head of the Five Star Movement, lambasts *la casta*, or the 'political caste'. In France, Marine Le Pen denounces the self-interested 'EU oligarchy'. In Britain, Nigel Farage has shifted his target from the EU to the political class. A growing number of populists are preoccupied by the machinations of the deep state.

The populist right thinks of itself in radically different terms from the old right – as representing the people against the educated elite (which incorporates most of the establishment) rather than defending the existing order against socialist subversion. Thus Trump talks about 'the silent majority', Farage talks about 'the people's army' and Le Pen talks about 'the forgotten France'.

The battle between the meritocrats and the masses is complicated further by the fact that journalists are unreliable witnesses because they are overwhelmingly drawn from the cognitive elite but are frequently blind to their own biases. National newspapers used to recruit people from local newspapers who cut their teeth reporting local news. One of the best columnists in Britain, Frank Johnson, left school at sixteen and started his career as an office boy at the *North-West Evening Mail* in Barrow-in-Furness. One of the best interviewers, John Humphreys, left school even earlier, at fifteen, and became a reporter on the *Penarth Times*. Now journalism is becoming an all-graduate profession and you can pass effortlessly from university to a job in London without ever leaving your cosmopolitan bubble.

This cognitive bias is qualified in Britain by the existence of a vibrant tabloid press and in the United States by the existence of the megaphone that is Fox News. But they are very much traitors to their class. The gap between the media class and populist voters is so wide that members of the press corps were visibly shaken with surprise when Leave won the referendum and Trump won the election. Some burst into tears. The vast majority of British pundits (including the author of this book) expected a Remain victory. The director of the Princeton Election Consortium promised, a week before the election, to 'eat a bug' if Trump won more than 240 electoral votes.[5] Whether he did or not is, alas, not recorded.

Populist leaders have struck back against the media's cosmopolitan bias not just because they think doing so is a good source of votes but also because they are affronted by the way that journalists' ideological sympathies distort their coverage. Boris Johnson denounced the *Financial Times* and the *Economist* for their negative coverage of Brexit at the 2017 Tory Party Conference. German populists have repeatedly vilified the *Lügenpresse* – the lying press. American bloggers routinely denounce the 'lamestream media'. No one has been so skilled at taking the war to the enemy as Donald Trump. As well as routinely savaging the press for producing 'fake news', he forced journalists to sit in 'press pens' and encourages his supporters to bait them like caged animals.

Adding to the confusion, the populists have chosen some unlikely leaders for their fight. Trump is a billionaire who lives in a triplex in a golden tower in Manhattan and a country club in Florida. He inherited his money and attended private schools and Wharton Business School. Tucker Carlson, his loudest supporter on Fox News after Sean Hannity, is the son of a diplomat and stepson of the heiress to the Swanson frozen-TV-dinner fortune. Boris Johnson, the Conservative politician who did more than anyone to tip the balance in favour of Brexit, was a King's Scholar at Eton and a Brackenbury Scholar at Balliol College, Oxford, where he read classics. Christened Alexander Boris de Pfeffel Johnson, he was born in New York City, brought up in Brussels and belongs to one of Britain's most prominent political-cum-media clans. Dominic Cummings, who masterminded the Tories' 2019 electoral victory and dominated Downing Street until he fell out with his boss in November 2019, is an intellectual elitist who read ancient and modern history at Oxford and worries that the British establishment is not meritocratic enough: it recruits too many generalists (trained in subjects like ancient and modern history!) and not enough mathematicians and scientists. He speaks warmly of turning Britain into a 'meritocratic technopolis'.

Yet Trump is a winner with the soul of a loser, consumed by imagined slights to his fragile ego, hypersensitive to the pretensions of smarty-pants liberals, a man who spends many hours a day watching

Cable News, stuffing himself with cheeseburgers and seething with anger. Boris Johnson has created a popular following because, for all his elite education, he behaves like a yob, with a succession of mistresses, illegitimate children and broken promises. Cummings seethes with rage against the metropolitan establishment and presents 'the North' as a repository of wisdom.

Once again, the revolt of the masses is following the script laid down by Michael Young in *The Rise of the Meritocracy*. Young predicted that a small section of the meritocratic elite would break with the establishment and side with the angry populists. He even suggested that some of those breakaway leaders would come from Balliol College, Oxford. The one big thing that Young got wrong is that he expected these populists to come from the left whereas, today, most of them come from the right.

YELLOW JACKETS V. GLOBAL JUNKETS

Conservative anger against the cognitive elite has been mounting for decades. In Britain, Enoch Powell anticipated many of the themes of Brexit with his warnings against the European Union, rising immigration and a transnational elite that was willing to compromise British identity in pursuit of quick profits.[6] In America, the radical right dreamed of sawing the Eastern Seaboard off and letting it float into the Atlantic Ocean. During Barry Goldwater's 1964 presidential campaign, Ronald Reagan criss-crossed the country denouncing the idea that 'a little intellectual elite in a far-distant capital can plan our lives for us better than we can plan them ourselves'. Richard Nixon condemned 'feminine intellectuals' who betrayed core American values. Spiro Agnew, his vice-president, aided by silver-tongued speech-writers such as William Safire and Pat Buchanan, launched a fusillade of alliterations against the 'nattering nabobs of negativism', 'pusillanimous pussyfooters' and 'hopeless hysterical hypochondriacs'.[7]

In 1995, the historian Christopher Lasch published *The Revolt of the Elites and the Betrayal of Democracy*, which argued that America's elites were storing up trouble for the future. By revolting against what they regarded as crude Americanism, rejecting patriotism for globalism and the rituals of civic life for cosmopolitanism, they were betraying democracy and setting themselves on a collision course with the middle class. Three years later, Richard Rorty, a philosopher with impeccably liberal credentials, sketched his vision of the future: 'something will crack. The non-suburban electorate will decide that the system has failed and start looking around for a strongman to vote for – someone willing to assure them that, once he is elected, the smug bureaucrats, tricky lawyers, overpaid bond salesmen, and post-modernist professors will no longer be calling the shots.'[8]

Two events supercharged the revolt against the cognitive elites that has shaped today's politics. They did so because they struck at the foundations of the elites' claim to authority: that they possessed sufficient intelligence and expertise to make sensible judgements on behalf of the masses for the common good.

The first was the Iraq War and its calamitous aftermath. The Iraq War was all the more triggering for the populists because it was the brainchild of the Republican Party, the party which presented itself as the party of common-sense patriotism, rather than the Democrats: specifically the brainchild of neoconservative intellectuals who had started off as Democrats but who had gradually shifted to the right over the decades. Neo-conservatives occupied some of the most powerful positions in the Republican Party: Paul Wolfowitz was second in command at the Pentagon and Bill Kristol was an omnipresent Republican public intellectual as editor of the *Weekly Standard*, the White House's favourite magazine, and a go-to hawk for the Cable news networks. They also provided the strongest justification for the invasion of Iraq: that Saddam had weapons of mass destruction; that he had close ties with other terrorist powers, including al Qaeda; and that America had a duty to the world to pursue an interventionist foreign policy.

The disastrous aftermath of America's invasion of Iraq confirmed everything that the war's opponents had been saying. The weapons of mass destruction failed to materialize. De-Baathification produced anarchy. The opposition to the invasion proved remarkably tenacious. The democratization of Iraq released ethnic tensions that, however brutally, had been held in check by Saddam Hussein. In Britain, this disaster turned centrist Tony Blair's reputation toxic and transformed

Jeremy Corbyn from a marginal crank into the leader of the Labour Party from 2015 to 2020. In America, the Iraq debacle helped to promote both the Democratic left and the nationalist right, energizing Bernie Sanders's campaign, embarrassing Hillary Clinton's and empowering the Trumpists. For all their faults, the neoconservatives had been the flagbearers of both intellectualism and global engagement in the Republican Party. Their collapse helped to propel the rise of both anti-intellectualism and nativism. Trump combined a condemnation of the debacle ('we don't win any more') with hostility to the idea that America had to promote anything more than its own interests, crudely conceived.

The second was the financial crisis. Pro-globalizers had argued that financial liberalization was in everybody's interests. The bankers might get obscenely rich, but everybody else would be better off too. Financial liberalization might unleash bursts of turbulence, but wise men such as central bankers would be able to step in and impose order on chaos. The financial crisis blew these arguments to smithereens. The wizards failed to bring the crisis under control until it had destroyed billions of dollars' worth of wealth. The bankers continued to enrich themselves even as the global economy collapsed: AIG executives even insisted on receiving their annual bonuses, despite the fact that the taxpayer had been obliged to save the company from destruction. Even before Covid struck, Britain's Office of National Statistics (ONS) predicted that average living standards won't reach the level they were at before the financial crisis until the mid-2020s.

The Iraq War and the financial crisis both fit into a larger pattern: of experts pronouncing confidently on things that intimately effect the lives of the masses (bloodily so, in the case of the Iraq War) and getting it completely wrong. A 2003 Home Office report concluded that net immigration from Central and Eastern Europe would be between 5,000 and 13,000 immigrants a year. This helped to tip the Blair government's decision not to apply a brake to East European immigration. In 2013, the ONS estimated that the actual figure was about 50,000. By 2014, there were nearly 1.5 million workers from Central and Eastern Europe living in the UK.[9]

A succession of corporate disasters and scandals raised questions about the cult of pure intelligence. Long-Term Capital Management, a hedge fund, was supposed to be the perfect advertisement for brain-power, including the Nobel Prize-winning duo Myron Scholes and Robert Merton on its board. But in 1998 it made such a catastrophically wrong bet that the Federal Reserve had to organize a rescue. Enron famously prided itself on being run by 'the smartest guys in the room'. Jeff Skilling, one of the company's leading architects, was a product of the two great engines of the modern meritocracy – Harvard Business School and McKinsey. McKinsey advised the company throughout its decade-long transformation from a humble natural-gas pipeline company into a trading goliath. Enron hired 250 MBAs from the world's greatest business schools and tried to turn them into a 'new breed of tightly focused and vertically specialised petropreneurs'. But the company was forced to file for bankruptcy at the end of 2001 and Skilling and several other senior executives ended up in jail.[10]

The pro-business Bush administration was forced to pass the Sarbanes–Oxley reforms in 2002 to try to impose more discipline on the corporate sector. But scandals continued. In 2012, the Libor scandal revealed that bankers had been routinely manipulating the London Interbank Offered Rate (Libor) in order to line their pockets at the expense of mortgage holders. In the same year, Goldman Sachs, an investment bank that was once a byword for dignity, was accused of treating some of its clients as 'muppets'. 'Getting an unsophisticated client was the golden prize,' according to Greg Smith, a former employee. 'The quickest way to make money on Wall Street was to take the most sophisticated product and try to sell it to the least sophisticated client.'[11]

Other sections of the elite were also tainted. The British parliamentary expenses scandal of 2010 suggested that MPs were routinely fiddling their expenses in order to maintain lavish lifestyles (one MP claimed the cost of cleaning his moat). The phone-hacking scandal of 2011 demonstrated that some journalists were willing to break elementary moral rules, including hacking the phone of a murdered schoolgirl, Milly Dowler. The casualties of the crisis included David Cameron's director of communications, Andy Coulson, a former editor of the *News of the World*. All these scandals had one thing in common: they involved clever and well-connected people rigging the system for their own narrow benefit.

THE ROOTS OF RAGE

There is no doubting the force of the revolt against the cognitive elite. Hatred of 'smarty-pants' has trumped other forms of resentment, including class resentment. Cultural populism has trumped economic populism. Jeremy Corbyn, who tried to direct the fires of populism against the moneyed elite, is now on the backbenches. Boris Johnson, who directed it against the meritocratic elite, is in Downing Street. What lies behind all this fury?

Most obviously, marginalization. One way to understand recent history is to think of a queue for coffee: you are heading to Starbucks in the morning, desperate for a cup of regular coffee before you start laying bricks, when a young person in LuluLemon yoga clothes cuts in front of you and orders a skinny no-foam extra-shot latte made with almond milk – for twenty people. Then the line-cutter turns round and starts giving you a lecture on how you're a sexist, racist bully who needs to check your privilege before speaking. One of the most gripping scenes in *Brexit: The Uncivil War* (2019), Graham James's TV flim about Britain's EU referendum, featured a swing voter having an emotional breakdown during a focus group. She's listened to ardent Remainers, smugly ensconced in their metropolitan jobs implying that she's flirting with Leave because she's a racist, and she can't take it any more. 'The past few years have been fucking awful, if you must know! And all I hear all the time is . . . SHUT UP! Don't talk about it! Don't mention it – ever. Well I'm sick of it! I'm sick of feeling like nothing, like I have nothing! Like I know nothing. Like I am nothing. I'm sick of it!'

The meritocrats have seized control of almost every institution of any significance and, sometimes without realizing it, muscled aside anybody who doesn't share their world view. Few people would begrudge the meritocrats their success in wresting control of the civil service from dim-witted aristocrats in the mid-nineteenth century: you need a combination of brains and discipline to administer the modern state. Recently, however, the meritocratic revolution has advanced into more problematic areas. Businesses used to provide a ladder for people to climb from the shop floor to the corner office through practical success rather than academic qualifications. Now they are increasingly run by people with MBAs and a few years working for McKinsey. Journalism is becoming an all-graduate profession without any roots in provincial or working-class society. Most damaging of all is the marriage between politics and meritocracy.

The essence of democratic politics is that it's open to anyone, regardless not just of social pedigree but also of IQ and education. The great democratic reforms of the late nineteenth and early twentieth centuries removed successive barriers to equal representation erected by property, biology or education. The great left-wing parties earned their spurs by helping working-class people into Parliament. The Labour Party's original name was the Labour Representation Committee and, before the Second World War, for example, most Labour MPs were manual workers who had been sponsored by trade unions. When the first Labour government took office in 1924 it included a former invoice clerk (Ramsay MacDonald), a former mill hand (J. R. Clynes), a former foundry labourer (Arthur Henderson) and a former engine driver (J. H. Thomas). 'A constitution which enables an engine-driver of yesterday to be a Secretary of State today is a great constitution,' Thomas wrote, in a state of giddy wonder.[12] Ernest Bevin left school at eleven to take a job as a farm boy, and was subsequently a kitchen boy, a grocer's errand boy, a van boy, a tram conductor and a drayman before, at the age of twenty-nine, becoming active in the Dock, Wharf, Riverside and General Labourers' Union. Herbert Morrison, deputy prime minister in the 1945 Labour government, started life as an errand boy and shop assistant before working his way up to the top of the London County Council. Now, across the West, the old barriers to workers' representation are being replaced by new barriers, of educational qualifications, and working-class people everywhere have less reason to celebrate 'great constitutions'. Today, only 3 per cent of Labour MPs have roots in the manual working class – and the only ex-miner in parliament, Patrick McLoughlin, sits on the Conservative benches.

What we are witnessing is the birth of a 'diploma democracy' or 'political meritocracy'.[13] In many European countries, more than 80 per cent of MPs have university degrees – and the figure goes up to almost 100 per cent when you look at the most recent intake. In

Angela Merkel's third Cabinet, installed in 2013, fourteen out of fifteen ministers had the equivalent of a master's degree, nine had a Ph.D., seven had held some sort of job in a university and two had held full professorships before entering politics.[14] The problem of diploma bias becomes more marked as you move into multilateral institutions, which are as cognitively removed from regular voters as they are physically removed. More than a quarter of MEPs have Ph.D.s. It is conventional to agonize about the slowness of the rise in the number of women or ethnic minorities in Parliament. The simultaneous decline in the number of working-class MPs arouses little comment.

Parliaments are the tip of an iceberg of educational privilege. The political parties are ceasing to be mass-membership organizations and instead becoming professional bodies dominated by graduates (the Labour Party increased its membership to 500,000 under Corbyn, but this is still a fraction of what it was in the 1950s). Most NGOs are now run by professionals rather than by volunteers. Graduates are more likely than non-graduates to engage in political activities such as signing petitions or calling for boycotts. Even the bastions of the working class, the trade unions, are being colonized by knowledge workers: in Britain, the average trade unionist is a woman in her sixties with a higher qualification. This has important consequences for the political agenda: the 70 per cent who didn't go to university have different priorities from the 30 per cent who did. They are much more preoccupied by questions such as crime (which deserves stiff punishment), immigration (which needs to be curbed) and welfare scrounging (which must be stopped), and much less by the travails of refugees.[15] The populist revolution is, at its simplest, an appeal for attention: poorer people are grabbing the meritocrats by the lapels and saying, 'Listen to me: I've got something to say as well.'[16]

A second problem is condescension. Elite institutions are experts in massaging the egos of their inhabitants. Goldman Sachs describes itself as 'probably the most elite work-society ever to be assembled on the globe'. Harvard University calls itself 'a haven for the world's most ambitious scholars'.[17] The dean of Yale Law School tells each graduating class that they are 'quite simply, the finest new law graduates on the planet'.[18] It takes a strong character to listen to all this praise without becoming a self-satisfied snob. The most common complaint made by populists is that the elites look down on them in every imaginable way. Conservative journalists such as Laura Ingraham have earned a mass following because they are experts in playing on the resentment that such condescension evokes. In *Shut Up and Sing: How Elites from Hollywood, Politics and the Media are Subverting America* (2006), she captures it perfectly:

> They think we're stupid, they think our patriotism is stupid. They think our churchgoing is stupid. They think our flag-flying is stupid. They think having big families is stupid. They think where we live – anywhere but near or in a few major cities – is stupid. They think our SUVs are stupid. They think owning a gun is stupid. They think our abiding belief in the goodness of America and its founding principles is stupid.

Many members of the cognitive elite have been surprisingly willing to express their contempt for the unlettered masses. In France, Gilles Le Gendre, president of Macron's party in the National Assembly, told an interviewer that the government had probably been 'too intelligent, too subtle, too technical' in explaining its policies to the French people.[19] In Britain, Janan Ganesh, a *Financial Times* columnist, wrote that liberal Londoners, like their confreres in other sophisticated cities, 'look at their domestic stragglers and feel ... shackled to a corpse'.[20] In America, David Rothkopf, a professor of international relations and a former member of Bill Clinton's administration, has described Donald Trump's supporters as 'threatened by what they don't understand and what they don't understand is almost everything'. Late-night comedians got easy laughs by making fun of working-class Americans even as that class was ravaged by 'deaths of despair' and the opioid epidemic.

In Britain, the Brexit vote gave many liberals pause about the merits of democracy. Richard Dawkins, the author of *The Selfish Gene* (1976), said that 'it's unfair to thrust onto unqualified simpletons the responsibility to take historic decisions of great complexity and sophistication'. Nick Cohen, a columnist on the *Observer*, described the Brexit campaign as 'a know-nothing movement of loud mouths and closed minds'.[21] Writing about Clacton, a seaside town that voted heavily for Leave, Matthew Parris, a former Conservative MP and

Times columnist, declared that 'this is Britain on crutches. This is tracksuit-and-trainers Britain, tattoo-parlour Britain, all-our-yesterdays Britain . . . I am not arguing that we should be careless of the needs of struggling people and places such as Clacton. But I am arguing – if I am honest – that we should be careless of their opinions.'[22]

These problems are made even more infuriating by what often looks like self-dealing. This was at its most striking with the global financial crisis: bankers who preached the doctrine of capitalism red in tooth and claw during the boom years suddenly discovered the virtues of state intervention when they needed help. It was repeated with the Covid crisis, when buccaneering globalists such as Richard Branson discovered the virtues of state aid. You can also see it at work in the divisive issue of immigration. Though members of the cognitive elite like to see their pro-immigration beliefs as proof of their enlightenment (in a survey of British public opinion by Chatham House, 57 per cent of the elite thought immigration has been good for the country, compared with just 25 per cent of the general public), they also have material interests at stake. For them, immigration means cheap servants to raise their children (a necessity when two parents are both pursuing brilliant careers) and cheap service workers in bars and restaurants. For manual workers, it might well mean somebody who is willing to do their job for less money and no benefits. In the global cities where meritocrats congregate, service jobs are dominated by recent immigrants who are willing to put up with miserable wages, long hours and crowded living conditions.[23]

Members of the cognitive elite are adept at marking their own homework. Most financial service regulators have a background in the financial services industry. Senior corporate managers sit on each other's boards and determine each other's salaries. Senior politicians slide effortlessly into the private sector and are soon raking in the cash from industries that they recently regulated. George Osborne, Britain's former Chancellor of the Exchequer, gets paid £650,000 by Black Rock for four days' work a month. Sir Nick Clegg, Britain's former deputy prime minister, works for Facebook as head of its global affairs and communications team. Sheryl Sandberg, Facebook's COO, who got her start in life working as chief of staff for Larry Summers when he was head of the US Treasury, celebrated Sir Nick's appointment as someone who 'understands deeply the responsibilities we have to people who use our services around the world'.

THE NEW FLASHPOINTS

The rise of populism changed the great flashpoints of politics from economics pure and simple (who gets what?) to the intersection between economics and status (what sort of people get what?). What infuriated populists was not only that the cognitive elite has managed to capture control of all the best jobs, from well-paid berths in the private sector to tenured positions in the public sector. It was that they had managed to capture control of the status hierarchy as well. They had simultaneously increased their share of material rewards *and* their share of psychic rewards.

The most important flashpoint is the question of national identity. Populism around the world is driven by nationalists who want to prioritize the interests and culture of the nation against the interests and culture of transnational elites. What the masses hate most about the meritocrats is not that they're too rich. It's that they're insufficiently patriotic. Polls suggest that as many as seven in ten Republicans doubted that Barack Obama was born in the United States. Newt Gingrich, a former Republican Speaker of the House of Representatives, even argued that Barack Obama was 'the first anti-American president'. The meritocrats, on the other hand, are overwhelmingly cosmopolitan: they possess portable skills; study and work abroad; routinely deal with colleagues around the world; and pride themselves on taking foreign holidays and eating ethnic food. The most successful among them talk about 'living between two places'. For them, 'nationalism' is routinely coupled with modifiers such as 'bigoted' or 'narrow-minded'.

The two great populist revolts both hinged on the national question. The promise that won the 2016 referendum for Leave in Britain was the promise to 'take back control' from foreign bureaucrats and global forces. During his 2016 election campaign, Donald Trump repeatedly said that, unlike his rival and, by implication, unlike his Republican predecessors, he would prioritize American rather than global interests. 'The most important difference between our plan and that of our opponent,' he said, 'is that our plan will put America first. Americanism, not globalism, will be our credo.' His final campaign ad in 2016 featured images of George Soros, the hedge-fund billionaire, Janet Yellen, the chair of the Federal Reserve Board, and Lloyd Blankfein, the chairman of Goldman Sachs, while Trump opined that the 'global power structure . . . is responsible for the economic decisions that have robbed our working class, stripped our country of its wealth and put that money into the pockets of a handful of large corporations and political entities'.

A second flashpoint is expertise. In America, Donald Trump routinely denounced experts as toadies of the Democratic Party, provoking expert fury in return. In Britain, Michael Gove unleashed a tide of educated fury when he said, on 21 June 2016, that 'Britons have had enough of experts.' He later led government criticism of civil servants and leading lawyers on the grounds that they were all members of a London-based elite who – whatever their brainpower and qualifications – viewed the world through the same metropolitan filter.

THE FUTURE OF POPULISM

The Covid-19 crisis destroyed Trump's chances of re-election not just because it slowed the previously roaring US economy but because it highlighted his incompetence. Trump ignored the advice of medical experts and eventually sacked his chief medical adviser, Anthony Fauci. He sidelined global institutions and withdrew America from the World Health Organization. He made grandiloquent statements about Covid – it was 'totally under control' (22 January 2020), pretty much 'shut-down' (2 February), destined to 'disappear' (27 February), 'going to go away' (12 March) – and hinted that it was a hoax created by the 'deep state' in order to destroy his re-election chances. On 24 April Trump even suggested that people inject themselves with bleach.

By contrast, Boris Johnson's government re-embraced experts during the crisis. Mr Johnson stood routinely on platforms flanked by medical experts such as Chris Whitty, the chief medical officer, and Sir Patrick Vallance, the chief scientific adviser. He sang the praises of medical staff who saved his life when he was taken into intensive care with the virus. His ministers habitually referred to 'the science' in making decisions. The Johnson government remained ahead of the Labour Party in the opinion polls during the worst of the crisis, despite the fact that Britain had the highest level of 'excess mortality' in Europe.

Still, it would be a mistake from this to conclude that Covid marked the end of populism and the re-empowerment of the meritocratic elite. The fault lines that we have examined in this chapter remain in place: less-educated voters continued to form the heart of the Trump coalition even as better-educated voters voted even more emphatically against him: according to national exit polls, 67 per cent of whites without college degrees voted for Trump, compared with 33 per cent who voted for Biden. Trump also astonished liberals by winning 12 per cent of black voters and 32 per cent of Latino voters, again largely because of his appeal to people without university degrees.[24] The Brexit-supporting right of the Conservative Party continue to denounce 'the science', treating the lockdown as a mistake and the injunction to wear face masks (or 'muzzles', as they call them) as an unjustified example of Big Government tyranny. The post-Brexit Conservative Party continues to be more of a working-class than a middle-class party: a Survation poll in December 2019 showed that 50 per cent of degree-holders supported Labour, compared with 28 per cent who supported the Conservatives while 30 per cent of people with no qualifications supported Labour, compared with 45 per cent who supported the Conservatives.

The Trump presidency also radicalized the left to a degree that hasn't been seen since the late 1960s, with Bernie Sanders making a prolonged bid for the Democratic nomination and young radicals such as Alexandria Ocasio-Cortez trying to set the tone of the Congressional Democratic Party. The killing of an unarmed African-American, George Floyd, by a white police officer, Derek Chauvin, on 25 May 2020 provoked angry riots across America, particularly in the big cities, and turned Black Lives Matter into one of the most powerful forces in the country. The movement pointed out that by all sorts of measures America's racial disparities were no better than they were when LBJ launched the Great Society – and were in some ways worse. Both the wealth gap and the income gap between blacks and whites are the same as they were in 1968: black households still earn 60 per cent as much as white households. The incarceration rate for African-Americans has more than tripled since 1960. Why continue to pursue the policies of the civil rights era when they had so obviously failed?

As well as mobilizing thousands of people on the streets, Black Lives Matter popularized a new cohort of black intellectuals such as Ijeoma Oluo and Ibram X. Kendi and a new set of political terms such as 'white privilege', 'white fragility' and 'unconscious bias'. These intellectuals were as hostile to the idea of meritocracy as conservative populists were. They drew on many of the ideas that had been generated in the heat of the 1960s – the emphasis on the 'social construction of reality' and the preoccupation with group rights and experiences – and supercharged them with an unyielding focus on power.

The new radicals didn't have much time for abstract discussions of procedural justice. For them there are no objective standards that can be appealed to by all groups. There are only social constructs that reflect the interests of white power or black resistance. There are no innocent transactions between people from different races. There are only power plays in which both conscious and unconscious biases are at work. 'Racism' is not bigotry based on the colour of your skin, Ibram X. Kendi argues in *How to be an Antiracist*. Races are 'fundamentally power identities' and racism is the collective system that preserves white power. Anything that isn't explicitly anti-racist – like the notion of meritocracy – is *ipso facto* racist.

This philosophy leads inexorably to two conclusions. The first is that Martin Luther King's idea of a colour-blind society is a nonsense. People who claim not to 'see colour' are acting within a context of a society that is profoundly shaped by racial advantage and disadvantage. They are also influenced by all sorts of hidden prejudices that express themselves in 'microaggressions'. By not seeing colour you are not seeing the world as it is. The second is that 'meritocracy' is nothing more than an illusion designed to justify and perpetuate white power. This is not just because white people have better opportunities than black people because they have benefited from the legacy of slavery and exploitation, but also because supposedly objective standards are distorted by power. Black people are forced to study a curriculum that has been designed for the benefit of whites. They are measured against standards which are designed to justify and extend white power. Black failure is deliberately built into the system.

Even before the Black Lives Matter movement took off, many of these ideas had embedded themselves in academia – particularly in humanities departments and in the expanding cadre of administrators. The University of California, Los Angeles, has declared, in its official guidelines, that it is a 'racial micro-aggression' to say things like 'when I look at you I don't see colour'; 'there is only one race: the human race'; and 'I don't believe in race.' The University of Wisconsin-Stevens Point has advised staff that any comment that suggests 'you do not want to acknowledge race' is a problem. The University of Missouri's guide to 'inclusive terminology' has declared that the idea of colour blindness can be 'disempowering for people whose racial identity is an important part of who they are'. They had also begun to seep into corporations – particularly corporations in the knowledge-intensive IT and media sectors.[25]

The Black Lives Matter movement hastened the jump from academia to the rest of society. Companies not only increased their efforts to recruit more blacks but also required all employees to study white fragility and unconscious bias. *The New York Times* started to capitalize the word 'Black' and significantly increased the number of articles it devoted to ethnic minorities. The *Washington Post* capitalized 'White' as well as 'Black'. The National Museum of African-American History displayed a graphic claiming that 'white culture' puts a higher premium than 'black culture' on punctuality, politeness, respect for authority, scientific thinking and rationality. Rewarding these qualities is therefore racist.

The simultaneous rise of populism on the right and identity politics on the left poses an obvious danger: that society will divide even more sharply along racial lines, with blacks pointing to past injustices and (at least poorer) whites replying that the past thirty years has been a hell of stagnant wages and growing despair. Politics is increasingly a tribal affair in which the red and blue tribes accuse each other of heinous sins (racism or anti-Americanism, for example) and will have nothing more to do with each other. And given America's cultural power and habit of reaching the future first, this problem is spreading rapidly around the world.

*

The main message of this book is that the best way forward lies in the meritocratic idea rather than in collective rights or enforced egalitarianism – that is, in treating people as individuals rather than as members of groups; in distributing opportunities and jobs on the basis of ability and achievement; and in removing barriers to the free trade in ideas and talent. This is the philosophy that helped mankind to escape from the world of priority, degree and place with which we started this book. And this is the philosophy that has driven many great breakthroughs in justice from the GI Bill to the 1944 Education Act ever since.

But it also has to be conceded that the meritocratic revolution never went far enough, partly because meritocrats declared premature victory but also because meritocracy has significant blind spots to some forms of inequality. The Conclusion will address the question of how meritocracy can be brought up to date to cope with a world of growing discontent on both the left and the right. But before concluding, we need to look at the development of the meritocratic idea in a part of the world that is suffering from none of the West's agonized doubts.

Asia Rediscovers Meritocracy

Singapore is the closest thing the world has produced to a meritocracy. To the Western eye, the city-state looks like a high-tech version of Plato's Republic, with its caste of wise 'guardians', ensconced in their skyscrapers, presiding over the men of 'silver' and 'bronze'. To the Eastern eye, it looks like a high-tech version of the Confucian mandarin state. To many Singaporean students, it seems more like a giant exam factory. In both the National University of Singapore and the Nanyang Technological University, students have set up shrines to the normal distribution curve, which they dub the Bell Curve God, making regular offerings of food and candles. The National University has even set up a website, Facebook and Twitter account for the Bell Curve God so that students can pray electronically. 'As students, we are subject to the omnipotent, inscrutable force that is the Bell Curve God,' Dylan Lee Soon Yoong told the BBC.[1]

Singapore's economic model is built on two simple but bold ideas: that good government is essential to economic development and that 'good people' are essential to good government. The Singaporeans devote substantial resources to selecting the best and training them to rule the rest – an idea we have met throughout this book in many different contexts.[2] They spot talented youngsters early and provide them with a golden ladder of opportunity into the elite. The chosen are given generous scholarships to study abroad, usually in the United States. These scholarships have to be repaid, not with money but with a certain number of years of government service. Singapore benchmarks public sector jobs against private sector pay in top global companies such as McKinsey and Goldman Sachs – junior ministers and permanent secretaries can earn $1.6 million a year and the prime minister earns $3.1 million. These pay scales are strikingly similar to those of Victorian Britain, when ministers were paid spectacular sums by modern standards. They mean that able and ambitious people are more likely to go into public service rather than into the private sector, as in the West.

Lee Kuan Yew vies with Thomas Jefferson for the title of the philosopher king of the meritocratic idea. Lee was a model scholarship winner: he got the best school certificate results in Singapore in 1940, when the country was a colony of Great Britain, won a scholarship to Fitzwilliam College, Cambridge, and graduated with a double starred first in law. For Lee, intellectual ability was the most precious commodity in the world – and the idea that 'all men are created equal and capable of equal contribution to the common good' was the most dangerous illusion. It was only by harnessing the mental power of the vital few that a country, particularly a slither of a country like Singapore, could achieve national greatness. 'I am sorry if I am constantly preoccupied with what the near-geniuses and the above average are going to do,' he once said. 'But I am convinced that it is they who ultimately decide the shape of things to come.'

Lee took his Galton-like faith in genius to its logical conclusion. In 1983, he sparked a 'great marriage debate' when he suggested that elite men should choose highly educated women as wives. (His own wife had been a classmate of his and had beaten him on a couple of papers, in English and economics.) He established a matchmaking agency, the Social Development Unit, to encourage graduates to meet, match and hopefully hatch, and introduced a Graduate Mothers Scheme to encourage highly educated women to produce three or four children. (All this effort was, in fact, wasted, given the pattern of 'assortative mating' that we noted earlier and the state's dismal record in persuading people to have more children.) In 1994, he provoked a great democracy debate when he revived J. S. Mill's idea of a variable franchise. Surely a middle-aged family man with a stake in the future should have more votes than a young wastrel who is simply bent on sowing his wild oats – or a retiree just focused on his own failing health? (Again, this effort was wasted, given that Singapore's democracy is tightly controlled by the state.)

Lee frequently couched his meritocratic vision in Confucian terms.

He emphasized the importance of government by 'honourable men' (*junzi*) who can earn 'the trust and respect of the population' by governing wisely and benevolently. 'Over the last thirty years,' he said in 1987, 'one of the driving forces that made Singapore succeed was that the majority of the people placed the importance of the welfare of society above the individual, which is a basic Confucian concept.' He also argued that the Asian economic miracle represented a triumph of Confucian values as much as good economic management. 'If you have a culture that doesn't place much value on learning and scholarship and hard work and thrift and deferment of present enjoyment for future gain,' he said in 1994, 'the going will be much slower.'

For all his preoccupation with the state, Lee put the family at the heart of Singapore's development model. The care for the old and weak was the duty of the family, supported and supplemented by the state, rather than of the state alone. He believed that the West would destroy itself because it lacked Confucian discipline – the West's soaring welfare budgets (particularly for the care of the elderly) diverted investment from education, while its addiction to instant gratification undermined thrift and self-discipline. He bristled with contempt at the idea that people could dump their parents in an old people's home, their bills paid by the welfare state, so that they could 'get on with their lives'.

He also warned his fellow leaders against the personal corruption that was prevalent in so many emerging countries, particularly in Africa. 'First, we had to set the example,' he once noted, referring to his own time as prime minister, 'not only in being uncorrupt, but also in being thrifty and economical, and not travelling in grand style ... We wanted to trim the cost of government, so we ran a very spartan government. No wastage, no lavish entertainment, no big offices, we set the tone, the example they [the civil servants] followed.'[3]

Confucian Singapore drew on two other meritocratic traditions. The first was the Cambridge tradition that we came across in our chapter on Britain and which had been embodied in intellectual aristocrats such as Thomas Babington Macaulay (Trinity) and John Maynard Keynes (King's). Proud of his double first from Cambridge, Lee had an encyclopaedic knowledge of the achievements of other Cantabrian prodigies, including those of his eldest son, Lee Hsien

Loong, who scored *twelve* more alphas than his nearest competitors in the Tripos. The second is what might be termed the McKinsey tradition. Singapore's rulers, who spend their lives shuffling between the public and private sectors, are marinated in the management ideas that are produced by the great management consultancies. There is a strong technocratic element here: the elite see every problem as a technical problem to be solved by wise social engineers. There is also, alas, a witch-doctorish element: the elite is besotted with management buzz words and by the latest business gurus. Mandarins repeat ugly McKinsey formulae with the same dutiful reverence with which they once repeated exquisite poems.

Singapore's educational system is the fruit of Lee's elitist vision. Teachers are required to finish in the top third of their class (as they are in Finland and South Korea, which also shine in the education rankings). They are also offered all sorts of perks in order to attract high-flyers into the profession, such as full scholarships in return for promising to teach for at least four to six years and sabbaticals working in the Ministry of Education on policy.[4] Headmasters are often appointed in their thirties and paid far higher salaries than their Western equivalents. Selection and streaming are routine. A primary-school leaving exam determines both which secondary school you go to and which stream you enter. A secondary-school leaving exam determines which sixth-form college you go to. The schools tend to make a great fuss about exam successes, holding ceremonies for prize-winners and inscribing the names of scholarship-winners in gilded letters.

The city-state is much concerned with identifying children at the very top of the ability range. All children are assessed at the age of eight or nine in maths, English and reasoning. The top 1 per cent are transferred into a Gifted Education Programme which is run in nine primary schools up to the age of twelve. They can then choose if they want to go to certain secondary schools that also offer a Gifted Programme. These selected children are given 'personalized education plans' that include extra teaching in some subjects, advanced placement in some classes and access to self-taught online courses.[5]

At the summit of this system sits Raffles College. Founded in 1823 by Sir Stamford Raffles, alma mater to most of the Singaporean elite, including Lee Kuan Yew, Raffles is perhaps the world's most successful scholarship factory, sending about 40 per cent of its graduating class to elite universities in the United States, and dozens to Oxbridge, all for a fee of about $15 a month. Almost all of Raffles' students take advanced maths as one of their four A-level subjects; just 8 per cent focus on the humanities. About half of the students who go from Raffles to foreign universities every year sign bonds to pay back their college education through government service. Raffles also gives scholarships to hundreds of bright children from outside Singapore.

As well as its *upsides*, Singapore displays many of meritocracy's *downsides*. There is a problem with calcification: the same family names crop up in lists of top scholarship winners and office-holders, starting with the Lee family itself. There is also a problem with arrogance: Ngiam Tong Dow, a former top civil servant, has noticed 'a particular brand of elite arrogance creeping in. Some civil servants behave like they have a mandate from the emperor. We think we are little Lee Kuan Yews.' 'We are a tyranny of the capable and the clever,' one young blogger, the daughter of an MP, wrote proudly. 'If you're not good enough, life will kick you in the balls, that's just how things go ... Please get out of my elite uncaring face.'[6] (The girl's father intervened in the uproar that followed the publication of the blog, only to say that 'some people cannot take the brutal truth').[7] For a society that invests so much in education, Singapore has a mediocre record when it comes to generating new ideas, let alone in producing novels, paintings or music. Singapore is a land of intellectual one-upmanship – dropping names about which elite institutions you attended and what scholarships you won – rather than intellectual creativity. Conformity is more important than originality.

It combines meritocracy with an intrusive, and somewhat fussy, authoritarianism. The state tells people where they can live (in order to avoid ethnic enclaves) and even how they can pee (men have to pee sitting down after eleven in the evening). The rule of law can often seem arbitrary, given the government's influence over the courts. The state also keeps a watchful eye on its citizens and quickly clamps down on dissent. (A Singaporean taxi driver once told this author that the reason that there are so few police on the streets is that 'in Singapore we are all policemen'.)

Yet most poor people in the emerging world would be willing to put up with these inconveniences in order to experience Singapore's economic success. A small piece of swampland has one of the world's highest living standards, thanks to investment in human capital. An ethnic hodgepodge has been moulded into a clean and efficient state. Meritocracy-mad Singapore is also trying to do something about the downside of meritocracy. The government is rallying behind slogans such as 'compassionate meritocracy' and 'excellence is a mountain with many peaks'. The elite is trying to upgrade the status of vocational education, particularly in labour-intensive services such as hairdressing and beauty treatment. Development economists frequently talk about 'getting to Denmark', by which they mean creating a successful modern economy. But Singapore – a country with roughly the same size of population as Denmark but just sixty years' history as an independent country – has an income per person that is higher than Denmark's and a life expectancy that is two and a half years longer.

Singapore's experiment with meritocracy is a striking story in itself, because the city-state has taken the idea further than any other country and demonstrated that it can turbo-charge economic development. But it is even more important because Singapore provides a model for the world's greatest rising power, China.

RED MERITOCRACY

Thanks to Lee, Singapore has been consistent in its commitment to meritocracy since it broke away from Malaysia in 1965. By contrast, Communist China has veered from hysterical hostility to passionate support. Mao's Cultural Revolution, from 1966 to his death in 1976, was one of the world's most radical and bloodthirsty experiments in egalitarianism, vying with Cambodia's Khmer Rouge regime. The authorities pitted 'reds' against 'experts'. Universities abolished exams. The military abolished ranks. Red guards humiliated anybody in authority, forcing professors to till the fields and bosses to work on production lines.[8] Such was their lust for equality that they even denounced competitive sports and condemned 'trophy mania'.[9] China worshipped the collective – the greyer the better – and condemned individualism as a bourgeois deviation.[10] Tens of millions died, lives were ruined and, in many respects, the country collapsed.

Today, China is a land of 'trophy mania'. Everybody dreams of getting ahead – of being number one in school, of making a fortune as an entrepreneur, of rising up the ranks of the company – and everybody knows that getting ahead can mean trying harder and thinking smarter than the next person.

China has followed Singapore in trying to produce a meritocratic education system. Children compete to get into the best nursery schools so that they can get into the best secondary schools so that they can get into the best universities. Examinations regulate the race to get ahead. The most important of these examinations – the university entrance exam, or *gaokao*, that students take at eighteen – is in many ways a revival of the old-style mandarin examinations. More than 9 million students take the examination every year and competition is so fierce that the Chinese compare it to 'ten thousand horses crossing a river on a single log'.[11]

The test is demanding: a series of papers that together take nine hours over two days and test the student's knowledge of Mandarin, English, maths and either the sciences or the arts. Your overall score in the exam determines whether you get into university, which university you get into and which course you can study. The university you get into then determines what job you can get and what salary you can command. The authorities are so concerned to prevent cheating that, in Henan province in 2015, they flew drones over the examination hall to check for radio signals from smartphones.[12] The examination is treated with such reverence that lorries are banned from rumbling past schools when the examination is in progress and cars from sounding their horns.[13]

Chinese tiger mothers start preparing their children for university, either at home or abroad, while they are still in the womb. One of the country's bestselling books in recent decades was *Harvard Girl* (2000), in which a mother named Liu Weihua details the regimen that she used to get her daughter into the Ivy League. The regimen began before birth, with the mother forcing herself to eat a high-nutrition diet that made her sick. Liu Weihua started teaching her daughter to memorize Tang Dynasty poems before she was two. Things got even tougher for the young prodigy when she was in primary school: her mother took her to study in noisy settings to hone her concentration and forced her to clench ice cubes in her hands for fifteen minutes at a time to build her endurance.[14]

Evidence of other parents following such regimes can be found across the country. Infant formula is packaged as a 'brainpower booster', with one focusing on 'memory as a weapon', another on strengthening information retention and creativity, and a third on producing 'multidimensional intelligence'. McDonald's website is hosted by a Professor Ronald who offers Happy Courses for multiplication and language learning.[15] When Mattel, a toy company, opened a six-storey Barbie megastore in downtown Shanghai with a spa and a cocktail bar, it discovered that Chinese parents disapproved of Barbie's poor study habits.[16] Such evidence can even be found perched on children's noses. The proportion of sixteen- to eighteen-year-olds deemed to be short-sighted has increased from fewer than a third in 1970 to nearly four fifths today. And the problem is getting worse: 40 per cent of primary school children are now short-sighted, double the rate in 2000, and the problem is more marked among higher-income families, who are more likely to make their children study intensively.[17]

More generally, formerly collectivist China is now saturated with the spirit of competitive individualism. The state media preaches a doctrine of self-help that is reminiscent of Samuel Smiles. Rely on yourself! Embrace competition! Blaze your own path! China Mobile sells cell-phone service to the young with the slogan, 'My turf, my decision'. Older Chinese now call the current generation the 'me generation'. Whereas the older generation referred to 'our work unit', the younger generation refer to themselves.

POLITICAL MERITOCRACY

The Communist Party also claims that it is trying to promote political meritocracy: that is, a political system that aims to select and promote leaders on the basis of talents rather than on the basis of how many votes they can muster in an election. The Party presents this as a direct challenge to the Western faith in democracy, a faith that, in the Party's view, is being tested to destruction by populist leaders and ill-conceived referendums. Political meritocracy is not just an efficient way of allocating power in a developing country, in the view of many Party intellectuals. It is a challenge to the West's cherished view that history progresses towards the triumph of liberalism and democracy.

The Party claims it has constructed a system that ensures that the top jobs go to people on the basis of ability and grit. The road to the top is long and hard: you need to shine at the Central Party School, prove your administrative mettle running a province (which might be the size of several European countries) and, increasingly, prove your business mettle by running a state-owned enterprise. The Party's Organization Department, which specializes in human resources, but for an entire nation rather than a company, monitors your performance at every step. Provincial governors are evaluated on their success on a number of measures, such as promoting economic growth or eradicating poverty, and are rapidly downgraded if they fail to hit their targets.[18] University presidents are evaluated on their success in boosting student enrolments or improving academic results.[19]

Li Yuanchao, Minister of the Organization Department of the CPC Central Committee, provided a detailed description of the process used to select the secretary general of the Party:

> First, there was a nomination process, including retired cadres. Those who received many nominations could move to the next stage. Next, there was an examination, including such questions as how to be a good secretary general. Over 10 people took the exam, and the list was narrowed to five people. To ensure that the process was fair, the examination papers were put in the corridor for all to judge the results. Then, there was an oral examination with an interview panel composed of ministers, vice-ministers and university professors. To ensure transparency and fairness, ordinary cadres who work for the General Secretary were in the room, which allowed them to supervise the whole process. Three candidates with the highest score were selected for the next stage. Then, the department of personnel led an inspection team to look into the performance and virtue of the candidates, with more emphasis placed on virtue. Two people were recommended for the next

358

stage. The final decision was made by a committee of 12 ministers who each had a vote, and the candidate had to have at least eight votes to succeed. If the required number of votes was not secured the first time, the ministers discussed further until two-thirds could agree on a candidate.[20]

The Party has even taken to distributing membership cards (which open all sorts of doors) on the basis of academic achievement. Richard McGregor, a journalist with the *Financial Times*, recalls talking with three students at Tsinghua University, China's equivalent of MIT, in 2009. They reported that 'to be a party member is a symbol of excellence'; that 'if you are a party member, you will get more opportunities with government jobs'; and that, at both school and university, positions in the Party were offered as a prize for the best students.[21] In the age of rapid growth, the Party's institutional base has shifted from the factory and the farm to the university and the office.

The Party-State also uses examinations to select public officials. (Public officials include politicians as well as civil servants, since China has no rigid distinction between the two and no tradition of elections.) You have to pass a public service examination to embark on a career as an official. You have to take a succession of progressively harder examinations as you rise up the ranks. These public examinations are more like IQ tests than tests of knowledge expertise. Support for meritocracy is not always full-throated. The Party is, after all, the *Communist* Party, not the *Merit* Party. Marx and Engels believed in the egalitarian principle of 'from each according to his ability, to each according to his need'. But it is nevertheless gaining ground.

The Party leadership has a suitably Chinese name for political meritocracy: 'guardian discourse'.[22] This 'discourse' draws on two great traditions – one with deep roots in Chinese history and another more recent. Hu Jintao, China's leader from 2002 to 2012, began the Party's official embrace of Confucius, making the teaching of Confucianism compulsory in schools and founding Confucius Institutes, modelled on Germany's Goethe Institutes, across the world. Xi Jinping intensified the embrace, defining Confucianism, together with Buddhism and Taoism, as one of the 'traditional cultures' that define what it is to be

Chinese. Official attempts to promote Confucianism include a range of initiatives: quoting Confucius at the 2008 Beijing Olympics; sponsoring a 2010 feature film based on Confucius's life starring Chow Yun-fat, a Hong Kong action hero; teaching the Confucian classics in Communist Party schools; funding a Confucius Research Institute in Confucius's hometown of Qufu, in Shandong province, which holds a regular World Confucius Conference; obliging school textbooks to include 'boxes' that contain Confucian poems and maxims; and pouring significant resources into Confucius Institutes around the world. Confucius is supposed to provide an ethical model to an increasingly materialistic society as well as present a rather more appealing face to the rest of the world than, say, Mao, who, whatever his reputation in China, is recognized in the rest of the world as a genocidal monster.

The more recent addition is faith in engineering. In the wake of the collapse of the imperial state in the early twentieth century, policy-makers fixated on engineers, on the grounds that China's ossified Confucian tradition had condemned China to humiliation at the hands of Western powers and only engineers could reverse its fortunes. Today, engineers run the country. In 2002–7, all nine members of the Politburo Standing Committee under Hu Jintao were engineers; in 2007–12, all but one was. The proportion is lower today, but the man who really matters, Xi, studied chemical engineering at Tsinghua University. These engineers see social problems as engineering problems: policy-makers have no more need to ask what the people think than qualified engineers have to ask unqualified workers.

THE LIMITS OF POLITICAL MERITOCRACY

How much truth is there in this vision of a red meritocracy rising in the East? The idea is gaining considerable traction not just in China but abroad in the light of democracy's recent travails. Zhang Weiwei, of China's Fudan University, proclaims that the world is seeing a competition between two different political models – one based on meritocratic leadership and the other on popular election – and that 'the Chinese model may win'.[23] Kishore Mahbubani, a former dean of Singapore's Lee Kuan Yew School of Public Policy, says that China's system has thrown up 'possibly the best set of leaders that China could produce'.[24] Nicolas Berggruen and Nathan Gardels argue that Eastern meritocracy is a valuable counterbalance to Western democracy and its obsession with the short term ('one person one vote electoral democracy embedded in a consumer culture of immediate gratification is also headed for terminal political decay unless it reforms').[25] Nor is this style of thinking confined to theoreticians: Imran Khan, Pakistan's prime minister, praises the Chinese Communist Party for sifting 'through all the talent' and bringing it 'to the top'. 'It's a system based on meritocracy,' he says.[26]

Yet the idea that China is creating a political meritocracy took a severe blow when President Xi appointed himself president for life (or at least as long as he wants) in 2018. Before then, it was possible to argue that China had solved the biggest problem of autocracies (ageing leaders who won't retire) by insisting that its leaders change every ten years. Now, China looks more feudal than meritocratic. The full cost of this change has yet to be seen, but it's unlikely to be positive. Xi will remain in power in his dotage, just like (the singularly unmeritocratic) Vladimir Putin in Russia. Cronyism will put down deeper roots. Rising stars will find themselves frustrated while sycophants will flourish. It's hard to imagine that China's growing and educated middle class won't grow restless as the leadership ages and becomes increasingly out of touch.

Xi is the highest ranking of a cohort of Red Princes and Princesses whose parents and grandparents came to power with the revolution and have been intermarrying ever since. These royal families sit atop a system that is rife with favouritism and discrimination of every description. Rich parents use their connections to get their children into elite 'feeder schools' (known as 'keypoint schools') that excel at preparing their pupils for the exam;[27] almost all the senior figures in the Party are male; minorities such as the Uighurs in Xinjiang and the Tibetans in Tibet are treated like subject peoples.

On top of that, corruption is not just rife but frequently mind-boggling: in 2014, for example, the authorities discovered that Xu Caihou, the vice-chairman of the Central Military Commission, had the entire basement of his 20,000-square-foot house stocked with cash of various denominations that weighed more than a ton.[28] The Huran Report, a Shanghai-based wealth monitor, estimated in 2012 that the eighty-three richest delegates to the National People's Congress and the Chinese People's Consultative Conference had a net worth of over $250 billion.[29]

The commingling of power and money has reduced the efficiency of the state to well below Singapore levels. The World Bank's global governance indicators have consistently ranked China in the sixtieth percentile for government effectiveness and the fortieth percentile for the rule of law. The power–money dynamic has also helped to create one of the world's most unequal societies. One study found that the top 1 per cent of Chinese controlled a third of the country's assets.[30] Another calculated that Beijing has more billionaires than New York. The official estimate of China's Gini coefficient (a standard measure in which 0 means total equality and 1 means total inequality) was 0.48 in 2018, higher than anywhere in the OECD, and many unofficial estimates are higher. Some academics think that anything above the 0.5 threshold heralds social instability.[31]

The combination of rising inequality and growing corruption raises serious questions about China's future as an opportunity society. A lucky generation that came of age in the 1990s accumulated remarkable privileges – and then set about reinforcing their position with a combination of connections and corruption. Parents pay 'sponsorship' fees to get their children into top schools. In Beijing, the fees can be as much as $16,000, more than double the basic national salary.[32] Job-seekers also end up paying for jobs, much as they did in France before the revolution and Britain before the liberal reforms of the Victorian era. Paying for jobs has become such a problem that in 2012 the *Modern Chinese Dictionary*, the national authority on language, added the word *maiguan* – 'to buy a government promotion'.

This is very far from the 'political meritocracy' that the elite imagines. But before dismissing China as nothing more than yet another kleptocratic regime we need to remember two things. The first is that, for all its imperfections, the Chinese state has presided over a remarkable period of modernization. It has held the country together, despite cramming two centuries' worth of economic development into a mere fifty years, and constructed a network of airports, roads and bridges that makes the United States look backward.

The second is that China's educational system is producing remarkable results. China has constructed an (albeit imperfect) version of the Webbs' 'capacity-catching machine'. According to the biggest study of educational mobility in China, China's elite universities are doing a better job of recruiting the children of blue-collar workers than America's elite universities, which give half of their places to the children of the richest 5 per cent.[33] Selected cities such as Shanghai and Beijing compete with Singapore for the top slots in global rankings. China's universities are learning how to compete with the best in the world. A meritocracy it certainly isn't. But, for all its lapses into corruption and cronyism, China is using the meritocratic idea to drive a remarkable period of growth and to allow it to take its place among the other Asian tigers in terms of living standards.

ASIA MAJOR

If Singapore is the most striking example of an Asian country embracing meritocracy, and China the most significant, if also the most perplexing, you can find similar developments right across the world's most dynamic region, as countries try to re-engineer their governments to address more demanding challenges, or as they try to revitalize their education systems in order to improve their human capital.

Over the past thirty years, many Asian countries have put a growing emphasis on meritocratic principles in recruiting civil servants.[34] Governments emphasize the importance of breaking old systems of patronage and corruption, of recruiting people with stellar qualifications, of forging an elite class of civil servants who can spearhead modernization, and so on. Asian countries are trying hard to create an elite civil service caste comparable to the United Kingdom's fast stream. South Korea has a Senior Civil Service; Singapore has an Administrative Service; Thailand has its High Potential Performers; Malaysia has something called TalentCorp and the Malaysian Administrative Modernization and Management Planning Unit and has followed Singapore in providing the brightest young people with bonded scholarships whereby the government pays the cost of their education in return for several years of government service. They are also heavily influenced by a book by three McKinsey consultants, Ed Michaels, Helen Handfield-Jones and Beth Axelrod, *The War for Talent* (2001), though they find themselves struggling to compete with the private sector with its high pay, flexible career structures and air of excitement.

Asian governments continue to worship at the altar of examinations. A striking number of governments use exams not only to recruit entry-level civil servants but also to promote people up the hierarchy and to bring in mid-career people from outside. But the cult has been losing some of its lustre of late: questions have been selectively leaked, evidence has emerged of friends and relations being given higher scores in the interview part of the examination and, according to one survey, only 35 per cent of people in South Korea and Taiwan believe that recruitment is done on merit.[35] Moreover, there is a tension between selecting by examination and recruiting high-flyers. Most countries are trying to broaden the avenues of recruitment beyond multiple-choice tests in order to stave the flow of high-flyers into the private sector – paying more attention to academic achievements and work experience, exempting experts from tests and even targeting specific candidates for recruitment, before they are converted into McKinsey man or woman.

TIGERS BEHIND DESKS

It is impossible to travel in Asia without being struck by the cult of education. In India, 'toppers', as children who come top in examinations are called, are treated like child rock stars, with their pictures in the papers. In Vietnam, neatly uniformed children stride to school at eight o'clock on Sunday morning. In Japan, exam papers appear in the newspapers the day after the students sit them so that the citizenry can pore over them. In Hong Kong, a newspaper contains a letter from a paediatrician blaming an epidemic of spinal curvature on children's habit of carrying giant piles of books home with them. Look at any league table of educational performance and you can see East Asian countries clustered at the top.

The culture is saturated by exam-mania. Parents camp outside schools to pray for their children's success in exams. Examinees avoid eating seaweed soup on the grounds that its slipperiness means that they lose their laboriously acquired knowledge. In Japan, KitKat markets itself as a bringer of good luck in exams on the grounds that the chocolate bar's name in Japanese, *kitto katto*, sounds like *kitto katsu*, 'surely winning'. In South Korea, the Talmud has become a surprise bestseller because it is associated with cognitive development. According to Ynet, a popular Israeli news site, more South Korean families have a copy of the book than do Israeli families, and expectant mothers listen to audio versions in order to encourage cognitive development in their unborn children.[36]

The region's success is not the result of lavish public spending. Even in a rich country like Japan schools can seem shabby and ill equipped by comparison with their Western equivalents, and classes are intimidatingly large. In South Korea, schools invite parents with particular skills to give a few lessons a week in order to save costs. In Japan, schools cut down on overheads – and impart moral lessons into the bargain – by getting the pupils to do menial tasks such as serving meals and cleaning. In some countries, there are more schools than school buildings so that one school uses the buildings in the morning, another in the afternoon. The region's success is the result of a culture that puts an inordinate value on educational success.

The emphasis on examination success has given rise to a parallel educational system, a continent-wide tutoring and cramming industry. Families who can afford to hire private tutors, particularly in difficult subjects such as mathematics and Mandarin. In the South Korean film *Parasite* the first parasite who worms his way into a rich family's home is a private tutor. Cramming schools are ubiquitous: no sooner do children finish their regular schools than they troop off to cramming schools to supplement their knowledge (some cramming schools are so hard to get into that there are cramming schools to get into those cramming schools). Though it is easy to dismiss these schools as educational factories, some are actually quite innovative, experimenting with clever tools, such as diagnostic tests (which pinpoint weaknesses) and predictive tests (which show which universities are within your grasp) and paying successful teachers significant bonuses. At the very least, they increase the amount of resources society invests in education.

The standard criticism of Asian meritocracy is the criticism of the cramming schools writ large: that it sacrifices 'real' education for cramming. By 'force feeding the duck' teachers destroy their charges' childhood and rob them of any real pleasure in knowledge for its own sake. In fact, as with cramming schools, the reality is more interesting. A questionnaire given to students along with their PISA test revealed that students in Singapore, Shanghai and Japan report enjoying school more than their counterparts in Britain, America or Finland, and being more interested in the subjects that they were studying.[37]

Asians seem to exceed Westerners in their belief in one half of Michael Young's formula for meritocracy – effort. In her comparative study of Eastern and Western learning styles, *Cultural Foundations of Learning: East and West* (2012), Jin Li notes that Asian children are more resilient than their Western counterparts: they not only persevere for longer in the face of a difficult challenge, but frequently go out of their way to find challenges. Difficulty is a spur to effort, not an excuse for giving up.[38] She relates this to the Confucian tradition. Confucius argued that the path to virtue includes self-improvement through knowledge: working hard in order to master a body of learning and conquer a difficult problem is a fundamental part of becoming a moral individual. Confucians take pride in the hard work rather than just in the results of the hard work.

Asia is continuing to focus intently on the two components of Michael Young's formula for merit – IQ plus effort – at a time when a growing number of people are sceptical about both. If this book is right, and meritocracy was a key component of the making of modernity, then this suggests that the future is now being forged in the East rather than the West.

Conclusion

Renewing Meritocracy

The meritocratic idea made the modern world, sweeping aside race- and sex-based barriers to competition, building ladders of opportunity from the bottom of society to the top, and electrifying sluggish institutions with intelligence and energy. Discrimination on the basis of race and sex is now illegal across the advanced world. Women take up more than half of the places in most Western (and in many emerging-country) universities. Kamala Harris, a woman of Jamaican and Indian heritage, is vice-president of the United States, and may well follow Barack Obama to the Oval Office. None of that would have been possible without the meritocratic idea.

Meritocracy succeeds because it does a better job than the alternatives of reconciling the two great tensions at the heart of modernity: between efficiency and fairness on the one hand, and between moral equality and social differentiation on the other. It screens job applicants for competence. Vaccines save our lives rather than poisoning us because highly trained scientists develop them and other highly trained scientists test and regulate them. But, at the same time, meritocracy gives everybody a chance to put their name into the sorting hat.

THE GOLDEN TICKET

The comfortable idea that there is a tight link between liberal democracy and prosperity has been damaged, if not discredited, by the rise of China and other authoritarian modernizers.[1] Yet a glance around the world suggests that meritocracy is a golden ticket to prosperity. Singapore, perhaps the world's poster child of meritocracy, has transformed itself from an underdeveloped swamp into one of the world's most prosperous countries, with a higher standard of living and a longer life expectancy than its old colonial master. The Scandinavian countries retain their positions at the top of international league tables of prosperity and productivity in large part because they are committed to education, good government and, beneath their communitarian veneer, competition.[2]

By contrast, countries that have resisted meritocracy have either stagnated or hit their growth limits. Greece, a byword for nepotism and 'clientelism' (using public sector jobs to reward Party cronies), has struggled for decades. Italy, the homeland of *nepotismo*, enjoyed a post-war boom like France and Germany but has been stagnating since the mid-1990s. The handful of countries that have succeeded in combining anti-meritocratic cultures with high standards of living are petro-states that are dependent on the accident of geography rather than the ingenuity of their people. They will surely revert to poverty in the coming post-oil age unless they change their habits.

A raft of cross-country surveys reinforces this impression. The Organization for Economic Cooperation and Development has repeatedly demonstrated that high social mobility promotes economic growth.[3] Both the World Bank and Transparency International show that corruption is inimical to long-term prosperity. Nicholas Bloom, of Stanford University, and John Van Reenen, of the London School of Economics, have collected data on management practices in over 11,000 firms in 34 countries to produce a veritable Domesday Book of management. They demonstrate that countries that favour recruiting professional managers through open competition have higher growth rates than those that favour recruiting amateur managers through personal connections. America has the highest overall management score, followed by Germany and Japan. Rich-world laggards such as Portugal and Greece, and big emerging-market countries such as India, have a long tail of unmeritocratic and therefore badly managed firms.[4]

Two recent studies are particularly telling. Four economists at the University of Chicago's Booth School of Business have examined America's GDP growth per person in 1960–2010 in the light of the distribution of talent. They claim that roughly a fifth of that growth can be explained by the improved allocation of talent, particularly the opening of highly skilled professions to new talent pools. In 1960, 94 per cent of America's doctors and lawyers were white men. By 2010, that number had shrunk to 60 per cent.[5] That makes for both a more productive and a more just society.

Bruno Pellegrino, of the University of California, Los Angeles, and Luigi Zingales, also of the Booth School, have constructed a measure of countries' levels of meritocracy based on data from the World Economic Forum's survey of expert opinion on who holds senior management positions.[6] The WEF asks questions such as: are senior managers recruited on the basis of family connections or on merit and competence? Are senior managers willing to delegate authority to juniors? And are managers rewarded and promoted according to productivity? The authors also posit that a country's level of meritocracy in the business sector is related to its level of meritocracy in the wider society (quality of government, rigidity of employment laws, quality of judicial decisions, size of the black economy, vibrancy of the high-tech sector). They rank the world's advanced economies roughly in terms of their 'meritocracy score' ('roughly' because the data is based on perceptions, albeit the perceptions of experts): Sweden comes at the top and Italy at the bottom. More generally, Northern European countries cluster at the top, along with America and Japan, while Southern European countries lie at the bottom.

The authors show that countries with high meritocracy scores have enjoyed much more of a bonus from new technology than countries with low scores such as Italy. Italy's loyalty-based management style had no negative consequences for productivity growth in the decades before 1995. But when the IT revolution took off, loyalty-based management reduced Italy's productivity growth by between thirteen and sixteen percentage points. This suggests that the meritocracy dividend is growing along with the IT revolution: meritocracy is not just the secret sauce of economic growth in the long term but a secret sauce that is becoming more potent.

Studies of institutions point in the same direction as cross-country studies. Independent central banks are more successful at controlling inflation than are those beholden to governments and therefore voters.[7] Independent judges, appointed by technocratic merit commissions, produce sounder judgements than partisan judges, elected by the voters, in the sense that their judgements are much more consistent and much less likely to be overturned.[8] Public companies routinely outperform family companies unless family companies take the precaution of hiring professional managers.[9]

A good way to measure the virtue of meritocracy is to look at what happens if you remove it. New York's City College had a well-deserved reputation as the 'Harvard of the proletariat', taking thousands of poor adolescents, many of them the offspring of immigrants, and turning them into doctors, lawyers, academics and, in the case of nine alumni, Nobel Prize winners. In the run-up to the Second World War, City students included a host of people who went on to shape America's intellectual life, including Daniel Bell, Nathan Glazer, Sidney Hook, Irving Kristol and Irving Howe, who wrote a marvellous account of his City years in *World of Our Fathers* (1976). Then in 1970 the university introduced an open-access regime, admitting any-one who had graduated from the city's high schools. The result was a simultaneous boom in student numbers and a collapse in academic standards. By 1978, two out of three students admitted to the college required remedial teaching in the three 'R's.[10] Drop-out rates surged. Talented scholars left. Protests and occupations became common-place. In 1994, a task force, led by Benno Schmidt, pronounced the college 'moribund' and 'in a spiral of decline'. The college only began to recover after 1999, when it abandoned open admissions as a failed experiment.

TAKING TALENTS SERIOUSLY

The most powerful objection to the meritocratic idea is that the tal-ented don't *deserve* their talents. John Rawls argued that it's unfair to reward people because they are lucky enough to be born intelligent and hard-working, an argument that Michael Sandel also emphasizes, from a communitarian perspective, in *The Tyranny of Merit*.[11] Yet few people are so naturally gifted that they don't have to make an effort to master a difficult subject or skill when they would rather be amus-ing themselves. Even young Mozart had to practise. The more knowledge advances, the more even the greatest geniuses have to 'scorn delights, and live laborious days', to borrow a phrase from Milton, if they are to reach its frontier. Converting a raw ability into substantive expertise requires a rare combination of qualities: self-denial (we must train when we would rather be relaxing), investment (we must spend time and money cultivating our abilities), and risk-taking (a talent may wear out, lose market value or fail to materialize: after years of effort, we may find that we are simply not up to scratch). You need above-average rewards to induce people to engage in such a process of self-sacrifice and risk-taking. Reduce the rewards that accrue to outstanding talent and you reduce the amount of talent available to society as a whole.

Rawls ignores the importance of praise in motivating people to excel themselves. A Rawlsian might respond to a spectacular example of athletic success – a sprint by Usain Bolt or a gymnastic performance by Simone Biles – by shrugging his shoulders and pronouncing that it was all a matter of genetics or luck: Bolt inherited an ability to run fast, and Biles is a born gymnast. But this is not only wrong as a matter of fact: even if athletic achievement has a strong genetic component, hard work, training and effort also play a part. It is also counterproductive: one of the things that motivates sporting excellence is the roar of a crowd of spectators who are awestruck by athletes' ability to push nature to the limits. The applause is not only for the underlying natural ability but for the superhuman effort that turns natural ability into a world-beating performance.

More generally, Rawls ignores the importance of market incentives in turning raw abilities into social goods. Market incentives perform two functions: they encourage people to devote their time to turning their gifts into marketable talents and they direct people to areas where their talents can produce social benefits. Job security in the form of tenure can give academics an incentive to invest in acquiring specialized knowledge. Big pay-offs in terms of golden shares in start-ups can give young entrepreneurs an incentive to devote themselves to developing a world-changing algorithm. High executive salaries can persuade the mass of employees to make great efforts to become the next CEO.

Meritocracy, like the market, is a sophisticated process of information gathering. Intellectual competitions of various types – GCSEs and A-levels, university finals and job tests – help to reveal information about the most important of all economic resources: human capacity.[12] The process of revelation is not perfect, of course: some schools excel in training their pupils in exam techniques and some talented candidates wither under exam pressure. But there is a limit to how much even the best schools can go in turning a sow's ear into a silk purse. Skilled examiners – particularly academics looking for bright pupils – pride themselves on their ability to distinguish between polish and ability. Standardized tests (of which more later) can also help us to distinguish between raw ability and mere training. The more subject-focused tests can be supplemented by standardized tests, particularly early on in schooling, the better.

Meritocracy is also a valuable supplement to the market: while markets provide information about human preferences, examinations provide information about human abilities. Individuals get a sense of their strengths and weaknesses (including how they stack up against their peers). Schools get a sense of who will benefit from advanced teaching or which universities are within their reach. And governments get a sense of what intellectual resources are at their disposal. (One of the most striking results of the mass testing that followed the Second World War was that governments learned just how much talent was being wasted because so few people, particularly in the working class, had a chance of going to university.)

The most powerful argument for meritocracy, however, is moral rather than economic. What distinguishes human beings from mere lumps of flesh and blood is the fact that we possess talents and abilities that can be honed through hard work and commitment. It's certainly true that we are all of equal moral *sub specie aeternitatis* and that we possess a bundle of rights (to a vote or free speech) not because we are clever or useful but because we are human. On the other hand, people are also masters of their own fates and captains of their own souls. They fashion themselves by struggling against 'the fell clutch of circumstance' and the 'bludgeonings of chance'.[13] Treating people as mere atoms of equality or victims of circumstances infantilizes them, and perhaps dehumanizes them.

Paradoxically, treating people as moral equals also entails treating them as moral agents, who, by exercising their moral agency, can become socially unequal. Meritocracy is the ideal way of making sense of this paradox. By encouraging people to discover and develop their talents, it encourages them to discover and develop what makes them human. By rewarding people on the basis of those talents, it treats them with the respect they deserve, as self-governing individuals who are capable of dreaming their dreams and willing their fates while also enriching society as a whole. 'The ethical justification for meritocracy is not that people should be rewarded for their genes and upbringing,' says Peter Saunders, 'it is that everyone benefits when the talented are induced to hone their abilities to what other people demand in the marketplace.'[14] Few would dispute that the old world of patronage and connection debased everybody involved, not just by treating patrons as masters of the universe but also by treating job-seekers as interchangeable clients rather than as unique individuals with unique gifts. The new world envisaged by egalitarians and communitarians does much the same thing: by treating people as interchangeable atoms it turns institutions into omnipotent patrons that can dispense their rewards as they will.

Vivid evidence of the moral virtues of meritocracy is provided by migration. Gallup surveys show that 15 per cent of the world's adult population – some 750 million people – want to emigrate from where they live. The most popular destinations are all broadly meritocratic countries, with America at the top, followed by Canada, Germany, France, Australia and the United Kingdom. The most fled-from countries are all broadly anti-meritocratic – indeed émigrés repeatedly tell pollsters that the reason they left was to escape 'nepotism and corruption'.[15]

Professional people are particularly keen on migrating because, thanks to their qualifications, they have access to both international and local labour markets. Ivy League universities and global institutions such as the World Bank are stuffed with people with Greek or Italian surnames because able people want to shape their own lives rather than be dependent on others. Luigi Zingales is a case in point: he left home for the United States because, it seemed, the only chance of getting an academic job in Italy was to turn himself into the creature of a tenured patron – carrying his bag (*fare il portaborse*) for decades but still never knowing whether the professor would eventually bestow his favour on him or a wastrel nephew – whereas, in America, he knew he would be promoted on the basis of his publications and teaching.[16]

THE BLOWBACK

The Introduction discussed some of the current criticisms of meritocracy. These criticisms come from different directions and are often contradictory: we learn that meritocracy is both too *conservative* and too *disruptive*, for example, and that the cognitive elite is both deeply entrenched and horribly insecure. These criticisms are also oddly timed. Donald Trump's presidency underlined the dangers of weakening the meritocratic principle in government. Trump appointed relatives and cronies to powerful positions in his administration on a scale not seen in modern times, even allowing his daughter, Ivanka, to sit in for him for a while at a G7 summit. He hollowed out the executive branch by leaving senior jobs vacant, giving jobs to political appointees or denigrating expertise. During his presidency, more than a thousand scientists left the Environmental Protection Agency, the Department of Agriculture and other departments.[17] What mattered to Trump was not professional competence but absolute personal loyalty, whether it was forged by kinship, ideology or political dependence.

The survival of ethnic conflicts around the world demonstrates the danger of fixating on ethnicity: think of the fracturing of the Balkans along ethnic lines, the growing tension between Hindus and everyone else in Modi's India, and the persecution of successful minorities around the world, from the Chinese in South-East Asia to Indians in Africa. America's social justice movement is playing with some of the world's oldest hatreds as well as its oldest injustices. Moreover, the rise of China means that the West will have to fight harder to preserve its current economic and geostrategic position: diluting the meritocratic principle at the same time that China is emphasizing educational competition and rigorous performance measures in government is likely to hasten the West's decline.

Oddly timed or not, these criticisms are gaining traction because they contain a certain amount of truth. Inequality in most of the world *is* far too high for comfort. Examinations *can* seem like a tyranny. The cognitive elite *is* intolerably smug. Though meritocracy has always prided itself on its ability to provide opportunities for upward mobility, over the past four decades the barriers to entry have got higher. In the words of William Deresiewicz, a former Yale academic, 'our new multiracial, gender-neutral meritocracy has figured out a way to make itself hereditary'.[18] Predictably enough, growing sections of Western societies have become alienated and embittered.

Two criticisms in particular deserve sustained consideration. These two criticisms are sometimes at loggerheads with each other. They also demand very different responses. But the future of the meritocratic idea depends on society's ability to deal with them.

The first criticism is that the meritocratic idea is still very far from the reality. The meritocratic revolution that was such a striking feature of the post-war years didn't go far enough. The privileged preserved all sorts of advantages, ranging from formal advantages such as legacy admissions to more informal ones such as 'lucky breaks' for people who apply early or play particular sports. And from the 1980s onwards the revolution began to consume itself as merit made money and money purchased education.

The second criticism comes from the opposite direction: that meritocracy in its pure form is just too much for humanity to bear. Rousseau was one of the first to make this point. In his *Discourse on the Origins and the Foundations of Inequality among Men* (1755) he argued that the 'universal desire for reputation, honours and preferment' leads inexorably to an all-consuming desire to compare 'talents and strengths'. The more society does to universalize the competitive principle, the more it 'multiplies the passions' and sets up the mass of competitors for 'many catastrophes of every kind'. 'This frenzy to achieve distinction' may be responsible for 'what is best . . . among men' – our heroes and philosophers – but it is also responsible for 'what is worst': 'that is to say a multitude of bad things for a small number of good things'. Worst of all, competition 'almost always keeps us outside ourselves'.[19] Others, from John Adams to Max Weber to T. S. Eliot to the prophets of the counterculture, have worried about the social and psychological consequences of the rat race.[20]

The answer to the first of these problems is *more* meritocracy: we need to redouble our efforts to remove formal advantages for the rich while also developing better ways to distinguish between innate ability and mere learning. The answer to the second is *wiser* meritocracy. We need to civilize and direct the competitive principle. We also need to make sure that the 'winners' of the meritocratic competition have much more of a sense of responsibility to the wider society – and that the 'losers' have alternative paths to dignity and self-fulfilment. Let's start with the case for *more* meritocracy and go on to the case for *wiser* meritocracy.

WHY NOT THE BEST?

The most obvious case for more meritocracy is provided by America's elite universities and their habit of clinging on to their old snobbish practices despite a lot of warm words about 'diversity' and 'inclusion'. A recent study, based on evidence unearthed during a legal case brought by several Asian-American students against Harvard, discovered that more than 43 per cent of (mostly rich) white students at Harvard were given preferential treatment because they were 'legacies', athletes, on the dean's 'special interest' list or the children of faculty. The boost for these privileged white applicants is as big as the one provided for African-Americans through affirmative action – and three quarters of them would have been rejected if they had been held to strictly meritocratic standards. Similar practices are common across the Ivy League.[21]

When you eliminate old-fashioned favouritism you are still confronted with a difficult problem: how do you discover talented children in the population at large when the ladder of opportunity has so many rungs missing? And how do you give the best possible opportunity to such children once you have discovered them? The answer is to revive two ideas that were at the heart of the meritocratic movement until the 1960s: IQ testing and academic selection. These ideas were historically linked to a commitment to increase levels of social mobility and discover talent in neglected communities. Sidney Webb talked of 'driving shafts' into the lowest strata of society in order to replenish the elite with talent. This progressive vision needs to be returned to the heart of educational policy.

Academically selective schools have an impressive record in providing bright but underprivileged children with an escalator into the elite.

Britain's best grammar schools were founded to identify talent in provincial cities such as Manchester (through Manchester Grammar School) and Birmingham (through King Edward VI Grammar School) and provide it with educations every bit as good as Eton and Winchester. They honoured their founders' intentions. New York's elite academic schools had an equally good record of providing poor children, particularly immigrant children, with a high road to elite universities and professional success.

Selective schools are more successful than non-selective schools because they are in the business of educational transformation. They take their character from their most successful alumni rather than from their neighbourhoods. They transform their pupils' lives by pursuing clear goals, stretching them to the maximum, and reminding them, through both institutional memory and encouragement, of what they can achieve if they put their nose to the grindstone.

But how can schools make sure that they are selecting pupils on the basis of future promise rather than current polish? Achievement tests are backward looking, skewing selection in favour of children who have been well raised and well taught. They also bring with them the risk of burn-out: children who are overstuffed with knowledge while they are young, like prize geese, often fail to do much of anything with the rest of their lives. The best way to discover future promise is to test raw ability rather than either school-imparted achievement or 'the whole human being'. And the best way to test for raw ability is to use standardized tests of various sorts. Such tests help to 'read through' the veneer of culture and reveal raw brainpower by getting test-takers to perform a series of abstract tasks.

The standard criticism of this argument is that you can improve your performance on IQ tests by practising – and that the children likely to be doing the practising are affluent children who have access to expert help. In fact, research suggests that there is a strict limit on how much better you can get. A 2006 analysis of a large collection of studies found that coaching for the SAT produced an improvement of 50 points on a scale of 1600;[22] a more recent study found a 20-point improvement. Neither of these numbers is insignificant, but they are both small compared with other affluence-related advantages and much smaller than on tests of knowledge rather than reasoning.[23] IQ tests are thus significantly less socially biased than other ways of sorting children, such as scholastic tests (which favour the well taught) and teacher assessments or neighbourhood schools (which institutionalize selection by house price).

In Britain, talk about selective schools and IQ tests provokes heated argument about the 11-plus, with the left arguing that the 11-plus divided the population into sheep and goats on the basis of a crude pass–fail dividing line that varied according to the number of school places available across the country, doing life-long harm to the children who failed in the process, and the right retorting that it gave unique opportunities to bright working-class children who were identified early and given a life-changing opportunity. Both sides of the argument have a point – selection was certainly crude, but if you were on the right side of it, you were on an escalator to success.

The best way forward is to learn from both the successes and the failures of the past. Don't re-create a national system that makes an arbitrary division at the age of eleven. Create instead a highly variegated school system that has lots of different types of schools from technical schools to arts schools but also makes room for academically selective schools. The British government has already provided the material for this with school academies. The Brampton Manor Academy, for example, is situated in Newham, one of the poorest boroughs in London, with the majority of pupils from ethnic minorities and one in five eligible for free school meals. In 2021, the school nevertheless won more places in Oxbridge (fifty-five) than Eton (forty-eight). The sixth form is highly selective, expecting A-level applicants to have top grades at GCSE in the relevant subjects. It also cultivates a rigorously academic atmosphere, requiring all pupils to wear uniforms, offering intensive coaching for Oxbridge entrance exams as well as a wide range of extracurricular activities, and recording the names of successful candidates in gold letters.

The government could push the revolution further by allowing academies to select their pupils at eleven on the basis of IQ tests. Private schools could also be required to allocate a proportion of their places to children whose parents couldn't afford such a luxury: half sounds like a good starting point, certainly for the richer schools like Eton, Winchester and Marlborough. Private schools have abused their charitable status by abandoning Britain's poorer children and filling their places with the children of the international elite. They should lose their charitable status unless they are willing to resume their original purpose of educating poor scholars. Again, those poor scholars could be selected with the help of IQ tests as well as old-fashioned tests of knowledge.

One way to achieve this would be to create a system of fully funded national scholarships, awarded on the basis of a combination of IQ and social need, that would allow children to study at any school in the country. Primary schools would compete to discover and produce scholarship winners by scouring their neighbourhoods for talent. Secondary schools (including private schools) would compete to attract them because they would bring bright children with money attached. Such a system of scholarships would help to dissolve our current problem of social calcification by ensuring that a significant number of 'hidden Einsteins' from non-affluent homes were selected for a university-track education at an early age. And it would reduce the wastage of talent by giving schools an incentive to identify promising children.

National merit scholars might also be given free university educations in return for agreeing to spend a certain number of years working in the public sector. This would address the public sector's growing problem with recruiting high-flyers, particularly high-flyers in information technology, by providing them with a regular supply of brilliant young recruits. It would also repair the fraying link between public service and intellectual excellence. Thomas Jefferson produced a blueprint for such a system when he was governor of Virginia in 1779–81: the Commonwealth should educate 'natural aristocrats' at its own expense, sending them to boarding school and university as 'public foundationers', but should then recoup its investment by obliging them to serve in 'the offices of government'.[24] Singapore obliges scholarship winners to pay off their debt by working for the state. It is worth reintroducing the idea more widely in a West where public service is going out of fashion.

All this talk of IQ tests and educational selection inevitably raises emotive questions. Aren't IQ tests 'racist'? And aren't hard-edged examinations such as entrance exams and SATs heartless? In *Hard Times* (1854) Charles Dickens satirized the testing culture in the form of Mr Gradgrind, who was ready to 'weigh and measure any parcel of human nature'. Wouldn't this testing regime mean a return of Mr Gradgrind weighing every ounce of child intelligence? Before making the case for more political meritocracy to go along with more educational meritocracy, I want to address these two questions.

THE THIN END OF *THE BELL CURVE*

In 1994, Richard Herrnstein and Charles Murray published a highly controversial book called *The Bell Curve: Intelligence and Class Structure in American Life.*[25] The book did a disservice to the meritocratic idea in all sorts of ways, but two stand out: it argued that a truly meritocratic society would inevitably calcify into a caste society and it posited that the average IQ of black people is about ten to fifteen points lower than the average IQ of white people (which is in turn lower than the average IQ of Asian people). Both these arguments misrepresent the psychometric science upon which the book is supposedly founded.

It's certainly true that there have always been people who have drawn dark conclusions from psychometry, from Francis Galton onwards, as we saw in Chapter Eleven. But the dominant tradition among intelligence testers, particularly in Britain, has always been more progressive and optimistic: intelligence testers have been prominent advocates of social mobility, pre-school education and more enlightened treatment of the mentally handicapped and socially disadvantaged. There have been plenty of 'bell curve liberals' who believe that natural inequalities demand more progressive social policies, just as there have been plenty of anti-bell curve conservatives who find the idea that genes shape human nature repugnant.[26]

Herrnstein and Murray are wrong to imply that meritocracy will eventually lead to a static society. They repeat a common mistake in the nature–nurture debate: assuming that nature is a more conservative force than nurture. The truth is the opposite: it is nature rather than nurture that is the great disruptor. Parents can't guarantee that their children will be exactly like them because of the unpredictable dance of the chromosomes through genetic recombination and the statistical phenomenon of regression to the mean (the tendency of tall children to have slightly shorter children and short people to have slightly taller children).[27]

The Bell Curve is wrong to focus on group rather than individual differences for two reasons. The first is that group differences can easily be accounted for by environmental differences: Herrnstein and Murray concede that the environment accounts for anything from 20 to 60 per cent of IQ differences but then fail to acknowledge the fact that environmental differences can account for average differences in test results: African-Americans live, on average, in much poorer neighbourhoods than whites. The second is that group differences are far smaller than individual differences. Herrnstein and Murray focus on the small difference between averages in various populations. But the most striking fact revealed by IQ tests is the huge difference *within* populations. The differences that matter are the differences between individuals rather than the (purported) differences between groups.

Unfortunately, the noisy controversy over *The Bell Curve* has distracted public attention from an important scientific development: the growing consensus among specialists on the role that nature plays in shaping individual abilities. Robert Plomin, a leading researcher in behavioural genetics, argues that psychological differences, such as intelligence or depression, are about 50 per cent heritable and some physiological differences, such as weight, are 70 per cent heritable.[28] Twin and adoption studies have long pointed in this direction (indeed, the so-called Minnesota study of a hundred identical twins reared apart seems to point to a higher degree of heritability, given the extraordinary similarity of the IQs of separated twins).[29] Now we have another piece of evidence: the sequencing of the human genome has allowed us to detect the actual genetic basis of human differences. This doesn't mean that there is a single gene for this or that attribute – a fat gene or an addiction gene or a brilliance gene – but rather that thousands of small differences ('polygenic scores') can be aggregated together to predict psychological propensities.

The question of IQ brings us to IQ tests and other standardized tests.

HARD HEADS AND SOFT HEARTS

One common argument against standardized tests is that, Gradgrind-like, they reduce a child to a number. Why not take the 'whole child' into account rather than just their performance on an IQ test? And why not allow the people who know the child best after the parents – teachers – to have a louder say? Though this is superficially attractive, holistic assessment is, in fact, much more open to class prejudice than cold numbers.

Freddie deBoer, an American writer and self-identified Marxist, points out that, despite often being dressed in the language of social justice, 'whole person assessment' is, by its very nature, biased against the poor:

> The student who is captain of the sailing team, president of the robotics club, and who spent a summer building houses in the Global South will likely look more 'holistically' valuable than a poorer student who has not had the resources to do similar activities. Who is more likely to be a star violin player or to have completed a summer internship at a fancy magazine: a poor student or an affluent one? College essays are more easily improved through coaching than test scores, and teachers at expensive private schools likely feel more pressure to write effusive letters of recommendation than their peers in public schools.[30]

Thomas Chatterton Williams, an African-American writer who grew up in the South, makes a similar argument in favour of SATs. Traditional educational measurements would never have given him a chance to fulfil his potential, he says: even if he'd achieved a perfect grade point average (GPA) he would never have looked as good as a privately educated child with a perfect GPA plus lots of extracurricular activity and advanced placement courses. By contrast, SATs allowed him to shine. He not only got into Georgetown and New York Universities on the basis of his SATs. He knew he got there on his own merits rather than because the system was fixed in his favour. SATs are 'a lifeline for people who need to improve their circumstances'.[31]

The most common objection to educational selection is that it's too hard-edged. There is a measure of truth in this if selection means nothing more than dividing the population into 'successes' and 'failures'. But if selection means differentiation, you get a much happier result. In an ideal education system, children's abilities are matched to their challenges: nobody gains anything if low-performing students are left behind while teachers concentrate on the high-flyers or if high-performing students are left to idle while teachers focus on the rest. Selection is just a way of matching abilities to challenges that avoids the problem of super-sized and characterless schools.

The modern fashion for delaying differentiation for as long as possible in the name of second chances comes with significant hidden costs. Time is a costly resource: the more education becomes an endurance race to amass more and more qualifications, the more money matters. Richer children can afford to hang around at university for longer. They can tap their parents' network of friends for internships. They often rely on free board and lodging from their metropolitan parents until they find the right job. For all its brutality in eliminating the also-rans, the old scholarship system paid for poor children to go to university and made sure that they got professional jobs at the end of it. Sometimes it turns out, in practice, that hard heads have generous hearts.

POLITICAL MERITOCRACY

The West prides itself on its commitment to one person one vote. In practice, however, constitution-makers have almost always mixed democracy with a measure of meritocracy on the grounds that pure democracy is too volatile. America's Founding Fathers hedged the democratic House of Representatives with all sorts of restraints. Senators were elected for six years rather than Congress's two so that they were more distant from popular opinion. (Jefferson likened the Senate to a bowl into which coffee could be poured so that it could cool down.) Supreme Court justices were appointed for life so they wouldn't be influenced by anything other than the letter of the constitution and the spirit of justice. Many countries use second chambers to give a role to wisdom and experience in forming policy.

The European Union is particularly suspicious of crude majoritarianism because of the experience of Nazism. The European Commission is more powerful than the European Parliament. States have to forswear certain policies such as the death penalty and torture as a condition of joining; European law lays down various individual rights that cannot be overridden by the voters. The system of 'qualified majority voting' means that you need large majorities to get things done – you can't just cobble together majorities of just over half the population.

Recent years have seen the democratic spirit advancing at the expense of the meritocratic. America has made growing use of direct democracy through ballot initiatives. Party bosses have ceded power to Party members: Donald Trump would not have won the Republican nomination in 2016 if the establishment had been in charge. Britain has allowed its fate to be decided by two referenda (over Scottish Independence and membership of the EU) and handed the choice of Party leaders from MPs to members. Even the EU is giving more power to its parliament.

There is a strong case for reversing this trend. The 2016 EU referendum reduced a set of complicated questions about Britain's relationship with its most important trading partner to a binary choice. The result has divided the country, plunged British politics into a prolonged crisis and, according to most economists, reduced its potential growth rate. Charismatic populists such as Boris Johnson and particularly Donald Trump have also taken a heavy toll on the quality of government in their respective countries. Angela Merkel did a far better job of dealing with the arrival of Covid than either of them because she relies on expertise and doggedness rather than charisma.

The economist Garett Jones makes a powerful case that a bit less democracy is better democracy. 'The push for "one person, one vote", come what may, has had both benefits and costs,' he says, 'and in the twenty-first century we have enough data to make it clear that the costs are pretty high.'[32] Democracy can make it difficult to balance the budget because voters want to have their cake and eat it in the form of lower taxes and higher spending. Sweden has been successful at putting its pension system on a solid foundation because politicians asked independent experts to produce a long-term plan for reforming it and agreed to abide by the results. America's social security system is faltering because democratically elected politicians can't agree on how to fix it, with Republicans refusing to raise taxes and Democrats refusing to adjust benefits or the retirement age.

It is possible to reinforce political meritocracy without embracing far-fetched measures such as creating a second chamber of wise men and women or giving more votes to the educated: even Lee Kuan Yew waited until he left office until he floated his idea of variable franchises, in 1994.[33] The best way forward is to supplement democratic institutions with meritocratic institutions and democratic mechanisms with meritocratic mechanisms. Countries that have not adopted independent central banks, most importantly China, should make the leap. Governments should generally avoid referenda, but if they must use them, they should apply very stringent criteria for passing far-reaching changes: Britain's recent history would be very different if David Cameron had demanded a super-majority or instituted a two-stage process. Parties should wrest control from their members and hand it back to representatives who have to take into account broad constituencies rather than just the opinions of ideological activists: the British Labour Party would have escaped the nightmare of Jeremy Corbyn's failed leadership, and might well be in power today, if members hadn't been given the final say in choosing a leader. America should learn from Sweden's example in finding wise men and women who can draw up plans to sort out its entitlement problem free from the hurly-burly of day-to-day politics. None of this needs to threaten the basic principle of democracy: so long as everyone is clear that ultimate sovereignty continues to lie with the people, such measures, by increasing good government, can only strengthen the democratic principle.

The press has historically played an important role in acting as a meritocratic supplement to democracy by providing a diet of reliable information and informed comment. Not all the press, of course: the British tabloids have always been intent on exercising what Rudyard Kipling called 'power without responsibility – the prerogative of the harlot throughout the ages'. But enough of the press to make the system work. The serious papers pride themselves on employing informed journalists, offering op-ed space to independent experts and holding governments to account.

Today's commercial realities are making this more difficult. More than a quarter of American newspapers have closed in the past fifteen years.[34] Most broadsheets have cut back on their networks of foreign correspondents. Cable news channels are more interested in stoking partisanship than in reporting the news. Internet giants such as Facebook and Twitter have built their brands by providing platforms for anyone who wants to post on them, however bizarre their views and unfounded their claims, and have only reluctantly agreed to put warnings on the most outrageous content. They are thus double threats to informed opinion: they soak up the advertising revenues that used to keep respectable newspapers afloat while at the same time disseminating nonsense. Daniel Patrick Moynihan once said that 'people are entitled to their own opinions but not to their own facts'. Thanks to cable news and the internet, too many of his fellow Americans not only feel entitled to 'their own facts' but have news streams that are specifically designed to provide them.

To some extent, the problem is proving self-correcting: the educated public, tired of fake news and click bait, is gravitating to certain global brands that are associated with high standards such as the *Financial Times*, the *Wall Street Journal*, the *Atlantic* and the *Economist*. The more customers these brands attract, the more resources they can devote to hiring high-quality journalists, fact checkers and data crunchers. The market nevertheless needs to be supplemented by state intervention. The BBC, paid for by the licence payer, not only acts as a source of objective news in the United Kingdom. It has a positive impact on the supply of news in general, by providing smaller news organizations with information and acting as a model of objective reporting. The state of American cable news has reinforced the case for keeping strict rules, such as the ones that exist in Britain and have prevented Sky from degenerating into Fox News, demanding a balanced approach to presenting the news. When it comes to internet platforms (which have partly built their positions by stealing content from other news sources) governments could tax a proportion of their profits and use this money to pay for public news stations or to subsidize struggling newspapers.

So far, I've advanced a paradoxical thought: that one way to address the discontent being created by meritocracy is to strengthen meritocracy. Properly judged educational selection will prevent the elite from hardening into a self-perpetuating clique. A measure of political meritocracy will strengthen political institutions. Yet paradox can only get you so far: now we've powered up the meritocratic machine, it's time to present some ideas for producing wiser meritocracy.

POSITIVE DISCRIMINATION

In Chapter Fourteen, I discussed Lyndon Johnson's landmark speech at Howard University when he declared that you can't take people who have been hobbled by chains for years, put them at the starting line of a race and then fire the starting pistol. You need a measure of affirmative action to prepare them for the race. Classical liberals have always had problems with affirmative action, worrying that it perpetuates the very racial categories that it's designed to eliminate, but it's hard to escape Johnson's logic: equality of opportunity doesn't work if some people start a long way behind others not because of their individual merits but because they happen to be born members of a certain group. Sometimes collective wrongs require collective solutions.

The case for affirmative action is at its strongest for the group that LBJ was talking about at Howard: African-Americans. Slavery was an evil that was borne by one group of people precisely because of the colour of their skin – most obviously by African-Americans, who were brought to America as slaves, but also by all black people who were touched by the global slave trade. The Jim Crow laws perpetuated state-sanctioned discrimination. Long after Jim Crow was abolished, a combination of law and custom forced black people to live in 'black areas' (often with the worst pollution) not just in the South but in the North as well. Thanks to the legacy of slavery and segregation, black Americans not only earn 60 per cent less than white Americans but have much less accumulated wealth.

The case for affirmative action also applies to other groups that have been subjected to collective wrongs down the generations. These groups certainly include other ethnic minorities: the aboriginal populations of former European colonies are obvious examples. But it's wrong to treat all ethnic groups as equally deserving of special breaks. Why should recent immigrants be given extra opportunities when their host countries have already improved their life chances by giving them citizenship? There is no collective wrong to be rectified here. It's equally wrong to exclude some groups of white people from consideration just because of the colour of their skin: what matters is collective deprivation, not skin colour. In Britain, white working-class children are less likely to go to university than black children, and white boys do particularly badly. In the United States, some of the worst poverty is concentrated in the white-dominated Appalachian regions, as J. D. Vance documents so ably. If the aim is to level the playing field by compensating for collective disadvantages, then there is no reason that affirmative action should be defined exclusively by race.

Bill Clinton never tired of saying that affirmative action should be 'mended not ended' but failed to say exactly what 'mending it' meant. The best way to mend it is to shift the emphasis from numerical targets to enriched education. Numerical targets pander to the worst instincts of the higher educational establishment – they allow them to engage in a quantifiable pursuit of virtue without having to put their souls into the project. Yet numerical targets are both unpopular and counterproductive. The majority of Americans (including majorities of blacks) say that they are opposed to affirmative action[35] and, in the 2020 ballot initiative, a majority of Californians voted against it. A 2012 study by three researchers at Duke University found that more than 76 per cent of black freshmen at Duke intended to major in the hard sciences or economics but more than half of them switched track during the course of their studies, compared with just 8 per cent of white students so that, by their senior year, only 35 per cent of black males graduated with a degree in science or economics.[36] Lady Margaret Hall, Oxford, has pioneered a much better approach to the problem by recruiting disadvantaged children on the basis of their promise and then providing them with a fully funded foundation year of additional teaching in both their subjects and academic skills in general so that they can catch up with their classmates. Foundation-year students live in college along with other undergraduate and graduate students so that they are taken into the academic community.[37]

This is necessarily a costly remedy to the problem that can apply only to a small minority of the age group. The best way to help the poor as a whole is early childhood education. Multiple studies show that going to pre-school gives young children a leg-up in all kinds of learning, not just academic but also social skills, listening, planning and self-control. One study of a poor but ethnically mixed school area led by Arya Ansari, of Ohio State University, found that, on entering kindergarten, children who had attended pre-school were approximately eight months ahead of children who hadn't attended in academic learning and about five months ahead in skills such as listening, planning and self-control.[38] Another study, by James Heckman, a Nobel Prize winner, shows that pre-school education can continue to pay dividends more than fifty years later.[39]

Pre-school education is still unevenly distributed: only 34 per cent of American four-year olds attended pre-school in 2019, compared with 60 per cent in Canada and 90 per cent in Europe. Bringing laggards (primarily America) up to the level of the leaders would be a big advance for equality of opportunity. But more is better. Perhaps the best thing that could be done to advance equality of opportunity would be to create educational priority areas, defined by poverty, where governments focus educational resources on the youngest children.

We also need to look outside the world of educational policy. Housing reforms might produce rich results. Weakening zoning rules that make it difficult to build flats in high-cost cities would make it easier for poorer people to move to areas where jobs and good schools are more abundant. Abolishing mortgage-interest tax deduction, which helps already wealthy people to buy homes, would allow the government to increase the size of its housing programmes for the poor without putting more pressure on the Exchequer.[40]

With a bit of imagination new technology can also be used to equalize life chances. During the Second World War, Bletchley Park did an impressive job of discovering untapped female talent by recruiting people who could solve crosswords and other puzzles. Unit 8200 of the Israeli Defense Forces, an elite cyber-security group that is so exclusive global companies such as Google and Facebook compete to hire 'graduates' of the unit without expecting them to bother with university, does something similar today. The unit monitors children's performance in video games in the hope of identifying exceptional young people who aren't much interested in schoolwork but can produce remarkable scores. Providence, Rhode Island, has pioneered a successful way of closing the 'word gap' between poorer and richer babies by getting parents to wear devices that record how many words they say daily and then giving them regular advice on how better to talk to their children. Several companies, such as Reasoning Mind and DreamBox, produce 'adaptive' or 'personalized' learning machines that gather data on the individual performance of children and then automatically tailor teaching to their needs, providing children from whatever social class with personalized instruction.

Even if we can solve the problem of social calcification by boosting social mobility, we risk making another problem worse: the arrogance of the successful. In order to address this problem, we need to inculcate the successful with a renewed sense of public duty.

REMORALIZING MERITOCRACY

The triumph of the cognitive elite has coincided with the demoralization of the meritocratic idea. The successful have come to see their success exclusively in terms of just rewards for their superior abilities and effort.[41] They draw a sharp distinction between yesterday's elites (rentiers who made their money by inheriting it from Daddy or exploiting the poor) and themselves (high achievers who made their money by solving difficult problems and thereby improving the state of the world). Theirs is the creed of the irritating l'Oréal advertisement – 'because you're worth it'.

This demoralized view of merit is unsatisfactory, indeed corrosive. Oliver Goldsmith's most famous lines, in *The Deserted Village* (1770), seem to hang over today's meritocratic-plutocratic mix: 'Ill fares the land, to hastening ills a prey/Where wealth accumulates, and men decay.' Too many people see the cognitive elite as exemplars of incompetence and self-dealing rather than expertise and problem-solving. Financiers rig the financial system for their own benefit. Technologists are building 'surveillance capitalism'. Politicians earn millions cashing in on their public service. Many members of the elite themselves suffer from the demoralized view of success. Towards the end of his career, Clayton Christensen, a leading professor at Harvard Business School became so worried about the number of his pupils who had ended up divorced, miserable or in prison that he co-authored (with James Allworth and Karen Dillon) a book on *How Will You Measure Your Life?* (2012), urging business types to put more emphasis on basic morality.

The best way to deal with this problem is not to reject the meritocratic idea but to look back at its rich history. The meritocratic revolution that I have described in this book was as much a moral revolution as a technocratic one. The notion of meritocracy provided both a moral critique of the old order and a code of conduct for reformers who wanted to replace the old ruling class with something better.

England's meritocrats succeeded in dismantling Old Corruption without firing a shot because they were impresarios of moral outrage. They demonized sinecures and jobbery. They mocked Oxbridge dons for their deep potations and scant learning. They forced civil servants and parliamentarians to live up to higher standards of personal conduct. They told aristocrats that leadership was not a right they exercised on account of their birth but a responsibility they exercised on behalf of the common good. You can't treat the state as an object to be plundered, as the eighteenth- and early-nineteenth-century aristocracy did, they argued. That is a form of barbarism. You can't just tend your own estates and leave the government to take care of itself. That is irresponsible. You must be a high-minded guardian: win a seat in Parliament or win a job in the civil service and serve the public good. Charles Kingsley thought that a silent moral revolution had transformed the British upper class by 1850. 'The attitude of the British upper classes has undergone a noble change. There is no aristocracy in the world, and there never has been one, as far as I know, which has so honourably repented, and brought forth fruits meet for repentance; which has so cheerfully asked what its duty was, that it might do it.'[42]

Reformers directed the same austere message at the businessmen who, flush with commercial success, began to flood into local and national politics in the mid-nineteenth century. The literature of the period is full of sermons against self-serving business types who treated politics as a way of climbing up the social ladder or, still worse, lining their own pockets. Gladstone delivered numerous speeches in the 1860s and 1870s about the danger of 'plutocracy'. Robert Lowe warned of the dangers of 'a plutocracy working upon a democracy'. Newspapers thundered against arrivistes who wanted to degrade the 'government of the most worthy' into the 'government of the most wealthy'.[43] Trollope contrasted the vulgar Augustus Melmotte, who went into politics to advance himself, with the patrician Duke of Omnium, who did so out of a sense of duty.

'Duty' was indeed the key word of the Victorian moral lexicon. The mid-Victorians used this stern but inspiring term to persuade both the old aristocracy and the rising 'plutocracy' to put nation before self and effort before ease. Educators found that Plato and the Bible agreed on the importance of duty. Conservatives and Liberals, intellectuals and soldiers, Anglicans and Nonconformists, put their differences aside when it came to singing the praises of putting duty above self. Queen Victoria represented duty on the throne, just as Gladstone embodied duty in public life.

We need a similar moral revival today if meritocracy is to flourish again. This means addressing issues of injustice in modern terms: we need to recognize that the 'social justice' movement is sometimes on to something. But it also means addressing them in the same terms as nineteenth-century meritocrats. We can get a long way by reading the founder of meritocratic thought. Though Plato's ideas about abolishing private property and marriage are clearly far-fetched, he nevertheless put his finger on two of the problems that have transformed the burgeoning meritocracy of the 1950s and 1960s into a plutocracy: the tendency of politicians to feather their own nests when they retire, as David Cameron tried to do by lobbying on behalf of Lex Greensill, and the elite's ingenuity in finding ways to advance their own children. There is a whiff of the *Ancien Régime* today as a transnational elite masters these practices and treats national and international bodies as systems of outdoor relief for their families. We urgently need to erect barriers against this if we are to save global institutions from being held in justified opprobrium.

The case for re-moralizing the education of the elite is even stronger in China than it is in the West. The understandable pleasure that people who have lived in poverty take in new wealth often degenerates into grubbiness and corruption. The Chinese elite is beginning to address these problems by reviving the Confucian tradition, which it is carefully weaving into the national educational curriculum, as we saw in the previous chapter. It is also allowing some parents to send their children to special Confucian academies, such as the Si Hai Confucius Academy in Beijing, where they wear traditional Chinese garb, learn Confucian texts, visit Confucian shrines and organize their behaviour in accordance with Confucian rites. If there is a touch of cultural nationalism about this, rather like Narendra Modi's revival of Hindu religious themes in India, there is also something more – a sense that China needs to embrace its ancient traditions if it is not to become 'all elbows'. A group of intellectuals known as the New Confucians argues that the answer to the problem of improving civil life in China lies in recapturing Confucius's insight that the meritocratic elite's primary job is not to solve technical problems but to preserve and enrich civilization.

UPGRADING VOCATIONAL EDUCATION

The man who gave meritocracy its name understood that status is at least as important as income or class: the losers in the meritocratic race feel devalued not because they are paid less than the high-IQ types but because they are treated as less valued members of the community. Status is at the heart of the current unease about meritocracy on both the left and the right. Populists accuse the cognitive elite of looking down on them. Parents worry that their children will be denied high-status jobs on the basis of a handful of exam results. This problem is particularly marked in Britain and the United States, where the elites are besotted with a handful of academic institutions and vocational education is treated as an afterthought. Britain's system of vocational education is a patchwork of underfunded colleges and ever-changing qualifications. America spends far more on subsidizing (through tax breaks) its fabulously endowed elite universities than it does on its entire system of vocational education.

It is nevertheless wrong to think that all this is a problem of meritocracy per se, as so many of meritocracy's current critics seem to do. It is a problem of a policy that focuses on opening up elite institutions to all comers rather than on crafting different types of education for different abilities and aptitudes. The German-speaking world has avoided much of the current discontent with meritocracy, in terms of both angst in elite institutions and anger among populists, by giving an honoured place to vocational education. More than a quarter of young Germans attend technical schools and about half get apprenticeships when they leave school. It's not unusual to spend some time as an apprentice and then to go on to university.

Both America and Germany once gave more weight to practical education. In America, the land-grant colleges that were founded in 1862 and 1890 deliberately focused on practical subjects such as science, engineering and agriculture. Institutes of Technology (such as MIT) were designed to rival elite colleges in the practical arts. In Britain, the great cities built vocational schools and industrial colleges for the new working class. Quintin Hogg, a sugar merchant, philanthropist and sire of a Conservative dynasty, revived the Royal Polytechnic Institution, which had been founded in 1838 but had fallen into decay, and turned it into a great centre of technical education, with almost 7,000 students.[44] Two Conservative prime ministers, Stanley Baldwin and Neville Chamberlain, studied metallurgy at Mason Science College, the nucleus of Birmingham University (though Baldwin also studied history at Trinity College, Cambridge). Redbrick universities tried to carve out a niche teaching practical subjects rather than turning themselves into imitations of Oxford and Cambridge. The landmark 1944 Education Act envisaged three types of schools – not just grammar schools and secondary moderns but also technical schools. British higher education once included two types of institutions – traditional universities and more practical polytechnics.

In recent decades, however, both countries have strongly favoured academic education over vocational education – and thus selection by elimination over selection by differentiation. Governments entered into a race to send more than half their young people to universities. (Britain's polytechnics were turned into universities in 1992 as part of a drive to hit this number.) Universities realized that they could make money by offering higher degrees to supplement the now commonplace bachelor degrees. Academic league tables encouraged institutions to focus on attracting academic superstars and the pupils they brought with them.

The best way to address the current discontent with the educational meritocracy is not to fiddle with admissions to elite institutions but to upgrade vocational education, a recommendation made to the British government in the Augar Report on the future of tertiary education, published in 2019.[45] Upgrading vocational education means more than creating a fairer distribution of resources between universities and further-education colleges, though that is an urgent priority. It means rethinking conventional models of success. Policy-makers need to free themselves of the (often unconscious) assumption that manual work and vocational skills occupy a lower position in the status hierarchy than brain work and academic education. John Ruskin, one of the great Victorian advocates of the dignity of labour, argued that society should place equal value on 'hands, head and heart' – that is, on craftsmanship and compassion as well as academic studies. David Goodhart has persuasively expanded and updated this argument in *Head Hand Heart: The Struggle for Dignity and Status in the 21st Century* (2020).

Educational differentiation needs to be counterbalanced by equality of esteem. Schools and opinion formers need to stop stigmatizing or neglecting technical qualifications (the BBC has made a good start by reporting on results for technical qualifications as well as A-levels). Teachers need to stop forcing all their children into the same academic mould, instead adjusting their teaching to the 'material of which the man is made', as Ruskin put it. Policy-makers need to think in terms of several ladders to success, not just one ever narrower ladder marked 'cognitive ability'. In Chapter Ten I quoted Suzanne Keller saying that nineteenth-century America was successful because it was a pack of cards with an ace in every suit, whereas Europe tended to have just one ace and one suit. We need more suits.

Equality of esteem is not the pie-in-the-sky that it sounds. In 1956, two years before he published *The Rise of the Meritocracy*, Michael Young, together with Peter Willmott, wrote an article that is worth bearing in mind today. They pointed out that manual workers advanced a radically different conception of the status hierarchy from the professional elite, placing productive labourers at the top and non-productive office workers at the bottom.[46] 'I put builders at the top,' one man told them. 'They're building houses and today houses are needed more than anything else. Builders are actually working, not like all those people in old collar-and-tie jobs. All they do is push a pen along and look at books.'[47]

As so often, policy-makers need to catch up with the common sense of the people. Not everyone puts the same emphasis on academic prizes as people who write books on the defects, or indeed the virtues, of meritocracy. Many members of the cognitive elite (for example, bankers and journalists) are held in contempt by the vast mass of people, while members of the caring professions are revered: there is no 'clap for bankers' movement to rival the 'clap for carers' movement. Most people have other (and more profound) sources of self-esteem and self-fulfilment – raising their families, socializing with their friends, making a respectable living (in 2015, 71 per cent of Britons said that they had a 'good job', compared with 57 per cent in 1989).

Modern societies are also immensely creative when it comes to charting new paths of success. Growing wealth means that society can reward a wider range of talents. 'I must study politics and war that my sons may have liberty to study mathematics and philosophy,' wrote America's second president, John Adams, and they in turn must study those subjects so that their children can study 'painting, poetry, music, architecture, statuary, tapestry and porcelain'.[48] Or indeed bee-keeping, bread-making or yoga-teaching. These days, sports stars and entertainers can make millions. There are also ample rewards for all sorts of talents, from cooking to wine-tasting. It sometimes seems that there is no talent so recondite that you cannot make a living out of it. Matt 'Megatoad' Stonie earns more than $200,000 a year as the world's hot-dog-eating champion: he can eat more than sixty in ten minutes.

THE DEATH OF VENICE

Creating a more efficient 'capacity-catching machine'; re-moralizing the cognitive elite; upgrading vocational education: all this adds up to a formidable list of reforms at a time when the world confronts so many urgent problems. The decay of the meritocracy is slow. Elite universities continue to offer a first-class education. The plutocratic elite preserves some elements of meritocracy. The avenues of upward mobility haven't silted up completely. Why take time away from focusing on more obviously urgent issues such as the state of the health service? The answer is that slow decay can gather pace and become fast decay if you don't address it – and the decay of something as vital as the meritocratic spirit can doom an entire civilization. For a sense of what might happen to the West if it doesn't begin to revive the meritocratic spirit, we can turn, in conclusion, to one of Europe's most beautiful cities.

In terms of natural resources, Venice is unlucky, set in an insect-infested swamp in a land that normally abounds in milk and honey. Yet in the early Middle Ages Venice was the richest city in Europe, thanks to its unusual openness to talent. The city-state was ruled by a doge, selected by a council of wise men, rather than a heriditary ruler.

Social mobility was commonplace. Two Harvard economists, Daron Acemoglu and James Robinson, calculate that in government documents in the years 960, 971 and 982 new names made up 69 per cent, 81 per cent and 65 per cent respectively of those recorded.[49] Institutions became more inclusive. Elites competed to build some of the world's most spectacular buildings and patronize some of its most glorious arts.[50]

But competition is hard and uncertainty disorienting. In the late twelfth and early thirteenth centuries the most powerful families took to rigging the system in favour of their children. And in 1315 they succeeded in locking their position at the top of society for good by publishing the Book of Gold (*Libro d'Oro*) – an official list of Venetian noble families that was intended to keep the social order exactly as it was. Venetians called this *La Serrata*: the closure.

La Serrata spelt the end of Venice as the world's most successful city-state. A self-satisfied oligarchy used its power to hoard opportunities and strangle innovation. The *commenda* were banned. The state took over trade. Newcomers were kept out or down. The city lost its vigour. By 1500, the city's population was lower than it had been in 1330. By 1851, when John Ruskin published the first volume of his magnificent *Stones of Venice*, it was a byword for decline – 'a ghost upon the sands of the sea, so weak – so quiet, – so bereft of all but her loveliness, that we might well doubt, as we watched her faint reflection in the mirage of the lagoon, which was the City, and which the Shadow.'[51]

Advanced countries today are in danger of producing a slow-motion version of *La Seratta*. The honour rolls of the great universities are becoming contemporary versions of books of gold that record the names of the children of privilege (with a few members of approved ethnic minorities added for show). Elites are losing touch with the wider society. Economies are stagnating and political unrest rising. A sense of common purpose is fading. The West has succeeded in igniting or reigniting the meritocratic spirit in the past – and using that spirit for the common good rather than for narrow personal advantage. This happened in mid-nineteenth-century Britain, when government was revivified by open competition; in late-nineteenth-century America, when the promise of American life was rescued from the Gilded Age; and in the aftermath of the Second World War, when new educational opportunities multiplied. It is time to start doing so again if the West is not to succumb to Venice's sad fate and global leadership is not to pass inexorably to the Chinese-dominated world.

Acknowledgements

It is a pleasure to acknowledge the numerous debts that I have accumulated in writing this book. The *Economist*, my professional home for more than thirty years, has provided an ideal perch for thinking about the past, present and future of meritocracy. Several colleagues in particular have lent their professional expertise. Rosie Blau, Rob Gifford and David Rennie shared their expertise on China. I apologize if I've not always taken their advice. Sophie Pedder corrected some of my elementary errors on French history, politics and, indeed, spelling. Xan Smiley shared his unrivalled knowledge of the world of 'priority, degree and place', catching embarrassing errors of fact, interpretation and genealogy. Patrick Foulis answered a barrage of questions about business. Rachel Horwood, Idrees Kahloon and Steven Mazie supplied some US references. John Prideaux read an early draft and made many helpful suggestions; Arkady Ostrovsky countered my pessimism with even greater pessimism. Sabrina Valaydon, Ketna Patel and Fanny Papageorgiou were unfailingly helpful and understanding (and saved several printer/photocopiers from destruction). Andrea Burgess supplied me with a ceaseless supply of books from the London Library, despite the fact that they had no obvious relationship with my day job. I'm particularly grateful to Zanny Minton-Beddoes, the editor-in-chief, for smiling on my bookwriting habits.

Several academics provided ideas, information and general inspiration at a particularly important stage of writing: Luigi Zingales, of the University of Chicago's Booth School, Tyler Cowen, Garett Jones and Alex Tabarrok of George Mason University, and Jerry Muller of the Catholic University of America. Michael Sandel was kind enough to point out a number of slips and errors. I would like to record my debt to Keith Hope, who alerted me, many years ago, to the fascinating connections between Thomas Babington Macaulay, the British intellectual aristocracy and IQ testing. My greatest academic debt is recorded in the dedication.

I am enormously grateful to Stuart Proffitt for seeing the potential of a general history of meritocracy several years ago and guiding the book to completion, applying the spur whenever I shied at a jump and the reins whenever I was heading in the wrong direction. He is the very model of what a book editor should be. I am also grateful to Stuart's team at Penguin Random House, particularly Alice Skinner, Sarah Day, Richard Duguid and Annabel Huxley. Stephen Ryan performed stupendous feats of proofreading and fact checking. As always, I am much indebted to my agent, Andrew Wylie, and to his colleagues Sarah Chalfant and James Pullen for all their help.

My greatest debt is to my wife, Amelia, and my daughters Ella and Dora, for not only tolerating my preoccupation with this subject – well, most of the time, anyway – but also for demonstrating that there are things that matter far more than merit. Amelia proved, once again, that she is a talented editor and eagle-eyed proofreader.

The responsibility for all the remaining errors is mine alone.

Notes

INTRODUCTION: A REVOLUTIONARY IDEA

1 Both quoted in Michael J. Sandel, *The Tyranny of Merit: What's become of the Common Good* (London, Allen Lane, 2020), pp. 65–7, 79
2 See, for example, Tony Blair, *New Britain: My Vision of a Young Country* (London, Fourth Estate, 1996), p. 19
3 David Cameron, Conservative Party Conference Speech, 2012
4 David Lipsey, 'The Meritocracy Myth', *New Statesman*, 26 February 2016
5 Nikki Graf, 'Most Americans Say Colleges Should Not Consider Race or Ethnicity in Admissions', Pew Research Center, Fact Tank, 25 February 2019
6 https://www.chinadaily.com.cn/china/19thcpcnationalcongress/2017-11/04/content_34115212.htm
7 Sandel, *The Tyranny of Merit*, p. 107
8 Ibid., p. 84
9 Gregory Zuckerman, *The Man Who Solved the Market: How Jim Simons Launched the Quant Revolution* (New York, Portfolio, 2019)
10 'America's New Aristocracy', *Economist*, 22 January 2015
11 Peter Saunders, *Social Mobility Myths* (London, Civitas, 2010), p. 69
12 Alice Sullivan et al., 'The Path from Social Origins to Top Jobs: Social Reproduction via Education', *British Journal of Sociology* 69 (3) (2018), pp. 782–4
13 Abdel Abdellaoui et al., 'Genetic Correlates of Social Stratification in Great Britain', *Nature Human Behaviour*, 21 October 2019; 'Will Ye Nae Come Back Again: Migrants from Coalfields Take More than Just Their Talent with Them', *Economist*, 24 October 2019
14 Emma Duncan, 'Special Report: Private Education', *Economist*, 13 April 2019, p. 6

15 Jody-Lan Castle, 'Top 10 Exam Rituals from Stressed Students across Asia', BBC News, 3 March 2016

16 Tomas Chamorro-Premuzik, 'Ace the Assessment', *Harvard Business Review*, July–August 2015

17 See, for example, Robin DiAngelo, *White Fragility: Why It's So Hard for White People to Talk about Racism* (London, Allen Lane, 2018), p. 9

18 Ibid., pp. 40–43

19 Ibram X Kendi, *How to be an Antiracist* (London, The Bodley Head, 2019), p. 101

20 Ibid., p. 102; Wayne Au, 'Hiding behind High-Stakes Testing: Meritocracy, Objectivity and Inequality in US Education', *International Education Journal: Comparative Perspectives* 12 (2) (2013), pp. 7–19. For a sense of how deeply these ideas have penetrated the educational bureaucracy, see the blog by Alison Collins, the Board of Education Commissioner of the San Francisco United School District, particularly 'So, What's Wrong with Merit-Based Enrollment', https://sfpsmom.com/so-whats-wrong-with-merit-based-enrollment/

21 McKay Coppins, 'The Bow-Tied Bard of Populism', *Atlantic*, 23 February 2017

22 Daniel Markovits, *The Meritocracy Trap: The Tyranny of Just Deserts* (New York, Penguin Press, 2019), p. ix

23 David Brooks, 'Why Our Elites Stink', *The New York Times*, 12 July 2012

24 Steven Pearlstein, 'It's Time to Abandon the Cruelty of Meritocracy', *Guardian*, 13 October 2018; cf. Joel Kotkin, 'How Liberals are the New Autocrats', *Daily Beast*, 1 January 2016

25 The Sutton Trust, 'Access to Advantage', 7 December 2018

26 Raj Chetty et al., 'Mobility Report Cards: The Role of Colleges in Intergenerational Mobility', National Bureau of Economic Research, July 2017

27 Neil Bhutta et al., 'Disparities in Wealth by Race and Ethnicity in the 2019 Survey of Consumer Finances, FEDS Notes, 28 September 2020

28 In David Mamet's screenplay, the motivational speaker is Alec Baldwin.

29 Sandel, *The Tyranny of Merit*, pp. 184–8. Ron Unz made a similar case for a lottery, from a conservative perspective, in 'The Myth of American Meritocracy: How Corrupt are Ivy League Admissions?', *American Conservative*, December 2012

30 I have examined the history of IQ testing in England in some detail in *Measuring the Mind: Education and Psychology in England c. 1860–1990* (Cambridge, Cambridge University Press, 1994)

31 Alexis de Tocqueville, *Democracy in America*, trans. George Lawrence, ed. J. P. Mayer (New York, Anchor Books, 1969), pp. 457–8

32 Christine Korsgaard, *Self-Constitution: Agency, Identity and Integrity* (Oxford, Oxford University Press, 2009); Ulrich Beck and Elisabeth Beck-Gernsheim, *Individualization: Institutionalized Individualism and Its Social and Political Consequences* (London, Sage, 2002)

33 The 10th Earl's descendant, Jamie Niedpath, now the 13th Earl, taught Bill Clinton at University College, Oxford

34 James J. Sheehan, *German History 1770–1866* (Oxford, Clarendon Press, 1989), p. 507

35 Roy Porter, *English Society in the Eighteenth Century* (London, Allen Lane, 1982), p. 29

36 Quoted in ibid., p. 82

37 Walter Bagehot, *The English Constitution* (1867; Fontana edition with an introduction by Richard Crossman, 1963), p. 126

38 Quoted in Jerome Karabel, *The Chosen: The Hidden History of Admission and Exclusion at Harvard, Yale and Princeton* (New York, Houghton Mifflin, 2005), p. 30

39 Markovits, *The Meritocracy Trap*, p. 10; Shaila Dewan and Robert Gebeloff, 'Among the Wealthiest 1 Percent Many Variations', *The New York Times*, 14 January 2012

40 Schumpeter, 'Here Comes SuperBoss', *Economist*, 16 December 2015

41 J. S. Mill, *The Subjection of Women* (University of Oxford Text Archive), p. 104

42 Jonathan Rose, *The Intellectual Life of the British Working Classes* (London, Yale University Press, 2001), p. 61

43 J. R. Pole, *The Pursuit of Equality in American History* (Berkeley and London, University of California Press, 1978), p. 220

44 George C. M. Birdwood, *Competition and the Indian Civil Service* (London, 1872), p. 17. 'For my part,' he argued, 'I would give a boy very heavy marks for an illustrious father' (p. 16)

45 W. H. Mallock, *Aristocracy and Evolution: A Study of the Rights, the Origin and the Social Functions of the Wealthier Classes* (London, Adam and Charles Black, 1898), pp. 334–9

46 Karl Mannheim, 'Conservative Thought', in his *Essays on Sociology and Social Psychology*, ed. Paul Kecskemeti (London, Routledge & Kegan Paul, 1953), p. 107

47 Michael J. Sandel, *The Tyranny of Merit: What's become of the Common Good* (London, Allen Lane, 2020), pp. 27–9

48 Thomas Mann, *Buddenbrooks* (Penguin Books, Harmondsworth, 1957), p. 107

49 de Tocqueville, *Democracy in America*, p. 10

50 Joseph F. Kett, *Merit: The History of a Founding Ideal from the American Revolution to the Twenty-First Century* (Ithaca, NY, Cornell University Press, 2013), p. 15

51 Quoted in Joel Kotkin, *The New Class Conflict* (Candor, NY, Telos Press Publishing, 2014), p. 1

52 Matthew Goodwin and Oliver Heath, 'Brexit Vote Explained: Poverty, Low Skills and Lack of Opportunities', Joseph Rowntree Foundation, August 2016

53 Matthew Goodwin's analysis of the US Census. County ranking based on 2018 educational data

54 Nate Cohn, 'Why Trump Won: Working-Class Whites', *The New York Times*, 9 November 2016

I. HOMO HIERARCHICUS

1 David Herlihy, 'Three Patterns of Social Mobility in Medieval History', *Journal of Interdisciplinary History*, 3 (4) (Spring 1973), p. 623

2 David Priestland, *Merchant, Soldier, Sage: A New History of Power* (London, Allen Lane, 2012), pp. 3–8

3 Gail Bossenga, 'Estates, Orders and Corps', in William Doyle (ed.), *The Oxford Handbook of the Ancien Régime* (Oxford, Oxford University Press, 2012), p. 146

4 E. M. W. Tillyard, *The Elizabethan World Picture* (London, Chatto and Windus, 1943), p. 23

5 Ibid., p. 19

6 Keith Thomas, *The Ends of Life: Roads to Fulfilment in Early Modern England* (Oxford, Oxford University Press, 2009), p. 56; Michael Howard, *War in European History* (Oxford, Oxford University Press, 2009 edn), p. 4

7 Howard, *War in European History*, p. 4

8 T. H. Hollingsworth, 'A Demographic Study of the British Ducal Families', *Population Studies* 11 (1) (1957), pp. 4–26

9 *Divers Crabtree Lectures, Expressing the Several Languages that Shrews Read to their Husbands* (London, 1639). Quoted in D. E. Underdown, 'The Taming of the Scold: The Enforcement of Patriarchal Authority in Early Modern England', in John Fletcher and Anthony Stevenson (eds.), *Order and Disorder in Early Modern England* (Cambridge, Cambridge University Press, 1987), p. 118

10 Lawrence Stone, *The Crisis of the Aristocracy, 1558–1641* (Oxford, Clarendon Press, 1965), pp. 34–5

11 William Doyle, *The Old European Order 1660–1800* (Oxford, Oxford University Press, 1978), p. 86

12 Quoted in Daniel J. Boorstin, *The Americans: The Colonial Experience* (New York, Vintage Books, 1958), pp. 99–100

13 David Cannadine, *The Decline and Fall of the British Aristocracy* (New Haven, Yale University Press, 1990), p. 694

14 Roy Porter, *English Society in the Eighteenth Century* (London, Allen Lane, 1982), p. 71

15 John Galsworthy, *The Country House* (London, William Heinemann, 1927), p. 177

16 David Gilmour, *Curzon* (London, John Murray, 1994), p. 2

17 Doyle, *The Old European Order*, p. 85

18 Quoted in Lewis Namier, *England in the Age of the American Revolution* (London, Macmillan, 1930), p. 9

19 Stone, *The Crisis of the Aristocracy*, p. 22

20 Anthony Trollope, *The Prime Minister* (Oxford, Oxford University Press, 2011), pp. 35–40

21 Stone, *The Crisis of the Aristocracy*, p. 28

22 Douglas Allen, *The Institutional Revolution: Measurement and the Economic Emergence of the Modern World* (Chicago, University of Chicago Press, 2012), p. 41

23 Stone, *The Crisis of the Aristocracy*, p. 33

24 Hilde de Ridder-Symoens, 'Rich Men, Poor Men: Social Stratification and Social Representation at the University (13th–16th Centuries)', in Wim Blockmans and Antheun Janse (eds.), *Showing Status: Representation of Social Positions in the Late Middle Ages* (Turnhout, Belgium, Brepols, 1999), p. 173

25 Harold Silver, *The Concept of Popular Education* (London, Methuen, 1965), p. 23

26 Chris Bryant, *Entitled: A Critical History of the British Aristocracy* (London, Transworld, 2017), p. 125

27 William Casey King, *Ambition, A History: From Vice to Virtue* (New Haven, Yale University Press, 2013), p. 27

28 Ibid., p. 4

29 Ibid., p. 4, Burton quoting first St Ambrose and then St Bernard

2. FAMILY POWER

1 Both quoted in Jeroen Duindam, *Dynasties: A Global History of Power, 1300–1800* (Cambridge, Cambridge University Press, 2016)

2 William Doyle, *The Oxford History of the French Revolution 1660–1800* (Oxford, Oxford University Press, 1989), p. 28

3 Ibid., p. 43

4 F. Pollock and F. W. Maitland, *History of English Law before the Time of Edward I, 2 Vols.* (first published, 1895; Indianapolis, Liberty Fund, 2010 edn), Vol. 1, p. 208

5 Philip Mansel, *King of the World: The Life of Louis XIV* (London, Allen Lane, 2020), p. 213

6 Ibid., pp. 230–54

7 Adrian Tinniswood, *Behind the Throne: A Domestic History of the Royal Household* (London, Jonathan Cape, 2018), p. 66

8 Ibid., p. 67

9 Mansel, *King of the World*, p. 213

10 Robert Bartlett, *Blood Royal: Dynastic Politics in Medieval Europe* (Cambridge, Cambridge University Press, 2020), p. 61

11 Ibid., p. 72

12 Hilary Mantel, 'Royal Bodies', *London Review of Books*, 21 February 2013

13 Paul Webster, 'Size Did Matter to Marie-Antoinette', *Guardian*, 4 August 2002

14 Ibid.; Simone Bertière, *The Indomitable Marie-Antoinette* (Paris, Éditions de Fallois, 2014)

15 Bartlett, *Blood Royal*, p. 433

16 Ibid., pp. 109–10

17 Ibid., p. 111

18 Ibid., p. 14

19 Ibid., p. 52

20 Ibid., p. 3

21 Ibid., p. 48

22 J. M. Roberts and Odd Arne Westad, *The History of the World* (6th edn, New York, Oxford University Press, 2013), p. 602

23 Lewis Namier, *Vanished Supremacies: Essays on Europe and History, 1812–1918* (New York, Harper Torchbook, 1963), p. 113

24 R. J. W. Evans, *The Making of the Habsburg Monarchy, 1550–1700* (New York, Oxford University Press, 1979), p. 442

25 Walter Bagehot, *The English Constitution* (1867; Fontana edition with introduction by Richard Crossman, 1963), p. 110

26 Martyn Rady, *The Habsburgs: The Rise and Fall of a World Power* (London, Allen Lane, 2020), pp. 64, 72

27 Ibid., p. 94

28 Gonzalo Alvarez et al., 'The Role of Inbreeding in the Extinction of a European Royal Dynasty', *PLOS One*, 4 (4) (April 2009)

3. NEPOTISM, PATRONAGE, VENALITY

1 Adam Bellow, *In Praise of Nepotism: A Natural History* (New York, Doubleday, 2003), pp. 17, 191. This section relies heavily on this path-breaking book
2 Ibid., pp. 191, 196
3 Ibid., p. 52
4 Ibid., pp. 141–59
5 Adrian Wooldridge, 'To Have and to Hold: Special Report, Family Companies', *Economist*, 18 April 2015
6 Philip Mansel, *King of the World: The Life of Louis XIV* (London, Allen Lane, 2019), pp. 238–9
7 Ibid., pp. 241–50
8 Tolstoy, *War and Peace*, trans. and with an introduction by Rosemary Edmonds (London, Penguin, 1978), pp. 17–18
9 Lewis Namier, *England in the Age of the American Revolution* (London, Macmillan, 1930), p. 93
10 Richard Pares, *King George III and the Politicians* (Oxford, Clarendon Press, 1953), p. 14
11 Quoted in Harold Perkin, *The Origins of Modern English Society 1780–1880* (London, Routledge and Kegan Paul, 1969), p. 45
12 Adrian Tinniswood, *Behind the Throne: A Domestic History of the Royal Household* (London, Jonathan Cape, 2018), p. 151
13 Peter G. Richards, *Patronage in British Government* (London, George Allen & Unwin, 1963), p. 23
14 Duncan Campbell-Smith, *Masters of the Post: The Authorized History of the Royal Mail* (London, Allen Lane, 2011), p. 43
15 Quoted in Douglas W. Allen, *The Institutional Revolution: Measurement and the Economic Emergence of the Modern World* (Chicago and London, University of Chicago Press, 2012), p. 146
16 Ibid., p. 149
17 Diarmaid MacCulloch, *Thomas Cromwell: A Life* (London, Allen Lane, 2018), p. 168
18 Mansel, *King of the World*, pp. 241–50
19 Allen, *The Institutional Revolution*, p. 56
20 Ibid., pp. 1–2
21 Quoted in ibid., p. 173

22 Ibid., pp. 1–21

23 Blenheim Palace cost about $60 million in 2012's money.

24 Allen, *The Institutional Revolution*, pp. 146–71

25 Ibid., p. 14

26 Sir Robert Harry Inglis, *Reform: Substance of the Speech Delivered 1 March, 1831* (London, Hatchard and Son), p. 45

27 Roy Porter, *English Society in the Eighteenth Century* (London, Allen Lane, 1982), p. 128

4. PLATO AND THE PHILOSOPHER KINGS

1 Cf. A. N. Whitehead, *Process and Reality* (New York, Free Press, 1979), p. 39

2 Melissa Lane, *Plato's Progeny: How Plato and Socrates Still Captivate the Modern Mind* (London, Duckworth, 2001), p. 132

3 Plato, *Republic*, Bk 3, 415

4 Anthony Gottlieb, *The Dream of Reason: A History of Philosophy from the Greeks to the Renaissance* (New York, W. W. Norton and Company, 2000), p. 184

5 Ibid., p. 188

6 Plato, *Republic*, Bk 5, 465

7 Bagehot, 'What Would Plato Make of Boris Johnson?', *Economist*, 22 June 2019

8 Alan Ryan, *On Politics: A New History of Political Philosophy*, 2 Vols. (London, Allen Lane, 2012), p. 32

9 Aristotle, *Politics*, trans T. A. Sinclair (London, Penguin, 1962), p. 65

10 Simon Blackburn, *Plato's Republic: A Biography* (New York, Atlantic Books, 2006), p. 9. *The Republic* continues to sell well in the Penguin Classics edition

11 Aldous Huxley, *Brave New World and Brave New World Revisited* (HarperCollins, 2004), Chapter 2

12 J. S. Mill, *Dissertations and Discussions* (London, 1867), Vol. 2, p. 283

13 H. C. G. Matthew, 'Gladstone, William Ewart', *Dictionary of National Biography*, Vol. 22, p. 390, col. 2.

14 Andrew Hill, *Ruskinland: How John Ruskin Shapes Our World* (London, Pallas Athene, 2019), p. 155

15 Leslie Stephen, 'Jowett's Life', *Studies of a Biographer*, Vol. 2 (Cambridge, Cambridge University Press, 2012 edn), pp. 123–59

16 Lane, *Plato's Progeny*, p. 101

17 Peter Hinchliff and John Prest, 'Jowett, Benjamin', *Dictionary of National Biography*, Vol. 30, p. 760

18 Anthony Kearney, 'Hardy and Jowett: Fact and Fiction in *Jude the Obscure*', *Thomas Hardy Journal* 20 (3) (October 2004), pp. 118–23

19 Michael Howard, 'All Souls and "The Round Table"', in S. J. D. Green and Peregrine Horden (eds.), *All Souls and the Wider World: Statesmen, Scholars and Adventurers, c. 1850–1950* (Oxford, Oxford University Press, 2011), pp. 155–66

20 Geoffrey Kabaservice, *The Guardians: Kingman Brewster, His Circle, and the Rise of the Liberal Establishment* (New York, Henry Holt and Company, 2004), p. 33

5. CHINA AND THE EXAMINATION STATE

1 This story is told in Mary Laven, *Mission to China: Matteo Ricci and the Jesuit Encounter with the East* (London, Faber and Faber, 2011)

2 Ibid., p. 134

3 James Hankins, *Virtue Politics: Soulcraft and Statecraft in Renaissance Italy* (Cambridge, Mass., Belknap Press of Harvard University Press, 2019), p. 496

4 Ritchie Robertson, *The Enlightenment: The Pursuit of Happiness, 1680–1790* (London, Allen Lane, 2020), p. 621

5 William T. Rowe, *China's Last Empire: The Great Qing* (Cambridge, Mass., Belknap Press of Harvard University Press, 2009), p. 45

6 Laven, *Mission to China*, pp. 132–3

7 Rowe, *China's Last Empire*, p. 47

8 Hankins, *Virtue Politics*, pp. 498–9

9 Michael Schuman, *Confucius and the World He Created* (New York, Basic Books, 2015), p. xiv

10 Mark Edward Lewis, *China's Cosmopolitan Empire: The Tang Dynasty* (Cambridge, Mass., Belknap Press of Harvard University Press, 2009), pp. 202–3

11 Ibid., p. 204

12 Ibid., pp. 101–4

13 The ever-assiduous Têng Ssü-yu lists these in his 'Chinese Influence on the Western Examination System', *Harvard Journal of Asiatic Studies*, 7 (4) (Sept. 1943), pp. 308–12

14 Ibid., p. 279

15 Ibid., p. 281

16 Robertson, *The Enlightenment*, p. 624

17 Têng, 'Chinese Influence on the Western Examination System', p. 288

18 Ibid., p. 299

19 Robertson, *The Enlightenment*, p. 625

20 E. Backhouse and J. O. P. Bland, *Annals and Memoirs of the Court of Peking* (Boston, Houghton Mifflin, 1914), p. 322

6. THE CHOSEN PEOPLE

1 George Gilder, *The Israel Test* (New York, Richard Vigilante Books, 2009), p. 33

2 David Brooks, 'The Tel Aviv Cluster', *The New York Times*, 12 January 2010

3 Yuri Slezkine, *The Jewish Century* (Princeton, Princeton University Press, 2004), p. 225

4 Ibid., p. 52

5 Ibid., p. 53

6 Thorstein Veblen, 'The Intellectual Pre-eminence of Jews in Modern Europe', *Political Science Quarterly* 34 (1) (March 1919), p. 39

7 Hans Eysenck, *Know Your Own IQ* (London, Penguin, 1962) and *Check Your Own IQ* (London, Penguin, 1966); Nathan Glazer, *Affirmative Discrimination: Ethnic Inequality and Public Policy* (Cambridge, Mass., Harvard University Press, 1987)

8 Slezkine, *The Jewish Century*, p. 1

9 Paul Johnson, *A History of the Jews* (London, Weidenfeld Nicolson, 1987), p. 287

10 Ibid., p. 190

11 Norman Lebrecht, *Genius and Anxiety: How Jews Changed the World 1847–1947* (London, Oneworld, 2019), p. 186

12 Werner Sombart, *The Jews and Modern Capitalism* (London, T. Fisher Unwin, 1913), p. 261. First published in 1911 in German.

13 Johnson, *A History of the Jews*, p. 399

14 Bret Stephens, 'The Secrets of Jewish Genius', *The New York Times*, 27 December 2019

15 Quoted in Slezkine, *The Jewish Century*, p. 124

16 The classic statement of this position is Sombart, *The Jews and Modern Capitalism*

17 Lebrecht, *Genius and Anxiety*, p. 5

18 Marcus Arkin, *Aspects of Jewish Economic History* (Philadelphia, Jewish Publication Society of America, 1975). Cited in Jennifer Senior, 'Are Jews Smarter?', *New York*, 14 October 2005

19 Maristella Botticini and Zvi Eckstein, *The Chosen Few: How Education Shaped Jewish History, 70–1492* (Princeton, Princeton University Press, 2012)

20 Ibid., pp. 59–60

21 Ibid., p. 7

22 Johnson, *A History of the Jews*, pp. 340–431

23 Lebrecht, *Genius and Anxiety*, p. 3

24 R. Qamar et al., 'Y-Chromosomal DNA Variation in Pakistan', *American Journal of Human Genetics* 70 (5) (2002), pp. 1107–24

7. THE GOLDEN LADDER

1 The concept of sponsored social mobility was invented by Ralph Turner. See Ralph H. Turner, 'Modes of Social Ascent through Education: Sponsored and Contest Mobility', in Reinhard Bendix and Seymour Martin Lipset (eds.), *Class, Status, and Power: Social Stratification in Comparative Perspective* (New York, The Free Press, 1966), pp. 449–58

2 David Herlihy, 'Three Patterns of Social Mobility in Medieval History', *Journal of Interdisciplinary History* 3 (4) (Spring 1973), pp. 635–6

3 Tom Holland, *Dominion: The Making of the Western Mind* (London, Little, Brown, 2019), p. 123

4 Larry Siedentop, *Inventing the Individual: The Origins of Western Liberalism* (London, Allen Lane, 2014), esp. pp. 51–100

5 Herlihy, 'Three Patterns of Social Mobility', p. 624

6 Hilde de Ridder-Symoens, 'Rich Men, Poor Men: Social Stratification and Social Representation at the University (13th–16th Centuries)', in Wim Blockmans and Antheun Janse (eds.), *Showing Status: Representation of Social Positions in the Late Middle Ages* (Turnhout, Belgium, Brepols, 1999), pp. 162, 173

7 Francis Green and David Kynaston, *Engines of Privilege: Britain's Private School Problem* (London, Bloomsbury, 2019), p. 166

8 Daron Acemoglu and James Robinson, *Why Nations Fail* (New York, Crown, 2012), pp. 152–6; Chrystia Freeland, *Plutocrats: The Rise of the New Global Super-Rich and the Fall of Everyone Else* (London, Allen Lane, 2012), pp. 277–9

9 Robert Bartlett, *Blood Royal: Dynastic Politics in Medieval Europe* (Cambridge, Cambridge University Press, 2020), pp. 414–16

10 Ibid., pp. 416–19

11 James Hankins, *Virtue Politics: Soulcraft and Statecraft in Renaissance Italy* (Cambridge, Mass., Belknap Press of Harvard University Press, 2019), pp. 39–40

12 Ibid., p. 40

13 Isaiah Berlin, 'The Originality of Machiavelli', in Isaiah Berlin, *The Proper Study of Mankind: An Anthology of Essays* (New York, Farrar, Straus and Giroux, 1997), pp. 269–325

14 Philip Bobbitt, *The Garments of Court and Palace: Machiavelli and the World that He Made* (London, Atlantic Books, 2013), p. 77. Bobbitt's book is the clearest thing I've read on a notoriously opaque thinker

15 Ibid., pp. 81–2, 111–12

16 Machiavelli, *Discourses*, Book 3, Chapter 9. Quoted in ibid, p. 81

17 Bobbitt, *The Garments of Court and Palace*, pp. 123–4

18 Keith Thomas, *The Ends of Life: Roads to Fulfilment in Early Modern England* (Oxford, Oxford University Press, 2009), p. 46

19 Anthony Grafton and Lisa Jardine, *From Humanism to the Humanities: Education and the Liberal Arts in Fifteenth- and Sixteenth-Century Europe* (Cambridge, Mass., Harvard University Press, 1986), p. 141

20 See my essay on Erasmus, *Economist*, 19 December 2020

21 Jacques Barzun, *From Dawn to Decadence: 500 Years of Western Cultural Life, 1500 to the Present* (New York, HarperCollins, 2000), p. 21

22 Ibid., p. 42

23 Mary Laven, *Mission to China: Matteo Ricci and the Jesuit Encounter with the East* (London, Faber and Faber, 2011), pp. 135–6

8. EUROPE AND THE CAREER OPEN TO TALENT

1 Rafe Blaufarb, *The French Army 1750–1820: Careers, Talent, Merit* (Manchester and New York, Manchester University Press, 2002), p. 109

2 Darrin M. McMahon, *Divine Fury: A History of Genius* (New York, Basic Books, 2013), p. 109

3 William Doyle, *Aristocracy and Its Enemies in the Age of Revolution* (Oxford, Oxford University Press, 2009), p. 151

4 John Carson, *The Measure of Merit: Talents, Intelligence, and Inequality in the French and American Republics, 1750–1940* (Princeton and Oxford, Princeton University Press, 2007), pp. 18–19. The relevant Condillac text is *Treatise on Sensations* (1754)

5 Carson, *The Measure of Merit*, pp. 22–6

6 Helvétius, *Essays on the Mind*. Quoted in Carson, *The Measure of Merit*, p. 23

7 Carson, *The Measure of Merit*, pp. 24–5

8 Ibid., p. 25

9 Ibid., p. 24. The quotation is from John Adams's letter to Thomas Jefferson of 13 July 1813.

10 Ibid., pp. 28–9

11 Theodore Zeldin, *France 1848–1945: Volume 1: Ambition, Love and Politics* (Oxford, Oxford University Press, 1973), p. 428

12 McMahon, *Divine Fury*, p. 96

13 Ritchie Robertson, *The Enlightenment: The Pursuit of Happiness 1680–1790* (London, Allen Lane, 2020), pp. 486–9

14 Jay M. Smith, *The Culture of Merit: Nobility, Royal Service and the Making of Absolute Monarchy in France 1600–1789* (Ann Arbor, University of Michigan Press, 1996), p. 240

15 Albion W. Small, *The Cameralists: The Pioneers of German Social Polity* (Chicago: University of Chicago Press, 1909); Andre Wakefield, *The Disordered Police State: German Cameralism as Science and Practice* (Chicago: University of Chicago Press, 2009).

16 Anthony J. La Vopa, *Grace, Talent, and Merit: Poor Students, Clerical Careers, and Professional Ideology in Eighteenth-Century Germany* (Cambridge, Cambridge University Press, 1988), p. 172

17 Ritchie Robertson, *The Enlightenment*, pp. 667–8

18 S. E. Finer, *The History of Government from the Earliest Times: Volume III: Empires, Monarchies and the Modern State* (Oxford, Oxford University Press, 1999), p. 1431

19 Geoffrey Parker, *The Military Revolution: Military Innovation and the Rise of the West, 1500–1800* (Cambridge, Cambridge University Press, 1988).

20 Philip Mansell, *King of the World: The Life of Louis XIV* (London, Allen Lane, 2019), p. 275

21 Blaufarb, *The French Army*, p. 1

22 Smith, *The Culture of Merit*, p. 233

23 Roderick Cavaliero, *Genius, Power and Magic: A Cultural History of Germany from Goethe to Wagner* (London, I. B. Tauris, 2013), p. 30

24 Tim Blanning, *Frederick the Great: King of Prussia* (London, Allen Lane, 2015), p. 402

25 James J. Sheehan, *German History, 1770–1866* (Oxford, Clarendon Press, 1989), pp. 68–9

26 Blanning, *Frederick the Great*, pp. 267, 407

27 Hans Rosenbert, *Bureaucracy, Aristocracy and Autocracy: The Prussian Experience 1660–1815* (Cambridge, Mass., Harvard University Press 1958)

28 T. C. W. Blanning, *Joseph II* (London, Longman, 1994); Robert A. Kann, *A History of the Habsburg Empire, 1526–1918* (Berkeley, University of California Press, 1974), pp. 183–7; Saul K. Padover, *The Revolutionary Emperor: Joseph the Second* (New York, Robert O. Ballou, 1934). For parallel developments in Prussia, see Christopher Clark, *Iron Kingdom: The Rise and Downfall of Prussia, 1600–1947* (London, Allen Lane, 2006), pp. 312–44

29 Evgenii V. Anisimov, *The Reforms of Peter the Great: Progress through Coercion in Russia* (Armonk, NY, and London, M. E. Sharpe, 1993), pp. 188–90

30 Tibor Szamuely, *The Russian Tradition* (London, Fontana, 1989)

31 Samuel P. Huntington, *The Clash of Civilisations and the Remaking of the World Order* (New York, Simon and Schuster, 1996), p. 141

32 Jeroen Duindam, *Dynasties: A Global History of Power, 1300–1800* (Cambridge, Cambridge University Press, 2016), pp. 253–4

33 Isabel de Madariaga, *Russia in the Age of Catherine the Great* (London, Weidenfeld & Nicolson, 1981), p. 79. Quoted in Finer, *The History of Government*, Vol. III, p. 1419

34 Carson, *The Measure of Merit*, p. 79

35 Janet Polasky, *Revolutions without Borders: The Call to Liberty in the Atlantic World* (New Haven, Yale University Press, 2015), p. 44

36 Blaufarb, *The French Army*, p. 164

37 Ezra N. Suleiman, *Elites in French Society: The Politics of Survival* (Princeton, Princeton University Press, 1978), p. 19

38 Sheehan, *German History*, p. 429

39 Suleiman, *Elites in French Society*, p. 41

40 Theodore Zeldin, *France 1848–1945: Volume Two: Intellect, Taste and Anxiety* (Oxford, Clarendon Press, 1977), p. 151

41 Ibid., p. 150

42 Ibid., pp. 268–9

43 Carson, *The Measure of Merit*, p. 66

44 Zeldin, *France 1848–1945*, Vol. Two, p. 334

45 Ibid., p. 340

46 Ibid., p. 200

47 Ibid., pp. 269–71

48 Ibid., p. 310

49 Suleiman, *Elites in French Society*, p. 34

50 Zeldin, *France 1848–1945*, p. 339

51 Ibid., p. 271

52 Suleiman, *Elites in French Society*, p. 37

53 Alan Ryan, *On Politics: A New History of Political Philosophy*, 2 Vols. (London, Allen Lane, 2012), Vol. 2, pp. 647–51

54 S. J. D. Green, 'Émile Durkheim on Human Talents and Two Traditions of Social Justice', *British Journal of Sociology* 40 (1) (March 1989), pp. 97–117

55 Émile Durkheim, *The Division of Labour in Society* (London, Macmillan, 1933), pp. 375–7

56 Green, 'Émile Durkheim on Human Talents'

57 Carl von Clausewitz, *On War*, ed. and trans. Michael Howard and Peter Paret (Princeton, 1976), pp. 154–5

58 Sheehan, *German History*, p. 252

59 Ibid., p. 309

60 H. H. Gerth and C. Wright Mills, *From Max Weber: Essays in Sociology* (London, Routledge and Kegan Paul, 1970), pp. 240–42

61 La Vopa, *Grace, Talent, and Merit*, p. 172

62 Percy Bysshe Shelley, *A Defence of Poetry* (1821)

63 McMahon, *Divine Fury*, p. 115

64 Jacques Barzun, *From Dawn to Decadence: 500 Years of Western Cultural Life, 1500 to the Present* (New York, HarperCollins, 2000), p. 470

65 Ibid., p. 484

66 Friedrich Nietzsche, *The Twilight of the Idols*, Section 44

67 Eric Hobsbawm, *The Age of Revolution: 1789–1848* (London, Weidenfeld & Nicolson, 1962), p. 184

68 Ibid., p. 196

69 Thomas Mann, *Buddenbrooks* (Harmondsworth, Penguin Books, 1957), p. 107

9. BRITAIN AND THE INTELLECTUAL ARISTOCRACY

1 G. E. Aylmer, *The State's Servants: The Civil Service of the English Republic, 1649–1660* (London, Routledge and Kegan Paul, 1973), pp. 61–2

2 John Milton, 'The Ready and Easy Way to Establish a Free Commonwealth', in Stephen Orgel and Jonathan Goldberg (eds.), *John Milton: A Critical Edition of the Major Works* (Oxford, Oxford University Press, 1991), p. 336

3 Leslie Stephen, *The English Utilitarians, 3 Vols.* (London, Duckworth and Co., 1900), Vol. p. 59

4 Thomas Paine, *Common Sense* (first pub. 1776), p. 23

5 Thomas Paine, *Rights of Man* (first pub. 1791; ECCO-TCP: Eighteenth Century Collections Online, University of Oxford), p. 69

6 Paine, *Common Sense*, p. 23

7 Paine, *Rights of Man*, p. 71

8 Paine, *Common Sense*, p. 26

9 Paine, *Rights of Man*, p. 72

10 See Owen Jones, *The Establishment: And How They Get Away with It* (London, Allen Lane, 2014) for one attempt to do this

11 John Wade, *The Extraordinary Black Book* (1832 edn), pp. 212, 480

12 Quoted in Douglas W. Allen, *The Institutional Revolution: Measurement and the Economic Emergence of the Modern World* (Chicago and London, University of Chicago Press, 2012), p. 44

13 Jonathan Rose, *The Intellectual Life of the British Working Classes* (London, Yale University Press, 2001), pp. 16, 117

14 Adam Smith, *The Wealth of Nations*, 2 Vols. (first pub. 1776), Vol. 1 p. 270

15 Michael Sadler, *Essays on Examinations* (London, Macmillan, 1936) p. 53

16 Joseph F. Kett, *Merit: The History of a Founding Ideal from the American Revolution to the Twenty-First Century* (Ithaca, NY, Cornell University Press, 2013), pp. 84–5. Kett wrongly argues that William Gladstone was educated at Cambridge

17 Quoted in Simon Heffer, *High Minds: The Victorians and the Birth of Modern Britain* (London, Windmill Books, 2014), p. 471

18 Noel Annan, 'The Intellectual Aristocracy', in J. H. Plumb (ed.), *Studies in Social History: A Tribute to G. M. Trevelyan* (London, Longmans, Green, 1955), pp. 241–87. See also Noel Annan's *Leslie Stephen: His Thought and Character in Relation to His Time* (New York, McGraw Hill, 1955)

19 Zareer Masani, *Macaulay:. Britain's Liberal Imperialist* (London, The Bodley Head, 2013), pp. 1–18

20 Macaulay also has vigorous supporters in India. Zareer Masani dedicates *Macaulay: Britain's Liberal Imperialist* to 'my history teachers in Bombay who were proud to be Macaulay's children'

21 Keith Hope, 'The Political Conception of Merit' (unpublished MS in Nuffield College library), emphasizes Macaulay's role in the development of the meritocratic idea. See also Gillian Sutherland, *Ability, Merit and Measurement: Mental Testing and English Education 1880–1940* (Oxford, Clarendon Press, 1984), pp. 97–111

22 *Macaulay Report on the Indian Civil Service*, November 1854. As reprinted in Fulton Committee, *The Civil Service: Volume I: Report of the Committee, 1966–69* [Fulton Report] London, HMSO, 1968), Appendix B, p. 122

23 Thomas Babington Macaulay, '[Government of India] A Speech Delivered in the House of Commons on the 10th of July, 1833', in *The Works of Lord Macaulay*, 12 Vols.(London, Longmans, Green, 1898), Vol. XI, pp. 572–3

24 *Macaulay Report*, p. 123

25 Macaulay, '[Government of India]', p. 572

26 *Macaulay Report*, p. 127

27 '*The Northcote–Trevelyan Report on the Organisation of the Permanent Civil Service*, 23 November, 1853. As reprinted in the *Fulton Report*, Their picture of the existing system was, of course, exaggerated. Several departments had already instituted examinations and promotion by merit. See 'Competitive Examination and the Civil Service', *Quarterly Review* 133 (265) (1872), p. 243, and Edward Hughes, 'Civil Service Reform 1853–5', *History* 27 (June 1942), pp. 55–7

28 Northcote–Trevelyan Report, p. 109

29 Ibid., p. 111

30 Ibid., p. 112

31 Ibid., p. 114

32 'Sir Charles Trevelyan's Reply to Remarks by Capt. H. H. O'Brien, R.A., on Sir Stafford Northcote's and Sir Charles Trevelyan's Report upon the Reorganisation of the Civil Service'. As reprinted in Hughes, 'Sir Charles Trevelyan and Civil Service Reform 1853–5', *English Historical Review* 64 (January 1949), p. 72 col. b; Trevelyan to Delane (editor of *The Times*), ibid., p. 85; J. Donald Kingsley, *Representative Bureaucracy: An Interpretation of the British Civil Service* (Yellow Springs, Ohio, Antioch Press, 1944), p. 69

33 Cf. Trevelyan, *The Purchase System in the British Army* (2nd edn, 1867), pp. 2–3

34 Trevelyan's belief in prizes was so strong that, during the Irish Famine, he wanted to give prizes to the crews who caught the most fish or stayed out longest at night. Jenifer Hart, 'Sir Charles Trevelyan at the Treasury', *English Historical Review* 75 (January 1960), p. 101

35 Cf. Trevelyan's letter of 15 January. Quoted in Hart, 'Sir Charles Trevelyan at the Treasury', p. 99. However, Trevelyan was himself a nepotist, thinking that his own exertions justified the appointment of his relations and connections. See ibid., pp. 97–8

36 Trevelyan, 'Thoughts on Patronage', quoted in Hughes, 'Sir Charles Trevelyan and Civil Service Reform', p. 70

37 John Stuart Mill, 'Reform of the Civil Service' (1854), in *The Collected Works of John Stuart Mill: Volume 18: Essays on Politics and Society*,

Part I, ed. John M. Robson (Toronto, University of Toronto Press, 1977), p. 207. For the circumstances surrounding Mill's paper, see the Textual Introduction, p. lxxx

38 *Macaulay Report*, p. 120

39 Simon Green, 'Archbishop Frederick Temple on Meritocracy, Liberal Education and the Idea of a Clerisy', in Michael Bentley (ed.), *Public and Private Doctrine: Essays in British History Presented to Maurice Cowling* (Cambridge, Cambridge University Press, 1993), pp. 149–67

40 *Oxford University Commission, Report of Her Majesty's Commissioners Appointed to Inquire into the State, Discipline, Studies, and Revenues of the University and Colleges of Oxford* (London, HMSO, 1852), p. 149

41 Edwin Chadwick, *A Lecture on the Economical, Social, Educational and Political Importance of Open Competitive Examinations, for Admission to the Public Service* (London, Knight and Co., 1857), p. 31

42 *Oxford University Commission, Report* (1852), p. 150

43 Green, 'Archbishop Frederick Temple on Meritocracy', p. 156

44 *Oxford University Commission, Report* (1852), p. 152

45 *Cambridge University Commission, Report of Her Majesty's Commissioners Appointed to Inquire into the State, Discipline, Studies and Revenues of the University and Colleges of Cambridge* (London, HMSO, 1852), p. 156

46 Ibid., p. 202

47 Heffer, *High Minds*, p. 499

48 Ibid., p. 490

49 Anthony Trollope, *The Three Clerks* (London, R. Bentley, 1874), p. 126

50 Quoted in Hughes, 'Sir Charles Trevelyan and Civil Service Reform', p. 63

51 Edmund Fawcett, *Liberalism: The Life of an Idea* (Princeton, Princeton University Press, 2014), p. 83

52 Ibid., p. 73

53 James Grant, *Bagehot: The Life and Times of the Greatest Victorian* (New York, Norton, 2019), p. 231

54 David Marquand, *Britain since 1918: The Strange Career of British Democracy* (London, Weidenfeld & Nicolson, 2008), p. 29

55 Mathew Arnold, *Culture and Anarchy: An Essay in Political and Social Criticism* (New York, Macmillan and Company, 1883) p. 85

56 Karl Pearson, *National Life from the Standpoint of Science* (London, A. and C. Black, 1905), p. 54

57 Quoted in Bernard M. Allen, *Sir Robert Morant: A Great Public Servant* (London, Macmillan, 1934), p. 126

58 Report of the Schools Inquiry Commission (Taunton), *Parliamentary Papers 1867–8, Vol. 1*, General Report (London, HMSO, 1868), p. 27

59 Ibid., p. 92

60 Ibid., p. 96

61 Ibid., p. 95

62 Ibid., p. 595

63 Ibid., p. 158

64 *Report of the Royal Commission of Secondary Education* (Bryce), p. 167

65 Ibid., p. 171

66 Ibid., p. 221

67 Ibid., p. 224

68 Ibid., p. 305

69 *Report of the Departmental Committee on Scholarships, Free Places and Maintenance Allowances* (Hilton Young), Parliamentary Papers 1920, p. 19

70 Ibid., p. 25

71 Sheldon Rothblatt, *The Revolution of the Dons: Cambridge and Society in Victorian England* (New York, Basic Books, 1968), pp. 81–2

72 Ernest Barker, *Age and Youth: Memories of Three Universities and Father of the Man* (Oxford, Oxford University Press, 1953), p. 296

73 Willard Wolfe, *From Radicalism to Socialism: Men and Ideas in the Formation of Fabian Socialist Doctrines 1881–1889* (New Haven, Yale University Press, 1975), p. 9. For a latter-day assertion of this creed, see A. J. P. Taylor, 'The Thing', *The Twentieth Century* 162 (968) (October 1957), esp. p. 29

74 G. Bernard Shaw, 'The Transition to Social Democracy', in G. Bernard Shaw (ed.), *Fabian Essays in Socialism* (London, Fabian Society, 1889), p. 18

75 Norman and Jeanne MacKenzie (eds.), *The Diary of Beatrice Webb: Volume 1: 1873–1892* (London, Virago, 1982); Bertrand Russell, *Autobiography: Volume 1: 1872–1914* (London, Little, Brown and Company, 1967), p. 74

76 See, for example, Sidney and Beatrice Webb, *The Decay of Capitalist Civilisation* (London, Fabian Society and George Allen and Unwin, 1923), pp. 18, 20–21, 30–32, 184

77 S. Webb, 'Secondary Education', in E. J. T. Brennan (ed.), *Education for National Efficiency: The Contribution of Sidney and Beatrice Webb* (London, Athlone Press, 1975), p. 132

78 Ibid., p. 116

79 S. Webb, 'London University: Policy and Forecast', in Brennan (ed.), *Education for National Efficiency*, p. 160

80 Webb, 'London University', p. 142

81 Douglas Jay, *The Socialist Case* (London, Faber and Faber, 1947), p. 258

82 Rose, *The Intellectual Life of the British Working Classes*, p. 42

83 Ibid., p. 237

84 Ibid., p. 44

85 Bernard Donoghue and G. W. Jones, *Herbert Morrison: Portrait of a Politician* (London, Littlehampton Book Services, 1973)

86 Alan Bullock, *Ernest Bevin: Foreign Secretary 1945–51* (London, William Heinemann, 1960), p. 92

87 Rose, *The Intellectual Life of the British Working Classes*, p. 423

88 John Campbell, *Nye Bevan and the Mirage of British Socialism* (London, Weidenfeld & Nicolson, 1987), p. 303

89 Ibid., p. 68

10. THE UNITED STATES AND THE REPUBLIC OF MERIT

1 Myron Magnet, *The Founders at Home: The Building of America, 1735–1817* (New York, W. W. Norton, 2014), p. 17

2 Ibid., p. 193

3 Mark Twain, *The Adventures of Huckleberry Finn* (New York, Charles L. Webster, 1884), Chapter 23

4 Gordon S. Wood, *The American Revolution: A History* (New York, Modern Library, 2002), p. 9

5 Joseph I. Kett, *Merit: The History of a Founding Ideal from the American Revolution to the Twenty-First Century* (Ithaca, NY, Cornell University Press, 2013), p. 39

6 J. R. Pole, *The Pursuit of Equality in American History* (Berkeley and Los Angeles, University of California Press, 1978), p. 26

7 Ibid., p. 29

8 Both quoted in Adam Bellow, *In Praise of Nepotism: A Natural History* (New York, Doubleday, 2003), p. 267

9 Samuel P. Huntington, *Who are We? The Challenges to America's National Identity* (New York, Simon and Schuster, 2004), p. 63

10 Ibid., p. 64

11 Louis Hartz, *The Liberal Tradition in America: An Interpretation of American Political Thought since the Revolution* (New York, Harcourt Brace, 1955)

12 Jill Lepore, *These Truths: A History of the United States* (New York, W. W. Norton and Company, 2018), pp. 78–79

13 Kett, *Merit*, p. 15

14 Wood, *The American Revolution*, p. 100

15 Pole, *The Pursuit of Equality in American History*, p. 147

16 Kett, *Merit*, p. 19

17 Richard Hofstadter, *The American Political Tradition – and the Men Who Made It* (New York, 1948), p. 12

18 Adrienne Koch and William Peden (eds.), *The Life and Selected Writings of Thomas Jefferson* (New York, Random House, The Modern Library, 1944), p. 633

19 Ibid., p. 280

20 Ibid., pp. 729–80

21 Ibid., pp. 632–3; Thomas Jefferson, letter to John Adams, 28 October 1813

22 Koch and Peden (eds.), *Life and Selected Writings of Thomas Jefferson*, pp. 38–9

23 Thomas Jefferson, letter to John Adams, 28 October 1813

24 Quoted in William Egginton, *The Splintering of the American Mind: Identity Politics, Inequality and Community on Today's College Campuses* (New York, Bloomsbury, 2018), p. 186

25 Bellow, *In Praise of Nepotism*, p. 273

26 Ibid., p. 294

27 Pole, *The Pursuit of Equality in American History*, p. 47

28 Kett, *Merit*, p. 25

29 Pole, *The Pursuit of Equality in American History*, p. 47

30 From John Adams to John Taylor, 19 April 1814, National Archives: Founders Online, https://founders.archives.gov/documents/Adams/99-02-02-6282 (modernized)

31 From John Adams to Benjamin Rush, 25 October 1809, National Archives: Founders Online, https://founders.archives.gov/documents/Adams/99-02-02-5454 (modernized)

32 John Adams, *A Defence of the Constitutions of Government of the United States of America* (1787), Letter XXXI, archive.org/details/defenceofconsooadam/page/182/mode/2up

33 Ibid.

34 Adams, *A Defence of the Constitutions*, Letter XXV, pp. 116–17

35 John Adams, Letter to John Taylor, 5 March 1815

36 From John Adams to Benjamin Rush, 27 December 1810, National Archives: Founders Online, https://founders.archives.gov/documents/Adams/99-02-02-5585

37 Magnet, *The Founders at Home*, p. 272

38 The Federalist, No. 36 [8 January 1788] National Archives: Founders Online, https://founders.archives.gov/documents/Hamilton/01-04-02-0193

39 Magnet, *The Founders at Home*, p. 12

40 The Federalist No. 68 [12 March 1788], National Archives: Founders Online, https://founders.archives.gov/documents/Hamilton/01-04-02-0218

41 Alexander Hamilton's *Final Version of the Report on the Subject of Manufactures* [5 December 1791], https://founders.archives.gov/documents/Hamilton/01-10-02-0001-0007

42 George F. Will, *The Conservative Sensibility* (New York, Hachette Books, 2019), p. 234

43 Kett, *Merit*, p. 35

44 Ibid., pp. 35–6

45 Ibid., pp. 63–4

46 Bellow, *In Praise of Nepotism*, p. 337

47 Michael J. Sandel, *Democracy's Discontent: America in Search of a Public Philosophy* (Cambridge, Mass., Belknap Press of Harvard University Press, 1996), p. 156

48 Kett, *Merit*, p. 98

49 Andrew Jackson's Bank Veto, 10 July 1832, University of Virginia, Miller Center, Presidential Speeches, https://millercenter.org/the-presidency/presidential-speeches/july-10-1832-bank-veto

50 Walter Russell Mead, *Special Providence: American Foreign Policy and How It Changed the World* (New York, Alfred Knopf, 2001), p. 238

51 Pole, *The Pursuit of Equality in American History* (2nd rev.edn. 1993), p. 157

52 Kett, *Merit*, p. 95

53 Frederic Lincoln, 'An Address to the Massachusetts Charitable Mechanic Association' (2 October 1845), p. 20

54 Alexis de Tocqueville, *Democracy in America*, 2 Vols. (New York, Knopf, 1996), Vol. 2, p. 243

55 Ibid.

56 Ibid., p. 256

57 Sven Beckert, *Empire of Cotton: A New History of Global Capitalism* (London, Allen Lane, 2014); Alan Greenspan and Adrian Wooldridge, *Capitalism in America: A History* (New York, Penguin Press, 2018), pp. 73–9

58 Address before the Wisconsin State Agricultural Society, Milwaukee, Wisconsin, 30 September 1859, http://www.abrahamlincolnonline.org/lincoln/speeches/fair.htm

59 Lepore, *These Truths*, p. 701

60 Pole, *The Pursuit of Equality in American History*, p. 254

61 Walter Isaacson and Evan Thomas, *The Wise Men: Six Friends and the World They Made* (New York, Simon and Schuster, 1986), p. 40

62 Pole, *The Pursuit of Equality in American History*, p. 264

63 Jerome Karabel, *The Chosen: The Hidden History of Admission and Exclusion at Harvard, Yale and Princeton* (New York, Houghton Mifflin, 2005), p. 13

64 Bellow, *In Praise of Nepotism*, p. 320

65 Ibid., p. 323

66 Francis Fukuyama, *Political Order and Political Decay: From the French Revolution to the Present* (London, Profile Books, 2015), p. 144

67 Kett, *Merit*, pp. 117–18

68 Isaacson and Thomas, *The Wise Men*, p. 87

69 Kett, *Merit*, p. 174

70 W. E. B. DuBois, 'The Talented Tenth', in Booker T. Washington et al., *The Negro Problem: A Series of Articles by Representative American Negroes of Today* (New York, James Potter Co., 1903)

71 W. E. B. Du Bois, 'Strivings of the Negro People', *Atlantic*, August, 1897, https://www.theatlantic.com/magazine/archive/1897/08/strivings-of-the-negro-people/305446/

72 Fukuyama, *Political Order and Political Decay*, p. 156

73 Kett, *Merit*, p. 201

74 Ibid., p. 193

75 Fukuyama, *Political Order and Political Decay*, p. 152

76 Kett, *Merit*, p. 194; Will, *The Conservative Sensibility*, p. 41

77 Lepore, *These Truths*, p. 206

78 Kett, *Merit*, p. 196

79 Ibid.

80 Will, *The Conservative Sensibility*, p. 41

II. THE MEASUREMENT OF MERIT

1 John Carson, *The Measure of Merit: Talents, Intelligence, and Inequality in the French and American Republics, 1750–1940* (Princeton and Oxford, Princeton University Press, 2007), p. 241

2 Nicholas Lemann, *The Big Test: The Secret History of the American Meritocracy* (New York, Farrar, Straus and Giroux, 1999), p. 69. It is notable that Lippmann exempted Cyril Burt from his strictures on IQ testing.

3 Carson, *The Measure of Merit*, p. 249

4 Darrin M. McMahon, *Divine Fury: A History of Genius* (New York, Basic Books, 2013), p. 161

5 Ibid., p. 157

6 See Jennifer Michael Hecht, *The End of the Soul: Scientific Modernity, Atheism and Anthropology in France* (New York, Columbia University Press, 2003)

7 McMahon, *Divine Fury*, p. 158

8 Carson, *The Measure of Merit*, p. 103.

9 Stephen Jay Gould, *The Mismeasure of Man* (revised and expanded edition, New York, W. W. Norton & Company, 1996), pp. 124–7

10 Carson, *The Measure of Merit*, p. 132

11 A. Binet and T. Simon, *The Development of Intelligence in Children*, trans. E. S. Kite (Baltimore, Williams & Wilkins, 1916), and *A Method of Measuring the Development of the Intelligence of Young Children*, trans. C. H. Town (Lincoln, Ill., The Couries Company, 1912)

12 R. M. Yerkes, J. W. Bridges and R. S. Hardwick, *A Point Scale for Measuring Mental Ability* (Baltimore, Warwick & York, 1915); L. M. Terman, *The Measurement of Intelligence* (Boston, Houghton Mifflin, 1916); L. M. Terman, G. Lyman, G. Ordahl, L. E. Ordahl, N. Galbreath and W. Talbert, *The Stanford Revision and Extension of the Binet-Simon Scale for Measuring Intelligence* (Baltimore, Warwick & York, 1917); W. H. Winch, 'Binet's Mental Tests: What They are, and What We Can Do with Them', *Child-Study* 6–8 (1913–15); C. Burt, 'The Measurement of Intelligence by the Binet Tests', *Eugenics Review* 6 (1914), pp. 36–50, 140–52. For an annotated bibliography of the literature on the Binet–Simon scale before 1914, see S. C. Kohs, 'The Binet-Simon Measuring Scale for Intelligence', *Journal of Educational Psychology* 5 (1914), pp. 215–24, 279–90, 335–46

13 On Galton, see Karl Pearson, *The Life, Letters and Labours of Francis Galton*: Vol. 1 (Cambridge, Cambridge University Press, 1914), Vol. 2 (1924), Vols. 3A and 3B (1930); Francis Galton, *Memories of My Life* (London, Methuen, 1908); D. W. Forrest, *Francis Galton: The Life and Work of a Victorian Genius* (London, Paul Elek, 1974); and Daniel J. Kevles, *In the Name of Eugenics: Genetics and the Uses of Human Heredity* (New York, Alfred A. Knopf, 1985), pp. 3–19. A vivid

pen-portrait appears in Beatrice Webb, *My Apprenticeship* (London, Longmans, Green, 1926), pp. 134–5

14 Cyril Burt, 'Francis Galton and His Contributions to Psychology', *British Journal of Statistical Psychology* 15 (1) (1962), p. 14, n. 1

15 Francis Galton, *Hereditary Genius* (London, Macmillan, 1869), pp. 37–8

16 Ibid., p. 14

17 Ibid., p. 26

18 Ibid., p. 5

19 Francis Galton, 'Typical Laws of Heredity', *Proceedings of the Royal Institution* 8 (1877), pp. 282–301

20 See, for example, Francis Galton, 'The Anthropometric Laboratory', *Fortnightly Review*, new series, 31 (1882), pp. 332–8

21 Joanne Woiak, 'Karl Pearson', *Dictionary of National Biography*, Vol. 43, pp. 331–5

22 Hamish G. Spencer, 'Sir Ronald Aylmer Fisher', *Dictionary of National Biography*, Vol. 19, pp. 714–17

23 C. Spearman, "General Intelligence", Objectively Determined and Measured', *American Journal of Psychology* 15 (2) (1904), pp. 201–92

24 C. Spearman, *The Abilities of Man: Their Nature and Measurement* (London, Macmillan, 1927)

25 George Bernard Shaw, *Man and Superman* (Westminster, A. Constable, 1903), p. 219

26 Nicholas Griffin (ed.), *The Selected Letters of Bertrand Russell, Volume 1: The Private Years (1884–1914)* (Boston, Mass., Houghton Mifflin, 1992), pp. 126–8

27 Granville Eastwood, *Harold Laski* (Bristol, Mowbray, 1977), p. 4

28 'Sterilisation of Defectives', *New Statesman*, 25 July 1931, pp. 102–3

29 Carson, *The Measure of Merit*, p. 218

30 Clarence Yoakum and Robert Yerkes, *Army Mental Tests* (New York, Henry Holt, 1920), pp. 22–3

31 Joseph F. Kett, *Merit: The History of a Founding Ideal from the American Revolution to the Twenty-First Century* (Ithaca, NY, Cornell University Press, 2013), p. 129

32 Carson, *The Measure of Merit*, p. 256

33 Ibid., p. 229

34 Ibid., p. 255

35 Ronald Fletcher, *Science, Ideology and the Media: The Cyril Burt Scandal* (New Brunswick, Transaction, 1991) and Robert B. Joynson, *The Burt Affair* (London, Routledge, 1989). I have discussed the scandal in

some detail in *Measuring the Mind* (Cambridge, Cambridge University Press, 2010), pp. 340–58

36 Cyril Burt, 'Experimental Tests of General Intelligence', *British Journal of Psychology* 3 (1909), p. 176

37 Cyril Burt, 'Inheritance of General Intelligence', *American Psychology* 27 (1972), p. 188

38 Godfrey H. Thomson, 'A Hierarchy without a General Factor', *British Journal of Psychology* (8) (1916), pp. 271–81

39 Godfrey H. Thomson, *The Factorial Analysis of Human Ability,* (4th edn, London, University of London Press, 1950), p. 303

40 L. L. Thurstone, *Primary Mental Abilities* (Chicago, Chicago University Press, 1938). Cf. William Stephenson, 'Tetrad-differences for Non-Verbal Subtests', *Journal of Educational Psychology* 22 (1931), pp. 167–85; W. P. Alexander, 'Intelligence, Concrete and Abstract', *British Journal of Psychology Monograph Supplement* 19 (1935); A. A. H. El Koussy, 'The Visual Perception of Space', ibid., 20 (1935)

41 Francis Galton, 'The Possible Improvement of the Human Breed under Existing Conditions of Law and Sentiment', reprinted in Francis Galton, *Essays in Eugenics* (London, Eugenics Education Society 1909)

42 Ibid., pp. 3–17

43 R. A. Fisher, 'The Correlation between Relatives on the Supposition of Mendelian Inheritance', *Transactions of the Royal Society of Edinburgh* M. 52 (1918), pp. 399–433

44 'Autobiography of Lewis M. Terman', in Carl Murchison (ed.), *History of Psychology in Autobiography, Volume* 2 (Worcester, Mass., Clark University Press, 1930), pp. 297–331, https://psychclassics.yorku.ca/Terman/murchison.htm

45 Carson, *The Measure of Merit*, p. 188

46 Lewis M. Terman, 'The Intelligence Quotient of Francis Galton in Childhood', *American Journal of Psychology* 28 (1917), pp. 209–15

47 Lewis M. Terman (ed.), *Genetic Studies of Genius, Volume* 2 (Palo Alto, CA, Stanford University Press, 1925). The IQ estimates of the 301 geniuses are summarized in Table 12A, 'Individual IQ Ratings of Young Geniuses'.

48 Lewis M. Terman (ed.), *Genetic Studies of Genius, Volume* 1 (Palo Alto, CA, Stanford University Press, 1925), pp. 1–2

49 Jerome Karabel, *The Chosen: The Hidden History of Admission and Exclusion at Harvard, Yale and Princeton* (NY, Houghton Mifflin, 2005), p. 139

50 Ibid., p. 140

51 Ibid., p. 163
52 Ibid., pp. 166–99
53 Ibid., pp. 172–3
54 Ibid., p. 174
55 Ibid., p. 174
56 Lemann, *The Big Test*, p. 83
57 Gould, *The Mismeasure of Man*, esp. pp. 234–321
58 Liam Hudson's foreword to Leon Kamin, *The Science and Politics of IQ* (Hanondsworth, Perguin, 1977), p. ii
59 Lemann, *The Big Test*, p. 45
60 J. B. S. Haldane, 'The Inequality of Man' in his *The Inequality of Man and Other Essays* (London, Chatto and Windus, 1932), p. 12
61 J. B. S. Haldane, 'Biology and Statesmanship', in John R. Baker and J. B. S. Haldane, *Biology in Everyday Life* (London, George Allen and Unwin, 1933), p. 117
62 Haldane, 'The Inequality of Man', p. 22
63 McMahon, *Divine Fury*, pp. 201–2
64 Eustace Percy, *Some Memories* (London, Eyre and Spottiswood, 1958), p. 106
65 T. S. Eliot, *Notes towards the Definition of Culture* (1948; London, Faber and Faber, 1979), p. 101
66 Liam Hudson, *The Cult of the Fact* (London, Jonathan Cape, 1976), p. 47
67 Arno J. Mayer, *The Persistence of the Old Regime: Europe to the Great War* (London, Verso, 2010), p. 23
68 Ibid., p. 26
69 Ibid., p. 82
70 Andrew Carnegie, *Autobiography* (London, Constable, 1920), p. 301
71 George Orwell, *The Road to Wigan Pier* (London, Left Book Club Edition, Victor Gollancz, 1937), p. 153
72 Simon Heffer, *The Age of Decadence: Britain 1880 to 1914* (London, Random House, 2017), p. 95. In fact, Edward VII broke the Courtly would by becoming friends with quite a few Jews, such as Sir Ernest Cassell
73 Cyril Connolly, *Enemies of Promise and Other Essays* (New York, 1960), p. 221. See also Bertrand Russell, *Education and the Social Order* (London, George Allen & Unwin, 1932), p. 81
74 Sonia Orwell and Ian Angus (eds.), *The Collected Essays, Journalism and Letters of George Orwell, Volume 3: As I Please, 1943–1945* (London, Secker and Warburg, 1968), p. 6

75 Joseph A. Soares, *The Decline of Privilege: The Modernization of Oxford University* (Stanford, Stanford University Press, 1999), p. 32

76 Lemann, *The Big Test*, p. 143

77 Karabel, *The Chosen*, p. 322

78 Ibid., p. 115

79 Ibid., pp. 191–2

80 Ibid., p. 205

12. THE MERITOCRATIC REVOLUTION

1 See Angus Calder, *The People's War: Britain 1939–1945* (London, Pimlico, 1992), esp. pp. 351–7, 457–77, 545–6; Paul Addison, *The Road to 1945: British Politics and the Second World War* (London, Pimlico, 1994), esp. pp. 270–78

2 Addison, *The Road to 1945*, pp. 129–30

3 William Beveridge, *The Pillars of Security* (London, Allen and Unwin, 1943), p. 84

4 Francis Green and David Kynaston, *Engines of Privilege: Britain's Private School Problem* (London, Bloomsbury, 2019), p. 32

5 David Cannadine, *The Decline and Fall of the British Aristocracy* (New Haven, Yale University Press, 1990), p. 608

6 Ibid., p. 639

7 Trial by peers is featured in two films, *Clouds of Witness* (adapted for TV from the 1926 novel by Dorothy L. Sayers) and *Kind Hearts and Coronet* (1949)

8 Dean Blackburn, *Penguin Books and Political Change: Britain's Meritocratic Moment 1937–1988* (Manchester, Manchester University Press, 2020), p. 109

9 Ibid., p. 112

10 Peter Mandler, *The Crisis of the Meritocracy* (Oxford, Oxford University Press, 2020), p. 75

11 Ibid., PP. 156–7

12 Noel Annan, *Our Age: Portrait of a Generation* (London, Random House, 1991), p. 403

13 Blackburn, *Penguin Books and Political Change*, p. 118

14 Cannadine, *The Decline and Fall of the British Aristocracy*, p. 670

15 Eric James, *Education and Leadership* (London, Harrap, 1951), p. 38

16 Mandler, *The Crisis of the Meritocracy*, p. 56

17 Guy Ortolano., *The Two Cultures: Science, Literature and Cultural Politics in Postwar Britain* (Cambridge, Cambridge University Press, 2011), pp. 16–18

18 Green and Kynaston, *Engines of Privilege*, p. 84

19 Ibid., p. 88

20 Jerome Karabel, *The Chosen: The Hidden History of Admission and Exclusion at Harvard, Yale and Princeton* (New York, Houghton Mifflin, 2005), p. 195

21 Joseph F. Kett, *Merit: The History of a Founding Ideal from the American Revolution to the Twenty-first Century* (Ithaca, NY, Cornell University Press, 2019), p. 234

22 Karabel, *The Chosen*, p. 164

23 C. Wright Mills, *The Power Elite* (New York, Oxford University Press, 1956), p. 361

24 Ibid., p. 231

25 Karabel, *The Chosen*, p. 263

26 John W. Gardner, *Excellence: Can We be Equal and Excellent Too?* (New York, Harper and Bros., 1961), p. 115

27 Daniel Markovits, *The Meritocracy Trap: The Tyranny of Just Deserts* (New York, Penguin Press, 2019), p. 112

28 Ibid., p. 113

29 Tony Judt, *Postwar: A History of Europe since 1945* (London, William Heinemann, 2005), p. 290

30 Julian Jackson, *A Certain Idea of France: The Life of Charles de Gaulle* (London, Allen Lane, 2018), pp. 645–50

31 Ibid., p. 639

32 Ibid., p. 377

33 Ezra N. Suleiman, *Elites in French Society: The Politics of Survival* (Princeton, Princeton University Press, 1978), p. 41

34 Green and Kynaston, *Engines of Privilege*, pp. 85–6

35 Joseph A. Soares, *The Decline of Privilege: The Modernization of Oxford University* (Stanford, Stanford University Press, 1999), p. 9

36 Annan, *Our Age*, p. 9

37 William Waldegrave, *A Different Kind of Weather: A Memoir* (London, Constable, 2015), pp. 69–70. Waldegrave also notes that he needed his dinner jacket far more at Harvard than at Oxford

38 Harold Wilson, *Purpose in Politics* (London, Weidenfeld & Nicolson, 1964), p. 298

39 Quoted in Jonathan Rose, *The Intellectual Life of the British Working Classes* (London, Yale University Press, 2001), p. 89

40 Richard Hoggart, *The Uses of Literacy: Aspects of Working-Class Life with Special Reference to Publications and Entertainments* (1957; Harmondsworth, Pelican, 1959), p. 291. For his recollections of school and university, see his *A Local Habitation (Life and Times, Volume I: 1918–40)* (Oxford, Oxford University Press, 1989), pp. 156–220

41 Judt, *Postwar*, p. 391

42 Nicholas Lemann, *The Big Test: The Secret History of the American Meritocracy* (New York, Farrar, Strauss and Giroux , 1999), p. 139

43 Richard Hofstadter, *Anti-Intellectualism in American Life* (New York, Alfred Knopf, 1979), p. 256

44 William H. Whyte, *The Organisation Man* (1956; Harmondsworth, Penguin, 1960), pp. 190–201

45 Vance Packard, *The Pyramid Climbers* (1962; Harmondsworth, Penguin, 1965), p. 273

46 John A. Byrne, *The Whiz Kids: Ten Founding Fathers of American Business – and the Legacy They Left Us* (New York, Currency Doubleday, 1993)

47 See John Micklethwait and Adrian Wooldridge, *The Witch Doctors: Making Sense of the Management Gurus* (New York, Times Books, 1996), esp. pp. 3–23, 43–63 and 79–95

48 Schumpeter, 'Romney the Revolutionary', *Economist*, 14 January 2012

13. GIRLY SWOTS

1 Charles Moore, *Margaret Thatcher: The Authorized Biography: Volume One: Not for Turning* (London, Allen Lane, 2013), p. 134

2 Ibid., p. 136

3 Ibid., p. 22

4 Rachel Reeves, *Women of Westminster: The MPs Who Changed Politics* (London, I. B. Tauris, 2019), p. 4

5 Sir William Blackstone, *Commentaries on the Laws of England* (Oxford, Clarendon Press, 1766), p. 433

6 Jill Lepore, *These Truths: A History of the United States* (New York, W. W. Norton, 2018), p. 196

7 Deondra Rose, *Citizens by Degree: Higher Education Policy and the Changing Gender Dynamics of American Citizenship* (Oxford, Oxford University Press, 2018), pp. 27–8

8 Quoted in Stephen Jay Gould, 'Women's Brains', https://faculty.washington.edu/lynnhank/wbgould.pdf

9 G. R. Searle, *A New England? Peace and War, 1886–1918* (Oxford, Clarendon Press, 2004), p. 79

10 J. R. Pole, *The Pursuit of Equality in American History* (2nd revised and expanded edn, Berkeley, University of California Press, 1993), p. 386

11 Ibid., p. 387

12 Ibid., p. 381

13 Ibid., p. 391

14 J. S. Mill, *The Subjection of Women* (University of Oxford Text Archive), p. 104

15 Ibid., p. 27

16 Ibid., p. 101

17 Quoted and discussed in Phyllis Rose, *Parallel Lives: Five Victorian Marriages* (London, Daunt Books, 2020), p. 106

18 Mill, *The Subjection of Women*, p. 103

19 Ibid., p. 119

20 Lepore, *These Truths*, p. 339; Jill Lepore, *The Secret History of Wonder Woman* (New York: Knopf, 2014), *passim*

21 Richard White, *The Republic for Which It Stands: The United States during Reconstruction and the Gilded Age, 1865–1896* (Oxford, Oxford University Press, 2017), p. 553

22 Ada Wallas, *Before the Bluestockings* (London, George Allen and Unwin, 1929). The publishers remind us, in brackets on the title page, that Ada Wallas is Mrs Graham Wallas

23 Gillian Sutherland, *Faith, Duty and the Power of Mind: The Cloughs and Their Circle 1820–1960* (Cambridge, Cambridge University Press, 2006), pp. 107, 123

24 Duncan Campbell-Smith, *Masters of the Post: The Authorized History of the Royal Mail* (London, Allen Lane, 2011), p. 187

25 Sutherland, *Faith, Duty and the Power of Mind*, p. 125

26 Jenifer Glynn, *The Pioneering Garretts: Breaking the Barriers for Women* (London, Hambledon Continuum, 2008), p. 181

27 https://victorianpersistence.files.wordpress.com/2013/03/a-room-of-ones-own-virginia-woolf-1929.pdf

28 Sheila Rowbotham, *Dreamers of a New Day: Women Who Invented the Twentieth Century* (London, Verso, 2010), p. 2

29 Gillian Sutherland, *In Search of the New Woman: Middle-Class Women and Work in Britain, 1870–1914* (Cambridge, Cambridge University Press, 2015), pp. 4–5

30 Ibid., pp. 100–101

31 Michael Coolican, *No Tradesmen and No Women: The Origins of the British Civil Service* (London, Biteback Publishing, 2018), pp. 136–7

32 Campbell-Smith, *Masters of the Post*, p. 241

33 Richard Holmes was a prominent advocate of this view.

34 Jerome Karabel, *The Chosen: The Hidden History of Admission and Exclusion at Harvard, Yale and Princeton* (New York, Houghton Mifflin, 2005), p. 444

35 Ibid., p. 411

36 Ibid., p. 428

37 Carol Dyhouse, *Students: A Gendered History* (London, Routledge, 2006), p. 130

14. AGAINST MERITOCRACY: THE REVOLT ON THE LEFT

1 Daniel J. Kevles, *In the Name of Eugenics* (New York, Alfred A. Knopf, 1985), p. 164; R. A. Soloway, *Demography and Degeneration: Eugenics and the Declining Birthrate in Twentieth-Century Britain* (Chapel Hill, University of North Carolina Press, 1990), pp. 195–203

2 Lancelot Hogben, 'Introduction to Part I. Prolegomena to Political Arithmetic', in Lancelot Hogben (ed.), *Political Arithmetic: A Symposium of Population Studies* (London, Allen and Unwin, 1938), pp. 13–46

3 Lancelot Hogben, 'The Limits of Applicability of Correlation Technique in Human Genetics', *Journal of Genetics* 27 (1933), p. 393

4 Richard Titmuss, *Poverty and Population: A Factual Study of Contemporary Social Waste* (London, Macmillan and Co., 1938), pp. 40–42

5 L. S. Penrose, *Heredity and Environment in Human Affairs* (Convocation Lecture of the National Children's Home) (London: National Children's Home, 1955), p. 18. Penrose's son, Roger, shared the 2020 Nobel Prize in physics (the other half was jointly won by Reinhard Gerzel and Andrea Ghez).

6 L. S. Penrose, *The Biology of Mental Defect* (London, Sidgwick and Jackson, 1949)

7 Ibid., p. 240

8 Brian Simon, *Intelligence, Psychology and Education: A Marxist Critique* (London, Lawrence and Wishart, 1971), p. 132

9 Ibid., p. 237

10 A. H. Halsey, 'Provincials and Professionals: The British Post-War Sociologists', *European Journal of Sociology* 23 (1982), pp. 150–75

11 J. W. B. Douglas, *The Home and the School* (1984, London, Panther, 1972), pp. 89–97

12 Franz Boas, *The Mind of Primitive Man* (New York, Macmillan, 1911), *passim*

13 Otto Klineberg, 'An Experimental Study of Speed and Other Factors in "Racial" Differences', *Archives of Psychology* 93 (1928); Otto Klineberg, *Negro Intelligence and Selective Migration* (New York, Columbia University Press, 1935)

14 C. Brigham, 'Intelligence Tests of Immigrant Groups', *Psychological Review* 37 (1930), pp. 158–65

15 Margaret Mead, *Sex and Temperament in Three Primitive Societies* (New York, William Morrow and Company, 1935), p. 280

16 The classic analysis of this difference is Ralph H. Turner, 'Modes of Social Ascent through Education: Sponsored and Contest Mobility', in Reinhard Bendix and Seymour Martin Lipset (eds.), *Class, Status, and Power: Social Stratification in Comparative Perspective* (New York, Free Press, 1966), pp. 449–58

17 J. E. Floud, 'Social Class Factors in Educational Achievement', in A. H. Halsey (ed.), *Ability and Educational Opportunity* (Paris: OECD, 1961), p. 93

18 John Carson, *The Measure of Merit: Talents, Intelligence, and Inequality in the French and American Republics, 1750–1940* (Princeton and Oxford, Princeton University Press, 2007), pp. 261–2

19 Michael Young, *The Rise of the Meritocracy, 1870–2033: An Essay on Education and Equality* (1958; London, Thames and Hudson, 1961)

20 This was not the first science fiction to satirize scientifically selected mandarins. See also Gerald Heard, *Doppelgangers* (1947), C. H. Sission, *An Asiatic Romance* (1953) and David Karp, *One* (1953)

21 Claire Donovan, 'The Chequered Career of a Cryptic Concept', in Geoff Dench (ed.), *The Rise and Rise of Meritocracy* (Oxford, Blackwell Publishing, 2006), p. 62

22 Paul Barker, 'A Tract for the Times', in ibid., p. 37

23 Ibid., pp. 36–44

24 R. H. S. Crossman, 'Towards a Philosophy of Socialism', in R. H. S. Crossman (ed.), *New Fabian Essays* (London, Turnstile Press, 1952), pp. 28–9. See also G. D. H. Cole, *Fabian Socialism* (London, Allen and Unwin, 1943), p. v

25 W. T. Rodgers, *About Equality* (London, Fabian Society, 1954), p. 1

26 C. A. R. Crosland, 'The Transition from Capitalism', in Crossman (ed.), *New Fabian Essays*, p. 65

27 Margaret Cole, 'Education and Social Democracy', in ibid., p. 109

28 Roy Jenkins, 'Equality', in ibid., pp. 85–6

29 Anthony Crosland, *The Conservative Enemy* (London, Cape, 1962), pp. 173–4

30 David Halberstam, *The Best and the Brightest* (New York, Random House, 1972), pp. 41, 44

31 John Rawls, *A Theory of Justice* (Cambridge, Mass., Harvard University Press, 1971), p. 15

32 Michael Young, 'Down with Meritocracy', *Guardian*, 29 June 2001

33 Marc Tracy, 'Steve Bannon's Book Club', *The New York Times*, 4 February 2017

34 Michael Anthony Lawrence, 'Justice-as-Fairness as Judicial Guiding Principle: Remembering John Rawls and the Warren Court', *Brooklyn Law Review* 82 (2) (2016), https://brooklynworks.brooklaw.edu/blr/vol81/iss2/5/, argues that the Warren Court adopted many of Rawls's basic principles *before* he wrote his book.

35 Peter L. Berger and Thomas Luckman, *The Social Construction of Reality. A Treatise in the Sociology of Knowledge* (Garden City, NY, Anchor Books, 1966). Berger bitterly regretted writing this book in his later years.

36 Basil Bernstein, 'A Socio-Linguistic Approach to Socialization: With Some Reference to Educability', in his *Class, Codes and Control, Volume I: Theoretical Studies towards a Sociology of Language* (London, Routledge and Kegan Paul, 1971), p. 151

37 Pierre Bourdieu and Jean-Claude Passeron, *Reproduction in Education, Society and Culture* (London, SAGE Publications, 1990)

38 For a convenient summary of this evidence, see Julian Le Grand, *The Strategy of Equality: Redistribution and the Social Services* (London, Routledge, 1982)

39 Edmund Burke, *Reflections on the Revolution in France and Other Writings*, edited and introduced by Jesse Norman (New York, Everyman Library, 2015), p. 490

40 William Morris, *News from Nowhere or An Epoch at Rest. Being Some Chapters from a Utopian Romance* (London, Reeves & Turner, 1891), p. 99

41 Arthur J. Penty, *Towards a Christian Sociology* (1923), p. 183

42 R. H. Tawney, 'British Socialism Today', *Socialist Commentary*, June 1952. Reprinted in R. H. Tawney, *The Radical Tradition* (Harmondsworth, Pelican, 1966), p. 176

43 Michael Young and Peter Willmott, 'Institute of Community Studies, Bethnal Green', *Sociological Review* 9 (2) (1961), pp. 203–13; and Peter Willmott, 'The Institute of Community Studies', in Martin Bulmer (ed.), *Essays on the History of British Sociological Research* (Cambridge, Cambridge University Press, 1985), pp. 137–50

44 Michael Young and Peter Willmott, *Family and Kinship in East London* (London, Routledge and Kegan Paul, 1957)

45 David Kynaston, *Modernity Britain: A Shake of the Dice, 1959–62* (London, Bloomsbury, 2014), p. 5

46 C. Wright Mills, *White Collar: The American Middle Classes* (New York, Oxford University Press, 1951), p. xvi

47 https://ushistoryscene.com/article/free-speech-movement/

48 http://www2.iath.virginia.edu/sixties/HTML_docs/Resources/Primary/Manifestos/SDS_Port_Huron.html; Sam Roberts, 'The Port Huron Statement at Fifty', *The New York Times*, 3 March 2012

49 Jill Lepore, *These Truths: A History of the United States* (New York, W. W. Norton & Company, 2018), p. 652

50 Quoted in William Egginton, *The Splintering of the American Mind* (New York, Bloomsbury, 2018), p. 26

51 Paul Goodman, 'The Politics of being Queer', in Taylor Stoehr (ed.), *Nature Heals: The Psychological Essays of Paul Goodman* (New York: Free Life Editions, 1977), p. 216

52 Catharine A. MacKinnon, 'Whose Culture?', in *Feminism Unmodified: Discourses on Life and Law* (Cambridge, Mass., Harvard University Press, 1987), p. 65. Quoted in David Frum, *How We Got Here: The 1970s: The Decade that Brought You Modern Life – for Better or Worse* (New York, Basic Books, 2000), p. 274

53 Anthony Crosland, *The Future of Socialism* (London, Jonathan Cape, 1956), p. 272

54 Susan Crosland, *Tony Crosland* (London, Coronet Books, 1983), p. 148

55 A. H. Halsey, Obituary, *Daily Telegraph*, 17 October 2014

56 Brian Jackson, *Streaming: An Educational System in Miniature* (London, Routledge and Kegan Paul, 1964), pp. 20–21

57 Crosland, *The Future of Socialism*, p. 261

58 Philip M. Williams, *Hugh Gaitskell: A Political Biography* (London, Jonathan Cape, 1979), p. 783

59 Crosland, *Conservative Enemy*, p. 181

60 Marion Mills Miller (ed.), *Great Debates in American History, Volume VI* (New York, Current Literature Publishing Company, 1913), p. 13

61 Frum, *How We Got Here*, p. 259
62 Ibid., p. 262

15. THE CORRUPTION OF THE MERITOCRACY

1 Michael Hicks, *Bastard Feudalism* (London, Longman, 1995)
2 Darrell M. West, *Billionaires: Reflections on the Upper Crust* (Washington, DC, Brookings Institution Press, 2014), p. 126
3 Peter Thiel, with Blake Masters, *Zero to One: Notes on Startups, or How to Build the Future* (London, Virgin Books, 2014)
4 Julia Carrie Wong and Matthew Cantor, 'How to Speak Silicon Valley: 53 Essential Tech-Bro Terms Explained', *Guardian*, 27 June 2019
5 Daniel Markovits, *The Meritocracy Trap: The Tyranny of Just Deserts* (New York, Penguin Press, 2019), p. 114
6 Emma Duncan, 'Special Report: Private Education', *Economist*, 13 April 2019, p. 3
7 The Sutton Trust, 'Elitist Britain 2019: The Educational Backgrounds of Britain's Leading People', p. 5
8 Ibid., p. 12
9 Francis Green and David Kynaston, *Engines of Privilege: Britain's Private School Problem* (London, Bloomsbury, 2019), p. 96
10 'America's New Aristocracy', *Economist*, 22 January 2015; 'How the Internet Has Changed Dating', *Economist*, 18 August 2018
11 Jeremy Greenwood et al., 'Marry Your Like: Assortative Mating and Income Inequality' (NBER Working Paper No. 1989)
12 A. Lareau, *Unequal Childhoods* (Berkeley, University of California Press, 2003)
13 Betty Hart and Todd R. Risley, 'The Early Catastrophe: The 30 Million Word Gap by Age 3', *American Educator* 1 (1) (spring 2003), pp. 4–9
14 Markovits, *The Meritocracy Trap*, p. 122
15 'America's New Aristocracy'
16 Amy Chua, 'Why Chinese Mothers are Superior', *Wall Street Journal*, 8 January 2011
17 Jennifer Medina, Katie Benner and Kate Taylor, 'Actresses, Business Leaders and Other Wealthy Parents Charged in US College Entry Fraud', *The New York Times*, 12 March 2019
18 Luis Ferré-Sadurní, 'Donald Trump May Have Donated over $1.4 million to Penn', *Daily Pennsylvanian*, 3 November 2016

19 Daniel Golden, *The Price of Admission: How America's Ruling Class Buys Its Way into Elite Colleges – and Who Gets Left Outside the Gates* (New York, Three Rivers Press, 2007)

20 Anthony Abraham Jack, *The Privileged Poor: How Elite Colleges are Failing Disadvantaged Students* (Cambridge, Mass., Harvard University Press, 2019), *passim*

21 Ibid., p. 149

22 Ibid., p. 151

23 Jacques Steinberg, *The Gatekeepers: Inside the Admissions Process of a Premier College* (New York, Viking, 2002), pp. 124–36, 219–20

24 Lauren A. Rivera, *Pedigree: How Elite Students Get Elite Jobs* (Princeton, Princeton University Press, 2015)

25 Ibid., p. 94

26 Adrian Wooldridge, 'Special Report: The Rise of the Superstars', *Economist*, 15 September 2016

27 Ibid., subsection on 'the dark arts'.

28 Ralph H. Turner, 'Modes of Social Ascent through Education', in Reinhard Bendix and Seymour Martin Lipset (eds.), *Class, Status, and Power*, pp. 449–59

29 Isabel V. Sawhill, *Generation Unbound: Drifting into Sex and Parenthood without Marriage* (Washington, DC, Brookings Institution Press, 2014)

30 These numbers are all taken from ibid. See also Isabel V. Sawhill, 'Beyond Marriage', *The New York Times*, 13 September 2014

31 Anne Case and Angus Deaton, *Deaths of Despair and the Future of Capitalism* (Princeton, Princeton University Press, 2020)

32 'Race in America: Staying Apart', *Economist*, 11 July 2020, pp. 14–16

33 J. D. Vance, *Hillbilly Elegy: A Memoir of a Family and Culture in Crisis* (New York, Harper, 2016), p. 81

34 Ibid., p. 89

35 Ibid., p. 127

36 Ibid., p. 95

37 David Goodhart, *The Road to Somewhere: The New Tribes Shaping British Politics* (London, Penguin, 2017), p. 202; Office of National Statistics Estimated number of Parents in Families with Dependent Children by Ethnic Group of the Parent, UK, 2016', 12 October 2017

38 Darren McGarvey, *Poverty Safari: Understanding the Anger of Britain's Underclass* (Edinburgh, Luath Press, 2017), p. 155

39 Ibid., p. 62

40 Ibid., p. 154

16. AGAINST MERITOCRACY:
THE REVOLT ON THE RIGHT

1 Hillary Rodham Clinton, *What Happened* (New York, Simon & Schuster, 2017)
2 Geoffrey Evans and Anand Menon, *Brexit and British Politics* (Cambridge, Polity Press, 2017), p. 84
3 Ibid., pp. 81–2
4 Daniel Markovits, *The Meritocracy Trap: The Tyranny of Just Deserts* (New York, Penguin Press, 2019), p. xvii
5 Ibid., p. 67
6 Bagehot, 'The Shadow of Enoch Powell Looms Ever-Larger over Britain', *Economist*, 6 April 2017
7 I have told this story in John Micklethwait and Adrian Wooldridge, *The Right Nation: Conservative Power in America* (New York, Penguin Press, 1994), pp. 27–131
8 Richard Rorty, *Achieving Our Country* (Cambridge, Mass., Harvard University Press, 1998). The *New York Times* reviewer, Christopher Lehmann-Haupt, decided to take issue with precisely this passage
9 Evans and Menon, *Brexit and British Politics*, p. 15
10 Adrian Wooldridge, *Masters of Management: How the Business Gurus and Their Ideas Have Changed the World – for Better and for Worse* (New York, HarperCollins, 2011), pp. 10–11
11 Simon Goodley, 'Goldman Sachs "Muppet" Trader Says Unsophisticated Clients Targeted', *Guardian*, 22 October 2012
12 David Marquand, *Britain since 1918: The Strange Career of British Democracy* (London, Weidenfeld & Nicolson, 2008), p. 39
13 Mark Bovens and Anchrit Wille, *Diploma Democracy: The Rise of Political Meritocracy* (Oxford, Oxford University Press, 2017)
14 Ibid., p. 3
15 Ibid., p. 6
16 Roger Eatwell and Matthew Goodwin, *National Populism: The Revolt against Liberal Democracy* (London, Pelican, 2018), p. 31
17 Markovits, *The Meritocracy Trap*, p. xi
18 Ibid., p. 8. Mr Markovits agrees with the dean. 'An elite degree therefore represents relentlessly demanding, ambitious and successful training. And no prior elite has ever been as capable or as industrious as the meritocratic elite that such training produces. None comes close.'
19 Tony Cross, 'Is the French Government Too Intelligent', Radio France Internationale, 20 December 2018

20 Janan Ganesh, 'Europe Could See More Catalonias', *Financial Times*, 23 October 2017

21 Nick Cohen, 'Vote Leave Campaign Poisonous', *Observer*, 19 June 2016

22 Matthew Parris, 'Tories Should Turn Their Backs on Clacton', *The Times*, 6 September 2014

23 Michael Lind, *The New Class War: Saving Democracy from the Managerial Elite* (New York, Portfolio, 2020), p. 21; Drew DeSilver, 'Immigrants Don't Make up a Majority of Workers in Any US Industry', Pew Research Center, 16 March 2017

24 https://www.nytimes.com/interactive/2020/11/03/us/elections/exit-polls-president.html. For a vintage expression of liberal outrage see Charles M. Blow, 'Exit Polls Point to the Power of White Patriarchy', *The New York Times*, 4 November 2020. For an intriguing exploration of what might be going on, see Michael Lind, 'Race, Class and the Two Melting Pots', *Tablet*, 4 November 2020

25 Andrew Sullivan, 'We All Live on Campus Now', *New York*, 9 February 2018

17. ASIA REDISCOVERS MERITOCRACY

1 Jody-Lan Castle, 'Top 10 Exam Rituals from Stressed Students across Asia', BBC News, 3 March 2016

2 Graham Allison and Robert D. Blackwill, with Ali Wyne, *Lee Kuan Yew: The Grand Master's Insights on China, the United States and the World* (Cambridge, Mass., MIT Press, 2013), p. 32

3 Michael Schuman, Confucius and the World He Created (New York, Basic Books, 2015), pp. 184–5

4 Lucy Grehan, *Cleverlands: The Secrets behind the Success of the World's Education Superpowers* (London, Unbound, 2016), p. 136

5 Maggie Fergusson, 'The Curse of Genius', *1843*, June/July 2019

6 Daniel A. Bell, *The China Model: Political Meritocracy and the Limits of Democracy* (Princeton, Princeton University Press, 2015), p. 126

7 Grehan, *Cleverlands*, p. 128

8 See, for example, Jung Chang and Jon Halliday, *Mao: The Untold Story* (London, Jonathan Cape, 2005), pp. 534–40, 566

9 Evan Osnos, *Age of Ambition: Chasing Fortune, Truth and Faith in the New China* (London, The Bodley Head, 2014), p. 39

10 Ibid., p. 39

11 Ibid., p. 66

12 Grehan, *Cleverlands*, p. 164

13 'The Class Ceiling', *Economist*, 2 June 2016

14 Osnos, *Age of Ambition*, p. 65

15 Tom Doctoroff, *What Chinese Want: Culture, Communism and China's Modern Consumer* (New York, Palgrave Macmillan, 2012), pp. 105, 127

16 Osnos, *Age of Ambition*, p. 39

17 'Losing Focus', *Economist*, 11 November 2014

18 Nicolas Berggruen and Nathan Gardels, *Intelligent Governance for the 21st Century: A Middle Way between West and East* (Cambridge, Polity Press, 2013), p. 45

19 Ann Lee, *What the US Can Learn from China: An Open-Minded Guide to Treating Our Greatest Competitor as Our Greatest Teacher* (San Francisco: Berrett-Koehler Publishers, 2012), p. 62

20 Daniel A. Bell, 'Political Meritocracy is a Good Thing: The Case of China', *HuffPost*, 21 October 2012

21 Richard McGregor, *The Party: The Secret World of China's Communist Rulers* (New York, HarperCollins, 2010), p. 31

22 Daniel A. Bell, *The China Model* (Princeton, Princeton University Press, 2015), p. 138. But see also Andrew J. Nathan, 'Beijing Bull: The Bogus China Model', *National Interest*, 22 October 2015

23 Zhang Weiwei, 'Meritocracy versus Democracy', *The New York Times*, 9 November 2012

24 'Embarrassed Meritocrats', *Economist*, 27 October 2012

25 Berggruen and Gardels, *Intelligent Government for the 21st Century*, p. 9

26 Mumtaz Alvi, 'It's a System Based on Meritocracy: Imran Fancies Chinese Model', *News International*, 1 November 2020

27 'The Class Ceiling'

28 Branko Milanović, *Capitalism, Alone: The Future of the System that Rules the World* (Cambridge, Mass., Belknap Press of Harvard University Press, 2019), pp. 108–9

29 Osnos, *Age of Ambition*, p. 258

30 Rosie Blau, 'The New Class War: Special Report, Chinese Society', Economist, 9 July 2016

31 Timothy Beardson, *Stumbling Giant: The Threats to China's Future* (New Haven, Yale University Press, 2013), p. 157

32 Osnos, *The Age of Ambition*, p. 252

33 Chen Liang and James Lee, 'Silent Revolution: The Social Origins of Peking University and Sochow University Undergraduates, 1952–2002'; I was sent a slide show based on this paper, which appeared in Chinese.

34 Ora-orn Poocharoen and Alex Brillantes, 'Meritocracy in Asia Pacific: Status, Issues and Challenges', *Review of Public Personnel Administration*, 33 (2) (2013) pp. 140–63

35 Ibid., p. 150

36 Ross Arbes, 'How the Talmud became a Best-Seller in South Korea', *New Yorker*, 23 June 2015

37 Grehan, *Cleverlands*, pp. 265–6

38 Ibid., p. 15

CONCLUSION

1 John Gerring, Philip Bond, William T. Barndt and Carola Moreno, 'Democracy and Economic Growth: A Historical Perspective', *World Politics* 57 (3) (2005), pp. 323–64; James Kanagasooriam, 'A Brave New World?' 15April2020,https://medium.com/@jameskanagasooriam/a-brave-new-world-563c05e34f3d

2 Adrian Wooldridge, 'Northern Lights: Special Report, The Nordic Countries', *Economist*, 31 January 2013

3 OECD, 'A Family Affair: Intergenerational Social Mobility across OECD Countries', https://www.oecd.org/economy/public-finance/chapter%205%20gfg%202010.pdf

4 Nicholas Bloom and John Van Reenen, 'Measuring and Explaining Management Practices across Firms and Countries', *Quarterly Journal of Economics* 122 (4) (2007), pp. 1351–408; Nicholas Bloom, Raffaella Sadun and John Van Reneen, 'The Organization of Firms across Countries', *Quarterly Journal of Economics* 127 (4) (2012), pp. 1663–705; Schumpeter, 'Measuring Management', *Economist*, 18 January 2014

5 Chang-Tai Hsieh et al., 'The Allocation of Talent and US Economic Growth', *Econometrica* 87 (5) (September 2019), pp. 1439–474

6 Bruno Pellegrino and Luigi Zingales, 'Diagnosing the Italian Disease', https://faculty.chicagobooth.edu/-/media/faculty/luigi-zingales/research/pellegrinozingalesdiagnosingtheitaliandisease512019.pdf. I am most grateful to Professor Zingales for sending me this paper

7 Alberto Alesina and Lawrence H. Summers, 'Central Bank Independence and Macroeconomic Performance: Some Comparative Evidence', *Journal of Money, Credit and Banking* 25 (2) (1993), pp. 151–62

8 Garett Jones, *10% Less Democracy: Why You Should Trust Elites a Little More and the Masses a Little Less* (Stanford, Stanford University Press, 2020), pp. 78–17

9 Randall Mock et al., 'Management Ownership and Market Valuation: An Empirical Analysis', *Journal of Financial Economics* 20, (January–March 1988), pp. 293–315; Nicholas Bloom, Raffaella Sadun and John van Reneen, 'Family Firms Need Professional Management', *Harvard Business Review*, 25 March 2011, https://hbr.org/2011/03/family-firms-need-professional

10 Edward B. Fiske, 'After 8 Years of Open Admissions City College Still Debates Effect', *The New York Times*, 19 June 1978

11 Fredrik deBoer, *The Cult of Smart: How Our Broken Education System Perpetuates Social Injustice* (New York, All Points Books, 2020), also makes the same case from a Marxist perspective. For another example of the application of Rawls-style reasoning see Gordon Marshall and Adam Swift, 'Merit and Mobility: A Reply to Peter Saunders', *Sociology* 30 (2) (1996)

12 S. J. D. Green, 'Competitive Equality of Opportunity: A Defencse', *Ethics* 100 (2) (October 1989), pp. 5–32, esp. pp. 20–21

13 William Ernest Henley, 'Invictus', was written in 1875 and first published in 1888

14 Peter Saunders, 'Meritocracy and Popular Legitimacy', in Geoff Dench (ed.), *The Rise and Rise of Meritocracy* (Oxford, Blackwell Publishing, 2006), p. 192

15 https://news.gallup.com/poll/245255/750-million-worldwide-migrate.aspx; Evangelia Marinakou et al., 'The Brain Drain Phenomenon in Higher Education in Greece: Attitudes and Opinions on the Decision to Immigrate', https://repository.uwl.ac.uk/id/eprint/1542/

16 Luigi Zingales, *A Capitalism for the People: Recapturing the Lost Genius of American Prosperity* (New York, Basic Books, 2012)

17 George Packer, 'The President is Winning His War on American Institutions', *Atlantic*, April 2020

18 William Deresiewicz, *Excellent Sheep: The Miseducation of the American Elite and the Way to a Meaningful Life* (New York, Free Press, 2015), p. 210

19 Victor Gourevitch (ed.), *Rousseau: The Discourses and Other Early Political Writings* (Cambridge, Cambridge University Press, 1997), p. 184

20 H. H. Gerth and C. Wright Mills (eds.), *From Max Weber: Essays in Sociology* (New York, Oxford University Press, 1958), p. 240; T. S. Eliot, 'Education in a Christian Society'(1940), in his *The Idea of a Christian Society and Other Writings*, with an introduction by David Edwards (London, Faber and Faber, 1982), p. 146; T. S. Eliot, *Notes towards the Definition of Culture* (1948; London, Faber and Faber, 1979), p. 101

21 Peter Arcidiacono et al., 'Legacy and Athlete Preferences at Harvard', 22 December 2020, http://public.econ.duke.edu/~psarcidi/legacyathlete. pdf; 'A Judge Finds There is Nothing Wrong with Harvard Admissions', *Economist*, 5 October 2019. Allison Borroughs, the judge in the case, argued, amazingly, that giving less weight to athletics would mean that 'Harvard would be far less competitive in Ivy League inter-collegiate sports, which would adversely impact Harvard and the student experience.'

22 John P. Hausknecht et al., 'Retesting in Selection: A Meta-Analysis of Practice Effects for Tests of Cognitive Ability', Cornell University Digital Commons, 1 June 2006

23 Brian S. Connelly et al., 'Balancing Treatment and Control Groups in Quasi-Experiments: An Introduction to Propensity Scoring', *Personnel Psychology* 66 (2) (2013), pp. 407–42

24 Thomas Jefferson, 'Notes on Virginia', in Adrienne Koch and William Peden (eds.), *The Life and Selected Writings of Thomas Jefferson* (New York, The Modern Library, 1944), esp. pp. 263, 265

25 Richard J. Herrnstein and Charles Murray, *The Bell Curve: Intelligence and Class Structure in American Life* (New York, The Free Press, 1994). See also Richard Herrnstein, 'IQ', *Atlantic* 228 (3) (September 1971); Richard Herrnstein, *IQ in the Meritocracy* (London, Allen Lane, 1973)

26 Adrian Wooldridge, 'Bell Curve Liberals: How the Left Betrayed IQ', *New Republic*, 27 February 1995

27 R. A. Fisher, 'The Correlation between Relatives on the Supposition of Mendelian Inheritance', *Transactions of the Royal Society of Edinburgh* 52 (1918), pp. 399–433

28 Robert Plomin, *Blueprint: How DNA Makes Us Who We Are* (London, Allen Lane, 2018). See also Steven Pinker, *The Blank Slate: The Modern Denial of Human Nature* (London, Allen Lane, 2002) and Judith Rich Harris, *The Nurture Assumption* (London, Bloomsbury, 1999)

29 Thomas J. Bouchard Jr et al., 'Sources of Human Psychological Differences: The Minnesota Study of Twins Reared Apart', *Science* 250 (4978) (12 October 1990), pp. 223–8

30 Freddie DeBoer, 'The Progressive Case for the SAT', *Jacobin*, 30 March 2018

31 Shannon Watkins, 'Goodbye Meritocracy, Hello ... What?', https://www.jamesgmartin.center/2020/04/goodbye-meritocracy-hellowhat/

32 Jones, *10% Less Democracy*. For connected arguments see Bryan Caplan, *The Myth of the Rational Voter: Why Democracies Choose Bad Policies* (Princeton, Princeton University Press, 2007)

33 Fareed Zakaria, 'Culture is Destiny: A Conversation with Lee Kuan Yew', *Foreign Affairs* 73 (2) (March–April 1994), pp. 109–26

34 https://www.usnewsdeserts.com/reports/news-deserts-and-ghost-news papers-will-local-news-survive/the-news-landscape-in-2020-trans formed-and-diminished/

35 Nikki Graf, 'Most Americans Say Colleges Should Not Consider Race or Ethnicity in Admissions', Pew Research Center: Fact Tank, 25 February 2019

36 Peter Arcidiacono, Esteban M. Aucejo and Ken Spenner, 'What Happens after Enrollment?: An Analysis of the Time Path of Racial Differences in GPA and Major Choice', *IZA Journal of Labor Economics* 1, Article no. 5 (October 2012)

37 https://www.lmh.ox.ac.uk/prospective-students/foundation-year

38 Arya Ansari, 'The Persistence of Preschool Effects from Early Childhood through Adolescence', *Journal of Educational Psychology* 110 (7) (October 2018), pp. 952–73

39 https://heckmanequation.org/resource/research-summary-lifecycle-bene fits-influential-early-childhood-program/

40 'Race in America: Staying Apart', *Economist*, 11 July 2020, pp. 14–16

41 Michael J. Sandel, *The Tyranny of Merit: What's become of the Common Good* (London, Allen Lane, 2020), p. 60

42 Charles Kingsley, *Alton Locke* (London, Chapman and Hall, 1850), p. 62

43 Jonathan Parry, '1867 and the Rule of Wealth', *Parliamentary History*, 36 (1) (2017), pp. 46–63

44 Ethel M. Wood, *The Polytechnic and Its Founder Quintin Hogg* (London, Nisbet, 1932)

45 Department for Education, *Independent Panel Report to the Review of Post-18 Education and Funding* (London, HMSO, 2019)

46 Michael Young and Peter Willmott, 'Social Grading by Manual Workers', *British Journal of Sociology* 7 (4) (1956), pp. 337–45

47 Ibid., p. 342

48 John Adams to Abigail Adams, 12 May 1780

49 Daron Acemoglu and James Robinson, *Why Nations Fail* (New York, Crown, 2012), pp. 152–6; Chrystia Freeland, *Plutocrats: The Rise of the New Global Super-Rich and the Fall of Everyone Else* (London, Allen Lane, 2012), pp. 277–9

50 Acemoglu and Robinson, *Why Nations Fail*, p. 153

51 John Ruskin, *The Stones of Venice, 3 Vols.* (1851–3; New York, National Library Association, 2001), Vol. 1, p. 1

Index